The Society
of the Sacred Heart:

History of A Spirit
1800 – 1975

Margaret Williams, RSCJ

THE SOCIETY
OF THE SACRED HEART

History of A Spirit
1800 – 1975

Darton, Longman & Todd

First published in Great Britain in 1978
by Darton, Longman and Todd Ltd
89 Lillie Road, London SW6 1UD

© 1978 Margaret Williams RSCJ

ISBN 0 232 51395 3

Printed in Great Britain by
The Anchor Press Ltd and bound by
William Brendon & Son Ltd, both of Tiptree, Essex

Contents

Foreword

The present book is the history of a spirit. It is not so much an account of the Society of the Sacred Heart in factual sequence as a study of the growth of its spirit from the beginning to the present day, as seen in significant events, in currents of thought, in dynamic personalities. Its purpose is to trace the continuity between the past and the present, in view of the future. Such a study is called for by the sudden and drastic developments that have taken place in the Catholic Church and in religious life since Vatican Council II.

In the first section, "Roots," the Society is placed within the framework of the Church at work in human history, since nothing can be understood apart from its relation to a larger whole. This will reveal the forces that caused its appearance in 1800. Its formative years, covered by the life-span of the foundress, Saint Madeleine Sophie Barat, are considered in the light of the often-asked question: "What would she do if she were here today?" This period is given with relative brevity, as several biographies are available. [1] The central section, "Growth," shows the development of the Society through the past one hundred years at greater length, since this period is less well known and since the events and the mentality of successive epochs will clarify today's problems by showing their causes. The last section, "Life-Sap," treats of the spiritual force that alone assures continued identity to a living organism: the Society's life of prayer.

Although it is primarily the study of a spirit, this book also aims to give the sound factual information needed for further study of a history still in the making. For this the notes and appendix may prove useful to other writers. Much demands to be written concerning the Society of the Sacred Heart: biographies, histories of movements and of provinces, studies of its many-faceted mission and of its spirituality. Much existing material waits to be translated or rewritten. The present book may serve as a spring-board.

It is, of course, inadequate for the vast field covered and for its all-embracing end. Every reader will find omissions among the events and persons selected for fuller treatment; every country will find unbalance. Will its tone be found overtly optimistic? If so, the author pleads guilty. It has been written with faith and with love, and (hopefully) with honesty. The faith rests upon a statement of Vatican Council II: "Religious life has a necessary role to play in the circumstances of the present age." [2] The love rests upon a life-time spent in the Society of the Sacred Heart, long study of its history, and wide contacts with its present situation. The honesty lies in recognizing the danger of proving a point by "slanted texts"; faith and love mean facing the whole truth. In the words of Mabel Digby: "The courage to condemn ourselves when necessary is, by that very fact, the surest pledge of renewal." [3]

The hope that follows faith, love and honesty is based upon certain assumptions: that the Society of the Sacred Heart, in its origin, its charism, and the life of its foundress, is part of the design of God for his kingdom on earth; that in its Providence-guided growth it is, like the Church itself, a "community of sinners," liable to every human mistake, earnest in its efforts to follow the divine thought; that the present call to renewal is authentic and imperative; that, through its past development and present changes, the Society keeps continuity of identity and of mission; finally, that all its members are co-responsible for its future.

Mother House
Feast of the Sacred Heart, 1976

PART ONE

ROOTS

1779–1865

One of the soldiers pierced
his side with a lance, and
immediately there came out
blood and water.

Jn 19:34

Two Poles

This is a book about renewal. It tells the story of the Society of the Sacred Heart, first called into being to take part in the renewal of faith following the French Revolution. For one hundred and seventy-five years the Society has shared the perennial mission of the Church to "keep renewing the world." [1] It is now caught up in the current renewal of the Church itself following Vatican Council II.

"Renewal of religious life turns upon two poles of which the axis is the Gospel. These are: the spirit of the Founder and the Church alive today." [2] The Gospel moment upon which the renewal of the Society turns is the moment to which John the Evangelist gives such emphatic witness: the piercing of Christ's Heart on Calvary. The founder is Saint Madeleine Sophie Barat who said: "We have a common mission with the Church," [3] and again: "Wind up your clock; it needs it." [4] "Today" is the moment at which the Society, with the Church, has "experienced with the force of a call to conversion the need of a new life, a fraternal life open to others in the spirit of the Gospel." [5] It becomes imperative to search for identity by tracing continuity between the two poles, remembering that "Tomorrow began Yesterday." [6]

Chapter 1

Design

> Yahweh's plans hold good
> forever, the intentions of
> his heart from age to age.
>
> Ps 33:11

The psalmist knew the human heart, and the heart of God. He knew the polarity between stability and change. We crave what holds good forever, and we must grow from age to age.

At a General Chapter held in 1970 the Society of the Sacred Heart met to discern its place in the divine plan at a critical moment. It recalled a saying of Saint Madeleine Sophie: "If I could live my life over again, I would obey only the Holy Spirit and act according to him."[1] These words have the ring of a death-bed judgment on a finished life. Actually, Madeleine Sophie was thirty-two years old when she wrote them, and as she died at eighty-five she had time to fulfill the wishful thinking of her youth. What of her "second life"? May we interpret this to mean something that she never thought of: that it is being lived now, in the Society after her? This supposes that it be lived according to the Holy Spirit. She expected as much. When very old she (for whom no generation gap existed) said to a group of the very young:

> The first person to be placed as a foundation stone of our little Society did not amount to much. . . . It is you who are the hope of the Society; one day you will be its foundation stones. When we die how glad we shall be — yes, glad — to leave behind us to sustain the Society those who are devoted to it, who will fulfil the plan of God for it. When we have disappeared you will carry on, better than we have done, the work that we began.[2]

So the second — and still unended — life is in continuity with the first. There is a life-principle in evolution. Sometimes there comes in a living organism a change so sudden, so radical, that the old life seems lost in the new. Is it the same life? The past then takes on a new significance. As T. S. Eliot put it:

> To know the past is to become most acutely conscious of one's place in time, of one's own contemporaneity. . . . The historical sense involves a perception not only of the pastness of the past but of its presence, . . . a consciousness not of what is dead but of what is living.[3]

This is what Vatican Council II (responsible for precipitating the drastic upheaval called "renewal") asks of the Church itself and of each religious order. The search for identity involves a search for that life-principle always evolving from the past through the present into the future. It requires both "a return to the original inspiration behind a given community" and "an adjustment of that community to the changed condition of the times."[4] Life is a mystery, and the mysterious name for the life-principle of a religious order is "charism," gift of the Spirit. And:

> There is a variety of gifts but always the same Spirit; there are all sorts of services to be done, but always the same God who is working in all of them. The particular way the Spirit is given to each person is for a good purpose.[5]

A gift is something to be used; it is expendable. In modern parlance: "Charism is the power of creative revolution as an eruption into history."[6] The charism in action is the "spirit" which gives to the organism its solidarity and expresses its nature. Mabel Digby spoke of the spirit of the Society of the Sacred Heart as its "life-sap"[7] and as:

> . . . a precious gift which the Society wishes above all to conserve and to transmit to the future, "the spirit of the Society," as we love to call it. It is not the spirit of any one person but the spirit of the work which our Foundress has left to us. A spirit means that which is most subtle and most intimate, the best in a religious body; it is something undefinable which blows like the Holy Spirit where it will.[8]

Madeleine Sophie was intransigent where the spirit of the Society was concerned:

> I would rather – and I say this often to Our Lord – that the Society should not exist, that it should be destroyed, than to see it come down from its true end for which it was formed, which is the greater glory of the Sacred Heart and the salvation of souls.[9]

* * *

The spirit of a living being cannot be understood apart from its ultimate purpose which is always in relation to some larger whole.
Madeleine Sophie saw the Society as integral to God's kingdom now
being built on our spinning planet, and she prayed: "Your kingdom
come, your will be done in the Society of the Sacred Heart as it is in
heaven." Similarly, the Chapter of 1970 projected the pattern of the
Society against:

> . . . this world, the home of the living God. Christ is here, hidden at the very
> heart of the world. Here where he died his risen life is gradually penetrating the
> whole of history. He is here in that unconscious expectation that is working in
> the whole of creation, here at work in men's efforts to build a world of justice and
> of brotherhood.[10]

In this design the Society is situated in the Church and in religious
life as these unfold through historic events.

In such a perspective the life-span of the Society has not been long;
the obvious dates are: November 21, 1800 to the present day. The
matter is not so simple. Madeleine Sophie, she who had no little insight into the divine ways, gave an earlier date for the birth of the
Society:

> Jesus brought it forth on Calvary when from his pierced side there flowed, with
> his blood, the ultimate pledge of his love for us.[11]
> There are many orders that bear our name and it is probably the wound in the
> side that they must express. How happy we are in coming forth, so to speak,
> from that divine Heart.[12]

She knew well the writings of Saint Augustine and would have
been acquainted with the passage in which he saw the birth of the
Church at the same moment:

> Adam slept that Eve might be made, Christ died that the Church might be made.
> Eve was formed from the side of the sleeping Adam; the side of the dead Christ
> was struck by the lance that the sacraments from which the Church is formed
> might flow forth.[13]

She saw further that: "It was then that the devotion to the Sacred
Heart was revealed; it was then that our Society was born." [14] Three
concepts fused in her vision of that moment on Calvary: the Church,

the Society, the devotion to the Sacred Heart. She drew her own conclusions:

> Our Lord himself is the Founder of this little Society. If it is the work of God he will sustain it, for he could not contradict himself and fail to give the help that he has promised to us as to the Church, with which we have a common mission.[15]

The Foundress thus saw the Society of the Sacred Heart, in the divine thought, as coeval with the Church, part of the same salvific plan, the same paschal mystery. It emerged into history only when "the signs of the times" called for it. She said: "It was the void caused by the absence of Christian education after the Revolution, and the sight of the attendant evils, that determined our foundation."[16] The Society came into being in response to a need and, after it had determined its own identity, received from the Church a mandate for its mission on December 22, 1826, when the Apostolic Approbation was given by Leo XII. By this it was "marked with the seal of the Holy Spirit,"[17] as Madeleine Sophie affirmed.

It did not, by that fact, then reach full growth. In her book *The Society of the Sacred Heart*, written in 1913, Janet Stuart says:

> As the individual so the religious Order is tried in the school of life; but its school is the contemporary events through which the whole Church passes, and in which her saints are formed, her champions tried, and her religious Orders tested and proved and drawn on in the way of perfection.
>
> These religious Orders, in their rise and growth, must pass through vicissitudes similar to those through which individuals are tried and trained up to their full power. . . . Their life is not allowed to remain primitive and uncomplex, as it was for most of them in the earliest years.[18]

She implies that the early years of the Society were its childhood, and speaks of the years in which she was writing as "the awkward age" of adolescence, the "critical moment" when those who were the last links with the foundress had passed away. And there will be:

> . . . stages of further growth and periods of quiescence to be gone through, each with its own alarms; is the growth true to its kind? Is the quiescence normal rest or inertness? . . . To catch the rhythm is a great advance towards understanding the whole of a mind or life.[19]

It is interesting to ask: what age has the Society now reached, in the nineteen-seventies? Considering the current emphasis upon "maturity" the expected answer might be "legal majority." The

Chapter of 1970 calls it "true co-responsibility for the building of community in order to accomplish the ecclesiastical mission of the Society in a dynamic fidelity to its charism." [20]

As for the duration of the Society, Janet Stuart wrote sixty years ago:

> Of all the virtues that religious can least afford to lose, that of hope seems the most needed. Dismal things are often said as to the future of religious life in the modern world. Some think that the existing Orders cannot keep their footing, that they will have to pass away and give place to other forms of good "better adapted to the needs of today." Those who know religious Orders from within cannot accept these dark prophecies. . . . We know, there is a heavenly vigour in these germs and these old, deeply-rooted stocks. We cannot fail to know that we have a message to give, and still more a power to exercise by prayer and sacrifice which is a force that the Church counts on beyond all earthly help. [21]

Madeleine Sophie never claimed prophetic powers but she showed her habitual thought more than once. When driven from Paris by the revolution of 1830 she said to the distressed community:

> The monarchy has fallen but the Church cannot fall, and you belong to the Church. Have confidence, Jesus Christ is watching over you and not a hair of your head will perish during this trial which the Society will survive, for it is destined to endure until the combats at the end of the world. [22]

So she faced indefinite extension in time and space, knowing that the Society would not be alone but in solidarity with the People of God:

> Pius IX has said that he wishes to see our little Society spread through the universe. This wish shows that he has understood the scope of our vocation and trusts that we shall correspond to it. . . . Do we not feel the exhilaration which seizes every Christian and every religious when she says: "I am in the bark of Peter, I belong to the body of the Church, I do what I can to extend and beautify it?"[23] . . . Let us forget our personal interests to think only of those of the Society, which has no other aim than to serve the Church in doing the work of the Heart of Jesus. [24]

*   *   *

To understand how the character of the Society of the Sacred Heart was determined by the moment of its appearance in history it must be seen in relation to religious life as a whole.

All Christians are called to live the Christ-life in plenitude, and religious life is one distinctive mode of doing so. Religious orders have basic elements in common: all are communities of men or women who follow a personal call to live the Christ-life together, according to the Gospel counsels of chastity, poverty and obedience, pledged thus to seek union with God through prayer and the service of men. It is the total consecration of a life by a perpetual profession ratified by the Church. Each order has a distinctive way of reaching this end, a charism leading to a mission of its own.

Vatican Council II has underlined the close connection between religious life and the Church as the People of God in chapter six of the Dogmatic Constitution *Lumen Gentium,* and has called for renewal of that life in the Decree *Perfectae Caritatis. Lumen Gentium* says:

> The Counsels are a divine gift, which the Church has received from her Lord and which she ever preserves with the help of his grace. Church authority has the duty, under the inspiration of the Holy Spirit, of interpreting these evangelical counsels, of regulating their practice, and finally of establishing stable forms of living according to them.[25]

This vigilance was exercised from the earliest centuries, but only took legal form in 1215 when the Fourth Lateran Council decreed that each order would receive its mandate by an Apostolic Approbation of its Constitutions. Church law, as codified at the Council of Trent, established a Commission for all that concerned religious life, and the Code of Canon Law as clarified by Pius X formed it into the present Sacred Congregation of Religious. There results a certain tension between legal control and the charismatic freedom that marks the foundation and growth of the religious orders. This tension is inevitable; it keeps the balance and is, in the long-run, beneficial, since authority too is "under the inspiration of the Holy Spirit."

Lumen Gentium uses an analogy:

> Thus it has come about that various forms of solitary and community life, as well as different religious families, have grown up. Advancing the progress of their members and the welfare of the whole Body of Christ, these groups have been like branches sprouting out wondrously and abundantly from a tree growing in the field of the Lord from a seed divinely planted.[26]

The roots of this tree are deep in the soil of the Gospel, for the evangelical counsels "are based upon the words and example of the Lord"[27] who "summoned those he wanted."[28] Above the soil the trunk rises in a straight line towards the transcendent, drawing up the essential life-sap: consecration, prayer, self-giving in charity. Each new order has drawn from earlier ones, adapting, assimilating, rejecting. There have been abuses and decadence, divisions, reforms, new beginnings. These branches have spread out in successive ages with a consistently wider thrust into the surrounding atmosphere of human events, a further penetration into the world, each bearing its own fruit "for the healing of the nations," [29] like the Tree of Life seen in the Book of Revelation.,

The Acts of the Apostles show the first – the ideal – Christian communities and the first – the ideal – pastors; "these remained faithful to the teaching of the apostles, to the brotherhood, to the breaking of bread and to the prayers." [30] Then the Church moved outward from the Palestine of the Chosen People into the stormy history of "the peoples." Baptism meant facing martyrdom; heroism was normal and expected of all. The faithful worshipped in the catacombs and the great Doctors explored dogma. The first observance of the evangelical counsels as a way of life took the form of consecration to Christ by voluntary chastity, the sacrifice of love for Love. Young women, living at home, bound themselves by vow, as seen in the Ceremonial for the Consecration of Virgins dating from the second century. The treatises of Saint Ambrose show the mystic significance of their act; they became *sponsae Christi*. Communities formed; Cesarius of Arles wrote the first constitutions for religious women, *Regulae ad Virgines*, in 534. The tradition has come in a straight line to the present day. Since Vatican II the vow of chastity has been placed first in the formulas of consecration, by a sure instinct for history and for essential values.

In the meantime the first Christian hermits, led by Anthony and Paul, had taken to the Egyptian desert, fleeing an evil world for the world's own good, wondering, in their solitude, "if new roofs are still rising in the ancient cities."[31] They sought union with God by the shortest, most obvious and most rugged road. The eremitical life was "a sign of contradiction." It lasted barely two centuries, but its essence – radical separation, solitude, silence and penance – passed into the very fibre of religious life. The uncompromising forms gradually yielded to others both more winning and more demanding. For before the death of Anthony the solitaries had been called into communities by Pachomius;[32] monasticism began with the writing of his Rule in 320. The virtues needed for community living – obedience, forbearance, corporate poverty, social awareness – were more searching than those needed by men eating their own dates under their own palm trees.

Then Saint Benedict wrote his Rule in 530, in the light of a vision in which he saw "the whole world gathered together as it were under one beam of the sun." [33] From Monte Cassino, Benedictine monasticism spread over Europe, and within it many distinct orders developed. It dominated throughout the Middle Ages, with its motto, "Pax," cloistered, contemplative, controlled by rule and bell, given to study, hospitality, manual work and the splendour of the liturgy. The Divine Office was its gift to the Church. These lovers of beauty, "living peacefully in their homes," [34] were the missionaries carrying the faith to new lands, the civilizers, educators and artists of Christendom.

In the thirteenth century the mendicant orders renewed by their evangelical simplicity the religious life that had grown top-heavy with privilege, power and form; their innovations startled their times. Friars, no longer cloister-bound, were met on the highways, in the market-places, penetrating society. There were Franciscans sharing the joyous freedom of the poor man of Assisi, preaching to birds and fishes and men, to "Brother Fire, glad and strong, to Sister Water, humble and precious and pure." [35] There were Dominicans, seekers of wisdom, trained teachers and spiritual guides, "Dogs of the Lord" tracking down truth. Francis and Dominic put their shoulders to the tottering wall of the Church, as in Giotto's painting of the dream of Innocent III. There were Carmelites, come to Europe from the fountain of Elias on Mount Carmel, whose aim was "to live for the sake of Jesus Christ and serve him with purity of heart" in contemplation fruitful for their brother men. The rules of these orders, with a new note of democracy in government, were all approved in the early thirteenth century.

In time the mendicant orders also needed renewal; "the friars" are the villain of the piece in Langland's *Piers Plowman.* For the history of religious life is marked by a rhythm of human weakness pursued by a divine ideal. There was failure to see the Spirit at work in a new form; the monks were suspicious of the friars, authority was suspicious of innovation. Jealousies, misunderstandings, the anguishing cross-purposes of those set on doing God's work, pruned the tree of religious life.

The Renaissance brought classical humanism into Christian thought-patterns; the discovery of the new world drew Europe out of herself, opened a road to the ancient cultures of the East and called all the religious orders to the missions. The Reformation shook the Church into auto-reformation at the Council of Trent and Sixtus V put religious life under stricter legal control. In 1534 Saint Ignatius of Loyola placed his prayer-rooted, militant apostles at the service of the papacy, especially by the work of education. These clerks regular were neither monks nor mendicants, and once more tradition-centred authority was slow to recognize them, with their strongly centralized government, their abandonment of Office in choir, their bold fusion of contemplation with tireless action. But the Society of Jesus sensed the needs of the future; it stimulated many new congregations that sprang up under the vigorous attritions of the Counter-Reformation.

What of women religious all this time? They were present, mostly behind grilles. Most medieval orders for men had a second order for women, with dynamic foundresses like Saint Scholastica and Saint Clare, or courageous reformers like Saint Teresa of Avila. Women were not yet ready to follow the consistent outward thrust of the orders for men. Saint Ignatius did not wish to have a women's counterpart of the Jesuit order. A change began in the seventeenth century when social conditions cried out for what only a woman could give. The Ursulines responded with schools, as did the Visitation nuns, though both remained within papal enclosure. Then Saint Vincent de Paul declared that the streets were cloister enough for the Sisters of Charity. Conflict was again roused; his Sisters were not "nuns". He did not mind what they were called; they were needed — on the streets. Mary Ward's Institute of Mary, uncloistered, waited two centuries for approbation. But the evolution went on. By the late eighteenth century there were many active congregations of women but because of the Constitution of Pius V, *Circa Pastoralis* (1556), their members were not considered "true religious." By the time the French Revolution had disrupted the very structures of society there seemed no limit, despite canonical ambiguities, to the forms that a life consecrated by the vows of religious could take.

The Society of the Sacred Heart, appearing in 1800, would have, necessarily, both obligations to the past and responsibilities to the future. "Uniting missionary dynamism to the search for total consecration, it raised, in a way more pressing than ever before, the question of the enlarged apostolate of women religious." [36] It inherited a network of traditions which had grown from one another: separateness from the world in a modified cloister, office in choir, monastic customs in community, prayer energizing the work of education on the Jesuit pattern – all implemented in a woman's way at the dawn of women's "liberation." Some of the tensions inherent in the very nature of the Society, and some of the problems that she would face later on, come from this historical inheritance.

These traditions were tenaciously alive, but the *ancien régime* had been shattered and it was morning for the Church. The Society was considered novel. Gregory XVI said: "Because of my monastic training there are many things in the rule of the Sacred Heart of which I would not approve. But it is the work of God and I would not change a word of it." [37] And because all the religious orders in France had been swept away in the Revolution, the Society was involved from the beginning in "renewal."

* * *

It is apparent that each new order, while sharing something of the mission, life-style and spirituality of the earlier ones, has its own role to play. But this is not enough to account for its separate existence. Only its proper charism can give to a corporate group the uniqueness of a personality. In the case of the Society of the Sacred Heart the name holds the clue to its identity. Devotion to the Sacred Heart "is marked by characteristics which do not allow us to mistake therein the finger of God," [38] say the Constitutions. Once again, the year 1800 is significant, for the history of religious life and that of devotion to the Sacred Heart had run parallel for centuries and were then fused.

The phrase "Sacred Heart" holds ideas basic to human life as well as to Christian revelation; the heart of a man is a universal symbol. Physiologically it is the life-giving organ; the ceasing of its natural action brings death. Though not the seat of the emotions it records them. Psychologically, as all emotions revolve around love, "heart" is a single term for that many-levelled driving force of life. The heart is the focal point of the affective life, of the love-moved thought that makes a man what he is. The language, the poetry, the art of all races from earliest times recognize in a man's heart the sign of his total personality, be he lion-hearted or chicken-hearted, large-hearted or heartless.

Revelation lifted the language of human experience to the divine plane. In the Bible the heart expresses that savouring knowledge that becomes wisdom. The Old Testament speaks anthropomorphically: "The anger of Yahweh will not turn aside until he has performed and carried out the decision of his heart." [39] When the Son of God became the Son of man, his heart was as the heart of his brothers, the symbol of a human life which in him, by virtue of the hypostatic union, is divine. The phrase "Sacred Heart" holds the dogmas of the Incarnation and Redemption. In the words of Bossuet:

> See what a heart is the heart of Jesus, see what is the mystery of Christianity. That is why the summary of our faith is expressed in these words: "We have believed in the love of God for us." [40]

And Pius XII concludes: "Devotion to the Sacred Heart is so important that it may be considered, so far as practice is concerned, the perfect profession of the Christian religion." [41] And Jesus Christ has shown the way to this practice in his own character sketch of himself: "Shoulder my yoke and learn from me, for I am gentle and humble of heart."[42]

The roots of the devotion are found in the same scene on Calvary which symbolized the birth of the Church and of the Society, when John witnessed the piercing of Christ's side, and when "fountains of living water" [43] flowed with his blood. In the Patristic Ages (c.250–600) theologians such as Origen, John Chrysostom, Augustine and Gregory the Great developed the doctrinal implications of the scene in metaphors drawn from Scripture, especially from the Song of Songs. The wound opened by the soldier's lance is "the cleft in the rock" [44] where souls of prayer take refuge:

> "Thou has wounded my heart, my sister, my spouse." This word is to be taken simply, for by mentioning the wounded heart is expressed the greatness of the love of Christ for the Church.[45]

In the Middle Ages the devotion remained cloistered, fathomed by mystics. They knew with Saint Bernard that: "The iron pierced to his soul and his Heart has drawn near to us. . . . Its secrets lie open through the cloven body." [46] They learned from Saint Gertrude how to lean, with John the Evangelist, upon Christ's Heart "in which all the treasures of beatitude lie hidden." [47] The contemplatives knew these treasures, and a literature of passionate experience flowered. In the fifteenth century the devotion left the cloister; it left Latin for the vernacular and was popularized in art forms and manuals of prayer. In the Counter-Reformation it became "the sword of the Spirit" and went overseas with the missionaries.

Jesuit spirituality drew the devotion into itself to such an extent that the Society of Jesus and devotion to the Sacred Heart were almost identified. Ignatius himself opened the way by the orientation of the Spiritual Exercises and by the "Anima Christi." As Jesuits became leading directors and spiritual authors, the devotion spread into all walks of life.

The seventeenth century was the Golden Age of the devotion in which its two main "schools" appeared, not in opposition but complementary. These were the "Ecole de France" and the "Ecole de Paray," (so named by Henri Brémond).[48]

The first owes its origin to Cardinal de Bérulle (1575–1629), founder of the French Oratorians, called "Apostle of the Word Incarnate." It was further developed by Monsieur Olier (1608–1657), founder of the Sulpician Seminary, and by John Eudes (1601–1680), founder of the Congregation of Jesus and Mary. He composed the first mass in honour of the Sacred Heart and wrote *The Admirable Heart of the Mother of God* which treats also of the Heart of her Son. Many Jesuits were attracted to this school which stressed "the spiritual heart" rather than the heart of flesh, and which contemplated the inward "states" of the God-man, his dispositions, thoughts and feelings. It was marked by adoration and self-emptying before the Word-made-flesh "who emptied himself". One attractive element was all pervasive in the prayer of this school: it saw the love of Christ's Heart in all the scenes of the Gospel and in his extended life in the members of his Body the Church. It was a devotion to "Jésus intériorisé":

> In the Heart of Jesus you will enter into the enjoyment of all that he is, the intercourse, the give-and-take between him and his Father. That which Jesus wrought in his Heart has spread through the Church, has made it expand and grow great. . . . The mysteries of Jesus and all that concerns him are not things past and done with, but living and present.[49]

It was this spirituality that was to enter most profoundly into the Society of the Sacred Heart.

Margaret Mary Alacoque (1647–1690), the Visitandine mystic of Paray-le-Monial, gave to the devotion of the Sacred Heart the forms that would mould it for the next three centuries, so well-known and wide-spread as to be practically identified with the devotion itself in the popular mind. Through the "Great Revelations" were given: the Holy Hour, the First Friday, the nine promises, the passion-centred reparation and, above all, the appeal of love for love: "Behold this Heart which has so loved men that it has spared nothing even to exhausting and consuming itself in order to show them its love." [50] These elements too were to enter the Society of the Sacred Heart as ways of expressing the deep interiority of the devotion.

Most important was the request for a feast of the Sacred Heart by which the devotion would take its place in the official life of the Church. Ninety years of struggle and of testing passed before this was granted, during which the devotion was quietly making its own way into the life of the people at all levels, growing from the grass-roots, circling the globe with the missionaries sponsored by ecclesiastical authority. At the same time it was opposed by very diverse forces: Voltairian rationalism and Jansenist rigour. Paradoxically, Jansenism, with its dark legalism, had been growing in France side by side with the devotion of love and of confidence. The Jesuits took up the cause and fought for the institution of the feast; the Jansenists fought back with every weapon of threat and raillery. The authorities in Rome moved cautiously. The requests made through Jean Croiset, S. J. and Joseph Gallifet, S. J. were repeatedly refused. This drove them to studies which proved that the devotion was doctrinally sound and that it had inspired sanctity for centuries. The time then came for the release of its full power. On January 26, 1765, Clement XIII issued a Brief sanctioning devotion to the Sacred Heart and permitting the feast.

Then the devotion underwent its baptism of blood. The Society of Jesus was suppressed in 1773, the French Revolution broke out in 1789, and the revolutionaries joined the Jansenists in attacking the Heart of Christ. Priests, nuns, young girls like Victoire de Saint Luc, [51] went to the guillotine for its sake. It became a political symbol when Sacred Heart badges were worn by the peasants of Vendée who rose in counter-revolution. A heretical Synod of Pistoia called it a new form of Nestorianism which separated the humanity from the divinity of Christ. The image of the divine Heart was ridiculed and blasphemed; in mockery, the heart of the atheist Marat was worshipped with incense after his murder. Then the tide turned when in 1794 Pius VI gave full doctrinal sanction to the devotion in the Bull *Auctorem Fidei.*,

Deep beneath these surface storms the fusion between religious life and the devotion to the Sacred Heart had come about. Saint Francis de Sales, as early as 1609, had said that the Visitation order had "the privilege and incomparable grace of bearing the title of Daughters of the Sacred Heart." [52] Catherine de Bar (Mother Mechtilde of the Blessed Sacrament) founded the Adorers of the Blessed Sacrament in 1652. They were devoted in the Bérullian way to intimacy with the "interior dispositions" of the Heart of Christ, as were the Adorers of the Heart of Jesus at the monastery of Sainte Aure. The Congregation of the Sacred Heart of Ernemont, founded in 1668, was the first religious order to bear the name of the divine Heart. Those that began during the Terror, like the Religious of the Sacred Hearts and of Perpetual Adoration founded by Joseph-Marie Coudrin, were marked by an intense sense of reparation, of offering as victim, of adoration of the Blessed Eucharist. The atmosphere of the cloister was warm at the beginning of the nineteenth century.

* * *

During the tumultuous close of the eighteenth century Madeleine Sophie Barat was growing up in the quiet town of Joigny. The forces that we have just seen at work in the devotion to the Sacred Heart, as it made its way into the life of the People of God and into religious life, reached a climax at that turning point into our modern world: the revolution that cleared the air for democracy. Only fourteen years before her birth the Decree of Clement XIII had integrated devotion to the Heart of Christ into the Church's liturgical cycle. How was it to be integrated into the social order? Voltaire and Rousseau had died only one year before her birth; deism was moving into atheism and the Church was challenged to confront the industrial revolution. What part would Christian women play in the coming social evolution? In her girlhood she saw all the religious orders in France suppressed. What would religious life be like after the Terror?

These questions were in the air that Madeleine Sophie breathed, unconscious as she was of their full import for her own life, for her unknown role as foundress. They shaped the young girl personally, as they shaped the young men, still seminarians, still unknown to her, who were dreaming of a new Society to confront the future. Most potently, they shaped the Society of the Sacred Heart itself when it came into being and took into itself this rich heritage while straining towards the unknowable.

As she looked back in later years Madeleine Sophie became keenly aware of what the Society had received, of what had prepared it for its own creative mission. Her writings abound in references to great founders, from Pachomius to her own contemporaries; she drank in the spirit of the great mystics, workers, educators, innovators, in that long line. She traced pertinent developments in spirituality and apostolate, in order to learn and to do. She had that historical sense that "sees the past not as dead but as living", and she kept her eyes on the horizon: "Why can we not say to the universe, 'Know his Heart'?"[53] She saw her "little Society" as the least in this unfinished evolution, and she was very sure that it was "a divine thought."

Chapter 2

Vision
1779–1800

Then I heard the voice of the
Lord saying: "Whom shall I
send? Who will be our messenger?"
I answered: "Here I am. Send
me." He said: "Go!"

Is 6:8–9

Under the Old Testament, in times of urgency, prophets were given
vision then sent on a mission to give it reality. Under the New Testament Christ called apostles, gave them his own vision and sent them
out to found his kingdom. At the turning point into modern history
Madeleine Sophie Barat received the mission "to glorify the Heart of
Jesus" (as expressed today: "to reveal the love of God-made-man") [1]
by the foundation of the Society of the Sacred Heart. She refused the
title of foundress – rightly, since she had never thought of founding it.
Others have given her the title – rightly, since in her person the
charism of the Society was most manifest, and since she guided its
growth for sixty-five years. The vision was first given to another and
she, with many co-workers, gave it reality.

At no period has Society history been the biography of a single person. The Society is made up of "living stones making a spiritual
house." [2] The Chapter of 1970 saw it as "made up of all the religious
of the Sacred Heart . . . sharing the responsibiity of accomplishing the
mission of the Society in the Church." [3] Some have a larger share of
the prophetic vision; all co-operate in the work. This reflects the same
"interpersonal mystery" that gives unity to Christ's body, the
Church. It calls for the handing on of inspiration from thinkers to
workers, the intermeshing of generations, the pooling of gifts, the
gearing of efforts separated by time and place. It brings about salutary

clashes, misunderstandings, cross-purposes, a resolution of themes
into harmony. So it was with the Society of the Sacred Heart as it
passed from vision into reality. Three persons stand out: Léonor
François de Tournély[4] (1767–1797), Joseph Désiré Varin[5]
(1769–1850) and Madeleine Sophie Barat.

*   *   *

The first spark was struck by a "youth movement"; when students
get together things happen. In the Oratorian Seminary of Saint Sul-
pice in Paris, before 1789, an alert group of seminarians met in secret
and formed an "Association of the Sacred Heart". The moment was
frightening; factories were first staining the air with smoke, hungry
people were throwing up barricades in the streets, voltairian
philosophers were defying the whole of revelation. The seminary,
founded by Monsieur Olier in the seventeenth century, was vibrant
with devotion to the Sacred Heart, then under violent attack. The
group prayed and wondered what they could do to reveal Christ's
love to the desperate world. Their director said of them: "Just wait!
These young men will some day found a society that will do great
things for the Church. They are turning over in their heads the most
astonishing plans and they live like saints." [6]

They were a group of very diverse enthusiasts. Léonor de
Tournély was gentle, scholarly, sensitive, drawn to inward solitude;
Joseph Varin was military-minded, impulsive and outgoing; Charles
de Broglie was practical and impulsive, the son of a Maréchal de
France; Louis de Sambucy de Saint-Estève was a brilliant planner —
and future trouble-maker. All represented the *ancien régime* at its best,
before it passed away: traditions of *noblesse oblige* fostered in gracious
châteaux and carried out in chivalrous service. But Joseph's restless
nature drove him home; as he left Paris he heard shouting over the fall
of the Bastille. The others were hastily ordained. Léonor and
Charles were for staying in the city and meeting martyrdom but
their director said: "Go! God has great designs for you."

The pilgrims left Paris in July, 1791, and were soon joined by
others. In the group were Xavier de Tournély, Léonor's brother,
Jean le Blanc and Fidèle de Grivel, historian of their movements. They begged their way to Luxembourg, then cannon fire
drove them to Antwerp. They prayed and studied, in the throes of
war, hunger and confusion. What could they do while waiting to take
up the ruined work of Christian education? Charles de Broglie said:

"We must go into some solitary place and there form ourselves to the spirit and practice of religious life. . . . We shall adapt the customs and rules of Saint Ignatius." They had the Constitutions of the Society of Jesus, convinced that it would soon be reconstituted. At Easter-time in 1794 they made a retreat in a Capuchin monastery at Antwerp to seek light.

> One day the Abbé de Tournély, in prayer before a crucifix, was lovingly contemplating the open side of the Saviour; all his thoughts and all his feelings turned to the Heart of Jesus on fire with love for men. He felt strongly pressed to give to the new congregation the name: Society of the Sacred Heart. [7]

The fellowship approved, and Father de Tournély became the first superior of the Fathers of the Sacred Heart.

In July, Joseph Varin visited his friends "just in passing," but after receiving communion at Léonor's mass he said: "I am never leaving you." The high-hearted cavalier joined the militia of Christ. He later learned that on that same day his mother had died on the scaffold, offering her life for Joseph. He was with the new society when they vowed their lives to the love of Christ at Leitershoven on October 15, 1794. They took for their motto the words describing the first Christians: "One heart and one mind," [8] and made it their own by the added phrase "in the Heart of Jesus." They had the courageous faith to dedicate their society to the Heart of Jesus at a time when it was a "sign of contradiction," and to base their rule on that of the Society of Jesus when it had been officially suppressed.

The group grew and was driven from town to town by the backwash of the revolution. Their mode of life, in which Trappist and Carmelite elements were blended with the Ignatian, was austere, contemplative, studious and gay. Father de Tournély was a man of prayer, with the motto "calm of heaven." In 1795 a further inspiration came to him: they must found a parallel order for women with the same name and spirit. "Good Master," he said in prayer, "I am not alone; I have brothers. Let me tell them of this and if they approve I shall not hesitate." He sought community discernment, giving in his description of the Society-to-be all the essential elements of its charism:

> It is destined to be devoted to the Heart of Jesus, and to awaken the love of Jesus in souls and the light of his teaching in minds. For this it will enter into the sentiments and interior dispositions of that divine Heart and will reveal them to others by means of education. [9]

The search for a foundation stone was carried on by the trial and error method. Actually there are four other women who have a claim to the title of foundress prior to that of Madeleine Sophie Barat. All of them had gifts for it, but not the better gift: the fulness of the charism adumbrated by Father de Tournély.

The first was the exiled Louise Adelaide de Bourbon Condé[10] (1757–1824), known as "the wandering princess." She had made earlier trials of religious life and now accepted Father de Tournély's offer. She accompanied the Fathers of the Sacred Heart to Vienna in 1796, and settled with a few homeless Sisters of Charity in an abandoned Visitation monastery. Father de Tournély called them "Servants of the Sacred Heart"; they were cloistered but planned nonetheless to undertake both education and the care of the sick. Their spirit is seen in a letter written by the Princess:

> The whole spirit of the house is a spirit of love and of tenderness for our Lord and for his august Mother. All is done for love and leads to love; that is the first idea that we had in forming this little Society. It seems that the house must be a burning centre of love.[11]

But she could not grasp the wholeness of a vocation that calls for deep prayer not apart from but in the midst of distracting work done for love at cost to self. In another letter she wrote:

> I have never had the least attraction for an enterprise which will require a multitude of business affairs and of difficulties all of which will fall upon me. Nothing is more contrary to my taste for solitude.[12]

She left and followed her own authentic call, and after many adventures founded the contemplative order of Saint Louis of the Temple, the prison in which her family had met death. The Sisters of Charity found a reopened convent of their own order, and the project failed. Father de Tournély was not shaken: "It is God who wills this Society. I may have been mistaken about the means but this Society will be." He died at Haggenbrunn where the Fathers of the Sacred Heart had opened their first school, on July 9, 1797, at the age of thirty.

In later years Madeleine Sophie, who had never seen Father de Tournély, said:

> We must be penetrated with this consoling truth, that from the earliest days the Society has recognized for its founder the one who received from God the first

revelation concerning it. He was a saint. . . . He knew only in a general way of the establishment of a Society that would be consecrated to the Heart of our Lord, and which would do its utmost to spread the knowledge and love of that Heart through the entire universe.[13]

Father Varin became superior of the Fathers of the Sacred Heart. He sent an outline of their aims to the exiled Pius VI who answered with a letter of approval that opened to them a serious mission:

> We hope that you will contribute powerfully to consoling the Church in the desolation in which she is now plunged, and win over to her the many enemies who now persecute her. For that, much labour awaits you, and the task which must be fulfilled is strenuous and difficult. Prepare for it by prayer, by the practice of virtue and by study.[14]

In the meantime another association of priests called the Fathers of the Faith had been formed at Spoletto by Nicolas Paccanari, a quixotic dreamer known to history as either a saint or a quack. The two groups had similar aims: the work of education and the restoration of the Society of Jesus, but they differed on one essential point: consecration to the Heart of Christ was not the primary inspiration of the Fathers of the Faith. Paccanari, still a deacon, came to Haggenbrunn and Father Varin fell under his exotic influence. The fusion took place under Paccanari's leadership on April 18, 1799, and the Fathers of the Sacred Heart ceased to exist as such.

The two men agreed about a parallel order for women which Paccanari had already beheld, he claimed, in a vision. Its name was to be "Dilette di Gesù," and the foundation stones were ready. Another royal personage, Marie-Anne of Austria,[15] a sister of the Emperor Francis II, was the second claimant to the title of foundress of the Society of the Sacred Heart. She and her two maids of honour, Louise and Léopoldine Naudet,[16] made their act of consecration in Prague, on May 31, 1799, feast of the Sacred Heart. The little group then moved to Padua and, in August, 1800, to Rome where a plan for the new order was drawn up. It was to be based on the Rule of the Society of Jesus with an apostolate of education in both boarding and free schools, and of retreats. Its members were to be cloistered, and to maintain perpetual adoration of the Blessed Sacrament. The focus did not fall upon the Heart of Christ, and in this the new institute departed from the vision of Father de Tournély.

In the spring of that same year Father Varin set out for Paris, on foot, seeking a foundation stone for the French branch of the Dilette di Gesù. The new century dawned hopefully. Pius VII succeeded Pius VI who had died in captivity; he startled the Church with his words: "Be good Christians and you will be good democrats." The Consulate had replaced the Directory under the "Constitution of the Year VII" and Napoleon was enforcing order. Churches were opening; renewal was at hand. In June Father Varin dodged into Paris with no passport, set up a chapel in an attic, worked in the reeking hospitals by day and gathered disciples by night.

One of these was a solemn young priest from Joigny, just out of prison, named Louis Barat. He asked to join the Fathers of the Faith as soon as he had found a place in life for his little sister, Madeleine Sophie – a good classical scholar twenty years old who wanted to be a Carmelite. She was now in Joigny, gathering grapes at the vintage time. At the end of the month Sophie came back to Paris, and in a flash Father Varin saw what he wanted:

> I went to see her and found a very small and frail-looking young girl, extremely modest, who did not dare to raise her eyes. Yet the inner conviction that had come to me when her brother spoke of her for the first time became more intense and the light shone more vividly. "What a foundation stone!" I said to myself. [17]

*   *   *

Madeleine Louise Sophie Barat was born in Joigny in northern France, on the night of December 12, 1779,[18] while a fire was raging in the nearby street. She was later called "a child of fire" in many senses. She was baptized at dawn in the Gothic church of Saint Thibault, with her eleven-year-old brother Louis[19] for godfather. Joigny was a tranquil medieval town clinging to a hillside near the river Yonne. The *maison Barat* on the Rue des Puits-Chardon (today the Rue Davier) was a small, simple, hard-working Christian home, typical of the sturdy class in whose hands lay the making of a new social order. Jacques Barat was a barrel-maker who owned a vineyard beyond the town wall; he was a silent, sensible man, illiterate. His wife, Marie-Madeleine Foufé, was an emotional woman of slightly more education. The house, two rooms wide and two storeys high, boasted a staircase instead of the usual ladder leading to the attic room that was given to Sophie for her own. Marie-Louise, aged ten, completed the austerely affectionate household.

Sophie soon enlivened them all. "Don't talk to me about vivacity; I am Burgundian!" She was quick and gentle, shy and impulsive, ready to give of her keen mind, her warmly sensitive heart. She was happy outdoors in the woods and vineyards, and in the firelit family room where she learned to be a good housekeeper. Her volatile nature was moulded by her mother's training, the discipline of her brother who took his duties as godfather only too seriously, and most of all by the inward pressure of God on her responsive nature. The name Sophie means Wisdom. "I was seventeen months old when I perceived that I existed.[20] . . . I had a real grasp of God's greatness." [21] At catechism class the reality of Christ seized and moved her to the depths. She made her first communion in the spring of 1789, when "among other extraordinary favours I received the gift of understanding Scripture." [22]

Sophie never went to school. While she longed to be at play in the vineyards she was kept hard at her books by Louis, himself a brilliant student in the seminary in Sens and then stern professor in the Collège St. Jacques in Joigny. He passed on to his little pupil the best educational traditions of the *ancien régime,* and soon her vibrant mind awoke; she experienced what she learned: "I was fire and flame for the art and valour of Greece!" [23] She learned from primary sources; history and literature were her best subjects:

I love the heroic; there at least one has room. The mind expands at ease and the heart is alive. . . .[24] In the midst of the evils and upheavals of those days, by comparing them with what my memory held of ancient and of modern history, I reached those considerations in which the designs, the judgments and the punishments of God were unveiled to my mind; I adored the decrees of the divine will instead of worrying about them.[25]

No-one could see to what use a country girl would put the mathematics, astronomy, modern and classical languages that completed her curriculum:

My poor parents had to bear a lot of blame from the neighbours for what my brother taught me!" "What foolishness," they said, "to teach a frail girl studies so far above her condition! That little Sophie, with her head in her books and her hand holding a pen is getting useless ideas stuffed into her memory!" But what gave my brother the strength to disagree with his counsellors? Evidently, it was the Sacred Heart!" [26]

Her studies were not carried on in peace. Soon after her first communion the post-riders brought bad news from Paris: the National Assembly, the fall of the Bastille, the Commune and *The Rights of*

Man — at the expense of the rights of God. Christians were wrenched by appalling contradictions, by dark ambiguities. By October the royal family was in prison and revolution washed even over peaceful Joigny. For the next six years Sophie was moulded by suffering. Louis fled from home — straight into Paris and into prison. Sophie kept house, found food, saved her mother from breakdown by her loving tact, and went on with her reading. But what was she to do with her life?

She had been sure of her vocation at the age of five. But she had never seen a nun and now the National Assembly had outlawed them. As a little girl she had made a doll's house in the form of a Carmelite cell — the sign of her dream. Now the Carmelites of Compiègne had gone singing to the scaffold. But, whether she could be a nun or not, Sophie gave herself to God at the age of fourteen by a vow of perpetual chastity.

Another sign then came from Paris. Somehow Louis had found two pictures — likewise outlawed, one of the Sacred Heart of Jesus and one of the Immaculate Heart of Mary. At sight of them Madame Barat lost her Jansenistic fear; she hung the pictures on the wall of the Barat home. Eighteenth-century art did not show the person of our Lord manifesting his Heart; the picture would have been like that first drawn, crudely, by Margaret Mary Alacoque, the heart surrounded by thorns and surmounted by a cross. Praying before these pictures in the firelit family room Sophie first learned the meaning of that symbol of divine love incarnate, and the closeness of the heart of Mary to that of her Son.

Then in the wild spring of 1794 the Terror abruptly ended and Louis came home. He saw that Sophie had grown into a wise young woman, centre of her home and comfort of her neighbours, "admired and made more of than if she had been a queen." She must complete her studies — in Paris. Terrified, Sophie resisted until her silent father spoke out; it was right for her to go.

For the next four years Sophie lived cooped up in a narrow house on the Rue de Touraine in the numb, exhausted city as a new age came to life around her. Louis, now a priest, gathered a group of young women seeking some form of dedication; they were: Octavie Bailly,[27] a gentle, prayerful girl like Madeleine Sophie who became her close friend, Marguerite whose last name is unknown, and Marie-Françoise Loquet,[28] an older woman with a reputation for competent catechetical work, the author of allegorical novels such as

The Journey of Sophie and Eulalie to the Palace of True Happiness.
They prayed and studied together but Sophie took her own pace.

It was an extraordinary preparation for an unknown work. She read Scripture, theology, the Fathers of the Church in the original languages, the works of the great mystics. Louis put her through a severe ascetic training, with penances that permanently harmed her health, with conscience-searching that drove her into scruples and ended by leaving her transparent to God's light. She experienced the piercing action of "the dark night of the soul." Such severity might have warped her sensitive nature but for her sense of humour: "I got used to it, and what made me suffer at first ended by making me laugh."[29] Louis thwarted her highest dreams: "You, Sophie! You'll never be a saint!" "Very well," she retorted. "I'll get even by being very humble."[30]

When the convents began to reopen Sophie once more dreamed of Carmel. But she had read the life of Francis Xavier and a new dream cut disturbingly across the old: to be sent and spent for others. She also read the life of Margaret Mary Alacoque and the devotion of love took deeper hold on her. Where find a vocation that would unite these attractions?

Every autumn Sophie went home at vintage time to be with her ageing parents. She became the guide and comfort of her married sister, Marie-Louise Dussousoy, ten years her senior, to whom she wrote:

Have a little confidence in God; he will help you. It is time that you answered his voice. I see that he is asking something more of you than what you are giving him each day; the troubles that he sends you are a proof of this. Tell me about it, dear sister. Open your heart to mine. O, if you only knew how I feel for you! I would like, if it were possible, to carry part of your burden.[31]

Her five year old nephew, the future Abbé Louis Dussaussoy, remembered to the end of his long life what Sophie was to him:

The gracious and modest beauty of my aunt, her gentleness, her sweet and melodious voice, exercised a real fascination over me. Her image is deeply engraved on my heart, like a statue of virginity or the incarnation of that wisdom whose name she bore. . . . We wandered together over the smiling slopes that overlook the charming and poetic valley of the Yonne. There she taught me, spoke to me of God and of his love, told me uplifting stories suited to my age, sang hymns to me or recited sacred poetry. At the sound of her voice, under the charm of her words, my whole being yielded to her and to all the

impressions that she wished to make on me. . . . An understanding of goodness,
beauty and truth entered through all my senses. [32]

When Sophie went back to Paris after the vintage of 1800 she knew
that a decision must be made about her life; it was then that she
found Father Varin waiting for her.

*   *   *

The point of no return was quickly reached. Under Father Varin's
guidance – gentler but no less demanding than that of Louis – Sophie
learned to walk in his way of "courage and confidence." One day he
asked her outright what she wanted to be. "A Carmelite." "No. The
gifts God has given you, the education that you have received, are not
meant to be kept in a cloister." Then for the first time Sophie heard
the story of Father de Tournély's desire, and of the Dilette di Gesù. "I
will think about it." "When the will of God is known there is
nothing to think about." [33] Sophie's consent was her irrevocable
"Fiat." Her companions also agreed, and Father Varin began their
religious formation.

Before dawn on the Feast of the Presentation of our Lady,
November 21, 1800, they gathered in the attic chapel. Over the altar
hung a painting of the Virgin Mother and her Child: on the side walls
were pictures of the Sacred Heart and of Saint Ignatius and his companions making their first vows. The ceremony was the same as that
followed by the Dilette di Gesù the year before; [34] the text of the act of
consecration was the same. The four candidates were dressed in
white. Father Varin offered mass; at the moment of communion each
made her oblation before the upraised Host: a temporary vow of
chastity (to which Sophie was already bound), an offering as victim
for the glory of God and the good of one's neighbour, a promise to
observe the rules of the Institute and (in all probability) an act of
dedication to the Heart of Christ. Each received a medal of the
Sacred Heart bearing on one side the legend: "I have come to cast fire
on the earth," and on the other: "My heart is joined to yours." Mass
closed with the Te Deum, the kiss of peace, and tears of joy. As
Sophie said later: "As I had never before seen a ceremony of dedication to religious life, this one, simple as it was, made a deep impression
on me." [35]

As the Dilette di Gesù in Italy ceased to exist four years later, that
day was the true beginning of the Society of the Sacred Heart. And

as, of the four young women present, Madeleine Sophie Barat alone persevered, she became that day its true foundation stone. "But as for me, I knew nothing, I foresaw nothing, I accepted what was given me."[36]

Looking back from the twentieth century it is possible to see, perhaps even more clearly than Father Varin did then, Madeleine Sophie's fitness for her role. The following is a retrospective portrait of the one who then gave herself over to the design of God, "the thoughts of his heart from age to age:"

Saint Madeleine Sophie, you are someone, someone who takes on importance for us because you are seen as human and accessible. While studying the beginnings of the Society we understand the message of the opening of the nineteenth century; a time of urgent re-christianization, calling for initiative, for experiments, animated by a vivifying breath. In this dynamism we discover: the desire of announcing Jesus Christ; a sense of Christian and religious responsibility; a focus upon the one thing necessary — salvation; a dominant generosity. We cannot but admire this missionary zeal, and recognize how closely the pressing need of the nineteenth century meets that of the twentieth: the need of workers who believe in their call.

At this challenge the figure of Madeleine Sophie stands out as a paradoxical person who can be thus resumed:

She attracted by her good qualities and even by her defects, which can be summarized as physical frailty contrasting with a tenacity amounting to iron firmness (perhaps even to authoritarianism).

The complexity of her character is remarkable. She had the qualities of sensitiveness, of imagination, of warm-heartedness, of keen intelligence, of good sense rooted in the soil of Burgundy.

This rich endowment, the factors of her formation, the influences that played upon her, made of her:

— a person of great cultivation who remained simple and close to her origins;

— a very sensitive person, finely perceptive to the point of disquiet (and even of scrupulosity) while remaining clear-eyed, open, available to others;

— a Christian inclining to over-severity, yet an active lover of life, able to transform everything into service:

— a person thirsting for silence, for solitude, for recollection, drawn to contemplation, and at the same time a friend making endless contacts in which, with a certain tact, a certain sense of fitness (diplomacy even), she felt at ease with great and humble people;

— a person longing to give herself wholly to God as in the Carmelite vocation, yet ready with great suppleness of faith to welcome the will of God, unhesitatingly, as seen in the needs of the Church and of the France of her day.

One feature of her spiritual make-up stands out with special clarity: her expendability under the Holy Spirit whose action was often manifested in difficult circumstances, by silence, by withdrawal, even by absence, sometimes by flight. Madeleine Sophie leaned upon God alone in prayer, always her first reaction.[37]

Chapter 3

Reality
1800–1865

Wisdom has built herself a
house; she has erected her
seven pillars.

Prov 9:1

The House of Wisdom appears in the Office composed for the
Beatification of Madeleine Sophie Barat in 1908: "By her desires
and prayers that house was seen to rise, founded on faith, erected by
hope, cemented by charity." [1] The sixty-five years during which she
laboured to build the Society of the Sacred Heart will here be considered from the outlook of the present day. "Do not come down
from her high thoughts; she has the genius of her times," [2] said Father
de Ravignan while she was still living. She has the genius of our times
— for us. We can learn much from the way in which she confronted
the questions of her day which adumbrated those of our own. She
once described her order as: "A Society of religious women whose
rules and spirit are adapted to the needs of the times." [3] As Janet Stuart
said in 1914:

> We should act today according to Montalembert's suggestion: it is not for us to
> do what our fathers did but to do what our fathers would do if they were here to-
> day; not what our Mother Foundress did in her time but what she would do if
> she were here today. [4]

The date does not matter.

We shall also learn that the beginnings were not a Golden Age of
classic perfection in which a blue-print for times to come was made.
Those years too knew search and experiment, trial and error.
Geneviève Deshayes wrote of 1802:

We were beginning, but we advanced like people walking in the dark. It was the way of Providence which has always led us thus, only lifting the veil of God's will little by little.[5]

In adapting the mentality of one age to that of another an understanding of the developing meaning of key-words is vitally needed. Awareness of semantic change belongs to the historical sense. It is not a question of "a new name for the same old thing"; a new name would not have been given if there had not been growth in the idea. Our predecessors did not hear a word as we do. Madeleine Sophie showed perception of this when she said of the "logical or literary analyses" with which her brother had crowned her own studies:

> At bottom these were true exercises in philosophy, but that word, stripped of its true meaning and debased by the false doctrines of voltairianism harmful to Jesus Christ and to eternal life, could not then be used. [6]

What about "democracy" or "liberty," even "equality," upon which thought and action hinge today as they did then?

Style too can colour thought. Madeleine Sophie's writings use the grammar, the vocabulary, often the metaphorical language of her eighteenth century education with which the twentieth century reader is not comfortable. Translation, especially if faithful, is another hazard, not only to sympathy but to truth.

* * *

It may be well to look first at the way in which the spirit of the Society of the Sacred Heart first became embodied in a written code. The Chapter of 1970 saw the exigencies of renewal as "summed up in the central theme of our Constitutions: unity and conformity with the Heart of Christ."[7] There is more concern today for a living organism than for the structures that control it, and that very concern demands understanding of the relation of spirit to letter. Janet Stuart faced the question:

> The Constitutions are to us only as Scripture is to Doctrine; we have beside them the living tradition that makes the rule of life. . . . Some vital spirit, quickening the Rule, had been in its first flower even before the Rule was written. The letter cannot serve without the spirit, but the spirit can flourish, at least for a time, without the letter. . . . Only from living soul to living soul can the original spirit

be handed down. . . . By the living tradition and the written law the Institute has come to its full growth with a marked personality of its own and some essential principles of construction which are found in the written rule.[8]

Madeleine Sophie knew from experience that only by sharing "from living soul to living soul" can a spirit take form in a code; the process belongs to the interpersonal mystery. One day in 1846, sitting among her first counsellors, she said to the novices:

What would I have done at the age of twenty-one, just out of the small home of a barrel-maker, if these had nót come to help me with their counsels and lend a hand? If I worked with Father Varin on our Constitutions, it is to the religious understanding of Mother de Charbonnel and Mother Desmarquest that you owe the practical development and moral strengthening of the Society of the Sacred Heart.[9]

The same truth is apparent in the current renewal of religious life. A study of the Jesuit attitude today recognizes that:

The charism maintains the structure and the structure maintains the charism. . . . It is the actual union of wills [among the members] — this mutual love — at any given moment of history which is the source of being of the Society [of Jesus]. The Constitutions, as Father Futrell remarks, are not the source of the being of the Society. The Society existed before the Constitutions were written or approved. And the being of the Society is not something that exists *in* the Constitutions. The Constitutions are, rather, the juridical instrument of the conservation of the Society's being. They are the concrete description of the process of the coming into existence of the Society through the actual unifying of its members for the apostolic end at any historical moment.[10]

For the first fifteen years of its life the Society of the Sacred Heart was gradually shaping a definite code. The original group stayed in Paris for a year and searched for the spirit by communal discernment. Father Varin recorded:

Every morning after mass we conferred together upon our Society. One of the first questions asked was: "What shall be its spirit" With one voice we all said: "Generosity!" A strong and generous love for Jesus Christ; that is what we felt must be the characteristic of the spouses of his Heart.[11]

The early *Mémoires* add:

It was there that the true foundations of the Society of the Sacred Heart were laid, under the standard of him whose work it was to do. It was there that Jesus

Christ gave it a *mot d'ordre*, impressed upon it a seal that was his own: a spirit large, strong and generous, filled with sweetness and with inflexible courage.[12]

Sophie, the youngest, with no idea that she was foundress, had the most far-reaching intuitions. In her old age she once revealed to her community, in a reminiscent mood, what had come to her as she prayed alone in the attic chapel:

The first idea that we had of the form to be given to our Society was to gather the greatest number possible of true adorers of the eucharistic Heart of Jesus. As we emerged from the Terror and from the abominations which the revolution had committed against the Blessed Sacrament, all hearts that had remained faithful to God — and they arose on all sides once the churches were opened — beat as one. . . .

And so I come to the primordial idea of our little Society of the Sacred Heart: to gather together young girls to establish a community which night and day would adore the Heart of Jesus outraged in his eucharistic love. But, I said to myself, when we shall be twenty-four religious able to replace each other on the priedieu to keep up perpetual adoration, that will be much but very little for so noble an end. But if we had pupils whom we could form to the spirit of adoration and of reparation, that would be different.

And I saw those hundreds, those thousands of adorers before a universal monstrance, lifted up above the Church. That is it, I said to myself before a lonely tabernacle, we must vow ourselves to the education of youth. We must lay in souls the solid foundation of a living faith in Jesus in the Blessed Sacrament, combat the traces of Jansenism which leads to impiety, and, with the revelations of Jesus Christ to Margaret Mary concerning the reparative and expiative devotion to the Sacred Heart in the Blessed Sacrament, we shall raise up a throng of adorers from all nations and to the very ends of the earth.[13]

Sophie had seen far in the year one of the Society; her vision foretold a community rooted in prayer, expressing the love of the Heart of Christ through a mission of education at the service of the Church, an international society reaching around the world.

For the moment the rules drawn up for the Dilette di Gesù were enough to guide the new community, but Father Varin looked behind them to the primary inspiration. The records say:

Father Varin did not look upon himself as founder (God forbid!) but as the successor of Father de Tournély whose lights and desires he had faithfully received. It was for him to transmit that spirit to us.[14]

He thus knew that the society would exist for one end only: to glorify the Heart of Christ by manifesting his love, that its rules would be based upon those of the Society of Jesus, that it would follow the Jesuit way of contemplation overflowing into apostolic service, that it would be devoted to an educational mission, though cloistered. He knew that all this must be adapted to a woman's way. He knew that its members, "living by the virtues of the Heart of Jesus," would "give themselves to prayer in order to receive from God light and grace."[15]

In that same year, 1800, another religious order was founded in Poitiers by Joseph-Marie Coudrin, the Religious of the Sacred Hearts and of Perpetual Adoration, known as the Society of Picpus. He was helped by Suzanne Geoffroy[16] who later joined the Society of the Sacred Heart. There was current at the moment an apocalyptic prophecy, a mélange of fantasy and of inspiration, made in 1787 by Charles Nectou, S.J. When Madeleine Sophie came to know of it she took it seriously:

> There will be a society of women consecrated to the Sacred Heart of Jesus. Their end will be to appease the anger of God, to extend the devotion to the Sacred Heart and to work for the salvation of souls. The Sacred Heart of Jesus will be the centre which unites all its elements. This Society will be marked by great union among its members and by a vital desire to procure the greater glory of God. The spirit of Saint Teresa will reign in their houses, that of Saint Ambrose in their dealings with others.[17]

In October, 1801, the little group moved to Amiens to take over a struggling school on the Rue Martin Bleu Dieu. Geneviève Deshayes[18] and Henriette Grosier[19] joined them, and "how happy we were in that poor little place!" They renewed their consecration on November 21. Octavie Bailly held back, thinking of Carmel, but Sophie said: "I am not looking for what satisfies me but for what pleases my God. I shall stay and do what I can."[20] She made her profession on June 7, 1802. A school for the poor was opened and the establishment moved to the Rue Neuve.

Sister Loquet, obviously competent but dominant and erratic, was in charge. But "she was a person whom God had received into his paradise but whom he did not call to share our vocation. She had guided us but did not have the spirit God wished for us."[21] So the third-in-line for the title of foundress withdrew and Louise Naudet came from the Dilette to arrange matters. Madeleine Sophie Barat was named superior on December 21, 1802, for "she had that drawing power, that indefinable charm that Jesus had given to the one whom we felt should be our mother."[22]

At once she created an atmosphere of joy, confidence and union, forgetting her shy inwardness as her full power to love was released. The community was joined by Catherine de Charbonnel,[23] a dynamic and erudite aristocrat, by Félicité Desmarquest,[24] a practical and tranquil daughter of a Picardy farmer, both future "pillars of the Society," and by Anne Baudemont, a former Poor Clare, problematical from the beginning. On September 29, 1804, they moved to a large house known thereafter as *le Berceau*. With its high scholastic standards the school soon attracted many returned *émigrés*.

The first coadjutrix sisters, Madeleine Raison and Bartholémy Roux, then entered the Society. The distinction between choir religious and the coadjutrices had originated in the Middle Ages among the Cistercians, in the desire to open religious life to all who felt called to it in an epoch when differences of education and social status would otherwise have been a barrier. Such distinctions were still taken for granted at the beginning of the nineteenth century, and without the category of coadjutrix sisters many vocations marked by simplicity, by humble, hidden service like that of Nazareth, and often by high gifts of prayer, would have been lost to the Society.

At first the community had worn black silk dresses and a round cap, suitable for *maîtresses de pensionnat*, but now a religious habit, in a simple style of contemporary dress with a veil and fluted cap, was adopted. Father de Tournély had been insistent that the new society should wear a garb "simple, modest and poor, but not the habit of the older orders which repels people of the world."[25]

Although Napoleon's Concordat with the Holy See had freed the Church in France, his Decree of Messidor in June 1804, renewed the threat to religious orders and prohibition of solemn vows. In Rome Father Paccanari was in trouble, and the Fathers of the Faith in France separated from the "Paccanarists." This brought about the dissolution of the Roman house of the Dilette de Gesù (this group, later became the Sisters of the Holy Family of Verona); the French branch was now autonomous under the name of *Association Religieuse des Dames de l'Instruction Chrétienne*. The name *Dames de la Foi*, given by popular usage, was dropped. The term *Dame* was then equivalent to "religious" as well as "lady." The use of "Madame" as a term of address was a precautionary measure in the aftermath of the revolution; it was continued throughout the nineteenth century in a milieu which found it natural, and this gave rise to the misleading name "the Madames" for the religious of the Sacred Heart.

In December, 1804, Mother Barat journeyed to Grenoble, passing her twenty-fifth birthday in the coach. Here she took possession of an old Visitation monastery, Sainte-Marie-d'en-Haut, offered to her by Philippine Duchesne[26] who had been a novice there before the revolution. Mother Barat spent two years in this lofty solitude, and here the first written outline of the new society was drawn up, *Abrégé de l'Institut*,[27] in November 1805. In presenting the document to Bishop Simon of Grenoble Mother Barat wrote:

> The necessity of learning from experience has not allowed us until now to write out the plan and rule of our association. Keeping ever before our eyes the end to which we tend and the spirit which should animate us, we seek every day the means to attain them.[28]

By this act of seeking episcopal approval the Society took on the character, which it kept for the next twenty years, of a religious association of simple vows dependent on diocesan authority.

The Plan resembles a dry skeleton seeking life. Through prudence the name of the association is not given, but the motive of the love of the Heart of Christ is clear in the preamble:

> The members believe that they can do nothing that would be dearer to the Heart of Jesus Christ than to devote themselves to the education of children who were always the dearest part of his flock.[29]

The aim of the association is not only the perfection of its members but the salvation of others by education in both boarding schools and schools for the poor, and by the work of retreats. A vow of education is made by the choir religious. The Society has central government; it observes cloister and recites the Little Office of Our Lady in choir. It offers a simple life in common, without corporal austerities. Its spirit rests upon the virtues of purity of intention, detachment, zeal and *douceur* (sweetness, gentleness, kindness). Prayer is one of the principal means of reaching its end.

Of these points two were to become controversial: enclosure and office in choir. At that date a religious order for women without these elements in some form was unthinkable (as earlier canonical difficulties met by Vincent de Paul's Sisters of Charity and Mary Ward's Institute of Mary testify).

Cloister in the first years of the Society was ambiguous. Technically it meant papal enclosure, and this could no longer be combined with the work of education, as had been done under the *ancien régime* by some orders such as the Visitation. Yet the rules for semi-enclosure had not yet been formulated. In France it was not safe to be overtly "religious" because of Napoleon's disapproval; the nuns often went out to accompany the pupils or to do business. Mother Barat stopped in her own home whenever passing through Joigny (where she liked to catch her old father in his working clothes). She firmly removed the grilles from Sainte-Marie despite the tears of Philippine Duchesne who exclaimed: "O my dear grilles!" "Your grilles, my dear!" retorted Mother Barat. "Don't talk to me of grilles! Our intentions, our actions, cannot be shut up in grilles." Later, she wrote to Philippine then in the New World: "I ask you now, where would you be with grilles – in Louisiana?"[30]

Similarly, no congregation of women was dispensed from the recitation of office in choir, even those based on the Jesuit rule which did not require it. The practice first began in the Society at Grenoble. Mother Barat said regretfully in a letter written in 1839 when the matter was under discussion that it had first been adopted as a substitute for the perpetual adoration of the Blessed Sacrament which she and her first companions had desired. She knew only too well the difficulty of reciting office in a teaching order.

The first General Council (or Congregation)[31] of the Society of the Sacred Heart was held at the Mother House in Amiens, in the presence of Father Varin and of Abbé Sambucy de Saint-Estève, chaplain of the house. On January 18, 1806, Sophie Barat, already considered superior general, was confirmed in that office for life by a majority of one vote over Anne Baudemont.[32] This fourth near-foundress "was endowed with the qualities requisite in a superior yet lacked that gentleness and humility which reveal the disciple of the Heart of Christ."[33] On the other hand:

> Mother Barat possessed all the qualities proper for her office. Her close union with God, her gentleness, prudence, entire devotion to the Society, the tried wisdom of her government, the talents she showed at an age when others have only promise for the future, led us to believe that God had raised her up to direct our little family.[34]

Despite differences of opinion which threatened a serious rift, the Council worked on a first draft of the Constitutions, the text of which has been lost. It was probably an elaboration of the Abridged Plan made at Grenoble inspired by the Rules and Constitutions of the Religious of Notre Dame, founded by Jeanne de l'Estonnac in 1607, itself based on the Summary of the Jesuit Constitutions. The name first proposed by Father de Tournély, Daughters of the Sacred Heart, was enthusiastically accepted, but it could not yet be openly assumed and the name in use remained Religious of Christian Teaching.

In July, 1806, Mother Barat went to Poitiers where Josephine Bigeu[35] and Lydie Chobelet joined the Society and offered her the old Cistercian monastery of Les Feuillants. They were joined by a group of enterprising young girls from Bordeaux who had run away from home in an attempt to form a community. Among them was Thérèse Maillucheau.[36] Mother Barat stayed for two years in the idyllic setting of Poitiers, "my primitive Church." The Poitiers Journal,[37] written by herself, gives a refreshingly vivid picture of a spirit gradually forming into rule and custom. She said to the novices:

> "I have many things to say to you but you cannot bear them now." God will tell you what you must know. You are still children and he treats you as such. Jesus in his goodness is planning great things for his new-born Society; we must pray and sufer much.[38]

A draft of "The Statutes and Rules of the Religious of Christian Teaching," known later as "Statuts Primitifs," was drawn up by Father Lambert of the Fathers of the Faith and approved by the episcopal council of Poitiers. In the meantime Mother Baudemont at Amiens was pressing for approbation by the Emperor. Mother Barat said:

> I do not know whether it would be expedient for us to be approved; if it should make us less humble and consequently less pleasing to our Lord it would be better to remain little and forgotten.[39]

But the civil approbation was found necessary for the Society's existence, and an abridgement of the Statutes in the Form of "Nine Articles" was drawn up. Napoleon signed it in his tent on the battlefield of Osterode on March 10, 1807. His attitude was: "I want nothing Sacred Heart," but: "I want to see women who are believers, not reasoners, and who are useful." [40] His minister, Portalis, assured him:

> This Society is conformable to the spirit of a religion which consecrates all that is attractive; for its object is to cultivate those branches of instruction which can

contribute to the happiness of families and the betterment of the public way of life.[41]

Napoleon was less tolerant of men's associations; on November 1, 1807, the Fathers of the Faith were dissolved and Father Varin took refuge in Switzerland. Correspondence concerning the Constitutions became more and more difficult.

Three new houses were opened in 1808: Dooresele at Ghent in Belgium; Cuignières in the country, a refuge in case of persecution; and Niort near Poitiers. Mother Barat found it impossible to live habitually at Amiens where Mother Baudement and Monsieur de Saint-Estève were assuming the role of "founders". They tended towards more monastic forms of government and way of life, and were preparing their own version of the Constitutions. This version, while based upon the Rule of Saint Ignatius, introduced elements from Poor Clare, Ursuline and Basilian observances. It included sixty-six articles from the *Statuts Primitifs*, but departed notably from the original inspiration of consecration to the Sacred Heart. This document, known as *Règles des Dames de l'Instruction Chrétienne* is extant only in the form given it in 1814.

Mother Barat left Poitiers in the summer of 1809 and for the next few years travelled among her five houses in an effort to maintain unity. Both she and Father Varin did their best to work in harmony with the group at Amiens. At a meeting on February 2, 1811, their Constitutions were voted on and tentatively accepted by Mother Barat. Her way was openness to the opinions of others; as a woman of discernment she knew how to listen, pray, wait, and then act firmly. She presented the Constitutions to the professed religious in each house; they were received with sorrow and alarm.

> We felt that the Sacred Heart was not living in those Constitutions. We looked in vain in them for the strong, sweet spirit which had been the drawing force in our own vocation.[42]

As Mother Barat said: "The attempt at Amiens completely lacks integration."[43]

In the summer of 1812 Monsieur de Saint-Estève was imprisoned but it still seemed possible to reach a compromise. In September Mother Barat went to Chevroz where Father Varin was living with his sister, for quiet consultation. A little boy was watching them, the future Jesuit Ferdinand Jeantier:

For several hours after holy mass I would see Father Varin and Mother
Barat walking together in a very recollected way under the trees that surround
the château de Chevroz. The father was holding a notebook in one hand and a
pencil in the other; he walked slowly, making long pauses at one spot, writing
and erasing. I often said to myself that they were writing and correcting the Constitutions of the Society of the Sacred Heart. What charity there must be in those
Constitutions which were composed by minds, hearts, hands, even pens all suf-
fused with the fire of the love of the Sacred Heart![44]

On August 7, 1814, the Company of Jesus was reconstituted by
the papal Bull *Solicitudo Omnium Ecclesiarium,* and Father Varin
became a Jesuit novice, while continuing to help Mother Barat.[45] He
decided that no compromise with Monsieur de Saint-Estève was
possible, and that the Constitutions of the Society of the Sacred Heart
must be completely rewritten. The Abbé, released from prison, went
to Rome as secretary to the influential French ambassador, Bishop
Pressigny. From there he unleashed a storm that all but destroyed the
Society. His letters were threatening: he had founded a house in
Rome which had obtained the Pope's approval; those religious who
wished to remain loyal to the Holy See must join him there. Mother
Barat answered that it was for the Society to present its Constitutions
to the Holy See for approval, that it must have the name "Sacred
Heart" rather than the Abbé's chosen name, Apostolines. The crisis
sharpened. In December the house at Dooresele withdrew from the
Society; the superior, Mother Peñeranda, feared Gallicanism if
Mother Barat did not submit. The French members of the community
returned to Paris, the Belgian remained.[46]

Mother Barat fell ill and almost died. When she recovered she
went to Paris to work with Father Varin on the true version of the
Constitutions. Political events caused further confusion: Napoleon's
abdication and the accession of Louis XVIII, Metternich's "Restoration" at the Congress of Vienna, the "Hundred Days" and peace after Waterloo. At Amiens matters grew worse. Mother Barat was ill
again in July, and while recuperating at Cuignières received letters
from a mysterious "Stephanelli" in Rome threatening excommunica-
tion. Submission seemed to be the only course, "one that will drive
home the nails that fasten you to the cross,"[47] wrote Father Varin.
Mother de Sambucy and Mother Copina left Amiens for the convent
of Saint Denys which Monsieur de Saint-Estève had opened in Rome
near the Quattro Fontane (where Mother Baudemont joined them a
year later).[48] In time it became apparent that the letters signed
"Stephanelli" were no better than forgeries, being written by Mon-

sieur de Saint-Estève himself. Throughout these months of anguish Father Varin and Mother Barat continued to work on the authentic Constitutions. They were ready by the time Mother Barat summoned the Second General Council which met in Paris in the convent of Saint Thomas de Villeneuve from November 1 to December 15, 1815.

The Council was composed of the superior of each house with one member of her community chosen by Mother Barat; all had possessed the true spirit of the Society from the beginning: Josephine Bigeu, Henriette Grosier, Suzanne Geoffroy, Henriette Girard,[49] Philippine Duchesne, Geneviève Deshayes, Emilie Giraud[50] and Eugénie de Gramont.[51] The latter alone had been "of the opposition" and her views changed during the Council. It was a youthful gathering energized by a leader thirty-six years old; it was wise from past suffering and created its future with hope. Unanimously it accepted the Constitutions[52] that had grown out of the lived spirit of the Society:

> They brought to a head, after twenty years of searching (January, 1796–November, 1815) the primal thought of Father de Tournély. If this thought finally became actual it was because Sophie Barat, who had inherited it and fused it with her own inspiration, was able to uphold it constantly through the difficult hours when all human help failed. The Lord blessed her perseverance and her prayer. She could offer to her religious family a law of life which expressed its own charism. If she is not directly the author of the text, it can be said that it expressed what she had lived in the depths of her own soul since her consecration of November 21, 1800.[53]

Mother Duchesne wrote:

> The sixteenth of December, 1815, was the day of our rebirth, or rather the confirmation of our Society which had always desired to be able thus to glory in belonging, in name as well as in fact, to the Sacred Heart of Jesus. The day was passed in holy joy.[54]

Mother Barat then wrote her first circular letter to the whole Society:

> Our Society from the beginning has been essentially founded upon devotion to the Sacred Heart of Jesus, and it must be so devoted and consecrated to the worship of that divine Heart that all the works and all the functions that it embraces must tend to that as to its final end. . . . And so I close with these words with which our Constitutions close: *Cor unum et anima una in corde Jesu.*[55]

The cross and ring were adopted in place of the medal worn till then, and the decisions of the Council were accepted in harmony. Mother Barat said:

> We are very satisfied. The Society now has but one mind and one heart; everywhere we are "religious of the Sacred Heart"; everywhere we have the same Rules and Constitutions.[56]

After the Council the centre of government was transferred to a small house on the Rue des Postes in Paris, "where people come from everywhere and where all the business falls on me,"[57] said Mother Barat. A period of startling expansion was beginning, and the Third General Council met from August 18 to October 12, 1820 to consider the means of maintaining unity:

> As the regulations made in the past have been enlarged or curtailed as seemed best for the greater good of the pupils, different opinions have arisen on certain points, without our realizing it. And as one of our dearest obligations is to maintain uniformity it seems urgent, before the Society extends any further, to consolidate the existing houses by regulating all that contributes to their spiritual and temporal welfare.[58]

The Council focussed on the work of education; the School Rule and Plan of Studies were revised. A *Summary of the Rules and Constitutions*, drawn up by Father Varin, was ratified.[59]

The Mother House was then transferred to the Hotel Biron on the Rue de Varenne where the first mass was offered on November 6, 1820. This aristocratic house (which Mother Barat did her best to simplify) soon spread the reputation of the Society; the pace of expansion doubled. There were now eleven houses and Mother Barat was constantly on the road. Only papal approval could give the Society its mandate to move confidently into the future.

Josephine Bigeu went to Rome to negotiate. It was found that the Holy See was slow, for the moment, to give solemn approbation to any order founded in France, and had already issued a simple Laudatory Brief stating that: "The Society of the Sacred Heart deserves praise." But a formal request was sent to Leo XII:

> The Society desires to spread devotion to the Sacred Heart over the whole earth and set everyone on fire with divine love. . . . But since our Institute embraces various countries where our Society can do good, it is indispensable that we have

a uniform rule in the places to which we shall be called, and this uniformity can only result from the will and approbation of your Holiness.[60]

The Society was in many ways novel to the Cardinals of the old school, but even they saw that: "It is manifestly the work of God; let us fear to touch it." The approval was granted, and at an audience held in the Gesù on July 31, 1826, Mother Bigeu thanked Leo XII in the name of the Society. Mother Barat wrote in a circular letter:

> Without this approbation we could not have won the full confidence needed to extend the good which the Society seems destined to produce for the glory of God. Our Rules and Constitutions being marked by the seal of the Holy Spirit, and the practice of them having already led many of ours to a high perfection and a holy death, nothing was lacking to the veneration which we have for these rules but the sanction of the common Father of the faithful. . . . Each one can now say: I am sure of obeying the Church and of doing the will of God.[61]

The Fourth General Council met from September 29 to November 25, 1826. It was devoted to making the Society conform more exactly to the ideal set for it by Rome. By the approbation it had been placed among the congregations immediately dependent upon the Holy See. Henceforth a Cardinal Protector would watch over its interests in Rome; the first to be named was Cardinal Carlo Pedicini.[62] As solemn vows could not be made by religious without papal enclosure, a vow of stability was henceforth to be made at profession which was considered canonical compensation for papal enclosure. Semi-cloister was to be more clearly defined and more strictly observed than in the beginning. Mother Barat wrote: "Our Approbation is of the same nature as that of the Society of Jesus; it is without parallel for nuns without strict enclosure." [63]

Leo XII signed the Brief of Approbation on December 22, 1826. When it reached Paris Mother Barat reconvened the Council members to read it to them.[64] The vow of stability was first made on April 16, 1827. On April 22 civil approbation was given by Charles X. This document gave the Society legal but ominous protection, since the state controlled the rights of teaching orders so approved.

In the years following the Society took possession of the Trinita-dei-Monti and of Santa Rufina in Rome, opened a free school at the Rue de Varenne, and was driven by the revolution of 1830 to transfer the central noviceship from Paris to Montet in Switzerland. Houses multiplied in Europe and America. The Fifth General Council, which met from September 19 to December 1, 1833, followed this constructive rhythm. It stressed joy and charity in community, simplicity and order in the schools, and once more revised the Plan of Studies since to hold to routine through fear of innovation is "weakness of mind."[65] The number of assistants general was raised from three to four;[66] |the American houses were represented by Eugénie Audé.[67]

In 1835 the administrative centre of the Society moved to a small house on the Rue Monsieur at the other end of the grounds of the Hotel Biron which was fully occupied by the school. Mother Barat wrote:

> To consolidate the work of the Society we have decided to have our own residence, which will be the Mother House and the center of the government of the Society. All relations with the other houses will begin and end there. In this house we will place the central noviceship, the juniorate, the probation for the whole of France, also the general treasury, the secretariate and the archives of the Society. It will be our habitual residence.[68]

When the time came for the Sixth General Council Mother Barat knew that grave issues upon which opinion was acutely divided must be faced. It met from June 10 to July 5, 1839, at the Trinita-dei-Monti in Rome, and precipitated a crisis which tried the nature and existence of the Society as by fire. This arose over proposed modifications of the Constitutions. Pushed by strong-minded members like Elizabeth Galitzin[69] and Pauline de Limminghe,[70] the Council made forty-seven changes in an attempt to make the Constitutions resemble more closely those of the Society of Jesus.[71] Some were slight though significant, many were salutary, a few might have proved disastrous had they remained in force. Some were necessary, such as the establishment of provinces and the modification of the structure of the General Councils.

Mother Barat sensed the coming storm. On July 12 she consecrated the Society to Our Lady of Sorrows[72] before a fresco at the Villa Lante, and the Council closed.[73] Then the storm broke; division appeared everywhere, within and without the Society. The Decree which roused the most violent controversy was that which would have transferred the Mother House from Paris to Rome. The French bishops wrote their protests to the Holy See. The house at Paris, where Mother de Gramont was under the influence of Archbishop de Quélen with his gallican tendencies, was the centre of resistance within the Society.

The point which most closely touched the charism of the Society was the minimizing of the sense of consecration to the Sacred Heart. This was partly illusory, due to hasty and erroneous versions of the Decrees promulgated too soon. But there was a significant change of emphasis in the wording that expressed the aim of the Society:

> The end of this little Society, wholly consecrated to the greater glory of the Sacred Heart of Jesus and the propagation of its worship, is not only to seek the salvation and perfection of its members with the help of divine grace, but also to use every means, aided by that same grace, to seek the salvation of the neighbor.[74]

The *Summary of the Constitutions* states:

> This little Society is wholly consecrated to the glory of the Sacred Heart of Jesus and to the propagation of its worship; such is the end which all those who become members must propose to themselves. It is for this end that they contract the obligation of tending unceasingly towards their own perfection by the imitation of those virtues of which the Heart of Jesus is the centre and model and of consecrating themselves to the salvation of souls by inspiring them with a tender and solid devotion to that divine Heart.[75]

This change made Father Varin cry out in a letter to Mother Barat:

> Your Society would never have existed if it had not had, before all, the aim of working for the glory of the divine Heart of Jesus. . . . If you suppress this article there is only one thing left to do — change the name of the Society. And if, none-the-less, you keep the name, it will be a Society of the Sacred Heart, but it will not be the one that you saw born thirty-nine years ago.[76]

A period of three years trial of the new Decrees was agreed upon, while Mother Barat suffered, prayed and journeyed. In July, 1842, she called a General Council to meet in La Ferrandière in Lyons, saying: "I cannot doubt of the success of this important Council."[77] But Archbishop Affre of Paris put a stop to it on the grounds that he was the ecclesiastical superior of the Society — which he was not. In the confusion caused by lost letters to Rome the Council dispersed without having met. It was then that the French government asserted its rights, threatening to close all the houses in France if the Society did not immediately return to the Constitutions of 1826 upon which its civil approbation rested. Mother Barat was left alone at Conflans without the help of her most trusted counsellors. "My meditation is: 'Jesus was silent'."[78]

The matter was settled by a Decree of a commission of Cardinals with Archbishop Mathieu of Besancon acting as the Society's

representative, signed on March 4, 1843. The Constitutions of
1826 were restored, the Mother House was to remain in Paris, and
the provinces already established were to continue pending the next
General Council. Harmony returned; no house had been lost,
although some religious in the north of France had left the Society.
Mother Barat wrote:

> I would never have believed it, but holy people find it hard to agree among
> themselves until they have passed *per ignem,* that is, through the fire of the love
> of God – or through Purgatory.[79]

She felt that a lack of communication, of that frank dialogue, that
trustful willingness to listen so stressed later on by the Chapter of
1970, was at the root of both crises. In 1814 the superior of
Dooresele had refused even to read the documents from Amiens and
had not come to confer when invited. In 1839 Mother Barat said:
"Our Mothers who stopped my mouth so often when I made
reasonable objections did not want to understand."[80] When summoning the councillors in 1842 she asked them:

> . . . to act with that modesty that edifies, to express our views with humility
> and moderation, to discuss when necessary, but calmly, yielding readily when
> the right becomes evident, forgetting ourselves wholly to think only of the
> glory of the Heart of Jesus.[81]

In the misunderstandings that followed she wrote:

> You know that I am not stubborn, that I easily yield to reason. . . . You see
> that I enter into your views and gladly give in to what is reasonable, which
> means to understand each other, to agree.[82]

Time and again she said: "Together we shall come to an understanding," and when her call for dialogue was refused:

> God alone knows how we shall get out of this! . . . It would have been easy if
> all had been willing to come to an agreement and act in accord, to be at one as
> we have always been since the beginning of the Society.[83]

A visible seal was placed upon the harmony restored after the
storm when, in 1844, Pauline Perdrau[84] painted at the Trinita a
fresco of Our Lady in the temple, Mater Admirabilis, the Society's
"Treasure of calm and of serenity." It was soon reproduced in every
school, a centre of prayer and of inspiration.[85]

In that same year Luigi Lambruschini,[86] papal Secretary of State and extremely conservative in outlook, became Cardinal Protector, and the Society spread vigorously, though shaken by the Revolution of 1848 which closed the houses in Piedmont and Switzerland. The Society's Golden Jubilee was celebrated on November 21, 1850, and Mother Barat looked to its origin:

> Every religious order studies the spirit of its founder; the measure of its perfection depends upon its conformity with him. We must study the Heart of Jesus, his teaching, his virtues.[87]

She was anxious to put the capstone on the Constitutions, and in May, 1851, requested the approval of Pius IX for three essential points left pending since 1839: to establish provinces each in charge of a provincial superior; to change the General Council into a convocation of the assistants general and provincials; to allow the superior general to nominate by secret ballot a vicar general to govern during the interval between her death and the election of her successor. The requests were granted, but Pius IX asked for a significant change in the first: there were to be vicariates instead of provinces. This stressed centralization and lessened the autonomy of the superiors vicar, since a vicariate has not the same canonical standing as a province. It meant also that the General Councils, made up of ex officio members with no representative delegates, were not true chapters. These factors tended to a certain rigidity of government along the vertical line as time passed.

The Seventh General Council then met at Lyons from November 13 to December 5, 1851, representing the fifteen vicariates into which the Society was then divided. It revised the Decrees, the Ceremonial, the Custom Book and the Plan of Studies.[88] On August 15, 1853, Napoleon III gave imperial approbation to the modified Constitutions.

Since 1851 no major changes have been made in the Constitutions; regulations made by successive General Councils have taken the form of Decrees which have the force of law but can be altered or abrogated without touching the Constitutions. Cardinal Giusto Recanati,[89] who became Protector in 1854, said of them:

> They are in truth a masterpiece, inspired by the Holy Spirit, not only from the ecclesiastical point of view but as a work of legislation. The unity seen in them is admirable; the devotion to the Sacred Heart is the centre around which everything revolves and towards which everything converges.[90]

Who is the author of the Constitutions? The Abridged Plan which prefaces them is attributed originally to Father de Tournély, but the extant version has undergone development. The primary author of the main text is Father Varin; he was assisted at first by Father de Clorivière and in the final version by Father Druilhet. If Madeleine Sophie Barat did not actually write any of the text, she was its constant inspirer, reviser and critic, working with Father Varin at every step. Her spirit and her expression are all-pervasive.

The Constitutions consist of four parts treating of: 1) the admission of subjects; 2) the means of forming them at each stage to the virtues and perfection of their state; 3) the apostolic works; 4) government and the means of preserving the spirit of the Institute. The Special Rules follow. The text closes with the "Letter of Saint Ignatius on the Virtue of Obedience." The Summary, included in the text but printed separately and placed in the hands of each religious, is far more than the name implies. It not only streamlines and focusses the full document but adds some extremely significant passages, such as the beautiful section on the five virtues of the apostolic life: living faith, contempt of the world, humility, simplicity and modesty.

The parallels with the Constitutions of the Society of Jesus are evident: both are congregations of world-wide membership in which prayer animates the apostolate, both have strongly centralized government. The Common Rules were adopted verbatim, whereas those for Special Offices were re-expressed. Of this adaptation Mother Barat said:

> It was a divine thought for it did not come from us. Our Lord had this thought and he carried it out, giving to weak women like us the idea of adopting these rules, so holy and so wise, and of giving ourselves, as far as is possible for women, to a type of apostolate which had not been seen before. [91]

The rules and spirituality of some other religious orders are also reflected in the Constitutions. None of the four great monastic rules were drawn upon, though much of the way of life was monastic in origin; the influences came rather from the great religious houses in France before the Revolution. There were the women's orders which had carried on the work of education: Dames de Saint Thomas de Villeneuve, Dames de Saint Louis de Saint Cyr, Religieuses de Notre Dame and "Les Dames Anglaises." There were those through which the devotion to the Sacred Heart was kindled: the Visitation and the Oratorians who had educated Father de Tournély and Father Varin. The Religieuses de Sainte Aure influenced the Custom Book. There is (and here the personal influence of Madeleine Sophie can be felt) a strong affinity of spirit with the Carmelites of the Teresian reform, in the insistence of the Constitutions on profound prayer passing through the humanity of Christ.

It is the focus placed upon the Heart of Christ that makes the difference; his glory is the primary aim of the Society. Mother Barat said that a religious order named for it "must express the wound in the Heart."[92] And the key phrase, "Heart of Jesus," and variants of "the interior dispositions of the divine Heart," give to the Constitutions their tone, colour and power. The *Histoire des Constitutions de la Société du Sacré Coeur* says of them:

> What is original in the Society of the Sacred Heart? The unique personality of a living being which has assimilated this rich traditional substance and which emerges new in its originality. . . . It is not possible to separate the canonical aspects from the spiritual. These Constitutions realize, in fact and to a high degree, the union between the juridical and charismatic elements. Law here appears as the concrete expression of a spirituality and of a way of living it. [93]

In urging fidelity to them Mother Barat said:

> Do not depart, under pretext of something better, from the unity so desirable in a congregation which seems destined to spread over the universe if we are faithful to God's designs.[94]

* * *

The spirit which gave life to the letter can be seen in the concrete by exploring the way in which the Five Options of the Chapter of 1970 were lived, still unformulated, in the beginning of the Society. Christ's "prayer of lasting power" moved the Chapter to take "several fundamental options which converge on a single centre, the Heart of Christ." They are not new choices made in 1970; they are affirmations with a new accent of elements always present. One cannot be chosen and another left; they are interdependent. They are priorities, focal points of the Society's determination to keep her identity in renewal: internationality, educational mission, solidarity with the poor, solidarity with the Third World, evangelical community.

In considering these options in the time of the Foundress it may be well to re-arrange them. Community will be placed first as it was the first to arise; internationality will follow as it was implicit in community. These two concern the life of the Society in itself, in its membership. Education comes next, the Society's basic form of service. Solidarity with the poor was at first included under education; it will be considered here together with solidarity with the Third World (a concept which did not then exist although the reality was emerging) as "social awareness." These three concern the Society as it reaches out to the People of God.

Community life is a form of the "interpersonal mystery" lived from day to day. Janet Stuart said that two worlds, the seen and the unseen, the active and the contemplative, "meet together in the quiet place of community life which has its frontiers on the one and the other."[95] The Chapter of 1970 said:

> We commit ourselves to renewal, at depth, of our life as a community, convinced that this is the one condition essential to the future of our religious life and to a genuine response to the summons of the Church and the world. [96]

The earliest records show vignettes of community life vibrant with simple joyousness, when customs were still flexible. Madeleine Sophie remembered that after the ceremony on November 21, 1800:

> At dinner time Father Varin, my brother and Father Roger were at table with us. It was like the *Agape* of the first Christians, full of sweet and religious expansiveness. The meal was prolonged beyond our usual time. [97]

They began by facing with realism the difficulties inherent in community building:

> We agreed to banish from among ourselves the pettiness of convent life, the tricks of self-love, the sensitiveness, the antipathies which are the faults of half-hearted and divided persons.[98]

At Amiens community life encountered the exactions of the apostolate. Sister Geneviève recalled:

> In the evening, after the fatigues and exhaustions of the day, when the children were in bed, we found ourselves free. Then our souls swam as in a refreshing bath. I cannot express the charm, the sweet and pure joy, that we found in being delightfully together. It was our consolation in a great purity of union in God alone. We talked by the fire in the kitchen; our three heads drawn close together were a picture of happy confidences exchanged. Zealous Sister Sophie

spoke of her desire for the missions of Canada; Sister Grosier felt the same way. I listened in silence, having only enough zeal for France. [99]

They had found the secret early: community is togetherness in God alone; "what charity reigned among us!" Geneviève, who played the harp, composed a song on the text "How good it is for brothers to dwell together in unity," and "we all sang it while the candle-end burned down." Work grew with the school and its demands were met buoyantly. Catherine de Charbonnel was in charge of the studies:

> What good literary parties we had then, our Mother Foundress and I, when the school was in bed! Our fourth vow gave us strength to sit up at night, for the day was full of work and distractions. . . . Those who had the literary share sat up late to write verses. We called them "our bright nuns" and just before midnight gave them coffee well sweetened. [100]

There were financial worries as well, but:

> It never occurred to us not to get on with things as they were. "No money, no desires!" said a Desert Father. . . . Never will the relative well-being of the Society today give us the unheard-of pleasures forced on us then by poverty and — yes, let's use the word — privation. [101]

This state of affairs continued at Sainte-Marie where "we lived in pure contentment," said Philippine Duchesne. "We were happy to find some inconvenience in the form of snow that drifted in here and there," [102] and so recreations were held "in the painted room where we all gathered around the great fireplace." [103] The community joined in the fun of the children, with angular Sister Philippine as "It".

The Poitiers Journal gives the fullest sense of "an atmosphere conducive to the experience of God," [104] with prolonged prayer, mutual trust, irrepressible gaiety with strict observance. The novices were formed by daily community life, and: "How they talked! It was a pleasure to hear them." They sat around a candle in which they had stuck a pin to mark the time allowed to each to tell the palpitating story of her vocation. As Mother Barat said: "We all enjoyed our recreations very much; they were always too short. It is true that this is the only time when we can see each other and communicate in full liberty of mind and heart." [105] When she returned from a journey one evening:

On leaving the chapel we went to the garden. There we stayed until quite late in the coolness, relaxing the rule concerning bedtime for the first moments of our reunion. We passed the time in rejoicing at being together again and in saying: how good is the Lord! Finally, my sisters had composed some verses in my honour which they sang by the light of the moon. [106]

Their life reached out to take in the whole community of Poitiers: the children with whom they had picnics on the grass "because it does them so much good," Marie the *commissionaire,* the gardener, little Madeleine who minded their one cow. In the "Manresa" of the Society we see:

A life hidden and retired, a life of deep detachment from family affections, personal desires and self will, but at the same time a life full of liberty of spirit; a life of silence and of fraternal charity, of exterior simplicity and of profound renouncement; a life of retreat from the world and of reparative adoration, and at the same time a life of intense apostolate and of study. These are the aspects, contrasting and seemingly contradictory but in reality complementary, which would be the specific elements of the life of the religious of the Sacred Heart, a life in which the equilibrium between persons and activities, realized by the foundress, would always be difficult to maintain. [107]

Later on, when absorbed by administration, Mother Barat called the Hotel Biron "the Sacred Heart hotel" because of the comings and goings, and said of the scenes of welcome at the front door: "This does so much good! It strengthens our mutual attachment to a Society that lives wholly in its members and they in it, united thus in the Heart of Jesus where all comes to rest." [108]

Mother Barat knew well that the "communication in full liberty of mind and heart" which was her ideal, is exposed to constant friction:

It is not easy to please everyone. Let's do our best and stay in peace. [109] When you come to know the heart of man nothing in his ideas or actions will surprise you.[110] . . . We don't live with angels; we have to put up with human nature and forgive it. I have often told you this, but the people in whom you see such real faults don't agree with you and you think they deceive themselves. In such cases, for the sake of peace, I try to put myself in their place, and I only judge them by looking through their eyeglasses. . . . Each one has her own views which I respect though different from mine. I am more tranquil for having recognized the impossibility of pleasing everyone. There, I have given you my secret for keeping peace whatever happens. [111]

She knew what it meant to live with women: "We must put up with them and excuse them; still more we must find them charming." [112]

She made communication easy because she possessed the art of listening. A novice, Maria Tommasini, never forgot her few moments with Mother Barat:

> You felt that she was listening to you with her intelligence and with her heart; she let you see her feelings of pain, of pleasure, of astonishment, of approval, of indignation. In a word, you knew that she was interested in you. [113]

The friendships formed in the early Society were a means of building not only community life but the life of the Society itself. The only mention of friendship in the Constitutions is negative, a warning against that exclusiveness that is "the bane of communities." [114] In actual life these first friendships were the "true interpersonal relationships which give substance to our commitment to live the universal love of Christ" [115] seen by the Chapter of 1970. The *Orientations* of 1967 speak of community life as "a likeness to and sharing in the life of the Trinity in the mutual gift of love and service, in unity of action and distinction of function." [116] Mother Barat once wrote to three of her friends who were in the same community: "I want you three to be a trinity, like to the one in heaven." [117] They were Philippine Duchesne, Thérèse Maillucheau and Josephine Bigeu, persons of towering spiritual stature and of very different temperaments.

Mother Barat gave free play to her own remarkable endowment for friendship. She loved each person with a real and distinctive love, and did not fear selective relationship with "those with whom I feel at ease," with whom she sensed affinity.

> The only good quality recognizable in me is the constancy of my affections. I think that this is all the more true because I give my intimacy to few persons. [118] . . . It is sweet to find true daughters and sincere friends in one's troubles. This is my only prop in this world, and when the Heart of Jesus gives it to me I can enjoy it without anxiety. [119]

She drew from differing personalities the unique gift that each could offer to the Society. When Mother de Charbonnel's practical talents drew her off on long journeys Mother Barat said: "She will come back soon; I can't get on any longer without her. What an excellent Mother, and how good it is to live with her!" [120] And of Mother Desmarquest, who "brought Nazareth into the Society," she said: "All is in common between this Mother and me; she has my whole confidence."

The friendships with her "trinity" reached deep. To Philippine she wrote: "I feel the need of pouring out my heart into that of a friend to whom our Lord seems to have given the same desire to make him known and loved." [121] And after long separation: "My intimate affection for you has never lessened; neither time nor distance can diminish it. On the contrary it is ever increasing." [122] With Thérèse, who carried the spirit of Carmel with her, Mother Barat shared her own understanding of the Song of Songs, and when they were apart: "Often the thought of you occupies me before our Lord. It takes only a moment to tell him the needs of those who are dearest to us, and in this respect you hold the first place." [123] It was noticed that once, after parting from Thérèse, Mother Barat was unusually silent as she drove away in the coach, and kept her eyes closed. "How recollected she is!" thought the novice who travelled with her. But Mother Barat gave the real reason for her silence in a letter to Thérèse: "I suffered so much from leaving you, and my heart was so full when I thought of you, that I could scarcely speak. My whole being stayed with you." [124] Josephine was "one of those perfect souls in whom there is nothing to find fault." After her death Mother Barat went into solitude for ten days. "I have need of this time to pour out my heart before him who has sent me this sorrow. I have lost a friend who understood me, a person who supported me." [125]

Mother Barat was not dismayed by friction in even these ideal friendships. She wrote to Thérèse:

> Don't forget that despite the intimate union of our two souls we did not always agree. I often caused you pain in the short time that we were together, and I admit that it would be one of my heaviest crosses if this should happen again. All this does not mean, however, that we shall never live together. On the contrary, I find myself wishing for this, and I feel that I should be very much at ease with you — whereas I have to take so many precautions with others! [126]

She never withdrew her confidence from those who caused her pain; she saw through their strengths and weaknesses to the core of their best selves. She saw that they had greatly served the Society by the very challenge of their vision and zeal, even when these were misdirected. They remained her friends. To Mother de Limminghe, who had resigned as assistant general without informing her after the crisis of 1839, she only said: "Was not some consideration due to a mother who has been to you more of a friend than a superior?"[128] When Mother Galitzin recognized her mistakes: "Your letter was a balm to my poor heart, pierced for so long. This is the moment to surround me, more than ever, with your love and zeal."[128] When Mother de Gramont shut herself up in bitter regret for her disastrous opposition in both crises, Mother Barat wrote:

> Why, if you have something troubling you, do you keep silence about it; I have sometimes been obliged to cross your will? our Lord has allowed that we did not always have the same views as to what was best. But, believe me, I do not love you the less for that. I would be so happy to have an open understanding with you. And I can tell you, dear little Mother, that my other crosses would seem light if you were at peace with me. [129]

Mother Barat maintained this network of mutual affection by incredible energy in letter writing. "Correspondence absorbs me, but truly it is a fatigue that I love. Without this wonderful invention how could we live far from our dear ones?" [130] She wrote to a person who had gone away the day before: "I had to write to you at once, to tell you how sad I felt last night at spiritual reading when I looked at your place and saw only a chair!"

The influence of Mother Barat's friendships went on into the future, for she formed many with the very young. In her old age she wrote constantly to Mathilde Garabis[131] who was thirty years her junior:

> I admit, my daughter, that after our Lord you are my hope. That is because I know your heart, and the need that you feel to be my comfort. This, we must recognize, is true friendship: to forget ourselves. That is the character of yours.[132] ... Everyone knows that you are dear to me; so, to avoid jealousy, let us show to all that our union is solidly virtuous and apostolic. Then we shall inspire a holy rivalry! [133]

A religious community must be "a true presence in the human community which we wish to love and serve." [134] The Chapter of 1970 saw this as an evolution of the "necessary intercourse with persons of the world" [135] named in the Constitutions as one of the four means by which the Society carries out its mission. The form of this contact with the world was, until Vatican Council II, controlled by enclosure and by the rule of silence. Mother Barat showed far more liberty of heart in this difficult balance then did most of her contemporaries — and of those who followed her.

The closest circle of acquaintances was her own family. She wrote to her sister:

> I am in a desert when I do not know what is happening at home. Do you think that I am not interested in what concerns you? No, dear sister; it will never be so. Nothing will ever change the friendship I have for you. [136]

Her nieces (of whom four entered the Society), her erratic nephews for whom she found jobs, even a distant cousin in the army, all were followed with relentless love.[137] She formed ties, often lasting ones, with people met in the course of the day's work: the little boy whom she helped "because he is from my home town and because he is unhappy"; the doctor whom she delighted by listening to the endless tales of his exploits; the poor who left the back door the richer for her sympathy as well as for her alms; the relatives of her religious whose names she always remembered. Others were met on journeys where she always started a conversation with her fellow-travellers: the waitress at an inn whom she drew into a corner ("What is there between you and God, my child");[138] the old pupil whose life was rescued by a chance meeting on the road? the burly workmen in a coach who decided to "travel all the way to heaven" with her. Returning to her enclosed community she would recall to it the human community: "I have seen things today that would tear your heart."[139]

As the years passed and the communities grew in size, the life-style became more formal, more hierarchic in structure; the animating force became more maternal than fraternal. Mother Barat sometimes looked back wistfully. Of the spiritual conferences given by superiors with solemn formality she said: "That word has been kept, although it does not really describe the gatherings that we had in the beginning of the Society, since it means 'confer together,' and that is what we no longer do." [140] She wrote to Thérèse Maillucheau:

> I want to use the time that is left to me to plant deeply in the Society, which is so tried, that way of life that was basic in the beginnings: a humble and interior way which led to union of hearts and to charity like to that of the Heart of Jesus.[141]

*   *   *

The Chapter of 1970 said:

> An international community, one and necessarily pluriform, we want to live our new awareness of this communion, and to accept the practical consequences of co-responsibility and sharing at the international level. [142]

Madeleine Sophie, while still a novice, had sensed this option in the intuition that came to her in prayer when she had seen the future pupils of the Sacred Heart "by hundreds and thousands, drawn from all nations to the very ends of the earth." [143] She thus saw internationality as bound up with its educational mission and with its charism to reveal the love of Christ. In the first years at Amiens the Society of six members received a letter from a missionary in Madagascar asking for a foundation. Obviously it could not be accepted, but Madeleine Sophie said: "I knew by what happened to me interiorly that our Society should embrace the whole world, and this thought struck me profoundly as a call from God." [144]

Philippine Duchesne had been inspired as a child by the talk of a passing missionary, but when she entered the Visitation the desire was seemingly lost in the contemplative life. When she entered the Society it returned, irresistibly, as she prayed before dawn in the children's dormitory on January 10, 1806. She wrote of her experience to Madeleine Sophie who, by her election as superior general became "nailed to France" a few days later, and who answered:

> Your letter brought me very deep joy, touching as it did the most sensitive chord in my heart. Yes, that is what I have been asking for you ever since the Lord gave you into my keeping, and I have prayed for it so often and with such ardour because I was sure that our Lord wanted from you this devotedness, this entire sacrifice. I have still another reason of which I can now tell you; it is one of my secrets. Even before I knew of our little Society the desire of carrying the name of the Lord to unbelieving nations was in the depths of my heart. . . . Time has shown that I cannot cling to my hope. . . . But have I given up my project? The same desire increases every day, and I have been asking that one of my companions may carry it out, and that the Holy Spirit himself may prepare and lead her. [145]

For twelve years of waiting Madeleine Sophie fashioned the impetuous Philippine with gentle wisdom. They had both heard the same call; one was sent for the other. The interpersonal mystery was at work.

Philippine Duchesne sailed on the *Rebecca* on February 8, 1818, with Eugénie Audé, Octavie Berthold,[146] Catherine Lamarre[147] and Marguerite Manteau,[148] reaching Louisiana on May 31, feast of the Sacred Heart. She began the work of the Society in North America; her fellow-workers seemed to succeed and she to fail. Only in 1841 did she reach those of whom she had first dreamed — the Indians. After only one year at the mission of Sugar Creek "the Woman-Who-Prays-Always" (as the "little savages" named her) returned to Saint Charles where she died on November 18, 1852. She had been inspired by the classic missionary ideal of the Church, to extend the faith of Christ to unbelievers. Madeleine Sophie, who shared this ideal, went beyond it. "I want to make the whole universe Catholic,"[149] and "Why can we not say to the universe: 'Know his Heart?'"[150] The Chapter of 1970 has seen that in our divided world today: "It is more than ever essential that the movement of the Incarnation be prolonged and that the love of Jesus be revealed."[151]

Anna du Rousier,[152] who had been a child at school at Poitiers when Mother Duchesne had passed there on her way to America and who had been inspired by her vision, was present at her death. She received the great missionary's last blessing and with it a similar mission for South America. She reached Santiago, Chile, in the fall of 1854, and from there the Society spread through still another continent. Mother Barat wrote to her:

> Your country, Chile, becomes our own, and we are happy to help in making known and loved the Sacred Heart of Jesus, our Saviour, among all the social classes that you will teach.[153]

This rapid spread of the Society raised the question of adaptation early in its history. Would unity among houses and members so widely separated be possible without uniformity on all points? Would uniformity be possible in differing cultures? Even in Europe, as the Society entered neighbouring nations, Mother Barat wrote: "Study the customs of the country and follow them."[154] And again: "It is useful to know the spirit of a particular country and to act accordingly." Adaptation must be personal; a new-comer encounters "the faults of nations which we must put up with," for life in a foreign land requires "such complete self-forgetfulness, such detachment from creatures even in lawful matters that one must be determined to live in absolute self-sacrifice."[155]

The problem became more acute in distant lands. Mother Duchesne clung to uniformity, trying to do on the American frontier what was done at the Hotel Biron. But Mother Barat urged adaptation in many instances, and gave wide permission for local decisions, saying: "At this distance how can I judge? . . . Examine the Decrees of the General Councils, decide which are not practicable in America, and write this to me." [156]

This principle was followed with insight and determination by Aloysia Hardey.[157] Her baptismal name was Mary Anne, but while a novice at Grand Coteau she changed it for that of Aloysia, inspired by the example of Aloysia Jouve,[158] Mother Duchesne's ardent niece, of whom Mother Barat said: "It is thus that I dreamed they all would be." Aloysia had longed to go with her aunt to Louisiana, but died at the age of twenty-four, a missionary by prayer and suffering in the manner of Thérèse of Lisieux. Aloysia Hardey did the work that Aloysia Jouve had dreamed of doing in America. In the same year that Mother Duchesne went to the Indians she went to New York. From Manhattanville she founded twenty-five houses along the eastern seaboard, from Halifax to Cuba. She fused obedience and loyalty to an old-world Center with the courage to keep pace with a new world going its own way. She kept the balance between tradition and innovation, and Mother Barat wrote: "We shall always understand each other. . . . I shall appeal directly to you when I need enlightenment, and feel perfectly at peace." [159]

The first entry into a non-Christian culture was made in 1842 when Bishop Dupuch of Algeria wrote to Mother Barat:

> When I look with the eyes of faith upon the vocation of the religious of the Sacred Heart, when I realize the depth and sublimity of that vocation, I do not hesitate to declare that the Society is destined for a great, a divine mission in Africa.[160]

Mother Barat said: "This is one of the most important foundations we have yet made, for it is in an infidel country — and how glorious to be the first to carry to it knowledge and love of the Sacred Heart of Jesus!" [161] She sent Marguerite Chonez[162] to found Mustapha, "dwelling place of joy." The little house was threatened by constant disasters and difficulties, and Mother Barat, the realist, said: "We should not have gone there but the bishop electrified me. But now we shall stay, for one soul saved is worth more than our lives." [163]

Other calls from a distance had to be refused — for the time being: Bombay, Sydney, Martinique, Tunis, Palestine, Shanghai,
Burma (where the first apostolate would have been embroidery with
gold thread for the queen). When refusing the request from
Shanghai in 1854 she said:

> A zealous missionary said to me lately: "They are looking for you in China;
> there are many young girls there waiting for your religious to come in order to
> enrol under the banner of the Sacred Heart." Alas! I had to give up the
> thought and my heart is heavy. When there was question of America I en-
> trusted it without hesitation to Mother Duchesne, for I knew that she was ac-
> cording to the heart of God. And now that the harvest is so great, can I find
> no-one whom the divine Master wills to use to do great things? [164]

She saw the world-wide spread of her Society as a future reality:

> One evening Mother Barat came and touched me gently on the shoulder; then
> for two long hours she spoke to me of the love of God and of her desire to
> spread his glory. She had led me out onto the balcony where the moon was
> shining. She told me of her desires for far-away countries, and of plans which
> only came true after her death. [165]

While waiting Mother Barat fostered internationality in every
way possible, for this was a question of the very fibre of the Society.
Colonies sent on foundations were of mixed nationalities; the first
house in Poland joined German, English, French and Italian nuns.
Poles came later. She said of the Hotel Biron:

> Here are Mexicans, Russians, Wallachians, Chilians. Bring them up in the
> great truths of religion. Be sure of this: you will thus open convents of the
> Sacred Heart in each country from which these children come. [166]

She wanted to see the pupils world-minded and established the
Association of the Holy Childhood in every school. She had the
Church itself in mind, and supported Pauline Jaricot in her difficult
task of founding the Society for the Propagation of the Faith. She
had the sense of pre-evangelization; there were two Chinese
children at the Hotel Biron, and when they returned to China, un-
baptized, she did not lament but said: "They have gone back to
their own land carrying with them faith, hope and charity." [167]

*   *   *

The Chapter of 1970 declared: "At a time when the integral development of man is a task of special urgency, we reaffirm our educational mission as our service of the Church." [168] Father de Tournély had said that the Society must "enter into the sentiments and interior dispositions of the Heart of Jesus and reveal them to others by means of education." [169] It follows that education is integral to the Society's charism, and that the communication of "the light of Christ's teaching to minds" is the fruit of prayer. Madeleine Sophie saw this as part of her "primordial idea" of the Society: "We must vow ourselves to the education of youth." [170] The foundation of the Society was a response to "the signs of the times": "It was the void left by the absence of Christian education after the Revolution, and the attendant evils, that determined our foundation." [171]

Mother Barat, who spent only one year in the classroom, was herself a gifted educator — as the children knew when she visited their classes. Her sensitive, penetrating mind had been formed by her own direct-method education, and she communicated her enthusiasms: "We must know how to inspire in our pupils a passion for the beautiful; let us put history into their souls." [172] She roused them to personal effort: "What have you got in your head? Shut your eyes and think this out. Think!" [173] She was a Christian humanist, though she might not have consented to the name. Pauline Perdrau, herself an artist, noted:

> We can never know upon what aesthetic basis our Mother rested the gift that she had received from heaven, her way of looking at the things of God. The knowledge of how to perceive the beautiful seemed infused in her from her youth. . . . She wisely feared to appear over-poetic or over-enthusiastic, and for this reason her exquisite sensitiveness — that quality needed for great virtue as for great talent — remained in her like a covered fire. [174]

She encouraged personal research: "In the matter of education we women often know better than men. . . . Even if your efforts come to nothing, continue to take notes. Who knows how useful they may be?" [175] She followed educational questions intently: "I have read everything on the subject, at least in what is essential, and reasonable. In spite of that I see that there is still a void to be filled in our methods and plans" [176] (she was then eighty).

Mother Barat saw education as a work of faith, and strongly, ruthlessly, she gave priority to this supreme value. She was following the Constitutions: "Christian education is the first and most important means that the Society uses to honour the divine Heart of Jesus."[177] It will "make the reign of the Heart of Jesus flower in the world."[178] She said to the young teachers: "Whatever you teach do not fail to speak of Jesus Christ." [179]

> In these times marked by lack of faith and by indifference what is needed is to impress them by a revelation of the truths of religion. . . . What are the arts and sciences compared with the solid virtues which we must teach our children? So much sand which the wind whirls away . . . apart from the greatest of all interests, the only one, the salvation of souls.[180] Actually, true piety includes all the aspects of education, and we are falling short of our end if we neglect even the lest part of what constitutes a good education.[181]

During the revolution of 1848 mobs surrounded the school in Turin, shouting: "Your education is behind the times, your studies are elementary, you hold reason in swaddling bands. . . . Soon the wives of workmen will show up the fine ladies who spent their youth in your sumptuous convents." Mother Barat accepted the challenge:

> In this struggle concerning Christian education the Heart of Jesus asks from us not our blood but our brains. There is no question of flight from this task. The directors of institutions — Catholic, Roman and apostolic — tell us, poor women authorized by the Church to teach, that we must hold our own and then measure ourselves against the universities.[182]

Accordingly, she demanded excellence.

> [At Amiens] we had to find methods for forming our teachers to that elevation of judgment and of taste which we must at all costs stamp upon our studies. The Jesuit Fathers helped us to reach a standard as high as their own.[183] . . . Weak points in study and teaching harm the reputation of our Institute. There are complaints that our pupils make little progress, that some have fallen behind since coming to us, that the teachers are not qualified for their classes, and that some cannot spell.[184]

The Plan of Studies[185] was the result of collaboration of many gifted minds. The first version was drawn up at Amiens in 1805 by Henriette Ducis[186] and Catherine de Charbonnel. It incorporated the traditional sources of Christian education which had formed the first teachers of the Society: the monastic, found in the Cistercian Abbaye-aux-Bois; the Renaissance, in the Ursuline school on the

Rue Saint-Jacques; the Golden Age of French culture in Saint-Cyr, reflecting Fénélon and Madame de Maintenon; and, predominantly, the Jesuit *Ratio Studiorum*. But post-revolution schools were more democratic than before under the *ancien régime;* in the school at Amiens princesses and farmers' daughters sat side by side. Moreover, women were beginning to rival men; the fusion of inherited traditions was future-orientated. As Father Druilhet said:

> Formerly the education of girls was a religious and domestic matter. Things have changed; the movement that is sweeping us towards learning now concerns both sexes. It is not for us to criticize this, but to take from it all that can be used in attaining our chosen end. [187]

The *Plan* was flexible, and revisions were made in 1810, 1820, 1826, 1833 and 1852. Before the General council of 1864 Mother Barat wrote:

> We must not be blind to the fact that in these times of activity in which we live demands are made upon us and obstacles are encountered, so that certain modifications and a certain perfectioning become indispensable. Without questioning what concerns religious life and the spirit which our holy founder Father de Tournély and Father Varin left us, and which we must keep intact in the face of those elements in our work which might tend to weaken them, there are many points which still call for attention. Thus, education is no longer what it was a few years ago; the multiplication of institutes which follow the trends of the times make us seem behind-hand. God forbid that we should compromise with duty or sacrifice our principal end to these tendencies, but we must again examine what we can accord and review our Plan of Studies to modify and complete it. [188]

The *Plan* was thus left open-ended. It aims at giving a liberal arts education with theology at its core, structured on philosophy, literature and history, humanistic in content while integrating the sciences and the practical skills.

It was then the age of romanticism in art, literature and fashion. Mother Barat stressed the solid and abiding elements in education, and counteracted sentimentality by strong character-formation. The School Rule is firm in maintaining principles, yet creates a warm atmosphere of love in "the family of the Sacred Heart" where every pupil is unique and where every teacher "must become for their sakes gentle, patient, indulgent, in one word, a mother." [189]

A juniorate for the training of the young religious was begun in 1849 by Aimée d'Avenas,[190] the first mistress general of studies. Mother Barat wrote to her:

If only you knew how much the Society needs *saintes savantes* you would hurry up and become one. Here in the noviceship we have a number of saints but of *savantes* — not one! It is all very well to lay the foundations of solid virtue, but only the union of virtue with knowledge will give our work its perfection. Unite these two things and you will understand the whole extent of your vocation.[191]

And to the whole Society:

In the measure in which we are obliged, for the greater glory of God, to give more care and more importance to our studies, let all feel more and more strongly the need of being steeped in the love of prayer.... It is a mistake to think that a busy life, even when taken up with study, harms interior spirit. On the contrary, when it is regulated by obedience such a life facilitates and invigorates it.[192]

She felt that intellectual growth gives fibre to the spiritual life:

Let our classical methods cause faith to speak to reason in the future teachers of our boarding schools and free schools.[193] ... This is a question of true discernment, of the application of religious principles. We must busy ourselves with these things in order to respond fitly to the mission implied in our vow. Women and children must have some knowledge of current errors and form their own judgments in the light of Christianity, in order to conform intelligently to the enlightened teaching of the Church. The hour has come when we must give a reason for our faith. Let our teachers be trained to reason that our pupils may learn to do so.[194]

The Chapter of 1970 saw this as a vital need: "We must educate to a faith that is relevant in a secularized world and to a deep respect for intellectual values (*valeurs de l'esprit*)."[195]

In the century between Madeleine Sophie's day and our own the Plan of Studies has confronted so many changing countries and cultures that it may be asked whether it remains the basis of "Sacred Heart education" — if there still is such a thing. Yet through all the changes in specifics certain constants, inherent in the original thought of the Society, are found to persist:

— education is a work of Christian faith, the ultimate end of which is one with that of the Society itself;

— it is a person-by-person formation in which character development keeps pace with mental development;

— it creates a way of life involving all the actions and interests of the person;

— the curriculum is an organic whole based upon recognized

values, in which there is hierarchic interdependence among the disciplines;
– education has a living relation to the needs and structures of human society which is in continuous evolution.

The last of these five "constants" is the most variable factor, the one in which the Society of the Sacred Heart has most often failed to be true to itself. Education is always intermeshed with current social problems, and Mother Barat said in 1850: "Present day society will be saved by education; other means are almost useless."[196] The types of school established in the beginning necessarily reflected the social spectrum of that day, and as time passed these types tended to harden – which accounts for many present-day anomalies.

The boarding schools, *pensionnats,* were the primary work. They were for children of "good families" who could pay tuition, and only such received an advanced education at that time.[197] As a matter of fact these schools covered a fairly wide range of the social spectrum, depending upon their locality. In all of them Mother Barat called for simplicity and combatted snobbery. She believed in the cultivation of an élite among the *classe dirigeante,* and said:

> Usually we succeed with the upper classes and we should hold to this all the more since the education of the other classes is taken care of by a number of religious orders whose aim is precisely that type of education.[198]

She even accepted, against the grain, a few schools for aristocrats only. The Trinita dei Monti was for the Roman nobility, at the request of Pope Leo XII who wrote: "Your Institute is the most proper to give them an education in keeping with their rank." The King of Sardinia (shortly before losing his throne) asked for a similar school in Turin: "The present generation is too corrupt for us to hope to reform it; but at least we shall try to preserve the future generation." Mother Barat was too large-minded to discriminate at either end of the scale; the nobility too were called to be Christian women.

It was largely the Hotel Biron that gave rise to the reputation for social snobbery that has dogged the Society of the Sacred Heart ever since 1820, and Mother Barat said of it: "We are too high on our candlestick here! Our adversaries find reason for their animosity. . . . How many subjects we lose because of this reputation. Simplicity! Simplicity!"[199] Her attitude was:

Those who work with the rich should always be eager to work with the poor,
and those who work with the poor should never refuse to serve the rich, since
all souls are dear to Jesus Christ.[200] . . . We must do all the good that we can.
Spend yourself for the rich and poor alike.[201]

Gradually the *pensionnats* were supplemented by the *demi-
pensionnats*, or day schools. The first was opened at Marseilles in
1852. Day students were even admitted to some boarding schools,
though kept rigorously apart from the boarders. Then came *externats*
with a more democratic range. This growth of day schools followed
the slow rise of the middle class, of which Mother Barat said:
"There is an immense good to be done among this class; it has far
greater influence than is generally believed."[202]

In the Constitutions both *pensionnats* and *écoles*, or free schools for
the poor, are given as means "which the Society uses to glorify the
Heart of Jesus by working for the sanctification of our neighbor."[203]
For every boarding school there was at first a free school where the
enrolment was far larger. The *écoles* used the methods of instruction
given by Jean Baptiste de la Salle to the Christian Brothers. Mother
Barat had seen the need on her first journey to Poitiers; in every
village where the carriage stopped clamorous children crowded
round her and she promised their mothers to do her best. The Industrial Revolution was gaining speed and children were exploited
in the factories. Voltaire had said: "The populace is not worth
teaching." Mother Barat felt differently; she opened not only
schools but workrooms where young girls could learn crafts:

> We cannot accomplish any solid good without adding this work; the rest will
> be worth little without it. But I must confess that I have met with little sym-
> pathy in the house in Paris where they are too afraid of leaving the beaten
> track.[204]

In addition she opened eighteen orphanages, especially after
cholera epidemics. She wrote of one:

> This establishment appeals to me more strongly than other more glamorous
> foundations, precisely because of the spirit of poverty, humility and simplicity
> that reigns there. It seems to me that this work will draw us closer to the Heart
> of our divine Master, that humble and obscure beginnings are more in confor-
> mity with his spirit and more likely to draw his blessing on our Society. I shall
> envy those chosen for this work.[205]

And when one was found to be too much of a burden:

Shall we not answer before God if we allow to suffer or even perish this orphanage which is more needed than those establishments that we maintain at the price of great sacrifice? ... For the orphans are in absolute want, and truly we do not do enough for the poor.[206]

There were also special schools to meet current needs. A centre for forming catechists in mountain villages was begun at Pignerol in 1839, and a teacher-training college, the Maestranza, was opened in Chile when the foundation was made in 1854. There was a school for deaf-mutes at Chambéry that was allowed to remain open even when the government closed the boarding school in 1848, and for some years the Hotel Biron had a department for the physically handicapped, with orthopaedic equipment. There were some schools for little boys, and Mother Barat wrote:

I am collecting money just now to build a poor school for a foundation that has no resources for construction and the children none for their religious education. For us, is this not the work of works? I can see this at Marmoutier by comparing the little boys there with what they were a few years ago. So this is the most realistic work that we can do: undertake the education of all the social classes when divine Providence entrusts them to us.[207]

*   *   *

The Chapter of 1970 saw education reaching beyond school systems into related forms of the development of the human person and of his environment. It made two options, here grouped under the common aspect of social awareness:

In the light of the Gospel and of our social context we wish to stand in solidarity with the poor. Christ has made us his own; he emptied himself and gave his life to set us free. Henceforth we are caught up in a work which is essentially one of liberation.
At a time when mankind hungers and thirsts for justice our attitude must be one of solidarity with the Third World which suffers poverty and oppression. This solidarity will above all shake us out of our complacency.[208]

Madeleine Sophie Barat's way of living these two attitudes was conditioned by her social environment and by the rule of enclosure, but her thinking was open-ended. She put it briefly by quoting at opportune moments a favourite maxim: "Make arrows of all wood." She claimed that according to circumstances: "Our order is devoted not only to education but to all that is related to education as well."[209]

It is clear from the preceding study that concern for the poor was included in the Society's educational mission from the beginning. What about concern for social action and for the structure of human society itself?

Mother Barat herself was "of the people," from the simple home of a property-owning (and illiterate) artisan. "My father made barrels and I want every-one to know it." She had the simplicity, the freedom, the wisdom of the soil given by her Burgundian origins. Personally she transcended the social hierarchy of her day and was at ease on every level. She accepted it as a fact and deplored its limitations: "In convents all are on an equal footing. Why is the whole world not like that? It would be better governed and a happier place."[210] Her views were not widely shared by her co-workers, many of whom were from families endowed with the advantages and liabilities of the privileged class. Most vocations, after the first generation of religious, were from this very class, a trend which narrowed recruitment even while the Society was spreading widely. A reputation for aristocratic exclusiveness soon arose. Actually, many of Mother Barat's schools were housed in magnificent but dilapidated and hence inexpensive buildings:

> It is painful enough for me to live in old palaces, grandiose chateaux, abbeys and convents saved from revolutionary destruction, without ourselves building houses that are too beautiful. But for the sake of the children. . . ! [211]

This reputation was increased by two unhappy facts that remain true even in more democratic times: private schools operate on tuition, and excellence calls for costly preparation and equipment.

If the religious did not go out among the poor, the poor came to them. "They are the blessing of the house; I am at peace because they are well received here."[212] She gave alms with a recklessness that alarmed the keepers of the strong-box; when it was nearly empty she would say: "Give away what is left so that it will fill up again." When she had to make a choice between visitors she went to those at the back door. Each was received with interest, sympathy and respect; each felt his dignity as a person: beggars, tradesmen, stray children, rough-handed women, the unhappy. She challenged the community: "I have seen poor people without enough to cover themselves, whole families without a piece of bread. Compared to that, what do we do with our vow of poverty?"[213]

If the religious could not go out into the milieux of their pupils in the poor schools they reached their families in another way. Catholic Action as such had not yet been organized, but in 1833 Frederick Ozanam founded the Conferences of Saint Vincent de Paul, saying: "The religious question has become a social question." There gradually grew up in the Society a whole range of enterprises called "les oeuvres populaires." These first took organized form at Turin (in the school for aristocrats only) where Mother du Rousier set up a circulating library, catechism classes, a vocational course for orphans, the Congregations of Saint Anne and of the Consolers of Mary. They spread to other convents, where often a special chapel was erected for "les oeuvres," where retreats were given to groups of all sorts, men as well as women and children. The *demoiselles* in the boarding school, who could not then have gone out into the slums, helped their underprivileged sisters in the free school on the same grounds, and Mother Barat wrote in a circular letter to all the children:

> It is sweet to me to see the littlest rivalling the older ones in zeal, and trying, by their works and their little sacrifices, to relieve the suffering members of Jesus Christ. It is thus that you will prepare yourselves for the great mission that you must fulfil some day.[214]

Mother Barat was aware of the social repercussions even of works with a purely spiritual aim, such as retreats (named in the Constitutions as the third principal means by which the Society fulfils its end). It was begun tentatively at Amiens, and became fully organized at Turin 1832. It was then taken up in most of the houses. Mother Barat said; "There is no doubt that these retreats are one of the most efficacious means of bringing about a renewal in society."[215]

The Congregation of the Children of Mary, the primary purpose of which was to form a spiritual élite, had still wider possibilities for social action. The first sodality was formed in the Paris school in 1818. The rules were drawn up by Father Varin, the medal showed the Sacred Heart on one side and the Immaculate Conception on the other, with the legend "Cor meum jungatur vobis." The Children of Mary were formed vigorously to spiritual leadership by methods that would have tried the virtue of novices.

The adult Congregation, called "du monde", was begun at Lyons by Edmée Lhuillier, in February, 1832. The statutes were drawn up by Father Druilhet:

To help young girls and women in the world to persevere in faith, in piety, in charity, in modesty; to encourage them to accomplish the duties of their state in life; and to bring them spiritual help in the difficulties, consolations and sorrows of life.[216]

Mother Barat saw the social potential of this venture. She wrote to the first officers:

Your mission is sublime; I do not hesitate to call it an apostolate, for you must be apostles in the midst of a corrupt world. Bring back by your example those of your companions who have strayed, encourage those who are weak through human respect, save those who are a prey to hell. . . . My heart thrills to the thought of the good that will result from this work. [217]

As the Congregation spread:

This, it seems to me, is the mission of a Child of Mary: what we cannot do on account of our enclosure, that is your work. We have gathered you together like an advance guard to replace us in the world. [218]

The Congregation was influential in three areas: personal spiritual growth, works of zeal in the service of the Church, good example in social conduct. Each centre had its Jesuit director, its RSCJ directress, its canonical erection, its special function. Mother Barat could say: "In the cities where this Congregation is well established and well directed society is renewed; the men follow the women."[219] Conflicts with "the world" were inevitable and called for courage. As time passed precepts concerning dress and deportment became exacting; balls and theatres were distrusted, sometimes forbidden. Not all directresses were as flexible as Mother Barat who looked to principles:

It is useful to know the spirit of a particular locality and to act accordingly. Our Congregation has never been accepted in your province. They have certain ideas about conduct in the world which are generally accepted; it would be useless to attack them. We must simply strengthen our children in their religious principles without going into such particulars. Leave to confessors the question of dances.[220]

Very often *ad hoc* works of zeal arose unexpectedly, as when the coachmen who drove the Children of Mary to their meetings at the Hotel Biron were invited indoors for refreshments served with informal evangelization, and the event became a habit. Any undertaking that could fit into the Constitutions when need gave the sign was accepted. Mother Barat said to the novices:

> You are destined for an apostolate. Your mission is great; it is noble, it is divine. It is great because it embraces the universe, it is noble because by it we raise souls to God, it is divine because it comes from himself. [221]

At the same time she realized the danger of doing too much, though "my heart suffers from refusing works of zeal":

> Everything now moves with astonishing speed, with unhappy consequences for the activity of intellects which develop beyond physical and often moral strength. . . . We are almost forced to do more than we can. By our vocation we are more or less compelled along these same lines. By throwing ourselves forward without restraint and by going too far we face a danger that might be very harmful; yet by remaining behind we run the risk of being reduced to a life not our own. Our works would lag and subjects would look elsewhere for an outlet for their zeal, in works of charity for instance. [222]

It is clear that there was concern for social charity in the early Society; what about concern for social justice? Christ began his public life with the challenge: "It is fitting that we do all that righteousness demands."[223] In Scripture righteousness is both holiness and justice.

Madeleine Sophie grasped the concept of justice in this biblical sense; the just man is the holy man living in a right relationship with God and his fellow men. Her sense of justice was bound up with her innate sense of truth: "Only the true is beautiful." Her directives, reprimands, reflexions were keen-edged with truth. Such clear-sightedness could lead to injustice when ruthless or one-sided, but her insights were illumined by that charity which transcends merely legal justice. Justice was the root of her chosen virtue, humility: "When can I also be counted for nothing? At least I shall then receive justice."[224] For others, her justice was not that of strict measure but of generosity pressed down and flowing over; "We owe ourselves to others; all that we can do for them is a matter of strict justice."[225] In giving alms to a recurrent beggar she gave more than enough for food so that he might buy tobacco, for: "He has a right to his pleasures."[226] Her contemporaries saw in her the portrait of the just woman:

> Hers was a mind as strong as it was straight, seeing everything in the light of truth and adhering to it once she had seen it; yet it was a mind full of respect

and consideration for others, reaching its end with gentleness and choosing the means that would cause the least friction. Although she was admirable on all these points, yet the generosity of her heart was greater than all the rest. One could not find in her nor in her way of thinking anything that was not large, high and broad. . . . She favoured no-one at the expense of any other. [227]

With regard to social justice in the economic realm, a study called *The Society of the Sacred Heart, a Microcosm in a Changing World* [228] asks the question: why were no religious of the Sacred Heart found on the working man's side of the barriers during the revolutions of the nineteenth century? A clue is given: "Even saints are conditioned by their social milieux." It is a shock to realize that Philippine Duchesne, now beatified, bought and sold slaves, doubtless glad to give them a good home and the chance for baptism. She was following the custom accepted by bishops as well as by plantation owners; could she have seen it as a basic human wrong in that time and place?

But was the Society necessarily a part of the *status quo*? Men of good will were wrenched by the contradictions of the French Revolution. Were religion and legitimacy inseparable? Was *The Rights of Man* always to be pitted against the rights of God? It took exceptional vision to see that democracy could ever shake off atheism, not only anti-king but anti-Church. When Mother Barat, who lived through four revolutions with a like philosophy, said: "This smoke of liberty filters in everywhere, even into convents," [229] she was smelling the cannon fire of the Roman revolution that sent Pius IX into exile. When she heard the Marseillaise: "What pictures press into my memory and my heart!" [230]

The non-involvement in politics which she insisted on for religious was based on the values of cloister and a transcendent outlook:

> For what concerns civil governments our role is to keep quiet, wait and pray. One thing should fill our minds and possess us entirely: the desire to make up to the heart of Jesus for so much ingratitude. Governments are blinding themselves. It is God and God alone who can bring light. If they would only recognize the need of God! But no, alas! Pride takes the place of everything in our century. [231]

As she wrote to her nephew: "So, *mon ami*, be among the small number of the wise." [232]

Nonetheless, Mother Barat's interest in current events was keen: "The charity of Christ urges us, and the times urge us also." [233] She said at the election of Louis Philippe, unacceptable to the legitimists as "King of the French by the favour of God and the will of the people":

> I beg of you to recommend to everyone not to talk politics in the parlour nor with the pupils, or if you do so let it be in support of the present government, since God has given it to us and it would be folly to entertain other hopes. [234]

Her pliant views were not those of the majority of the Society who were die-hard royalists, especially at the influential Hotel Biron.

She could see beneath violence to its root causes. When caught in Lyons during an armed riot among the factory workers she said: "The working man asks for nothing but bread and work. This riot will give fresh increase to industry which is what this city needs." [235] Her reason for abhorring debts was the fact that under the system then in force the workmen were thereby kept waiting for their pay, and "A working man's salary is a question of justice. Pay your labourers and your tradesmen every month. This is essential." [236] When buildings were under construction:

> Tell me what state your debts are in and whether you can pay your workmen as you go along. Bad times are coming and they become doubly bad when we cannot give bread to those who have earned it by the sweat of their brow. This is a trial to which I can never become resigned, first, because we should never undertake anything above our means, and second, because it is against justice.[237]
>
> If I had known that you owed your workmen six thousand francs I would not have sent my money elsewhere. I would have sent it straight to you to satisfy the men, for I cannot bear that a workman should suffer because of us. It is an enormous injustice, and my heart has been suffering keenly since I received your letter.[238]

When injustice led to revolution and she was barricaded in the Hotel Biron she said:

> We must drop all personal and local pre-occupations, even those of family and country, to think of the dangers and sorrows of the Church, our Mother. Let ours be the politics of Holy Scripture. Reading the Psalms is our best daily newspaper; when we meditate on them we find them to be of our times. [239]

Experience had taught her that the Society is, by its very nature, ready to face crises:

> I see our Lord with the revolution like a fan in his hand, separating the wheat from the chaff. Father de Tournély conceived of our Society while the Fathers

of the Sacred Heart were fleeing from city to city. We were born in a time of social upheaval; we must learn to live through it safe and sound and to draw others through it. That is the generous and virile apostolate to which weak and timid women, fearful by nature, are called by the Heart of Jesus, under the protection of his Mother on Calvary, our Lady of Seven Sorrows. [240]

Her vision and her confidence widened with the internationality of the Society:

If we are driven out, well, the Heart of Jesus is great and all the earth is ours. Haven't we got America, Burma, even China? In the midst of the insecurity of human governments it is good to belong to him who alone is great. [241]

Under violent changes lie quieter but more radical changes of thought. Mother Barat, who was always vehemently orthodox and who could distinguish between principle and opinion, was alive to the intellectual issues of her day. She had seen the tragedy of de Lammenais, but she knew that Louis Veuillot and the editors of *l'Univers* were loyally bold Christians. When the *Syllabus of Errors* became the storm centre in 1864 she said: "The Holy See has spoken; let us listen, understand and obey." In order better to understand she asked Mother Goetz to consult theologians and make an outline. "We shall pray over this, and I shall make the Society study what we should know and what answers should be given." [242] In her old age her copies of journals were marked with red crosses next to articles by advanced Catholic thinkers: Bishops Pie, Parisis, Dupanloup, and leaders of the intellectual laity. Ozanam, de Falloux and Montalembert. Mother de Charbonnel took alarm: "These thinkers are troubling orthodox minds." But Mother Barat met the disturbances of her times with a ringing challenge to the faith of the Society:

If we could only profit by these bad times to detach ourselves from everything and unite ourselves to the Sovereign Good, without any trace of earthly affection! Alas! So many lessons, sacrifices, difficulties have so far produced nothing more than a conviction. Hurry up; time presses; our Spouse is at the door and he knocks. God! how loudly he knocks sometimes! We must be either stupid or sunk in a lethargic sleep not to rush forward to meet him. Let us not be among the foolish virgins; we have had enough of that in the past. How we suffer now to see so many scandals and to hear so many abominations! How can our children stand against this torrent, the rich and the poor?

We are not ourselves filled with that strong faith which would give to our words the power of a two-edged sword. Was this double sword ever more needed? Hearts are growing heavy, even hard. If we offer only that measure of virtue which was enough in other days for those naturally Christian – and who make the same of others – we have missed our end. In extraordinary times extraordinary virtues are called for. [243]

* * *

After the Golden Jubilee of the Society Mother Barat travelled little and looked ahead. She built a large new Mother House, plain and stately, along the Boulevard des Invalides on the western side of the Hotel Biron; it was to remain the Centre for fifty years. From there she governed in strenuous peace for the last fifteen years of her life while wars shook the fast spreading Society. At her desk she said to her secretary: "Open the window! I want to hear the children shouting. I have given my life for them." While praying she was heard to whisper: "Jesus, it is time for us to see each other."

The Eighth General Council was held from June 17 to July 22, 1864. In summoning the members she said:

> If I could have one wish it would be to gather together once more in this land of exile my old mothers and daughters who have helped me for so long and shared with their First Mother the constant work of our difficult mission, who have so often lightened my burden and consoled me by taking the hardest and most tiresome part of it. Yes, I want to see them again, to tell them of my feelings and of my gratitude, and to urge most earnestly those who will live after me to redouble their devotedness, if possible, and to strengthen our Society on the foundation of the solid virtus, especially those most proper to our vocation: humility, an ardent zeal for the salvation of souls, and an unlimited generosity that no obstacle can check when there is question of the glory of the Heart of Jesus. And as these virtues must be practiced until our last breath, who will have the needed courage and perseverance if not enlightened by the habitual action of the Holy Spirit, the tendency at least towards union with the Heart of Jesus, to maintain, strengthen and support this life of sacrifice and of renouncement which will assure the existence of the Congregation for the future which Jesus has prepared for it? [244]

The Council was mainly concerned with the *Plan of Studies* and the juniorate. Mother Barat's resignation was refused and Mother Goetz became her vicar general. [245] The councillors then said goodbye to her for the last time.

By the following year the Society had reached a membership of 3,539 religious in 89 houses in 17 vicariates. Mother Barat had founded, in all, 111 houses of which many had been closed, some by violence. When she finally laid down her quill she had written 98 circular letters (32 to all the religious and 66 to those in government) and 14,000 personal letters (to count only those now extant) of which only 2,707 have so far been published. Her last letter, written a few days before her death, closed with a postscript:

> I beg Jesus to bless you as well as your family. Pray for our immense needs. Ask for workers, but for such as our vocation calls for: generous souls who love Jesus suffering and who desire with him to save souls by the cross. [246]

On May 21, 1865, Mother Barat met the community with the gay words: "On Thursday we are going to heaven." That meant Ascension Day. She agreed to meet the first communicants the next morning in the garden, but when they kept rendezvous they saw the blinds on her window closed. She had been stricken with paralysis and lay alert but wordless until eleven o'clock on the night of Ascension Thursday, May 25, 1865.

A document was found dated April, 1863, a testament in which she gave an account of her long government and begged pardon for her failures. Mother Goetz sent its closing paragraph to the whole Society present and future:

> The mothers who succeed me, and all the members of this beloved family of the Sacred Heart, will profit by my avowal, will repair the breaches that I deplore, will redouble their zeal and will labour to strengthen ever more and more a true religious spirit among all, especially by the virtues dearest to the Heart of Jesus: humility, her close sister poverty, and lastly obedience which is the guardian and bond of all the other virtues. These, when dominant, will assure the prosperity and even the existence of the Society. I should ask for your prayers; I expect them from your charity. But I dare to rely most strongly upon the dispositions that I read in your souls; to continue, at the price of every sacrifice, and with persevering fidelity to our holy Rule, to spread as far as we can the knowledge and love of the Sacred Heart of Jesus, and to become in every place where we shall be the good odour of him whose name, despite our unworthiness, we bear. [247]

PART TWO

GROWTH

1865–1975

Well, I tell you:
Look around, look at the fields;
already they are white, ready for the harvest!
Already the reaper is being paid his wages,
already he is bringing in the grain for eternal life,
and thus sower and reaper rejoice together.
For here the proverb holds good:
one sows, another reaps.

Jn 4:35–37

Fidelity and Creativity

The growth of the Society of the Sacred Heart from the death of Madeleine Sophie Barat to Vatican Council II was shaped by two drives in strong polarity: fidelity and creativity.

When two nouns standing for opposites are joined by "and" polarity is inevitable. A resolution of forces can be brought about by changing one of the nouns to an adjective. Shall it be "creative fidelity" or "faithful creativity"? These attitudes were both present in the Society from the beginning. Madeleine Sophie stood for faithful creativity, called as she was to build for the future; she said: "We should have no other limits than the horizon." [1] Philippine Duchesne stood for creative fidelity, called as she was to carry another's vision farther afield; she followed the horizon but would have no change. Madeleine Sophie told this apostle of frontiers: "Times change, and we must change with them and modify our views." [2] It was her spirit that prevailed.

Throughout the century following her death the very desire to remain true to that spirit led to a shift of emphasis; it was creative fidelity that prevailed. The accent was placed heavily on fidelity through the periods of consolidation, confirmation and expansion, with resulting tensions in the periods of challenge and renewal. Was there, perhaps, an unconscious distortion of the original message because (as in television) while the transmission was faithful the reception was not, due to a change of atmosphere? The question goes deep, because in religious life fidelity to a way is involved in fidelity to God. The Chapter of 1970 dared to say: "To remain faithful today is, in a sense, to change." [3] It is faithful creativity that again prevails. Where should the accent be placed?

Chapter 4

Consolidation
1865–1895

I, Wisdom, am mistress of discretion,
the inventor of lucidity of thought.
Good advice, sound judgment belong
to me, perception to me, strength to
me. . . . By me monarchs rule and
princes issue just laws.

Prov. 8:12–13, 15

When Josephine Goetz first took her place in the governing body
of the Society as vicar general, she was overheard murmuring this
stabilizing text. It characterized the epoch that was beginning. The
thirty years from 1865 to 1895 were to be a time of consolidation
marked by discretion, strength and law-observance, in fidelity to the
past. Three superiors general of strikingly different temperaments,
with generalates of very unequal length, shared a common historical
backdrop, a common mentality, and a common goal: to consolidate
the Society entrusted to them by Madeleine Sophie Barat. They
were: Josephine Goetz (1865–1874), Adèle Lehon (1874–1894)
and Augusta de Sartorius (1894–1895).

Janet Stuart said of the contemporaries of the Foundress who
outlived her, in a tone half playful and wholly serious:

> Looking back on our First Mothers we see that they "served the cause" as
> much by what they were as by what they did; such great and grave per-
> sonalities, so responsible, so high-toned and mature, people of such weight, so
> capable of giving advice because they always kept themselves under the dis-
> cipline of strong principles. They thought so deeply and reasonably — nothing
> foolish or flighty was to be found in them.[1]

The impression is that of an ancestral portrait gallery. These aloof figures, correct and venerable, must be known to be loved. Madeleine Sophie knew and loved them all; she passed the Society into their hands with trust. They governed during an extremely unified period when the first inspiration had become tradition and when tradition was becoming custom with almost the force of law. They looked back for security rather than forward to "future shock." Perhaps a remark made by Mother Barat in another context could be applied to them: "They were too afraid of anything that departed from the ordinary course, or from a certain custom to which they clung."[2] The keynote had been struck in the eulogies pronounced by bishops at the time of the Foundress' death: 'Keep what you have!" For the next thirty years any upset in the *status quo* was feared as a sign not of life but of disintegration.

The last quarter of the nineteenth century is, possibly, the moment least sympathetic to the last quarter of the twentieth, to judge by the antithesis between all matters from women's dress to Church Councils. Vatican II with its open window is a far pendulum swing from Vatican I with its definitions, its cautions, its anathemas. To find varying, even opposing, values given to the same term – "authority" for example – is disconcerting. It is worse to find that values now called into question – "blind obedience" for example – were then the ideals. In the Society, perspective is further blurred by the literary form in which its history has come down to us; the records repel by a platitudinous and fulsome style. We must transcend the language and seize the thought before being "turned off," and this requires penetration into the history of ideas of which semantic change is a record. It takes broad-mindedness to understand the narrow-mindedness of our antipodes-in-time.

Outwardly the times were not so disturbed as those of Madeleine Sophie Barat. "No era has been so completely self-satisfied as the late nineteenth century,"[3] and this was the air breathed by "our First Mothers." After the shock of the Franco-Prussian War and the Unification of Italy that made the Pope the "prisoner of the Vatican" there was quiescence, a "Victorian complacency" guarded by an uneasy balance of power. Beyond Europe there was "Big Business" in the United States, democratic effervescence in Latin America, colonial paternalism and partition in Africa, a new nationalism in Australia and New Zealand, an open door from West to East with the Meiji Restoration in Japan. But under the self-satisfaction explosive forces were brewing. The first international meeting of the United Workers of the World was held in the same month as Mother Barat's last General Council, June, 1864. Communism was released.

In the realm of thought the nexus between evolution and social justice had been "discovered"; *The Origin of the Species* had appeared in 1858. Its implications were met by *Rerum Novarum* in 1891, for in the Church the denouncements of Vatican Council I were followed by the stimulating Encyclicals of Leo XIII. The Holy See, no longer dependent on the good will of rulers, became a powerful, highly centralized religious government, and loyalty among Catholics was articulate. The first Christian Syndicates and the Catholic Centre Party in Germany appeared. There was a renaissance of Catholic scholarship in the university world. In mission lands heroism was once more "the seed of the Church" when the Uganda martyrs died in 1882.

The affairs of the Society of the Sacred Heart were watched over in Rome by two cautious and conservative Protectors, Charles Augustus de Reisach[4] (1868–1869) and Raffaele Monaco La Valetta[5] (1870–1896). The Society was spreading rapidly in a paradoxical way. It circled the globe, yet its spread was limited to countries where western culture and the industrial system were unquestioned. It responded to current events while assuming an attitude of aloofness. The desire for consolidation led to a passionate effort to keep uniformity at almost any cost; yet this sameness was achieved by adventuresome persons each of whom was an "original" aiming at a common goal in a characteristic way. Never have the members of the Society been asked to model themselves on some-one else, for: "Copies of even the best models are deplorable,"[6] said Janet Stuart. Even when impersonality and conformity were ideals, many creative personalities were involved in exciting journeys and challenging friendships. And despite unashamed conservatism the Society kept up with technical advance. Mother Barat had seen the coming of the steam age; distrustful at first, she ended by riding with amazed delight on primitive railroads. Her successors confronted the electric age; life was clarified by light bulbs and complicated by telegrams. Mother Lehon listened, at a hilarious community gathering, to the raucous phonograph record sent from the United States with greetings for her Golden Jubilee – incomprehensible in every sense!

Society statistics[7] for this period show tremendous vitality. In Mother Barat's time the membership had risen in a straight line from 4 (of whom 1 alone persevered) to 3,539, in a space of sixty five years. In the next thirty years the pace doubled; there were 6,649 religious in 1895. (Membership was to remain on the plateau of the six thousands until our own day.) Vocations rose steadily; the number of novices reached its peak in Society history in 1894: 680. The number of houses rose from 89 to 137 in 20 vicariates. In interpreting these figures the age level must be taken into account; it too had been rising. Yet despite the venerability of "our First Mothers," the age pyramid was still solidly based on youth.

At a time of extreme mobility such as the nineteen-seventies consolidation is looked upon as "hardening of the structures." What becomes of a living body if its primitive spirit passes into a set of habits? When does this happen? The process can be seen at work in this period when constructive and constrictive forces were both at play. The year 1894 marks a high point, to judge from a letter written by Juliette Désoudin just before the General Council:

> Pray with us for this solemn and inspiring assembly. All the older members have disappeared; a new generation is called upon to decide the fate of the Society, the conservation or weakening of its spirit. . . . What a need we feel for prayer that this Society may be placed in hands strong enough to tighten its laws instead of enlarging them, especially at a time that seeks its own ease on principle and in a spirit of independence! The gathering will count about twenty-two members, of whom only three or four have seen our Mother Foundress when they were novices. Actually, I am the only one who knew her as a superior. You understand me.[8]

"Hardening" is a pejorative word; used of a living organism it means death. But "strengthening" is a word of life. Perhaps consolidation is a needed phase in the life of a body which must go through more than one epoch. It seems that in those conservative years a strength was given to the Society without which it could not undergo the radical unfolding called for at a later time. Only perspective can recognize the harm done by "hardening". The Chapter of 1970 claimed that:"Now that certain exterior resemblances have vanished, the essential reality seems all the more clear."[9]

One cause of the vitality of those days, despite forbidding elements, was the tangible presence of the Foundress after her death. During her own long government she had personally moulded her first four successors as superior general; when she died Josephine Goetz and Adèle Lehon were by her side, Augusta de Sartorius was superior at Blumenthal, Mabel Digby was mistress general at Marmoutier. She became a living force in the memory of those in government until 1911, and in the memory of hundreds in the Society. She was made known to those who had not known her by the fact that the Cause for her Beatification, begun in 1872, called for constant study of her life and writings and for response to her example; prayer to her was seen as efficacious by undoubted miracles granted. Her omnipresence was powerfully felt. And if we seek to know her attitude towards legalistic hardening, there is an anecdote that speaks for itself. She, very old, enjoyed the very young, and liked to waylay for a moment's talk the little boy who brought the milk each day to the Hotel Biron. One day he came early and she missed him. The following conversation with the virtuous young portress (Maria Zoepffel) [10] is on record:

> "Did the little milkman come this morning?"
> "Yes, Reverend Mother."
> "And what did you say to him?"
> "Oh! Nothing! It was the time of greater silence!"
> "What? you were heartless enough to let that poor child go without any sign of kindness? What does greater silence mean to him? O Maria! Never forget that no-one should leave our houses without taking away a word of God." [11]

*   *   *

Marie Josephine Goetz [12] was elected superior general on September 8, 1865, a small, dark-eyed Alsatian, vivacious and intensely controlled. She was then only forty-seven years old, but the Foundress had said: "Josephine has the age of wisdom. She is anchored in humility — with breadth of mind." Forty years earlier, when Mother Barat had felt that she could bear her burden no longer, she had prayed to be shown her successor. That night she saw in sleep a little girl who looked at her meaningfully, and heard a voice say: "She who is to take your place is not yet eight years old."

Josephine was born at Scheldstadt on March 7, 1817. Left an orphan, lively and intelligent, she was brought up with severe love by "tante Odile." At the Sacred Heart school at Besançon, self-willed and self-righteous, she waged a cold war with authority until the day when an intuition of God's reality overwhelmed her at her desk in the study-room; she saw that humility is beautiful. She made the unusual choice of the choir of angels known as the Thrones for her patrons: "This mysterious name spoke to me of repose, stability, equilibrium in the spiritual order, and it brought a strange peace to my soul." She threw herself headlong into prayer and penance, headed the "Associates of the Sacred Heart," a fervent élite, and used her power for leadership for the good of the school. One of her teachers said of her: "If she enters the Society, there is a ready-made superior general!" When Mother Barat visited Besançon Josephine felt the call to religious life in her presence. She entered the noviceship at Montet, Switzerland, in October, 1834.

This house, opened as a refuge after the revolution of 1830, formed a generation of outstanding leaders in the austere beauty of mountains near the snow-line. Josephine all but ruined her health by self-added austerities, and followed to the letter the uncompromising line set by Mother Henriette Coppens:[13] "Say 'yes' to grace and 'no' to nature." After her vows in February, 1837, she learned common sense through work in the school at Montet, and then went back to Besançon where, as mistress general, she learned human nature through unruly children. Legend still points to the statue of the Infant Jesus that shed tears over their conduct – and Josephine who witnessed to this was not imaginative. By the time she reached Conflans for her probation (delayed for years because she could not be spared) she had formed the governing habit of her life: "Before each act I turn to the Holy Spirit and make a choice. I wait for his 'toc'." She was professed on March 5, 1847, having chosen to live face to face with God in prayer. The sense of duty was all-powerful in her, "acting from moment to moment under the impulse of the Spirit."

The next seventeen years were spent at Conflans where she was mistress of novices, and after 1854 superior as well. It was a fresh, silent place high on a bluff where the Seine and the Marne flowed together. She claimed to be "gros Jean," a country bumpkin. Father de Ravignan, her demanding director, thought differently:

> Mother Goetz has, underlying her good sense, a penetrating intelligence. Her timid manner hides the powers of a vigorous heart and the most generous courage. She has all the gifts, but most of all that of discernment of spirits. She assists at her first movements.[14]

She was a person of paradoxes. "Antitheses suited her turn of mind," and brought swift alternations of vehemence and calm to her expressive face. Some persons feared her rectitude, her gravity, her directness. She had an austere attraction for the liturgy of Ash Wednesday, and said: "We are governed by Ecclesiastes: vanity of vanities!" But few could resist the warmth of heart that lay behind the uplifted finger, the penetrating look relieved suddenly by a sparkle of fun. She enjoyed "serious amusements." When she spoke of God "her face became literally alight, her clear, profound gaze was luminous; I could feel the effect of something more than human acting in her." Her favourite word for herself was "insignificant."

Her workroom had a grilled window facing north; it was brightened by her own ardour, for "I am working with my mind on fire." She called it "my laboratory," for she had discovered "a little science of the soul" as old as man but then known by a new name, psychology. "My mind is swimming in truth," she said when reading the *Summa* of Saint Thomas into which few women then ventured. "I am devouring luminous pages and beautiful passages; I am taking notes for the future." She liked logic because "right thinking is the basis of the spiritual life." She went on to Dionysius the Areopagite, since "if the subject of the mystical life is the human soul, its object is God," and from there "let us pass into action." She made an outline for philosophical studies which was later incorporated into the *Plan of Studies*. It was the basis for her training of the novices:

> At my own risk I shall draw those entrusted to me towards the love of wisdom, that savouring knowledge of God and of his attributes and his mysteries, according to the capacity of each intelligence. For the intellect must understand and penetrate before wisdom judges, compares and acts. This is the program I am drawing up in my laboratory; it remains to make out a classical and methodical itinerary.[15]

Of the novices she said: "Give us a true Christian and we shall soon form a true religious," and to the individual: "Stay yourself. It is your own God-given nature that you must raise to the supernatural." She said bluntly: "I like correct saints, and to be correct one must be corrected. I want you to be perfect and I shall spare no detail." She acted accordingly. In prayer she led them straight to the Christ of the gospel and then stood aside. She wanted them to teach catechism "in an adventuresome way."

When Mother Goetz was named superior her usual diffidence made her pour out a flood of protests and self-accusations. Mother Barat said soothingly to those present: "Please forgive her; she doesn't mean to tell lies." This habit of self-humiliation at awkward moments made others uncomfortable. But Mother Goetz soon rallied, and her capacity for organization came into play, helped by her methodical use of time. "It seems to me that I have compartments in my brain into which I put my ideas; I can pull them out when I need them." She re-organized the three communities, two schools and orphanage at Conflans, erected new buildings and remodelled the chapel.

In the spring of 1864 she was named assistant general (secretly at first) succeeding Mother Coppens who had died the year before. Each week saw her precise little figure, carrying a neatly rolled umbrella, arrive at the Mother House to share in the deliberations. After her nomination as Vicar General at the Council of 1864 she lived at the Mother House. For one year she had charge of the probation which she called "the school of the heart." Mother Barat named her "my minister of interior affairs," and said to her helpers:

> Pass on your experience to Mother Goetz: she is capable and has a good head. Don't keep back anything; she will tell me what would otherwise tire my old memory. What a rest for me to have her! I can pray in peace. . . . I have nothing to hide from my little vicar general. At my age I may become mute at any moment.[16]

When that dreaded moment came Mother Goetz was in anguish during the four months of her government as vicar general. But after her own election as superior general she said: "I have received the *toc* of the Holy Spirit for my mission." She sensed that her generalate would be short: "My mission is clearly defined. I must in no way innovate, but clarify, strengthen and teach what is not yet fully understood."[17] And: "I feel drawn to innovate nothing, to start no movements of change in the beautiful uniformity of our laws."[18]

The Ninth General Council which elected her met only briefly, from September 8 to 16, 1865.[19] It established the elementary juniorate at Conflans, and organized the probation on an international basis; probanists from all over the world would assemble at the Mother House twice a year.

The next five years were peacefully energetic. Mother Goetz went to Rome and was "confirmed" by Pius IX. He reopened the thorny question of the transfer of the Mother House to Rome, but Mother Goetz, frightened, obtained an indefinite delay. She then carried out the unfinished business of Mother Barat. A retreat house known as "La Maison des Anges" was built on the Boulevard des

Invalides; it was also a centre for the Children of Mary and for
grandes pensionnaires from all over the world. The first retreat for
superiors at the Mother House was held in September, 1866,
followed by a council of studies. At Conflans a burial crypt was
made in the garden; it became a shrine holding the bodies of many
of the first builders of the Society. An unexpected favour from
heaven was given on December 14, 1866, when a novice, Mary
Wilson, who was dying at Grand Coteau, was miraculously cured
by the intercession of Saint John Berchmans who appeared to her in
vision.

Mother Goetz travelled diligently; in the first year she visited
thirty-two houses. Blunt and without eloquence, she trusted the
savoir-faire and ready tongue of Mother Lehon, "mon Aaron," who
travelled with her. At Blumenthal a scene took place which was
later recognized as prophetic. Mothers Goetz, Lehon and de Sartorius, superior of the house, attended a school reception at which
six-year-old Maria de Loë presented a gift of a holy water font.
Four superiors general were together in the same room. When at
home Mother Goetz worked relentlessly at her desk, closing her
door for long hours of thoughtful study, fighting neuralgic
headaches, only too conscious of her burden. Sometimes for relief
she would walk under the linden trees of the Hotel Biron with
Pauline Perdrau, talking of the past, projecting the future.

In 1869 the body of Father de Tournély was found in the village
churchyard at Haggenbrunn; it was transferred on November 20 to
a shrine in the newly founded house in Vienna. A renewed contact
with the primitive charism of the Society thus came about. Maria
Mayer,[20] superior at Vienna and the first vicar of Austria, came often to visit Mother Goetz as an intimate friend. Together they
spoke of the experience of God with which the superior general was
favoured at this time, of "the ways of grace that she had followed
until then, and those along which the Heart of Jesus now led her,
since he carried in her place the burden of her heavy office." [21]
Mother Goetz formulated her own thoughts on the spirit of the
Society in definite terms; it has four marks:

> Devotion to the Sacred Heart characterized by practical conformity to the sen-
> timents and affections of our Lord; intelligent insight into the Rule; love of the
> Society as a whole; esteem for all its works. [22]

Mother Goetz went to Rome in March, 1870, and in July
Vatican Council I opened. "I am archi-orthodox," she remarked,

exulting in the strong stance of the Council with regard to error and liberalism, synonymous terms to her. To Pius IX she offered in the name of the Society "the promise of a filial submission that will be absolute, to Holy Church and to its august Head," seeing in all authority "the instrument and the organ of the will of God." She drew a telling parallel:

> The unity of authority in catholicism maintains its primitive purity; Rome is its centre and we submit without rationalizing (*raisonnements*) to its decisions. In the same way this unity must exist in the Society of the Sacred Heart. Our centre is the Mother House; all directives that come from there must be sacred for us.[23]

On July 18 the dogma of the infallibility of the Pope was defined.

Suddenly, sharp events cut across history. Garibaldi marched on Rome, the temporal power of the papacy vanished, and Vatican I was suspended — until Vatican II could take up its unfinished business. Then the Franco–Prussian war broke out. It drove Mother Goetz to Laval where she could keep in touch with the Society while Mother Lehon guarded the Mother House through the bombing, the horse-meat diet and the terrorism of the siege of Paris.

In her refuge Mother Goetz guided a small probation and worked on a detailed re-editing of the Decrees of the General Councils until her right arm was paralyzed with cold. Anxiety and hardship broke her health, while around the Mother House the siege turned into the horrors of the Commune. They died away and Mother Goetz returned in July, 1871. She saw that it was impossible to hold the next General Council at the right time, so she prepared the agenda with the remark: "I shall not be there."

Mother Goetz' circular letters are incisive. They project with earnest brevity the basic ideas of Madeleine Sophie Barat: charity resting on fundamental obedience, humility and solid virtue. In the letter written after the death of Mother Desmarquest in March, 1869, she upheld fidelity to "our religious law" with its whole code of observances as a guiding principle. Speaking of the long life just ended:

> Are not such moving memories destined by Providence to preserve us from that mobility and inconstancy which come from the wind of revolution which destroys, overturns, changes, innovates? ... Far from us should be that changeableness which decides too quickly and follows the impressions of the moment, which throws itself without the help of prayer into works of zeal but gathers no lasting fruit because the blessing of heaven has not filled it. ... Un-

doubtedly there are certain improvements, in education for example, from which we cannot hold aloof. But these should never be the effect of personal initiative in such or such a house, since our actions must keep the mark of constant uniformity. If these improvements are recognized as necessary they can be proposed, and after mature examination can be adopted by general consent. Stamped with the seal of authority they will receive God's special blessing.[24]

From this it is an easy step to the narrower principle that: "We must tend as far as possible to keep uniformity in custom as well as unity of spirit in the Society."[25]

The most compelling of Mother Goetz' letters was written at the desolate moment following the war:

We can hope that God's protection will still be with us if we try, by corresponding more and more fully to the designs of his love, to grow in the spirit and virtues of our holy vocation, spirit and virtues eminently fitted for the needs of our times when hatred and forgetfulness of God, opposition to his laws and contempt for authority call for the exercise of love, of devotedness, of reparation and expiation which form the essence of the cultus paid to the Sacred Heart of Jesus. There is a general conviction that Christian society owes its salvation to the devotion to this divine Heart.[26]

The letter goes on to show that any religious whose personal way is anxious, painful and complicated, whose spirituality is sterile, will find light, strength and joy in the open Heart of Christ; that the Society has a mission to communicate this love to others; that public events call for a renewal in love.

In her very simple conferences Mother Goetz was clear and cool in tone, balancing negative with positive: "I am always struck by the sterility of those in whose lives there is no union with our Lord. Those united to him are capable of anything." The advice that she gave to superiors was practical; she aimed at "noble simplicity" in the life of the community and of the school, even to the shape of the children's hats. For the children themselves her ideal was: "Duty before all else, duty always."

Early in 1872 Mother Goetz called for all the letters of Madeleine Sophie Barat, and for testimonies to her holiness. Ecclesiastical tribunals were set up at the Mother House and in Rome where witnesses to the life of the Foundress gave their depositions. In the following year Mother Goetz again went to Rome to give her own testimony. Exhausted, she went to rest in the new house at Pau where she made a pilgrimage to the grotto of Lourdes nearby. But while she was there her peace was shattered by the May Laws of the Kulturkampf in Germany which closed five of her houses at one blow. She returned to the Mother House where, sitting in the garden with the community, she listened to Monsignor Louis Baunard reading aloud his biography of Madeleine Sophie Barat. She knew that her own work for the Society was done.

This work is summarized in the *Histoire Abrégée de la Société:*

> The task of the second generalate was one of strengthening and of completion. . . . Gifted with light and prudence to lead the Society not by new ways but by the understanding and practice of the laws already laid down, Mother Goetz was vigilant and firm to assure that nothing should weaken them, yet kind and gentle in winning hearts. In her hands the work begun took definite form: imprecise regulations were made precise; the Society became rooted in the love of its traditions, its past, its origins. Mother Goetz left her religious family more penetrated than ever with the spirit of the Foundress, more anchored than ever in its primitive spirit.[27]

Her own legacy was passed on through definite channels: the intellectual elevation of education by emphasis on philosophy and by teacher training; the clarification of a way of life by the editing of the Decrees; and unity of formation by the outline of instructions for novices known as "Exercise" which was followed thereafter in all countries. Her personal influence has perhaps been obscured by the way in which she is presented in her early biography which stressed her disconcerting humility and rigourism, and her static attitudes. But by nature she was refreshingly original and had the daring to move ahead, as seen in her enthusiasm for studies not then fit for women. She took leadership at a moment when initiative was not called for, and she threw her energies into consolidation. It requires vision to transmit the work of someone else to the future as a living thing ready for growth. If Mother Goetz lacked the warm humanness of Mother Barat, she was attractive in her own right and she was true to herself: straight, loyal, self-spending. In her forthright way she obeyed "the *toc* of the Holy Spirit who is driving me on." For her: "Christ is the way of all our undertakings, the truth of all our thoughts, the life of all our works."

In Advent, 1873, Mother Goetz spent ten days at the Hotel Biron, joyously sharing all that she had to give, saying: "Those who faithfully accept every opportunity for self-emptying quickly reach the life within, the possession of God." Struck by paralysis after

Christmas, she died on January 4, 1874. She had named her "Aaron," Adèle Lehon, as vicar general.

*   *   *

Adelaide (or Adèle) Aimée Thérèse Lehon[28] was a Belgian, tall and frighteningly thin, quick in speech and movement, with keen eyes and a generous smile. If Mother Goetz seems never to have been old, Mother Lehon seems never to have been young. Mature from childhood, she was in her sixty-eighth year when she began a generalate that was to last for twenty years; inevitably it was stamped with her own vigorous conservatism.

Adèle was born on December 9, 1806, in Antoing, Belgium. Her home was a château administered by her lawyer father for an absentee prince. A sympathetic but austere upbringing helped the frail child to live by will power. She first went to school with the Ursulines; at sixteen she appeared, against her will, at the Sacred Heart school at Amiens where she kept rigidly aloof. She criticized the régime, complaining that the silverware was washed at table in cold water. The next day the water was hot; her criticisms had been respected. Won over, she threw herself headlong into fervent austerities that had to be chastened. She saw that her adversary was her own domineering nature. The battle would be long and she chose for her patron the long-lived Saint John the Evangelist, apostle of love. Religious life, she knew, would be hard, and she liked the hard way.

She entered the Society at Lille on June 9, 1829, and passed her noviceship in a whirlwind of the unexpected. From Lille she went to Paris where she took the habit on October 4 and was set on her way by Mother Barat: "Are you ready for anything? God alone – and souls!" The revolution of 1830 scattered the novices and Adèle found herself at Autun, then at Besançon, then at Middes (the temporary house preceding Montet). Soon the tall novice was helping her companions to struggle through the snow on Mount Cenis, on her way to Italy where a noviceship was to be opened. She made her first vows at the Trinita on February 2, 1832. The novices then moved to Santa Rufina in the noisily crowded Trastevere. Adèle was ready for responsibility and her profession was advanced to August 25, 1833, so that she could become mistress of novices. Her hand was strong and she wore no velvet gloves, but if she asked much she gave more. She was loved because of, not despite, her *franchise sans voile.*

In 1838 Mother Lehon became superior at Santa Rufina. For the next thirty years she was identified with Italy until "I can scarcely speak French." She made the blunders of the over-honest, and after the crisis of 1839 she experienced the pain of a misunderstanding with Mother Barat due to a rumour that the Italian houses were about to separate from the Society. Her own loyalty soon became apparent, and from then on Mother Barat leaned on "my dear Adèle."

Mother Lehon was then sent to make foundations in the Papal States, at Loretto near the holy house brought from Nazareth (says legend) by angel hands, and at Saint Elpidio on the Adriatic. Life in these country houses was simple but menacing. Mother Lehon was at Loretto during the revolution of 1848 when her courage and humour saved both houses from the Carbonari who blundered in and out with their guns and threats. She was not there during the revolution of 1860 when these houses were lost.

After one year as superior at Lemberg in the Polish sector of Austria, Mother Lehon attended the General Council of 1851. She returned to the Villa Lante as superior vicar of Italy and mistress of novices, and was soon a familiar sight at the Vatican as the Society's representative.

Mother Barat guided her from a distance, and began by releasing her from the self-inflicted troubles arising from her own tense nature:

> As for yourself, my daughter, be more free and have confidence in Jesus; believe that your present state has physical causes and do not be worried by it. Only refuse voluntarily nothing of what our Lord asks of you and this good Master is powerful enough to do his work with a broken instrument as well as with a good one. The essential thing is to keep oneself small and always in his hands.[29]

Mother Barat poured out her own troubles to this friend in whom she found relief: "There! You see what is tormenting me. Reassure me if you can and tell me your own plans."[30] She thanked for gifts of money and personnel and then called for more, "as I know your generosity" before the needs of the poor children in Dublin. She counted on Adèle's understanding of the difficult people who were making things hard for the Society and longed to have her at the Mother House, since "I always turn to you when I am in trouble." These troubles were more than personal; they came from a sense of the Society's responsibility to the world:

America is restless; the commotion is becoming general. It makes one remember the words of our divine Master when he told his disciples of the signs that would point to what was to come. How this outlook should inflame our zeal, our love for the divine Heart and for souls! How many defections there will be, and what a prodigious number of the elect! We must prepare them, instruct them, put deep in them the devotion to the Sacred Heart. If the salt loses its savour, if the lamps of the world burn out, woe to us! The Spouse will arrive in the night of this world. Let us work with more ardour than ever, first for our own perfection and for that of those around us, and then for the souls of those entrusted to us. The hope of the Church is in the young. [31]

In 1864 Mother Lehon was elected assistant general, and for one year was at Mother Barat's side as "my minister of external affairs," and local superior of the Mother House. She kept the latter charge even though she travelled widely. Otherwise she disappeared in humble work, and Mother Goetz remarked: "Mother Lehon went out of herself long ago and has never gone back." During the war of 1870 she claimed the post of danger by right: "I've been through several revolutions; I'm not afraid. I'm Belgian, I'm calm, I'm old." She was bold enough to put her head through the guichet and say with a pistol under her chin: "No! You can't come in." She was adroit enough to slip compromising papers into her own pocket under the very nose of the *Citoyen* who dropped them on the table as he read them. When all was over she went to Rome to give her testimony for the Cause of Madeleine Sophie Barat, returned to Paris just before the death of Mother Goetz, and found herself vicar general.

In this role she administered the Society incisively; never had she been more severe with herself and with others. But when she was elected third superior general on May 1, 1874, she wrote on a slip of paper headed "Treasure of Truth": "You are now sacrificed, given over to others, at the service of all. Ask rather than command. No more imperatives."

The Tenth General Council met from May 1 to 21, 1874. It approved of the Decrees as edited by Mother Goetz, of the Rule of the Children of Mary as revised by a commission and of that of the newly established Affiliées, and appointed a new commission of studies. [32] Several proposals discussed are interesting today in view of recent changes and emphases. One concerned structures:

The Council took up several questions with relation to government, with the aim of lightening the burden of the superior general and of modifying the form of the general congregation in order to make it more representative. Should the vicariates be enlarged and the vicars given wider scope for action? Should an elected delegate accompany each vicar to the general congregation? [33]

These proposals were recognized as "good in principle" but were rejected on the grounds that the strongly centralized forms then in force were satisfactory, and that "the times through which we are passing are unfavourable to change, and any innovation is a danger."

Another suggestion, originating outside the Society, was the founding of a special house of prayer near Geneva, where the community would live a purely contemplative life.

Our Mothers considered that the establishment in our Society of houses especially consecrated to adoration and reparation would be quite in harmony with the spirit which our venerated Mother Foundress has left to us. But when they examined more closely the conditions laid down by those who are asking for such a house, they found that they could not be carried out. The intention was to create a congregation quite separated from ours, to exchange the vow of education of youth for a vow as victim, to remove from the superior general the right to recall into apostolic life the religious who would have been set aside for adoration.... The present proposition will thus be refused, without relinquishing the possibility of undertaking something analogous under more favourable conditions. [34]

A very positive note was struck in a decree concerning the formation of the young religious:

We must never forget that the equilibrium of a human being depends upon the degree of maturity and of development that she can and must attain, and that to fail to favour this development is an injustice to the whole religious society which would have profited from her perfectioning. [35]

The *Histoire Abrégée* has drawn a perceptive contrast between the second and third superiors general:

It would be difficult to find two people more unlike in mind and character. While Mother Goetz tried to penetrate the future for which she was preparing, Mother Lehon lived for the present moment. The one, brushing aside all secondary considerations, found hours for work and solitude in which to study and answer the problems of the hour; the other kept in touch with the least details of the present business and counted on common sense and on inspiration from on high to solve all difficulties. Mother Goetz was present at her own first movements; Mother Lehon asked pardon for the vivacity that escaped her. Mother Goetz could not bear to be behind in her work, Mother Lehon saw no reason for being in a hurry. They even differed in their mode of government. Mother Goetz, while motherly, was very methodical; Mother Lehon was inspired by circumstances with familiar ease. [36]

Mother Lehon saw her mission in a practical light, and touched the keynote of consolidation:

> I am old, I am lacking in talents. When I was named superior general I said to myself: I have neither the virtues nor the talents of our two first mothers, but I shall set myself to keeping the Rule, and I shall see that it is kept by others. I shall serve the Society thus.[37]

She became known as "our living Rule" while she took for herself a gentle role of service:

> I am the servant of the servants of Jesus; I must serve them everywhere, always. To be disturbed, interrupted by no matter whom, is good for the servant who cannot always please her masters.[38]

Her knowledge of the windings of the human heart was specific; she faced people with realism and forgave easily: "laissez tomber!" Extremely mortified and contemptuous of self, she grew in warmth towards others. Gradually her somewhat sombre and over-anxious spirituality gave way to confident joy, until: "Gratitude is the habitual sentiment of my soul." For: "It is the Holy Spirit who is the Master; we fulfil the wishes of the Spirit of Jesus."

In November, 1878, Mother Lehon had her first audience with the new Pope Leo XIII whom she strikingly resembled in appearance and venerability. He said: "There is a difference only of an 'h' between Léon and Lehon. We shall fight the good fight together." Despite this militant tone, which she herself sometimes adopted, Mother Lehon's government was quiet, with few startling events. Forty-two new houses appeared; the globe was circled. Yet she travelled less and less with advancing age and quietly controlled events from the Mother House. In 1878 the body of Father Varin was transferred to the crypt at Conflans. On July 5, 1879, the Cause of the Foundress was formally introduced in Rome, and from then on public honour could be paid to Venerable Madeleine Sophie; the session "Fama Sanctitatis" took place ten years later. Mother Lehon celebrated her Golden Jubilee on August 25, 1883; it was outdone in splendour only by her Diamond Jubilee. For the Jubilee of Leo XIII in 1888 the Society gave him a large painting of Judith, now in the Vatican; the subject was chosen by the Pope. When Mother Lehon fell ill in 1886 Mother Augusta de Sartorius was named vicar general to assist her in government.

The circular letters and General Councils of this time all strike the same note: a desire to guard the Society's heritage and to make it fructify by a very literal fidelity:

> Our way has been traced for us; we have before us sure and clear models, and I know that all desire to be more and more moved by that primitive spirit of charity, of zeal, of abnegation, of entire devotedness to the interests of the Heart of Jesus that is our legacy.[39]

And so: "I want none of our traditions to be lost,"[40] and "the Society has only to to on from good to better."[41] This optimism was shadowed by a fear of what might happen if the *status quo* were disturbed. This was not personal timidity; it was the air which Mother Lehon breathed. She herself was quick to point out the least abuse; she attacked with vigour "la mollesse," the softness so opposed to her own virility:

> Let us make no mistake; this fault which dominates our times finds its way into the holiest places and causes in some religious persons an excessive love of well-being, a fear of suffering, of trouble, of fatigue, a craving for pleasure. What then becomes of mortification, of that renouncement without which one cannot be a disciple of Jesus Christ?[42]

She said nothing startling, but self-evident truths were repeated so earnestly that their intrinsic power struck home.

The Eleventh General Council should have been held in 1880, but on the advice of Cardinal Monaco La Valletta it was postponed until 1884 when it met from February 29 to March 19. The Twelfth General Council followed, April 17 to May 11, 1890. Both were concerned largely with the "necessary concessions" needed for an expanding apostolate.[43] At both Mother Lehon offered to resign, but the offer was not accepted; she had won the affectionate trust and veneration of the Society. She asked of all what she had set as her own ideal: "Even in the smallest things, the very smallest things, be responsive to the Spirit of Jesus Christ." None could feel this to be beyond them.

Trouble appeared on the horizon after 1885; legal harassment of religious orders by fiscal control would eventually prove more deadly than violence. Inspectors were turning up in the French houses and Mother Lehon wrote:

> I am the first to urge you to pray that these evils may be averted. But I must add with our Venerable Mother: do not think that such danger fills me with anxiety.

O no! A single point of our Rule neglected, a breach of charity tolerated, would be far more painful to my heart; this would make me grieve before God. For as long as we remain faithful to our religious code we have nothing to fear from attacks from without. In the face of a law which aims to despoil us let us become more poor in desire and in practice; before calumnies let us be more humble; if our teaching is criticized let us make it more solid.[44]

She had become almost completely blind, with nothing left of rigour in her serenity. She wrote to the Society:

I beg of you, throw out anything that might trouble charity. Let us renew ourselves in the master virtue. Let us fear the least word or action that might harm it. Let the reputation of each of our sisters be dearer to us than our own. Far from us the small rivalries, the antipathies of nation for nation, of vicariate for vicariate, which are signs of a small heart, unworthy of the great and noble Heart of Jesus. Charity must be our mark if God is to bless us.[45]

October 2, 1893, marked the climax of Mother Lehon's long generalate. The body of Madeleine Sophie Barat was taken from the crypt at Conflans and found to be intact. Mother Lehon, unable to see, was led to her side and took the loved hand in her own:

With what ardour I promised in the name of us all that we would strengthen our generous efforts to be her true daughters. . . . How could I not pray that this little Society which she founded would remain immovable in its principles and its forms![46]

The body of the Foundress, freshly clothed, was then replaced in the crypt.

Mother Lehon's last conference asked that "the Heart of Jesus will hold all our hearts in unison, till they make but one with his own." She died in the light of Easter week, March 28, 1894.

*   *   *

The longest generalate was followed by the shortest. "I shall be but a passer-by," said Augusta von Sartorius.[47] She was a dignified German, serene and attractive, gifted with "incomparable kindness, the sweetness of the strong." What she gave in passing was more than enough: the communication of the spirit of the Society by the radiant personality of a woman of prayer.

She was born at Aachen, Germany, on August 1, 1830, and baptized Pulchérie - Augusta - Marie - Caroline - Josephine - Hubertine.

Augusta was enough. The French form of her surname has always been used in the Society, *de* for *von* Sartorius. Her childhood was passed in the lively, gracious, God-serving home of a doctor. Life revolved around the gifted and charming eldest daughter. While following her studies at home she cared for her crippled half-sister and her orphaned niece and nephew. The parish priest counted on her to run the Holy Childhood Association and the Children of Mary, while the sick poor thought that she was all theirs. So did her family when they gathered around her at the piano. Through all this devotedness her contact with God was growing silently deeper; her sensitive nature met him easily in a sunset over the Rhine or in a Gothic shrine of our Lady in the peaceful country-side.

Augusta was twenty-five before the thought of religious life surprised her. Could her home and parish get on withut her? Disturbed by this conflict of duties she set off in a snow storm for the Sacred Heart convent at Blumenthal for a retreat. "How can one see what is due to God and not give him everything?" was her decision. She entered the Society on November 17, 1855, and at Conflans received the impress of Mother Barat and Mother Goetz. She returned to Blumenthal for her first vows on February 28, 1858, and was promptly named mistress general. Too much the saint at first to please the children, she was just beginning to win them when a fire destroyed the school building.

Augusta went to Paris for her profession, made on October 20, 1863. Back in Blumenthal she became superior, and received from Mother Barat a life-plan for the responsibilities that mounted ahead:

> I can hardly use my eyes and so I can only write a few lines now and then. It would have been a joy to me to speak at length with you, dear daughter, in order to console you in the trials that you had to offer to the divine Heart. As I could not follow the impulse of my own heart I have scribbled a few lines already known and practised by you, but one cannot too often read and meditate upon them, and strive to follow them. I know that you will try to carry them out with all your power. . . . Goodbye, dear Sartorius; pray for your mother.

Enclosed on a slip of paper:

> I hold my life from Jesus, my God and my Saviour. I have understood this marvellous truth, and with all my will I have consecrated to him my entire being. So if I come from him I must be in him, there to live and die, having given to him all my actions in order to say with the great apostle: "I live, no, not I,

but Jesus Christ lives in me." This is an invitation from your mother general to tend with all your strength towards this divine life. [48]

Augusta took the words to heart as troubles came fast upon her. "These things bring us nearer to our Lord. . . . They bring freedom from a whole host of impressions that invade our inner life and cause trouble." The first problem was her health. She almost died in 1868 and never thereafter had respite from the headaches and giddiness that would come upon her at any moment. "I must accept the state of my health, make as little of it as possible, and carry it off gaily." So she offered to go to Chile. "No, not to Chile," said Mother Goetz, adding prophetically, "to Louisiana someday."

Mother de Sartorius held on to her dangerous post at Blumenthal through the Franco-Prussian war and the cholera. She then went to Marienthal in Germany where the anti-clerical war bred by the Kulturkampf attacked first the Jesuits then the "Jesuitesses." An official hand had scribbled on the broken seal of one of her letters: "Do what we can, we cannot get rid of the mice." The decree of expulsion was a biting parody of all the principles of religious life, and pinpointed their harmful effect upon the state. It reached Mother de Sartorius on May 25, 1873. "I salute you, banished community," she said in giving the news. The packing had already been done, and she was soon in Blumenthal again, greeted by the dog who had also been banished into Holland. The German Children of Mary wrote a letter promising perpetual loyalty to all they had been taught.

For the next eleven years her zeal and her ill health spurred each other on as she served as superior at Blumenthal, Moulins and Bois l'Evêque where she gave impetus to the social action among the mining families. School children, workmen, visitors, all felt the influence of this balanced woman who lived for others and who had the power to draw out their best selves. To her communities she revealed the source of this power:

Let's begin by praying. Prayer gives strength and perseverance; it is the mystic bridge thrown over the depths that separate us from God. . . . He is waiting for us, he draws us on, he is ready to give. So drop everything else and be filled with one thought: I am before God. Then be led by the Holy Spirit. Sometimes we simply talk to Jesus, sometimes we unite ourselves to the thoughts of his Heart, sometimes we stay peacefully at his feet, looking at him. [49]

In October, 1884, Mother de Sartorius risked her life in the long sea voyage to America, as superior vicar of Louisiana where Philippine Duchesne was still a living memory. She then took a primitive train through the bayou land to Saint Michael's. She adapted easily to the strange ways of this new world in the throes of reconstruction after the Civil War. She watched the slow Mississippi from the gallery where she sat with Bishop Gibbons, learning of the heroic days of the Church in the United States. She won the hearts of the negroes. An old former slave known as "Mother Duchesne's Liza" loved her lavishly and corrected her English. The new vicar gave herself to her adopted land, cheerfully hiding her physical suffering, sharing her inner peace. Then, in July, 1886, she was recalled to the Mother House to become assistant general and to act as vicar general during an illness of Mother Lehon.

When the tomb of Mother Barat was opened Mother de Sartorius noticed the absence of a profession ring. She slipped her own on the finger of the Foundress where it stayed until a new one was provided. She again became vicar general on the death of Mother Lehon, and when the Thirteenth General Council assembled she reminded the members that she could not be sure of more than fifteen minutes of life at any moment. They consulted Cardinal Richard upon the wisdom of electing her, and he replied: "You should choose her even if you only keep her for two years because of the good she will do the Society." She became superior general on July 22, 1894, and the Society kept her for less than ten months.

The Thirteenth General Council met from July 22 to August 12, 1894. It raised the question: is a revision of the Constitutions needed? The answer was: not now. Mother de Sartorius described its work in her first circular letter:

> We have looked over the loved field of the Lord to uproot and to cut down the few abuses that may easily have crept in by the easy-going ways of poor human nature of which the enemy of all good takes advantage, and which come also from a certain impulsiveness which today drives us towards a false and exaggerated liberty. We have thus tried to strengthen and draw closer the bonds of our submission to the Holy See and to its august Head.[50]

A decree expressing this submission was adopted.[51]

After the Council Mother de Sartorius went to Conflans for a retreat during which she renewed her earlier vow of abandonment to the good pleasure of God. "This is the time for saying 'yes,' for accepting my charge with love." She then went to Rome for an audience with Leo XIII who said: "You will have the spirit of Mother Barat and Mother Lehon." Back in Paris she wrote to her director: "Many things have changed in me. . . . The spirit of devotion to the Sacred Heart, as our Lord himself has revealed it, has so seized me that I live altogether in this atmosphere."

The few things that she had time to do were symbolic. She acquired the small house in Joigny where Madeleine Sophie Barat had lived as a child; it was kept in its simplicity and the attic room became a chapel. She instituted daily exposition of the Blessed Sacrament at the Mother House which Mother Barat had always desired. She called in all the letters written by Philippine Duchesne in preparation for her Cause. In her few circular letters and conferences she lingered on the primitive spirit:

> We have a unanimous desire to keep the traditions of our first Mothers, and the primitive spirit of the Society which has made it what it is and which must remain sacred for us. . . . It is a spirit not only of generosity and devotedness but of love, simplicity, humility, interior life. In a word, it is a spirit opposed to that of the world which threatens to enter even into religious houses. [52]
>
> The primitive spirit is a spirit of love. . . . To keep it let us remain united; let us form but one heart, let us put up with things, forget ourselves, and count as nothing those trifles that harm fraternal charity. [53]

In the spring Mother de Sartorius went to Conflans where she was heard praying aloud at the grave of Mother Lehon: "Help me, Mother. I can do no more." She returned, spent, to the Mother House where she died on May 8, 1895.

* * *

The "pillars of the Society" who had worked with Madeleine Sophie Barat were gradually joining her in the crypt at Conflans, and others were taking their place in government. Their strong personalities and long lives had done much for consolidation. When Félicité Desmarquest died in 1869 Mother Goetz spoke of her in terms that well describe them all:

> One of her characteristics was calmness, that perfect self-possession based on the Rule and on duty; there was nothing arbitrary in her balanced judgment. What wisdom and perfection in all she did! [54]

She was followed in 1871 by Elizabeth Prevost [55] whom Mother Barat had called "my second self." Complex Pauline de Limminghe spent the last years of her troubled life at Jette where she died in 1874. It was said that she had burned, in fulfilment of a promise, letters that would have told us much of the spirituality of Mother Barat. Pauline Perdrau spent her old age at Layrac, writing out the notes that she had taken on Mother Barat and Mother Goetz over the years. These memoirs were only published in 1936, in two volumes entitled *Les Loisirs de l'Abbaye.*

Mother Barat had called her assistants general "the four wheels of our chariot." They formed her private council and each had charge of the vicariates of a given region, grouped according to language. The list of forty-nine assistants general up to 1970 shows that most of them came to office after wide experience and remained for long years. While startlingly different in personality they were extremely unified in outlook, stressing tradition, controlling adaptation, supporting the action of the superior general with intense loyalty.

Aloysia Hardey, who had done so much to root the Society in North America, was called to the Mother House in 1872 as assistant general. She travelled constantly through Europe and three times returned to the United States with the mission that had always been hers: initiative within tradition in new environments. She started several new works, such as parlour boarders in Paris and an "apostolic school" in Beauvais to foster vocations. This last was among her few failures. She was future-orientated:

> Everything in the world has need of renewal because everything has within itself the germ of decay. Hence the necessity of religious renovation, which means a renewal of fervour, of fidelity in pursuing the end of our vocation. The law of sterility, of advancing age, is attached to persons and things; it leaves its impress all too soon. So it is in the moral order. There is a decline which fastens itself upon our thoughts, our desires, our resolutions. Hence the need of having spiritual things presented to us in a novel manner. [56]

Mother Hardey helped the international probations to feel as she did: "I have always considered the whole Society as my home." She would say: "Of ourselves we are worth little; it is the Society that gives us worth and reputation." And: "Every time you look at a crucifix pray that union and charity may reign in the Society." She died on June 7, 1886, and Mother Lehon wrote:

> I wish to recall how, noble, generous and straight was her character, how kind, compassionatae, strong and invincible in trial was her heart, how devoted she

was to the interests of the Society and to the glory of the Heart of Jesus, active in working for them and at the same time filially submissive to the voice of obedience.[57]

Two other assistants general were in office only briefly but stand out as attractive personalities. Natalie de Serres[58] was at the same time mistress general of studies, a gentle yet vigorous semi-invalid:

> She worked all her life and to the end, beyond her strength which she kept up by moral force. A straight, sure judgment, a rare intelligence, an unwearied devotion to our Society, made her dear and precious. [59]

Clémence Fornier was a perceptive spiritual guide; remarkable answers to prayer at the time of her death confirmed her title of "holy Mother Fornier":[60]

> Kindness, indulgent kindness, joined to a firmness full of prudence — for this she is remembered by all those whom she helped. She busied herself lovingly with the humble as well as with the great, with the poor as with the rich, because to her everyone was great.[61]

Adèle Cahier was one of those dynamic desk-workers who have played a unifying role in the Society. The first secretary general had been Philippine Duchesne; she was not a gifted writer. Henriette Ducis who succeeded her was the worthy daughter of a poet. Of the next in office, Mother Galitzin, Mother Barat said: "Writing is what you do passably well." The ideal was then found in Adèle Cahier who reigned in the secretariat from 1845 to 1865, making sure that Society history would be authentic. Calm and tireless, she was a demanding perfectionist, feared and loved by her aides.

Mother Cahier became assistant general in 1865 and ceased to be secretary general, but she continued her work with the archives. She had been Mother Barat's right hand; it was not easy to be the same for Mother Goetz for, says her biographer: "By the law of nature and of Providence these two suffered reciprocally, not so much *from* one another (since neither willed it so) but *because of* one another." Mother Cahier produced her massive life of Madeleine Sophie Barat in two volumes, and it was a blow when Mother Goetz decided that it was not suitable for the public. She loyally gave over her material to a more popular writer, Monsignor Louis Baunard, while her own work was published just before her death for the Society only. She spent her last energies in classifying evidence for the Beatification of Mother Barat, and the joy of the introductiion of the Cause coincided with her Golden Jubilee in 1879. She died on April 21, 1885.

All that came from her hands was done with care; each task was carried through. She feared neither trouble nor hard work. Rectitude was natural to her, and the spirit of faith that guided her made her realize that the least detail is important in God's eyes. [63]

Mother Cahier formed her two successors as secretary general. Amélie de Savonnières[64] held office for only one year, then Marie Dufour[65] took over for twenty-eight years. She was a gay, sparkling person of whom Mother Barat said: "It does me good to talk to someone so happy in her vocation." She maintained the "primitive spirit" in all that she wrote — which included biographies of the second, third and fourth superiors general and of several "pillars". (Is it surprising that the style of Society biographies became somewhat stereotyped?) In 1884 she originated *The Dove from the Ark*, the first of the newsletters which from then till now have helped the Society to keep in touch with itself. The opening number promised that: "This paper will appear whenever there is something to say." After her retirement in 1894 she still did her best. With a white apron over her bent form she modelled a bust of Mother Barat. It was not art, but Gagliardi, painter of the official portrait for the Beatification, said: "This has life; it speaks to me." The expulsions from the French houses sent Mother Dufour to Turin where she died in 1904.

The finances of a religious order involve not only the vow of poverty made by each member but corporate witness to an evangelical life. "We can't save souls without money," remarked Mother Barat wryly, and yet "truly pious people expect to see in a religious order poverty, simplicity and humility." [66] The treasurer general needs the gifts of a financier and the spirit of Saint Francis. Mother de Charbonnel first held the post, and Mother Barat said:

What strong virtues Mother de Charbonnel has! She has more than she needs of everything. I assure you, it's good to send her on foundations. . . . Give her a house and a little money and that's all. She'll get along with straw. [67]

Henriette Coppens next held the purse strings. She had the gifts of a builder, perception of the future and control of present resources.

Josephine Mahé[68] followed her, then Césarine Bulliat,[69] both for short terms. And then, in 1872, the irresistible Césarine Borget[70] took over as financial captain of the Society for the next forty-five years. She was a small, twinkling Savoyarde, childlike in her freshness, piety and simplicity. She hated money and figures and handled both with masculine power throughout the whole period of consolidation. Yet these twenty-three years were only the beginning; we shall meet her again in less placid times.

Juliette Désoudin[71] became mistress of probation as well as assistant general in 1865; for thirty years she moulded the Society of the future through the formation patterns that she set. Formerly the French probanists had come to Conflans while others made their probation in their own countries. The centralization established by Mother Goetz was a strong force not only for uniformity but for the deeper unity of minds and hearts through a common international experience. The phrase "Mother Désoudin said . . ." carried her dicta to many generations. A native of Metz, she was lively, original and impulsive; as a child she baptized a chance-met Jewish boy — to save his soul. After her profession she took charge of the school at Metz as "mistress general *hors ligne*," energizing not only the children but the whole city through the Children of Mary. At the Mother House each probanist felt the virility, tenderness and unflinching truth of her guidance, leading to the "vie à deux" with Jesus. The will of God became a challenge to freedom through full acceptance. When lamed by a fall she still remained omnipresent; her words lost none of their piquancy when underscored by a tapping cane. At her death on June 14, 1896:

> We have lost a faithful witness to the Society's past and a mother who placed on all our religious the traditional seal of the Sacred Heart as she received it from the founders and the formers. . . . May she obtain for us to base our perfection, as she did, on a constant fidelity to our religious law and on union with the divine Heart, in order to imitate our former mothers and to perpetuate those great models whom it is so painful to see disappear.[72]

If probation was a centripetal force in the effort for unity, the noviceship was a centrifugal force. The first ideal had been to have but a single centre; but this soon became impossible; each country came to have at least one noviceship of its own. Conflans was the central noviceship for France, but the novices were so numerous that in 1890 half of them were sent to Bordeaux. Since the formation plan of

Mother Goetz was used everywhere, unity became accentuated with wider dispersal.

Georgina Lévèque[73] was mistress of novices through the entire period of consolidation. At school at Besançon she was a leader who led others out of bounds; no-one could plan more daring good times apart from the school rule while remaining loyal and (secretly) fervent. After her profession she used these same attractive powers to lead generations of novices to say "I will" with joy, for "courage is the secret of sanctity." She looked back on the sometimes excessively severe training, with its arbitrary penances and humiliations, its imperatives and contradictions, that had been in honour earlier, and said: "I admire but I cannot imitate." The expulsions from France sent her over the Alps to Peschiera where she died in 1907.

* * *

Community life was tested by the rapid expansion of the Society at this time. A century later the Chapter of 1970 showed that community spirit is more than local:

> United with all the members of the Society and living by its spirit, the religious of the Sacred Heart belongs at one and the same time to three communities: the local community, the provincial community, the international community, and shares in the life of all three. She can thus go beyond herself and live a life open to the needs of the whole world.[74]

This implies that each form of community has its own role in the Society as a whole. Their interplay emerged clearly in the last quarter of the nineteenth century. The pluriformity stressed today was latently at work in a time of uniformity and centralization.

Uniformity was most persistent in the local community. As the Society spread, the life-style of those grouped within four walls in very unlike localities stayed amazingly the same. All gloried in the fact that persons going from one country to another would find every detail familiar; they would be at home. As Mother Lehon wrote:

> We have seen with gratitude to our Lord that despite difficulties of distance, of diversity of languages and climates, the Constitutions — and even approved customs — are everywhere in vigour, and that in changing countries our mothers and sisters find their homeland wherever the divine Heart is honoured in the same manner. We must try unceasingly to fortify this precious union between vicariates as between all the members of each community.[75]

The postulants in far-away lands found the régime not so much French as "religious". Adaptations to local custom were made more freely in the schools than in the communities where cloister safeguarded life from intrusion.

There were minimal concessions to climate; witness the bewilderment of Mother de Sartorius before a fan when it fell to her to refresh the bishop at his dinner — in Louisiana. Otherwise habit and the Custom Book kept the atmosphere of fraternal joyousness created by Madeleine Sophie Barat; they kept also the forms of her day which were due to pass away. How recognize the moment when spontaneity hardens into structure? Flexibility was not a grace in the eighteen-nineties. Yet a home-like spirit, revolving around the superior, counteracted rigidity. As Janet Stuart said some years later:

> The idea of governing a house of the Sacred Heart is not that of a formal administration, but more like that of ruling a family, practically all depends on the mother; so in a religious community the whole house takes its tone from the superior. . . . They must be the mothers of the family, and this is more than administration. They must be sensitively alive to the needs, and joys, and sorrows of each member of the community. These are not their "children" but their grown-up daughters.[76]

Yet, despite sameness in life-style, each house had its unique spirit, coloured by its locality, its students, its trials and achievements. Marmoutier was an idyllic retreat in "the land of saints"; Saint Charles kept the courageous simplicity of Philippine Duchesne; rural Roscrea sent its sturdy faith overseas in times of famine; urban Hammersmith hummed with "works"; Manhattanville pointed the way to higher studies. Houses, like people, have personalities, expressed corporately.

The role of the provincial community, unsignalized in the beginning, is today of primary importance. At first local superiors were directly responsible to the central government. When vicariates were erected in 1851, Mother Barat in her letters emphasized the authority of the vicars and urged dependence upon them. From then on vicariates came into existence as need arose. Houses founded in a new country were at first dependent upon the mother-land; when a sufficient number was reached the group became autonomous.

Vicariates were often regrouped, divided and reunited.[77] These changes reflect history: wars and treaties followed by shifting frontiers, colonial and missionary movements, conflicts between church and state. Each vicariate developed a character of its own that enriched the Society as a whole. The houses within a vicariate shared a common background, geographical, national and racial; conversely, some vicariates embraced people of more than one country or even race. Scenery, culture and the character of the people strengthened the bond, as does the interchange of subjects. Vicariates might develop special apostolates. The influence of the vicars, generally in office for very many years, has been strong. At first they were often "foreigners". These factors were just coming into play in the period of consolidation; they made for pluriformity even when uniformity was the ideal.

A centrifugal force felt to the fringes of the Society was the unobtrusive life of the Mother House, centre of the international community. All roads led back to "le trente-trois" on the Boulevard des Invalides. The three Paris houses together with Conflans formed a small "vicariate" dependent on the superior general. The central community lived in peaceful stability, "la douce bureaucratie de la Maison Mère." Its functions were more than governmental; it was the "family seat" of the Society, and each of the "great and grave personalities" who gathered at the front door to greet newcomers has stamped her character upon the Society. They became familiar to all as the young religious returned to their far-flung vicariates after profession.

* * *

Internationality in a religious order is a sign of the catholicity of the Church. In this period sixty-one houses were founded and eight new countries were opened to the Society of the Sacred Heart; the globe was circled. Every few years (or months) colonies speaking different tongues would set out for an unknown land to build a community and face a common work. None were sent at this time into non-Christian cultures; wherever they went they found a way of life basically Christian. Yet they felt like missionaries and were hailed as such. They set out with the zeal of a Xavier and covered like distances. Few saw their native land again. They were given to spreading not so much the faith as the knowledge of Christ's love. "I want to cover the world," Mother Barat had said.

Despite the uniformity that reached like a life-line to the ends of the earth, the mission principle of accommodation was recognized though not always followed. Mother Goetz said: "I am not sending you to America to reform others but to adapt yourselves to them." Mother Lehon said to those leaving for Lima:

> Become as Peruvian as the Peruvians; study and speak the language as perfectly as possible, so as to be taken for a child of the country. Show nothing in your manner that would jar on your sisters as foreign. Be slow to judge, slower to criticize, slower still to blame; such things must not be. Take up the customs and the way of life around you and don't try to make everything French.
>
> Forget your country to the extent that your sacrifice may lose nothing of its value through vain regrets, voluntary boredom, dreams that carry you to other shores than those to which you have come.
>
> Our All is in the tabernacle: our support, consoler, friend, spouse. Do not leave him for a moment in your hearts; visit him often in person. You will never be more an exile than he is. Joy always, joy everywhere, joy full and overflowing. Aspire to one thing only: to spend yourselves for him who has spent himself for you.
>
> Give up day-dreams and fix your mind on useful thoughts. Give up your own will, what your nature craves, by acting in just the opposite way. Give up your love of ease, of rest, of tranquillity, to be given over wholly to duty and to the good pleasure of God. But give not one hair of your head otherwise than for love.[78]

Of these directives the one concerning language was the most neglected. Otherwise they were faithfully observed by the valiant women who became the intercultural adventurers of the Society, weaving its internationality from one continent to another.

In Europe thirty-two houses were added to those founded by Mother Barat. In France, where there were seven vicariates, the new foundations were: Pau, near Lourdes, where the mild climate made it a place of rest (1874); the "maison des Anges" near the Mother House (1875); a city-house in Bordeaux (1891); and Joigny which soon became a place of pilgrimage (1894). Two houses formerly closed were re-opened, le Mans (1874) and Annonay (1890). The Belgian vicariate (created in 1851) at first included the houses in England, Ireland, Holland and Germany. In Belgium itself Bois l'Evèque was opened on a hill at the edge of industrial Liège where the "oeuvres populaires" flourished (1865), while near Brussels, Ixelles began its work for the very poor (1889). In Holland, Bennebroek welcomed the rural poor in a quiet village (1895). England and Ireland had been formed into an autonomous vicariate in 1858. There were: in London, Wandsworth (or West Hill), a training college (1874), new schools at Brighton near the sea (1877) and at

Carlisle near the Scottish border (1889), while at Hammersmith in the heart of London the former seminary of Cardinal Manning was transformed into a busy *externat* (1893). In Dublin a day school was opened on Leeson Street (1875).

In Spain, an autonomous vicariate since 1864, four new houses were opened: Seville began humbly in a poor quarter (1865); Saragossa was a boarding school (1875); in Madrid there were Caballero de Gracia and Saint Denys, the latter a gift of the munificent Duchess of Pastrana added to that of Chamartin which she had given earlier. In the Austrian vicariate (which dated from 1851) the foundation of a city house in Vienna (1868) was followed by that of Pressbaum in the country for the Austrian noviceship. (1892). In Italy (a vicariate since 1851) Portici was opened in uneasy proximity to Mount Vesuvius (1873), Florence in the centre of Italian art (1881), and Avigliana in the mountains (1889), while the Society returned to Turin, from which it had been driven by revolution in 1848, with the opening of a house at Valsalice (1883).

The five houses closed by the Kulturkampf in Germany and its political dependencies were Marienthal, Posen, Kientzheim, Metz and Montigny.. The last three remained (secretly) in the hands of small communities and were later reopened as schools.

The Society entered three new European countries. At Prague in Czechoslovakia a poor school and trade school grew up by the side of the boarding school (1872). A school called Philippineum was opened in Hungary, at Budapest (1883). In Scotland, the school at Aberdeen on the shores of the North Sea (1894) was soon attended by many Protestants as prejudice gave way to friendliness. An ancient statue of our Lady of Aberdeen was found and enthroned. Here there was soon a small teacher-training college for Highland lassies who had kept the Old Faith.

The European vicars of this period were remarkable women who had been formed by Madeleine Sophie Barat; her directives and loving relations with them can be followed through her letters up to her death. They then became virile transmitters of the first traditions, tenacious, austere, large-hearted, carrying her memory into the twentieth century. Many are outstanding. In France there was Alix de Kerouartz,[79] a Bretonne *à l'antique,* complex and scrupulously fervent, high-handed and high-hearted, who made adventures out of everything she did. There was Mathilde Garabis, Mother Barat's "particular friend," sunny and open-handed, given to pastoral pursuits. There was Esther d'Oussières,[80] known in youth as "Queen Esther," energetic and constructive.

Lucie Merilhou[81] had made the first English foundation at Berrymead in 1842, and transferred it to Roehampton in 1850. She became the first vicar of England-Ireland and then took charge of the Belgian vicariate, a measured and enterprising person. She was succeeded at Roehampton by Marcella Goold,[82] an Irish woman of originality and of profound prayer. Christina Gazelli[83] had moved in the court circles of Turin before she entered and was tempered by Mother de Rousier. As superior of many French houses and then vicar of Italy she "governed through Mary" and became known as the flaming "apostle of the Blessed Virgin." It was she who spread the custom of the lily procession on the feast of the Immaculate Conception throughout all the schools of the Society. Valérie de Bosredont[84] had entered with the Sisters of Mercy and then transferred to the Society. A person of enterprise, brilliant and serious, she became the first vicar of Spain, followed by Camille Parmentier[85] who guided the Spanish houses through a time of revolution. In Austria Maria Mayer was followed by Clementine de Gagern,[86] a woman of gentle and transparent spiritual power known as "joy-giver in the mystery of suffering," who at the same time showed practical energy in developing "les oeuvres." For a short time the houses in Poland, which formed part of the Austrian vicariate became autonomous (1864–1868) and were governed by Victoire Noizet,[87] a steady and courageous defender of religious liberty, who voiced the principle of her contemporaries in government: "The least recommendations of our Mothers are sacred oracles."

In the meantime North America had ceased to be a mission land in any sense, yet those who went there still felt like missionaries. Canada, where Sophie Barat had first dreamed of going, became a vicariate in 1864. The communities were bi-lingual and the schools had both French and English sections. The vicars were cosmopolitan. Thérèsine Trincano[88] was an Italian, with a clear head, warm heart and the power of stimulation; the influence of her Children of Mary was felt in Montreal, with the motto that she gave them: "No crinolines!" Clémence Cornélis,[89] a Belgian, strengthened the apostolic works of the vicariate. Stanislaus Tommasini, an Italian, opened a Canadian noviceship at the Sault. Ellen Mahony,[90] a Canadian of warm wisdom, became known as "Dean of Vicars," since she later governed the vicariates of Saint Louis, New York, and again

Canada. Amélie Schulten,[91] a German, fostered the government school known as College Street in Halifax.

Mother Barat had once said of the United States: "America is reason personified," but she liked better the American heart shown in "the generosity of your great country." She even liked American independence, thanks to Mother Hardey, though her circular letters to the American houses contained warnings against "negligent ways." Mother Goetz and Mother Lehon wanted as great a uniformity with Europe as possible — with "certain adaptations." Mother Goetz wrote:

> Studying as I do the various elements that go to form our Society, it seems to me that I find in your country certain natural qualities which, in God's providence, are capable of being the foundation of truly sublime virtues. In this I allude not only to the good sense and judgment, the persevering energy so essentially yours and which are powerful incentives to all that is great and good, but also to the striking generosity which is part of your nature, allied to a spirit of independence which at first sight might appear to be in direct opposition to religious abnegation, but which, to my mind, will be a strong and powerful help towards the perfection of obedience — and the same, I may say, of charity.[92]

Mother Duchesne's frontiers had melted away by now; the age of corporations was producing a consumer society. Immigration to "the land of the free" was at its height, and the Society was a small "melting pot" within the greater. Houses were governed by English, Irish, French and Maltese superiors — as well as American. But within the melting pot regional differences were becoming more marked as the Society reached out more widely.

This was a time of bitterness and pain for "the Deep South" after the Civil War. The vicariate of Louisiana had become autonomous in 1844 under the government of Maria Cutts,[93] an English woman and convert, strong and warm-hearted, who had been trained in France. She was followed by Amélie Jouve,[94] a niece of Philippine Duchesne who governed during the agonies of the Civil War and then returned to Europe. In 1864 the Missouri houses were joined to those in Chicago to form a Vicariate of the West (they again joined those in Louisiana in 1891 for two years only). Anna Shannon[95] then became vicar of Louisiana; she was a rallying point in the days of reconstruction. She had come from Ireland as a child and was formed as a novice by Mother Duchesne's ardent austerity, which only highlighted her own gaiety. She became a legend during the war years among white people and black, among soldiers blue and grey. "Halt!" said an armed guard during one of her good-will journeys. "But I go everywhere!" she retorted, parting their bayonets with her hands. No-one could resist the humour with which she solved problems, got food from nowhere and healed broken lives. Another tonic personality was Genevieve Gauci,[96] the first Maltese religious in the Society, who served as vicar in both the Louisiana and Chicago vicariates. She made one bishop exclaim: "The race of Mother Duchesne is still with us!"

A school was daringly opened in the heart of "the Baptist belt," in Selma, Alabama in 1882 (closed in 1891). Two schools were opened for the Spanish-French-American culture-blend in New Orleans, Mater Admirabilis (1876) and the Rosary (1887). The American bishops were pressing the education of negro children, a thankless task at that hyper-prejudiced date. At their request Mother Shannon opened the first Catholic school for negro girls at Saint Michael's (1868), followed by one at Grand Coteau (1875), while the Jesuits worked for the boys. The influence of these schools, poor as they were, spread through the plantations by means of sodalities for the parents, all ex-slaves. This "work of liberation" (the name given by the Chapter of 1970 to all education) was to become still more challenging in the years ahead.

In the vicariate of New York (autonomous since 1844) Sarah Jones[97] carried on the vigorous work of Mother Hardey. A convert and native of "Knickerbocker New York," she governed forthrightly. A network of houses spread rapidly. Some were day schools on city pavements: Walnut Street in Philadelphia (1865) transferred to Arch Street (1886); Massachusetts Avenue in Boston (1880); Madison Avenue in New York (1881). Some in ampler settings had both day and boarding students: Elmhurst in Providence (1872) and Grosse Pointe near Detroit, overlooking Lake Saint Clair (1885). Three were temporary: beautiful but remote Rosecroft in Maryland (1871); a parish school in Providence (1875); and a health centre at Atlantic City (1883).

In the new vicariate of the West the distances were greater: the network reached from Maryville in Saint Louis (1872) to North State Street in Chicago (1876), and to Omaha where two schools were opened: Park Place, later known as Duchesne (1881), and Saint Mary's parochial school (1886). Then a leap over the Rocky Mountains brought the Society to the Pacific coast with the foundation on Franklin Street in San Francisco (1887). A short-lived Central Vicariate, which grouped the houses in Chicago and Detroit, existed from 1887 to 1895.

Among the vicars of the West were intersting contrasts. Rose Gauthreaux,[98] a Creole from New Orleans, had been brought up in the orphanage of Saint Michael's and was trained for her responsibilities in New York, Canada and Chicago by Mother Hardey. Elizabeth Tucker[99] was an Englishwoman of "the Old Faith" who administered her houses, especially Eden Hall, in the way of a gracious abbess of the manorial tradition. Margaret Niederkorn,[100] a native of Luxemburg, came as a young girl to Chicago to be a "missionary" and had to overcome an active prejudice against the "aristocratic" Society before entering.

The continent was now spanned and enterprises reached out into American life in all directions. A call to spread the faith came in a form different from that heard by Philippine Duchesne; Protestantism was the challenge. In France "heretics" were looked upon with the same horror as were "Papists" in some parts of the United States. Admission of Protestant children to Sacred Heart schools was regarded in Paris as a threat to the piety and even to the faith of the Catholic children. Books by Protestant authors were placed on a private Index by the General Council of 1874. The Devil's Advocate in the Cause for Madeleine Sophie Barat's Beatification made the most of the fact that she had admitted "sectarians" to her schools. He was over-ruled by the fact that many conversions had resulted. A more lasting result was the breakdown of prejudice by good public relations. Ecumenism would have been more than suspect in those days, but the broad-minded charity of the religious for their "separated brethren" (even in areas like Selma and Boston) did the pre-ecumenical work of giving witness.

Yet Philippine's first dream was coming true in what might be called the Society's first "Third World mission," taking Third World to mean a suppressed minority struggling for its rights in the grip of poverty and oppression. The United States had two such worlds, those of the emerging Black Man and the vanishing Red Man. "It was for the sake of the Indians that Mother Duchesne felt inspired to establish the order in America," Mother Barat had said.

But Philippine had spent only one year among her "savages". After her withdrawal from Sugar Creek in 1842 a small group of religious stayed on the mission for forty years. They lived in literal solidarity with the Potawatomi, the "Fire-Makers," now beaten down to squalour. Their home was a log hut, mud-daubed and canvas-lined. Sister Mary Anne Layton[101] (the first American religious of the Sacred Heart) hid her horror with a smile when presented with a scalp. The superior, Lucille Mathevon,[102] was a Frenchwoman who had identified with pioneer America. "The Indians used her as one uses water, knowing that it will always be clear and flowing." She brimmed over with joy and song, composing *cantiques* in the Indian tongue.

But in 1848 the government forced the tribe to leave the reservation that had been given to them as "their land and home forever." Lucille led the reluctant "braves" on their trek, cutting down the tall prairie grass before them. At Saint Mary's, Kansas, she built "the sky-scraper of the prairies," a two-storey house, as a school for the Indian girls, where "our great hope is that the children will convert their parents." A government official reported:

> Saint Mary's Indian school seems to be in a prosperous condition, popular with the Indians and doing much good. The female department deserves particular mention for its efficiency in teaching the different branches of education. The exhibition of plain and fancy needlework and the embroidery executed by the pupils creditably attest to the care and attention bestowed by the sisters on these children of the forest. It is plain to me that their hearts are in their work.[103]

Yet doubts were expressed by bishops, and even by those within the Society, as to whether this life among the dispossessed was suitable for religious of the Sacred Heart. Mother Lehon defended it. But already the Indians were moving on; white children were forcing themselves into the school. The Journal of Saint Mary's records:

> Civilization has gradually crept in and the Indians are few and scattered now. We have had to follow the course of progress and abandon the type of education we have been giving to the Indian girls who are now received only as day pupils in the free school.[104]

Mother Mathevon and Sister Layton died in 1873 and six years later Saint Mary's was closed, a failure. But Mother Duchesne had looked beyond the Rocky Mountains, beyond the Pacific; the seed that she had planted to die on the prairies sprang up on the other side of the globe. Mother Lehon had been asked for a foundation in

New Zealand and said: "If it takes place, the pioneer colony will set out from Saint Louis," since religious had been freed for the work by the closing of Saint Mary's.

New Zealand, called "Land of the Long White Cloud" by the Maoris, had become a British colony in 1840. Already Marist priests were at work, one of whom had been cared for in illness in the Sacred Heart convent in Grand Coteau. He asked bishop Pompallier to send for the Society. The bishop on a visit to France, asked Mother Barat for help. She had to refuse (an act that she called "my constant cross, one that I can't get used to") but gave him hope and a copy of the newly painted picture of Mater Admirabilis. Later, Archbishop Redwood repeated the request to Mother Lehon, and in 1880 she entrusted the foundation in Timaru to Suzannah Boudreaux,[105] vicar of the Maryville-Chicago vicariate.

Suzannah was a native of Louisiana, the child of a poor family; she had been adopted by Mother Duchesne who aroused her own ardour in the little girl. She made her vows at seventeen and went to New York where for thirty years she worked with Mother Hardey, ready for anything and "taking people by the heart."

The colony of five reached Timaru on January 19, 1880. The archbishop and his congregation, most of whom had never seen a nun, installed them triumphantly in their lodging of one room made into three by curtains. The corner stone of their future home was blessed but Mother Boudreaux did not see the house rise; she died twelve days later. The school grew and did its quiet work in a quiet town.

New Zealand was reached from the west, Australia from the east. Australia had been settled as a British colony in 1788; the Church first came there in the person of fugitive Father Flynn, and in 1842 archbishop Polding had been installed in Sydney. In that same year he called on Mother Barat in Paris. She wrote:

I am continually undergoing assaults of zeal and of regret. I was interrupted in this letter by a call to the parlour to see the bishop of New South Wales who is asking for a colony in Sydney at once. Refusal or indefinite postponement, that is my usual answer. How painful — so many souls to be brought to Jesus Christ! As the language there is English, Ireland or England will give us the needed personnel.[106]

Forty years went by before England could find the promised nuns, this time at the request of the Hughes family whose daughters were at school in Paris. Lizzie, the youngest, liked Conflans so much that she precipitated matters by calling out to Leo XIII at a public audience: "Holy Father, please send my nuns to Australia!" Living at Brighton just then was Febronie Vercruysse,[107] a sturdy, realistic Belgian with great stores of love and energy. She had run the military hospital at Laval during the Franco-Prussian war and had spent eight years in England in charge of building operations. She led the group that reached Sydney on May 8, 1882, and settled at Rose Bay overlooking the glorious harbour.

Within a few years all the activities familiar to the Society were in full swing, and a second house was opened at Melbourne (1888) to the south. At first both Australia and New Zealand were dependent upon the Saint Louis-Chicago vicariate, but in 1888 the two countries formed an autonomous vicariate under Mother Vercruysse. Practical and loyal, she built up a sense of tradition until uniformity with the centre of the Society was gloried in by its most distant houses. By her side was the small, dynamic figure of Amélie Salmon.[108] When a young girl Amélie had received Mother Barat's blessing, and as she lived until 1938 she came to be looked upon as the last living link with the Foundress. As mistress general she gave the authentic "spirit of the Sacred Heart" to generations of Australian girls in a land vibrant with space, youth, enterprise.

Developments in the Latin American world were lively with the restiveness of new nations heady from their first experience of democracy. Philippine Duchesne had looked wistfully at Cuba, "the pearl of the Antilles," as she skirted it on her voyage to Louisiana, and Mother Hardey had founded the Cerro at Havana in 1858. This house became attached to the Louisiana vicariate in 1874. The Children of Mary were a power for good throughout the island, and much work was done among the poor. This called for a city house, and Tedajillo was opened in 1888, endowed by a benefactress with scholarships for needy girls. In the meantime Puerto Rico had welcomed the Society when Micaela Fesser[109] founded Santurce in 1880. She was a Cuban gifted with "ascetic energy" which she expended in enterprises throughout the Antilles. At first Santurce underwent the usual annoying (but non-violent) attacks on "Jesuitesses". In 1884 a new vicariate was formed of the houses in Cuba, Puerto Rico and Mexico, three very different countries which shared the stimulus of living on a perpetual religious-political volcano. It was entrusted to Mary Elizabeth Moran, [110]the pioneer of Mexico.

The Mexican foundation is bound up with one of the most piquant of the Society's "intercultural adventurers," Maria Stanislaus Tommasini, [111] from a simple, hard-working home in Parma. Her incurable gaiety bubbled up from a deeply sensitive and earnest nature. She literally sang and danced her way through adventures that began when she entered in 1843 and only ended when she danced for the novices at Kenwood just before her death at the age of eighty-six. She wrote her Memoires of the years between, during which she enlivened six countries, spoke in four languages and lost her heart to whatever land she was in.

The revolution of 1848 drove her from Turin to Paris, where Mother Barat welcomed the refugees:

> The Heart of Jesus has given us the joy of seeing each other; it is sweet and delightful and we are strengthened by our *cor unum et anima una*. Now we must reach out again – here, there, – winning souls at the price of another hard separation in these calamitous days . . . . God is wonderful in his providence. I was at my wits' end to find personnel when lo and behold! Monsieur Cavour sends us nuns already fortified by persecution. [112]

Maria was sent to New York where she became Mother Hardey's right hand as language teacher and mistress general of cosmopolitan Manhattanville. She learned Spanish from exiled Bishop Labastido who said: "Some day the Sacred Heart will come to Mexico and you will be one of the foundresses." She had a long wait. In 1870 she went to Havana as superior, and from there to the city house in New York. Then this volatile Latina governed the snowy vicariate of Canada for eight years, and from there moved light-heartedly to the hot bayou lands as superior of Grand Coteau.

Mary Elizabeth Moran, vicar of Louisiana, was an ardent expansionist; in 1883 she set out for Mexico where all religious were proscribed, and took Maria with her. They travelled in secular dress, their worldly disguise offset by an unworldly manner, but were recognized by a former pupil. Thanks to Maria's wit and daring they played the intricate game of finding a house without compromising Bishop Labistido. Ironically, it was dictator Porfirio Diaz who settled them in the second storey of a shop building in Mexico City, where an authentic Sacred Heart school soon flourished in this passionately Catholic country in the hands of brigands.

Mother Tommasini solved devious problems by straightforwardness, slipping in and out of the religious habit at need. By the time the new vicariate of Mexico-Antilles was formed in 1884 bishops all over Mexico and even government officials were clamouring for schools. Guanajuato was opened (1885) on the slopes of the mining mountains. Here Mother Tommasini not only enlightened the superstitious piety of the Indians but brought back people in high places to the practice of their faith, including a notorious bandit. The next year San Luis Potosi was opened, in feudal surroundings where the Indian children came in crowds, and here the first Mexican novice made her vows despite the law. Grand Coteau was annexed to the vicariate to serve as a noviceship (1885–1896). Mother Tommasini returned to Cuba for a short time, but was back in Mexico for the foundation of Guadalajara in 1895.

All this time the Society was covering enormous distances in the southern district. The nations of Latin America shared a common culture and language, yet each was unique; each had fought its way to independence under its own heroes, and they were now each other's rivals.

Ana du Rousier, who had made two foundations in Chile, Santiago (1854) and Talca (1859), returned to Paris for the General Council of 1864. Her rich experience and glamorous mission, her way of coping with political problems made Mother Barat say: "Don't go away until you have shown my assistants general all that you have known and gathered from two worlds." So the next two superiors general learned from her the nature of "missions" in lands already Catholic. She returned to Chile and opened a school at Concepcion. When the children assembled in May, 1865, the bishop encouraged the religious in language redolent of the times:

By generous abnegation you will give to the world virtuous young persons from whose heart as from the calix of a flower will arise the sweet perfume that they will spread abroad in their families and in society, which, purifying the surrounding air, will vivify generations to come. [113]

A house in the seaport of Valparaiso was opened (1870) to the blare of military music, "a custom of the country to which we must adapt." The "menace" here was Protestantism, introduced by the business world into this Catholic culture. At Chillan, near the moody volcano of that name, a second teacher-training college was begun (1874), together with the usual boarding and poor schools.

The rural population welcomed the nuns picturesquely, and Mother du Rousier at last had her wish of at least touching the Indians. An Auracanian chief enrolled his daughters, and assured their good conduct by a threat of marriage to the ugliest man in the tribe in the case of insubordination.

Mother du Rousier travelled in carriages that plunged through swollen rivers, or on foot over swaying bamboo bridges. It was harder to cross the social barriers between *haciendas* and huts; she had to work on separate social levels. She broke down prejudice against a religious order without papal enclosure; she virilized the warm latin devotion to the Sacred Heart. When the Society kept the Silver Jubilee of its coming to Chile the government gave free transportation to all the nuns to go to the celebrations in Santiago. She died on January 28, 1880.

Her work as vicar was taken up by Angelita Alentado, [114] a Cuban, quiet, serious and magnanimous, under whose government the Chilean vicariate became the most far-flung in the Society. She opened a second house in Santiago, Apoquindo (1885). This was a day school in the city which attracted children who would otherwise have gone to Protestant schools, "drawn by the seduction of the English there taught." She crossed the war-riddled boundaries of Chile into Peru and Uruguay. She was succeeded by Elizabeth Windhoff, [115] a German, a radiant and original personality, who was cured of a serious illness by the intercession of Madeleine Sophie Barat.

The foundation in Lima took place in 1876. The Peruvian government asked for a training college which was opened in a large sixteenth century building known as San Pedro, together with a boarding school. One of the great representatives of the internationalism of the Society was among the pioneers in Peru.

Jeanne de Lavigerie [116] (née Jeanne de Sainte Affrique) was born in Bordeaux in 1851, in a home indifferent to religion. But at school she annotated her geography book with fervent wishes to become a nun. After graduation her early vocation became obscured by doubts, and her friends were astonished by her marriage to Monsieur de Lavigerie during the dark days of the Franco-Prussian war. But within five years she entered at Conflans, wearing a widow's veil. "I came as soon as our Lord called me," she said. As a novice she heard another call, this time with no doubts. She offered to go to Peru to win the conversion of her irreligious brother; he went to communion by her side just before she set sail. In Lima she became mistress of novices and then superior. Her quiet, well-balanced judgment, her energizing love of Christ, gave her power over the ebullient children and the pleasure-loving Children of Mary. In 1895 she left Peru to become vicar of Mexico.

In 1880 the Society crossed the Andes and reached Buenos Aires in the midst of a civil war. An orphanage was added to the schools in this city house. Four years later Almagro was opened in the country. This rapid spread of the Society through the South American continent was speeded by high patronage both ecclesiastical and civil, by the generosity of influential women, and by the cooperation of other religious orders.

*　*　*

Towards the end of the nineteenth century education had become universal (in theory) in all the countries where the Society was at work; standards for every social class were rising sharply. Private schools had to compete with the state schools where education was compulsory, regimented, and *gratis*. The problem for the Society was how to keep the integrity — as uniformly as possible — of the "Sacred Heart education" now widely in demand, while meeting, independently, the requirements of national systems.

When Mother Goetz became superior general Bishop Pie remarked:

> With her humble and powerful intelligence and her virile firmness, Mother Goetz will lead her Society into the new paths of those masculine branches of learning of which women who rule over Christian homes must no longer remain in ignorance. [117]

He was right; her intuitions concerning formation, philosophical studies and teacher training all bore fruit. In her circular letters she placed studies in the first rank:

> Before the grave problems which face us everywhere we must understand as never before how important it is for our Society to keep, in its work of teaching, the solidity and the elevation by which it can reach the standards of present-day needs, and give to the young people educated in our houses — together with precious lessons in faith, duty and solid virtues — all the knowledge which they have the right to expect from our zeal in a strong complete and careful education. [118]

Mother Lehon never had direct experience in the school and she was not an intellectual. During her long government her interests centred on practical aspects of daily school life; experimentation was checked and a cautious, defensive attitude prevailed. The *Manual of Philosophy* so desired by Mother Goetz was only introduced in 1894.

One reason for this attitude was the conflict between independent schools and the universities. The question of diplomas for the teaching orders had arisen early. Mother du Rousier, from her experience on three continents, confirmed Mother Barat in her belief that the religious should take university examinations. Mother Goetz pressed them to do so, while the Kulturkampf showed their necessity for the very existence of some schools. But the church-state clash became ominous, and Mother Lehon wrote before the General Council of 1884:

> The requirements of the universities, the necessity of preparing for public examinations, have forced us to adopt certain books beyond our syllabus, and most often foreign to our spirit. A list of all these works which it seems necessary to consult will be sent to the General Council, with appreciations of each. We must understand that it is a sacred obligation to determine just how far we can go in the way of concessions, and where we must stop. [119]

The result was a tightening of the restrictions on reading and a careful control of libraries. Some mandates, if taken literally, would have required the superior of each house to read every book that found its way in! This suggests a certain anti-intellectualism, heightened by the fact that learning was often placed well below virtue in educational criteria. The reasons lie deeper. Universities were feared as social change was feared; both were too often actively anti-Christian. Moreover, they could not offer the values fostered in the *Plan of Studies*. But practice went ahead of theory (as in most situations), and more and more young nuns took the dreaded examinations; the effects were salutary.

All this gave impetus to the juniorate. The direct preparation of young teachers had been begun by Mother Barat in 1849, under Aimée d'Avenas, the first mistress general of studies. She composed text books, taught sparkling classes, and gave intellectual fibre to the Society's mission. The Elementary Juniorate was put on a strong basis by Mother Goetz in 1866. She appointed a Commission of Studies; this was not permanent, but Councils of Studies were held frequently from then on. This was to assure "a centre of uniformity, a principle of strength and consolidation."

The juniorate was in charge of Marie Ann Martin, [120] an "apostle of learning." Brilliant and enthusiastic, she saw in books, as had Madeleine Sophie before her, a revelation of the attributes of God and of his providence in human affairs. Among her star pupils was Maria Dagon, [121] a vibrant, warm hearted intellectual who, forgetting her ill-health, began the Advanced Juniorate in 1876. She died after two years, but Lucie Durand [122] continued her work for twenty. The latter "taught like a man" with a woman's heart; she was "fire and flame" for studies, and grounded the young teachers in philosophy, theology and the classics. These three were among the "saintes savantes" without whom, Mother Barat had said, the Society's vocation could not be fulfilled.

Not all promising teachers could go to Conflans and the French curriculum could not be followed in all places. Juniorates were organized in other countries, generally in houses of noviceship. They worked in close touch with the centre and incorporated the *Plan of Studies* into varied national systems. One important development was a new emphasis placed on the physical sciences, which were encouraged by Mother Digby as vicar of England. Her microscope was her delight; science was no longer a Cinderella. She also extended the work of teacher training till it was a recognized part of the Society's educational mission. From Wandsworth as from San Pedro the spirit of Sacred Heart education reached out through thousands of dedicated teachers into schools of all types, many officially "godless."

Democratization was slowly at work in a system undeniably marked by the "privilege" and social distinctions of the time in the *pensionnats* — which became known by as many names as there were languages spoken in them. The *écoles* were at first perpetuated on the same pattern as in the early days in France wherever social conditions called for this, as in some localities in Latin America. In other places the pattern changed rapidly. Most of the houses in the United States began with a "free school," but these were drawn into the parochial school system and varied with the status of the parish. Some became important centres of civic life, as in Chicago. But one after the other these schools were either closed or given over to "religious better suited for this work," which meant "uncloistered."

It is significant that a large number of the houses opened were day schools. The *externats* were at first distinctly "middle class," and even in *demi-pènsionnats* the day pupils were separated from the boarders through fear of "the world" or of indiscipline. Mother Lehon expressed "an extreme repugnance for day schools," and wanted the children to be kept at school as late as possible, and even on Sundays. These distinctions gradually faded out, and day schools of equal standing with boarding schools, or combined with them, became normal.

The demand for a typical "Sacred Heart School" was one of the causes for the rapid spread of the Society. At the time of the foundation in Peru:

> Several old pupils of our families in Paris, England, New York and Chile have contributed to an appreciation of our Institute, for these young people are distinguished in society for their polished behaviour, their attractive virtues and their social principles. [123]

A newspaper obituary to Mother du Rousier read:

> In Chile, thank heaven, women have always been well-educated. . . . In colonial times and in the first years of the republic the Chilean woman was trained exclusively in her own home, or occasionally admitted for training into certain monasteries. . . . But changing times and the diffusion of human knowledge have created new needs in Europe and in the Americas. In the clash of opinions and in the storm of errors which envelop the modern world, women must take a firm hold of the realm of virtue, of modesty, of domestic and social duties, by means of a strong, elevated and Christian education. From this has arisen the need of a more fundamental and varied plan of studies, one which has been established in Chile by the Society of the Sacred Heart. [124]

Another tribute came from the papacy itself. Leo XIII never forgot that as Cardinal Pecci he had taken part in a Literary Academy in the Sacred Heart school at Jette. As pope he said to Mother Lehon:

> What I appreciate in your education is its hall-mark of solidity, of that steadiness of mind which forms an unshakable foundation for the life of the soul. It is not surprising that children of good Christian families who come to you in their first innocence find at the Sacred Heart and keep always a tender piety and a felt devotion. But that is not enough; this piety must reach the intelligence; it must be based on strong teaching and enlightened by a profound study of truth. [125]

In all this talk of education, where are the children? They are visible in the profuse memoirs and diaries of the time. The first schools had been lit by wavering candles or oil lamps, throwing a glow over the distant scene; today's classrooms are brilliant with electricity. At the *fin du siècle* they were lit by gas, a hard, dull light. Yet the faces revealed are alive, eager, confident and sentimental. Uniforms in Mother Barat's day had been graceful and gaily colored. Now they had become sombre and straight-laced. Crinolines were giving way to bustles and both, together with curls, were frowned upon. Discipline counteracted sentimentalism. "Train them to put their duty before everything else, train them to bear adversity," said Mother Goetz.

The children in all lands had an extraordinarily similar love of their school. The title of "child of the Sacred Heart" was gloried in – too often with triumphalism. "We'll show the new nuns from France that we're as good as the Rue de Varenne," said the young Australians. Customs and insignia fostered this loyalty. "What would you do if you were to lose it?" said a proud father to the wearer of a pink ribbon. "I would die of shame," said the eight-year-old.

Yet we read of *crises d'insubordination* in even the best schools. Were they caused by a too rigid discipline? Or by a lack of natural contacts with the children's families? They were often precipitated by the departure of some loved mistress general, and remedied by the wisdom of her soon equally loved successor. The mistress general had a far-reaching influence for life, working for "consolidation" in the best sense. There were: Henrietta Kerr [126] at Roehampton, taking part in England's "Second Spring"; Josephine Augustin [127] at Beauvais, translating piety into efficacious action; Josephine Errington [128] who was powerful both in studies and in character training at Roehampton then at Manhattanville, where she first failed then more than succeeded with American youth, with her inspiriting motto "Surgite Eamus."

But there was an intellectual timbre to the charm and formalism of those decades at our antipodes of taste. Pauline de Flaujac, [129] whose pulsating poems to the Holy Child were set to music, acted as judge at a *Jeu des Roses* at Pau in 1887, where the contestants for a golden rose read their own essays. The prize went to "Point Rose n'est la Vie" on the sobering theme that life is white, black and grey. One girl present that June evening wrote in her memoirs fifty years later:

As I near the end of life's journey I understand more fully the nature of the training we received, and what pains the nuns took to develop in us true piety, and all our gifts of mind and heart. . . . They would say to us: "We are teaching you to learn for yourselves." Never-the-less they managed to send us away with a considerable sum of knowledge. . . . The affection that the old children bear to the nuns of the Sacred Heart is well known; numbers add their testimony to mine, for everything in us vibrates when we speak of the Sacred Heart, and our memories are as enduring as our gratitude. [130]

* * *

Awareness of social justice and of responsibility for the world's evils is central in the thinking of the Society today; not so a century ago. Efforts in holiness, in virtue, in doing good, seem often to have been self-contained within a person or a group, though Mother Goetz warned:

Far be it from us to hold aloof from the great Catholic problems, the progress of religion, the dangers to our faith, or its reawakening, and above all the destinies of the Roman Church to which we must be unreservedly devoted. [131]

She had seen Pius IX exiled after his attempts at a more liberal government of the Papal States; the experience created distrust of any social reform tinged with "liberalism." Yet the pope himself challenged the Society at an audience with the mother general: "Several times the pope came back on the evils of the times, on the necessity of prayer and of devotedness, and repeated: 'Do all the good you can'!" Mother Lehon was devoted to Leo XIII who had taken a progressive attitude. He opened the Vatican archives to scholars, and caused an intellectual awakening by *Aeterni Patris* on Thomism and *Divinum Illud* on Scripture study. But when at last *Rerum Novarum* appeared in 1891, reminding the Church that "the human condition must be respected," the response from the Society in the sense of any intensive undertaking or change of attitude was far from immediate.

Another factor in this social conservatism was the tenacious royalism of the "good Catholic families" from which the majority of the religious came. Although there was no question of "votes for women" at that date, the Society shared in the view of *non-expedit* that kept Catholics from the polls in Italy. When Leo XIII recognized the Third Republic and "Catholic socialism" was a fact, convents were often centres of reactionism, and Cardinal Lavigerie's famous toast to the government aroused no echoes.

Leo XIII declared to Mother Lehon: "I can say that I have never heard anything against your Society, for you have never given cause for blame to persons in the world. You have been till now unattackable." [132] This was gratifying but too sweeping to be true. Mother Barat had said fifty years earlier: "We are criticized for everything; we are severely blamed for the slightest and most inconsequential things." [133] The same reappears in Society annals, generally with regard to some bishop "who does not understand our customs." Cloister which prevented some needed work, or dependence for permissions on a distant Mother House, were the most usual causes of episcopal discontent. In most cases their lordships were won over to active friendship, but not always. A case in point is the stormy story of the Society's relations to Archbishop Manning. This far-seeing fighter for social rights had an invincible prejudice. When Mother Digby offered to open a school for the poor in London he refused it on the grounds that the Society was unfitted to work for the poor. When another bishop asked for a school because the Society was best fitted to teach the upper classes Mother Digby told him firmly: "We educate all social classes." This time he refused because of the rule of cloister.

This was, at bottom, the same problem that had disturbed Mother Barat at the Hotel Biron, "although I discount two-thirds of what is said," – a reputation for aloofness amounting to snobbishness. At a meeting of all the Catholic associations in Guadalajara, in the cathedral, each group was publicly prayed for; the Children of Mary of the Sacred Heart heard: "May they obtain Christian humility!" Perhaps in the late nineteenth century all criticism was attributed too easily to "misunderstanding." "Our reputation for pride is our humiliation," said Gertrude Bodkin much later.

Despite these negative elements the Society was, by its very name, caught up in the wider movement of the devotion to the Sacred Heart at this epoch. The social nature of the devotion was stressed as a force for unity and for zeal; it was "Cor Jesu, Rex et Centrum omnium cordium." After the bitter days of the Commune groups of French laymen made a national vow to build a basilica in honour of the Heart of Christ; the cornerstone was laid on the day chosen by Pius IX for the universal consecration of the Church to the Sacred Heart, June 16, 1875. The national consecration is written over the door of Montmartre: "Christo et ejusque sacratissimo

Cordi Gallia poenitens et devota." The consecration of other nations, made by civil governments, followed: the Tyrol, Ecuador, Portugal, Belgium, Ireland, Spain. Group consecrations of all kinds were made: factories, communes, employment groups, especially the "Society for the Social Reign of Christ." In rhythm with this the "popular works" of the Society expanded notably. Night classes, clubs with interesting names like "the Rooks" in Dublin, were formed, while the work of retreats went beyond the alumnae to include groups of girls and women of many walks of life. It was a question of activating the Constitutions which call for work to extend the love of the Heart of Christ "by every means in their power."

* * *

Spirituality, like climate, varies between such contrasting places as Scotland and the Philippine Islands, between such antithetical decades as the eighteen-seventies and the nineteen-seventies, yet the same spiritual life flourishes in each — with a difference. A widespread society shows telling variations.

There are sombre notes in this time of consolidation. Jansenism originating in the seventeenth century, had gripped the eighteenth; its long shadow fell across the nineteenth — and beyond. Religious orders were touched by its dark views of human nature and of God's mercy, by its scruple-raising fears. Madeleine Sophie had narrowly escaped being warped, and some of her contemporaries, like Adèle Cahier, suffered from its rigourism. "That heresy makes me more angry than I can say," said Janet Stuart later on, and she warned against "that shadowy ground that we must avoid, the cloud of Jansenism." [134]

Many religious had been brought up in homes where the training of conscience was strangling; fear of sin brought fear of the good things the abuse of which might cause sin. In the noviceship a kind of dichotomy between nature and grace placed an exaggeratedly high value on mortification. Sermons and spiritual reading fostered legalism. The General Council of 1874 recommended that "we must avoid placing the Bible in the hands of young religious" (following the protective measures of Vatican I). A few persons were daily communicants, as Madeleine Sophie had been, but the Eucharist was not "our daily bread"; superiors in all religious orders could forbid a communion, or allow an "extra" one. Spiritual direction too easily entered the realm of conscience (although this was warned against in the Constitutions). In 1890 a decree of the Sacred Congregation safe-guarded freedom of conscience. Passages which opened the door to control in these matters by superiors were then effaced from the Constitutions, the Decrees and the Custom Book (with a directive to do so "in pencil").

These cramping elements were more than offset by a glowing love of the Blessed Sacrament. In the warm joy of frequent Exposition and daily adoration, the prayer of the religious could transcend inhibitions and flower in authentic union with the God of love, strengthened by a discipline both accepted and voluntary. The now unpopular word "piety" must be stripped of its connotations – sentimentality, facile consolation and manifold "practices" – before the strong beauty of this gift of the Holy Spirit can be grasped. Costly acts and devotedness underlay the elaborate observances by which piety was kept at white heat: novenas, vocal prayers, processions to the shrines so lovingly and lavishly adorned.

All this was accentuated by the training given in the schools, where piety was the hall-mark placed upon the virtue of the authentic child of the Sacred Heart. It was carried into "the world" by the Children of Mary. But intransigence caused revolt in some cases, and non-conformists were dismissed from the Sodality. The General Council of 1890 advised discretion in the matter of "balls, theatres and other dangerous pleasures"; a *coup d'état* would do no good and the Children of Mary must make their own decisions with the help of their confessors. But the General Council of 1894 was restrictive:

> An Appendix has been added to the Rule of the Children of Mary which will make it possible to draw them back, prudently, to the first fervour of their Institute, which has for its end to be the precious "leaven in the dough," of the world, filled with the spirit of Jesus Christ. [135]

This Appendix became a source of friction and was removed a year later.

Despite tensions the Children of Mary were powerful for good in the spiritual climate of that day. Many stood out for personal holiness, and a bishop remarked: "When I want to start a good work I look around for a Child of Mary of the Sacred Heart." Madame de Luppe was president of the Sodality in France at the time of the fire in the charity bazaar in 1897. She and eight more working in the stalls aided others to leave the burning building, and perished. They were identified by their medals of our Lady.

A Third Order for the Society of the Sacred Heart had been proposed in 1839; the idea was urged by Mothers Galitzin, Lhuillier 'de Serres and Garabis. Mother Barat was in favour of it. Father Gautrelet, co-founder of the Apostleship of Prayer, helped to establish "The Association of the Sacred Heart," with its own Constitutions. The first group made their consecration at Moulins in 1862, under the leadership of Louise de Montaignac, a dynamic semi-invalid (whose Cause for beatification has been introduced). The General Council of 1864 suggested other forms for the Third Order, the first attempt was dissolved and the matter postponed, to Mother Barat's grief. It was actualized by Mother Goetz in 1869 as an "Association Affiliated to the Sacred Heart." This was not a true Third Order as had been first envisaged, but an association whose members share in the prayers and merits of the Society. Their Rule was approved in 1884, and small centres were established, in secrecy, as stipulated by Cardinal Monaco La Valetta. The most fervent among the Children of Mary were chosen to become Affiliées and bound themselves by solemn promise:

> To strive for my perfection by a more and more exact observance of the commandments of God and the duties of my state of life, and for this end I wish to be united in intentions and in prayer to all those who belong to the Society of the Sacred Heart. I make moreover the promise to maintain and extend among the faithful the devotion to the Sacred Heart of Jesus and to the Immaculate Heart of Mary. [136]

Many alumnae of the Society have fulfilled Mother Barat's wish that through them the kingdom of God might "flower in the world." At this time a wide-reaching work for the Church was begun by an alumna of Marmoutier, while she herself has disappeared behind it. Her vision touches today. Emilie Marthe Tamisier [137] gave her life to extending the social reign of Christ through the Eucharist. At school she became possessed by a master passion, love of the Eucharist. She asked to enter the Society, but Mother Barat sensed a mysterious call. "No, child, you are on the wrong path. God does not want you here."

Emily searched and blundered for years, knowing only that she must be the apostle of the eucharistic Christ not for herself but for the world. Guided by Father Eymard, this transparent but complex young woman acted upon laymen, priests, bishops, and finally Leo XIII helped at every step by the Children of Mary of the Sacred Heart as she went from city to city organizing pilgrimages and hours of adoration. Her efforts led to the first Eucharistic Congress, held at Lille in June, 1881. The work then left her hands as the great Congresses succeeded each other year after year around the world. She spent her old age sewing for the poor at Marmoutier. She left to the future her ardour for "the social reign of Jesus through a return to the Eucharist":

> Everything seems ready for the reign — no longer individual but social — of the Eucharist. Our great Congresses are spreading this truth of the sovereignty of God over peoples, of the universal royalty of Christ the redeemer and civilizer. They must become popular, they must reach the masses. We must form groups, individuals will be christianized, then families, then social groups, all regenerated by the Eucharist . . . . In every city there are fine types of Catholic life: men and women, old and young, learned and illiterate, who are only waiting for the impulse to be given. Make them come to know each other, to exchange their souls, their thoughts, their ideas, then group them round a church and around the Host. [138]

Chapter 5

Confirmation
1895 – 1914

If we live by the truth and in love,
we shall grow in all ways into Christ
who is the head.

Eph 4:15

"Confirmation" is a more vibrant word than "consolidation"; it implies testing, then placing a seal of authenticity. It has a sacramental ring; by confirmation the young Christian grows in the might of the Spirit. The years from 1895 to 1914 which carried the Society of the Sacred Heart into the twentieth century of christendom and the second of its own life, were charged with dynamism. Standing firm on the foundations laid, changing nothing, they aimed with Saint Paul, "to grow in all ways." Truth, with attendant fortitude, stands out in Mabel Digby; love, with resultant hope, in Janet Stuart.

The times were disturbing after the preceding complacency. Small wars broke out in the Antilles, in South Africa, in the Near East and in the North Pacific where Asia had entered the international scene. Then came the first world war, while the Hague Peace Conference strove for other ways of righting the world's wrongs. Science was drawing the earth closer together: the global age was beginning.

In the Church the Chair of Peter passed from the aged statesman Leo XIII to Pius X with his youthful motto: "Restore all things in Christ." Freemasonry, with Communism looking over its shoulder, confronted the Church, while the Church confronted Modernism within herself. Evolution was challenging Revelation. At the dawn of the new century Leo XIII consecrated the whole human race to the Heart of Christ, and asked: "Are you satisfied with what I have done, religious of the Sacred Heart?"

In the Society all the traditional structures remained, but when these felt the shock of a literal displacement during the expulsions from France a current of new vitality passed through them. Society statistics remained almost constant, in contrast to the spectacular increases in the preceding period. The number of vicariates remained stable at 20, the number of houses rose only from 136 to 140, while the membership dropped slightly from 6577 to 6497. But these placid figures are misleading; they hide a tumultuous turnover when thousands of religious were shaken from one country to another. There was, naturally, a sharp decline in the number of novices which dropped from 680 to 274, then rose to 316 by 1914. Lights and shadows formed a striking contrast and strong hands were needed on the rudder. Mabel Digby became the fifth superior general on August 25, 1895.

*   *   *

Mabel Josephine Digby[1] was born at Ashley House, Middlesex, on April 7, 1835. When she was six her father and mother agreed: "That child will be either a saint or a devil." She loved horses but not books; she let life educate her. She was fifteen when her family moved to Montpellier, and the young sportswoman was at home in the wit and grace of the French salons. Here Mrs Digby and her daughter Geraldine became Catholics. Mr Digby, a "gentleman of the old school," had a horror of Papists. In his anger he made the children choose between their parents. Mabel walked to his side: "I promise you to remain always a faithful Protestant."

But within a year she was struck down like Saul on his resolute road. Her friends plotted to pull her into church just in time to hear some famous mountain singers at benediction. Mabel sat down defiantly. When the monstrance was raised she fell prostrate, and remained motionless while the church emptied. Then she turned to Geraldine at her side: "I am a Catholic. Jesus Christ has looked at me." As her mother said: "God alone can subdue that unconquerable Mabel." She was baptized on March 19, 1853. Her godmother gave her a crucifix, saying: "You can never love him too much." At a retreat made at Marmoutier she determined to enter religious life. For four years she struggled with her father's displeasure, with her own ill health, with directors and superiors who recognized her vocation but forbade her to follow it. Mother Barat went over their heads when she read in a letter: "This young English girl is highly gifted with the spirit of prayer, and shows astonishing humility and childlike obedience. She is charming." Mabel entered at Marmoutier on February 19, 1957.

"Your little Digby interests me," wrote Mother Barat, and the novice went to Conflans to be formed by Mother Goetz. She had reason to remember later on what Mother Barat said to the white veils one day: "We have often been despised and persecuted, but this must be so, and I would no longer recognize the Society if it did not bear this mark of resemblance to its divine Master." Mabel was alone in the chapel once when she was startled to hear a soft voice praying aloud. It came from the tribune where Mother Barat, in retreat, thought that she was alone with God. Mother Goetz told Mabel to go back to the chapel at the same hour each day of the retreat; Mother Barat's spirit of prayer drifted down on her fourth successor.

After her first vows Mabel went back to Marmoutier as mistress general and showed astonishing power over the children. But each summer she returned to Paris to make her probation, in instalments, under Mother Barat's guidance. To her Mabel confided a secret anxiety concerning her father who had died suddenly in a railroad station. Mother Barat answered: "One day you will go to America. That will be God's sign to you that your father is saved." Mabel was professed on November 4, 1864, in the last group to receive the cross and ring from the hands of the Foundress. In her notes she underlined the words: "May the truth shine out more and more; our Lord knows why." Truth was the touchstone of her life, truth in thought, word and deed.

Mother Goetz placed Mother Digby in charge of Marmoutier. It had been an old Cistercian monastery going back to Saint Martin of Tours whose shrine it held. It was a ruin of the French revolution when Mother Barat acquired it in 1847 and built a school around the one archway still standing. Mother Digby brought to light ancient crypts which became chapels and raised a modern building for the children. She saved it during the flooding of the Loire and offered it as a military hospital during the Franco-Prussion war.

In 1872 Mother Digby was placed in charge of the English-Irish vicariate, and Roehampton entered on a golden age. She pulled

down, rebuilt, equipped and beautified an ideal home for the school
and noviceship. It became an active vicariate centre as new houses
appeared in England and Ireland. Mother Digby went from one to
the other, working to make "the Old Faith" shine out more brightly
and to break down the wall of separation between Catholics and
Anglicans that she understood so well. The Golden Jubilee of the
English foundation was kept in 1892.

Mother Digby paid the price in suffering for the flourishing
vigour of the vicariate, from a chronic heart condition and from the
headaches that had been her lot since the day when, riding on her
uncle's shoulder, she had struck her head against a doorway. She
welcomed and ignored physical pain and it rarely left her: "O bona
crux!" In 1879 she nearly died as the result of an accident, and was
instantaneously cured by the prayers of the household to Madeleine
Sophie Barat.

Until 1889 Mother Digby was also in charge of the novices; she
said: "Let truth be their queen as poverty was the Lady of Saint
Francis." Mother Goetz had given her the line to follow: "Make
them strong and supernatural." Accordingly, "she would propose
some inspiriting impossibility to be made possible." Strong,
searching discipline, in which "one realized that it was only another
string of one's instrument that she had selected to tune," was for the
sake of prayer:

> Her teaching about the inner life was in harmony with all that we knew or
> guessed about her own. "The only time when we can legitimately take the
> strain off is in prayer," she once said — and all that she taught us showed how
> God possessed the whole of her inner life and thought. But it was all to be on
> the simplest lines as far as her teaching went: study and imitation, self-
> annihilation before God — he is to be all and everything else nothing, especially
> self. Her favourite words for prayer summed it all up: "Tu solus sanctus, tu
> solus dominus, tu solus altissimus."[2]

Mabel Digby was born for government, through her clarity of
mind and strength of will. Power went out from the steady bearing,
the calm, unchanging expression, the penetrating blue eyes and
beautiful voice, power used humbly in service, with impersonality.
Someone said: "She is an admiral on his own quarterdeck; I am
somewhat afraid of her." Love came with the experience of her
heart, compassionate, generous and understanding.

Originally hers must have been a fearless, proud and rather solitary nature, blended from two strains. From her father came the genial side, the heart, the gay courage, the joy in life; from her mother the force of character, the queenliness, the penetrating judgment, the governing power. . . . God and the spiritual life, the means of union with him occupied her thoughts and interests, and when she entered the Society and had to take its double spirit of prayer and work her second book became human nature. She made a study of children in the years in which she was employed in the school, and of novices and nuns later on; she knew human nature in the world outside through her varied intercourse with all kinds of people under all kinds of circumstances . . . . She did not talk much, but how precious were her few words in throwing light, in giving counsel, in lifting up everything that had slackened or dropped, in opening new horizons. [3]

In 1894 Mother Digby attended the General Council that elected Mother de Sartorius; it chose her as assistant general and local superior of the Mother House. On September 8, our Lady's birthday, she said: "I have laid down Roehampton as a carpet beneath her feet." A year later she became vicar general on Mother de Sartorius' death, and on August 25, 1895, she was elected fifth superior general.

The Fourteenth General Council met from August 21 to September 6. [4] Mother Digby showed that her way of administration was to be drawn from the nature of the Society itself:

Our government is a government of centralized unity resting upon the spirit of faith in an authority coming from God and sanctioned by Holy Church. It is, fundamentally and in its inter-relationships, a spirit of truth and of charity, a spirit sincerely seeking the glory of God and the good of souls by the sacrifice of egotism and by constant devotedness; a spirit profoundly interior in its adoration, reparation, incessant prayer, in its energy in the face of suffering, in its search for the self-stripping of holy poverty, in the taste for self-abasement, remembering that for the spouse of Jesus Christ, humble, poor and crucified, his Heart must be an open book where we learn all things, each truth, each feeling, each rule of conduct. [5]

The Council again took up the question of a house of prayer: "From now on the Mother House will be this unique house of adoration, from which will radiate the influence of perpetual Exposition." [6] It calmly faced the threat of legal harassment in France: "Bound to the divine Heart as we are, his interests are our own; if we seek these interests alone, can the help of God fail us?" [7] Rome was watching the coming storm, ready to defend the interests of the religious orders. When Cardinal Monaco La Valletta died the following year Leo XIII appointed as Cardinal Protector the vigilant Angelo di Pietri[8] who wrote to Mother Digby: "Your spirit is a double spirit, contemplation united to devotedness. Be faithful."

Two contrasting strands were to run side by side throughout Mother Digby's generalate: one dark, woven of suffering and of loss, one bright with fulfilment. They were no more separable than Good Friday and Easter. She knew that her mission was to keep the integrity of the Society by "the sword of the Spirit."

The first five years, though ominous, were urgent with renewal as the Society's centenary approached. Mother Digby appealed to its members to balance the evils of the time with counterweights: want of conviction by truth, changeability by a sense of eternity, selfishness by generosity, over-activity by prayer. [9] At the Mother House she strengthened solidarity by means of superiors' retreats and meetings of educators. She journeyed throughout Europe despite the menace to her health. "They say that I may die in my armchair at any moment, so it might as well be on the train." The Paris winters were trying, so every December she went to Rome where visits to Leo XIII renewed her courage, and each spring set off for another country.

She had not forgotten Mother Barat's prophecy. During an illness when death seemed close Mother Désoudin was inspired to say: "Promise that you will go to America if you recover." She set sail on August 11, 1898. The route swept in a wide arc: through eastern Canada, mid-western United States, California, Mexico, Louisiana, then back to the eastern seaboard. The hub was Saint Charles where the spirit of Mother Duchesne touched her. By her side was Janet Stuart whose vivid letters to Roehampton told of the happenings in each house with its local colour: colonial, pioneer, Indian, Negro and Yankee; of the crossing of the Rockies and sunsets over the Pacific; of ghostly nights in the palace of Maximilian in Mexico City. Mother Stuart gave conferences on education as they went along. North America was welcoming a mother general for the first time. The communities remembered: "When I enter a house I look for the spirit of prayer." The children remembered: "Take always the straight course, come what will." The last month was spent at Manhattanville where all the superiors came together.

Mother Digby was back in Paris in May, 1899, with her thoughts fixed on the centenary. She had already begun a three-year preparation by circular letters, "to pay our debt of gratitude, to repair our faults and prepare for new blessings." The tone of her circulars was her own, weighty, uplifting, with a biblical ring; they were (said her contemporaries) "electrifying." The first preparatory letter, written from Rome on December 12, 1897, asked for an evaluation. The three points to be considered were: austerity in a life of work, submission of mind, harmony with the thought of the Church.

> According to the mind of the Church religious life consists essentially in the gift of self which is both determined and ratified by the vows of religion: determined as to the manner of giving, ratified as to its fulfilment and scope. Now we no longer possess what we have given away, and so we have handed over to the Society and to its service all ownership of ourselves. [10]

The next preparatory letter was written on November 11, 1898, from "the second sanctuary of the Society," the small room at Saint Charles where Philippine Duchesne had died. It dealt with the Society's reason for being:

> Each religious order has received from God its special treasure . . . . The devotion to the Sacred Heart includes all others since it is their source, "bread holding the sweetness of every taste," the riches of which are inexhaustible. [11]

Adoration, reparation and love are its expressions, and "by these means the nations and the world will be renewed."

> Our past is now in our Lord's keeping, with its imperfections and its shortcomings; our future is given with absolute trust to his love; the present is ours. There are some who despair of the present time, seeing it lost in indifference and desolation. Those who look more closely, enlightened by a faith which sees nothing as impossible to God, think otherwise. We know that grace triumphs when there seems no other help. Devotion to the Sacred Heart alone holds the promise that tepid souls will become fervent in practicing it. Hence the perfection of each one, her individual sanctity, is a leaven which will work in a debased world. This is the hope of the future. [12]

The following year Leo XIII accomplished what he called "the greatest act of my pontificate," the consecration of the human race to the heart of Christ at the dawn of a new century. His act was inspired by a former Sacred Heart pupil of Riedenburg, Maria von Droste Zu Vichering, [13] who had entered the Good Shepherd order as Mary of the Divine Heart. The pope, impressed, consulted his theologians: could he consecrate all men, believers and unbelievers, to Christ's love? The answer was drawn from Saint Thomas: all men are potentially members of Christ's Body, and Christ's Vicar may speak in their name. Leo XIII did so on the Feast of the Sacred Heart, 1899, for "in that divine Heart all our hopes should be placed, and from it the salvation of all men is to be confidently sought." [14]

Mother Digby responded in her third preparatory letter, written from Paris on November 18:

> The coincidence of our centenary with the consecration of the world to the Heart of Jesus is not only a powerful motive for confidence but should penetrate us deeply with the importance of our mission .... The spirit of a religious order lies in the great and simple idea of its origin: ours is a consecration to the glory of the Heart of Jesus containing the essence of our religious life; the rest is accessory, a means to that end .... May we understand the power of the divine call to the devotion to the Sacred Heart, so that each one of us may become "another Christ," living and breathing for his greater glory. [15]

As the cententary drew near she wrote on the theme of *Cor unum et anima una*:

> The richness, the strength and the beauty of the Society rest largely in the diversity of gifts, of minds, of ideas and of thoughts which are brought together in obedience to the Rule. No uniformity is prescribed, but all the elements of the beautiful are found: variety, order, proportion; these make the Society a living whole. The keeping of this unity, so precious in itself, calls for the cooperation of all its members. As a practical and important conclusion: all that is valuable in the spiritual order is gained only by sacrifice, and to keep unity we must bring our minds to it. [16]

As direct preparation for the Jubilee a practice of poverty was followed in all the houses. It was initiated by Alexandrine Dupautaine, [17] superior at Amiens and *doyenne* of those formed by Madeleine Sophie Barat, known as "the best of *bonnes mamans* and the most encouraging of saints."

November 21, 1900, was celebrated around the world by nuns, pupils, alumnae and friends in the old-time spirit of *congé sans cloche* — a bell-less holiday! As Leo XIII wrote: "The remembrance of past benefits urges the will to act with a more joyous energy."

In the meantime a counter-current had been running rapidly towards the destruction of all the houses where the Foundress had lived. The storm broke in 1901 with the Waldeck-Rousseau Law requiring that all religious congregations be authorized by the state and forbidding any non-authorized congregation to teach. Any order that did not conform could be dissolved, especially those with foreign administrators or with houses abroad. The alternative was secularization in the legal sense: the Society in France would lose its identity as a religious order and each French member her status as a religious. Mother Digby was intransigent. Strengthened by Leo XIII's "Letter to the Generals of Religious Orders in France" she refused secularization even before her petition for authorization had been refused by the government in January, 1902. She wrote to the Society:

> Let us be ready to pass through bad times without surprise and without trouble of mind, remembering that the crucible frees the true gold and trial reveals the precious metal in a religious body, purifying and solidifying it. A long peace is not without danger. Israel under its olive and fig trees forgot the wonders of the desert, the manna and the divine law. An assured peace breeds sufficiency, over-security breeds carelessness. With war and persecution come special graces. . . . No truce is allowed; no diplomatic agreement; no *modus vivendi* can be set up between Christ and the world, the flesh and the devil. [18]

She said: "We must not hold to our houses more than our Lord holds to them," and: "What would be the loss of them all in comparison to one deliberate infidelity on the part of one of us?"

Leo XIII died in July, 1904, and Pius X took the stand of his predecessor in two letters to France: *Vehementer Nos* condemning the law of separation published unilaterally, and *Gravissimo* deploring the appropriation of goods by the state. A law of 1904 made plain in its irony the basis of the attack on the religious orders:

> The congregations are societies bound by the triple vows of poverty, chastity and obedience. Thus it is clear that a member of a congregation is in servitude — not merely mental but actual . . . . We see men and women in the flower of youth absorbed by a single aim — that of religion . . . . Their influence is unbounded; they have the prestige, the aureole of consecrated beings. They do all in their power to form their pupils to the image of God and to the liking of the Church. [19]

The closing of the houses began in 1902 and ended in 1909. Seven vicars saw their vicariates dissolved while they went over the frontier. Forty-seven times the same scene was enacted — with local variations: a more or less suave liquidator appeared to take inven-

tory and was met by a statement of rights; the date of evacuation
was set; the heart-broken children went home after their last prize-
day; the house was stripped with the help of indignant parents and
neighbours; the community, heart-whole in its offering, scattered; a
few guardians stayed in the desolate place till the last day, then
locked the door behind them. "There's nothing to do; you could eat
your dinner off the floor," said the cleaners sent in by the new
owner, the government.

The Fifteenth General Council met in the midst of all this from
May 18 to 31, 1904, the year that saw the most closures. It
provided that the superior of each house evacuated should sign a formal protest. [20] Its sessions were overclouded by a certain internal
tension, augmented by unwarrented interference from without on
the part of some persons who called Mother Digby's mode of
government into question. The basic reasons for this are not clear
from the records. The Council members felt that the Society had
passed through a grave crisis, but the episode, unknown to the
religious at large, passed and left no mark on history.

The dispersals continued unrelentingly. At the Hotel Biron,
Juliette de Lapeyrouse,[21] who had governed "like an abbess of the
Middle Ages" for thirty-five years, died just before the emptying of
the "gilded palace." The Mother House was spared until July,
1907. It was stripped by then; Mother Digby sat motionless in the
chapel while the altar was being carried out. The body of Madeleine
Sophie Barat had been sent to Jette in April, 1904. The cedar tree
that she had planted eighty-four years earlier, "Mother Barat's
cedar," was cut down. It had grown no taller since the day of her
funeral when a pigeon had broken off its tip but its branches had
reached out ever more widely. From the dead trunk an altar was
made for the new shrine at Jette. Then the Mother House itself was
locked on August 10, 1907; inside a protest against injustice had
been written large on the wall.

For the next two years Mother Digby directed the Society from
Conflans, working at an old school desk in a bare room. New
vicariates were created abroad as the seven in France were ex-
tinguished; new houses opened as old ones closed. For some two
thousand five hundred French religious a home was found. "And
where are you going?" was Mother Digby's compassionate question
to a religious passing through Conflans. "I really don't know but it's
written on my trunk," was the cheerful answer. Conflan's turn came

last. The novices had already gone to Rivoli, the body of Mother Hardey was sent to Kenwood, that of Father Varin to Roehampton, and on July 30, 1909, Ixelles in Brussels became the Mother House. Mother Borget, now over eighty, was a heroine in all eyes, friendly and unfriendly, as she gallantly fought for the property and personnel of the Society. Did the liquidators know that she kept their names in a bottle of holy water?

Throughout this crucifying time an undercurrent of joy had been rising steadily. The places where Madeleine Sophie Barat had lived were empty but she herself was manifestly present. The Process for her Beatification had been going on quietly: The Antepreparatory Session (July, 1900), the Preparatory Session (May, 1902), that of the Heroicity of Virtues (January, 1905) and the Session of Miracles (December, 1907) and the *De Tuto* (January 14, 1908). Two cures among the many proven authentic were accepted: that of Nancy Bakewell, [22] a little girl in Saint Louis in 1876, and that of Marie Klippel, [23] a young nun at Riedenburg in 1882. A second exhumation of the body of Mother Barat took place at Jette on March 27, 1908, and Mother Digby wrote:

> During the hours that I passed by her open coffin I commended her little Society to her, urgently, so that even as her body has remained whole and intact, so she will keep her religious family ever united, preserved always from the corruption of relaxation and infidelity. [24]

As the long process drew to a close Pius X said: "It seems to me that the life of the Venerable Mother Barat and of the Institute that she founded reproduce the Christian life and the Church." In preparation for the ceremony of beatification Mother Digby wrote to the Society:

> It is not everything to belong to the body of the Society; it is more to belong to the soul. And what is the soul of the Society? Where is that élite which gives life to the whole, which carries the weight of it before God, which upholds it, in which the Spirit of truth reigns? Happily, it is not found in one rank or age or condition; it is spread through the Society like a leaven of holiness . . . . Such persons are everywhere; God alone knows their number and their names. What we do know is that we can each be of their number. [25]

The Beatification of Madeleine Sophie Barat took place in Saint Peter's basilica on May 24, 1908. Thousands of jubilant religious, students and friends of the Society and the two *miraculées* saw her picture unveiled and heard Pius X declare: "All that was done by her on earth is now confirmed in heaven." Mother Digby, too ill to travel, listened from Conflans to the world-wide "alleluia," and wrote:

> the Society is not a machine that functions from the start by a sort of mechanical process; it is a body, an organism in which each period of life has its own point of departure .... We are now at that grave moment when a generation that has not known the Foundress or seen her at work must take the responsibility of maintaining and extending the tradition and the primitive spirit. And it is at this moment, by the moving designs of God, that the Church formally gives us our Blessed Foundress as model and guide. [26]

Life was quieter at Ixelles. Many French children had followed the nuns into schools in England, Holland, Belgium, Italy and Spain. The student nuns had joined the novices at Rivoli. The Children of Mary were holding meetings in France as usual while their directors slipped over the border to help them, notably Marthe de Lavergne,[27] the mistress of novices-in-exile. Friends were keeping doors open for a future return by holding property for the Society. Mother Digby, after a serious illness, called the Sixteenth General Council. It met in Ixelles from August 11 to 28, 1910, and calmly turned its attention to the studies. [28]

Mother Digby herself was transparently at peace. Those who watched her said: "She had seen we knew not what and it made her long with a great and ever growing desire to be dissolved and to be with Christ." She spent motionless hours before the Blessed Sacrament to which she had been invincibly drawn since the moment of her conversion. It was while kneeling before the tabernacle that she was struck with paralysis. Just before her death on May 21, 1911, she repeated her "Alleluia!" She was buried at Roehampton on Ascension Day, May 25 and feast-day of the new Beata. She had named as vicar general Janet Stuart who came to Ixelles and wrote to the Society: "In her presence one breathed in the truth, strength and peace which she communicated during life; she will still communicate them." [29]

*   *   *

Janet Erskine Stuart [30] was born on November 11, 1857, the youngest of thirteen children in an Anglican rectory at Cottesmore in Rutlandshire. She was a serious, sensitive child who lost her mother at the age of two. "I had an old-fashioned, ceremonious home-training. Are homes more ceremonious where there is no mother?" But she was secure in the care of Dody, her invalid sister and in the affection of big brothers for whom she was "our Antigone." She was the comrade of her reserved and upright father to whom she gave "everything except her confidence." She was educated at home, indoors by thought-provoking books in many languages, outdoors by "the whole country-side with its fields and trees and hedges and gardens." She had unassuming power over others but lived her own life, full of questioning before mysteries: "What I was looking for without knowing it was God's thought for his creatures." She kept the self-made rule of hiding her own feelings, but "better if I had broken it a thousand times."

At the age of six Janet heard the story of Lazarus and went straight to the graveyard. "Having prayed with all my might I shouted as loud as I could: 'Mama! Come forth!'" Her disappointment was the seed of doubt, but "at the age of twelve I began to think and was happy ever after." She went through a faith crisis like that of adolescents a century later, during which she was challenged by her brother to find her *telos*, her end in life.

> I made up my mind that it must be found. The search lasted for seven years and was one of the happiest times of my life. It began by examining the grounds of my faith and they all melted away .... At twenty I reached a point that was more agnostic than anything else. I had left off praying and seemed stuck fast. [31]

But through friends "it came upon me like a flash that in the Catholic Church I should find my last end and the truth about whose very existence I was doubting." The search led her to Farm Street where she was received into the Church on March 6, 1879. She could never again live in her father's home.

The next three years were a search for the way to fulfil her *telos*. Under the breezy direction of Father Gallwey she explored a new world of prayer. He encouraged her love of beauty and wrote:

> I see so clearly how our blessed Lord is drawing his child to himself..... The day will come when he will take entire possession of you, and then for his sake you will find yourself compelled to speak of him to others in order to help those whom he loves. [32]

So Janet spent her days in hunting and fishing and her nights in prayer. The thought of religious life came slowly and she visited many convents, including Roehampton. She wrote out a penetrating statement of her ideals of religious life and spoke of the Society of the Sacred Heart to which she felt drawn because of its name, but which, she feared, "did not do enough for the poor." One spring day, while looking at a bed of blue hyacinths, "the word of the Lord came to me and I saw it all." She entered on September 8, 1882, at Roehampton. "What a place it is! There is life and light in everything and an atmosphere of God."

In Mother Digby's energetic hands the sensitive, beauty-loving intellectual soon learned that "shyness is not an apostolic virtue," and that "I must not judge as though I must necessarily be wrong." Mother Digby herself, so masculine in decisive action, came to lean on Janet's womanly gift of "the illative sense, the faculty of insight, in the high principles of human things an almost prophetic intuition." As a novice Janet surrendered her gifted personality to the way of obedience in "my own order which I love beyond words and in which I am so completely satisfied."

After her first vows she briefly enjoyed her favorite occupation: "To be a teacher! I should not have minded what I taught so long as I could catch someone and teach him something." On February 12, 1889, she was professed at the Mother House where "grace seized me and shook a little sense into me." Returning to Roehampton she first assisted and then replaced Mother Digby as mistress of novices. Perhaps the moment at which she did so is an unobtrusive turning point from an old to a new order in the Society. A few years later a newcomer from Japan could distinguish the young religious who had been Mother Stuart's novices from those who had been Mother Digby's. How? "Because they were so much more human."

The rest of Janet's life was spent in teaching her favourite subject: the art of the spiritual life. By this more than by government she was to leave on the Society of the Sacred Heart a mark which she would have called "heavenly-mindedness." Through dealing with the novices she became an instinctive rather than a scientific psychologist:

> The strength of women is in their character; their mission is civilization in its loftiest and widest sense. ... In two things we must establish them fundamentally, quiet of mind and firmness of will.[33]

She guided the novices with reverence, tolerance, humour and demanding love, in the open sunshine. She asked in return for generosity, persevering effort, self-development, while serving God "great-heartedly, thoughtfully, constantly."

In 1894 Mother Stuart became vicar of the English-Irish vicariate; she had to travel, appear in public and make decisions – at constant cost to her self-diffidence. But: "To be a joy-bearer and joy-giver says everything," as those who lived under her bracing government soon learned. Her influence, direct or indirect, was quietly powerful and asked much. It called forth great love while it provoked a counter-reaction in some who found the stimulus too constant. She herself admitted in later years that she had placed too high a value on externals.

She could now be an educator in a definite sense, concerned with public and private school systems and with teacher-training programs. Roehampton set up a printing press for Society literature under the direction of Rose Thunder, [34] and to this Mother Stuart became an important contributor. She was a Christian humanist with a gift for writing. Her plays, poems and essays (published only after her death) grew out of the community life that she made so interesting; she shared her thoughts and fancies on a spiritual level and in artistic form. Letter-writing (a rarely cultivated fine art) was a constant expression of this gift as well as an apostolate: letters of pure friendship, guidance in prayer or lively news-sharing with an undercurrent of reflection. All this adds up to a busy life, but Mother Stuart was never busy if "to be busy means to find it inconvenient to be interrupted."

The circle of influence widened as she travelled. She visited the houses of England and Ireland and many on the continent, especially in Rome where she gave evidence for the cause of Philippine Duchesne. After the journey through North America as Mother Digby's companion she went to South America as her representative in 1901, where she visited the houses in Puerto Rico, Cuba, Chile, Peru and Argentina. She had the satisfaction of once more mounting a horse to go up a slippery mountain through tropical rain to a country house called Colorado; here she and Mother de Lavigerie had "a good long talk about many holy things" until far into the night (ten o'clock!).

As Mother Stuart's life became more outgoing it reached inward more deeply. She who had the gifts of the genius and of the mystic shrank from all that was singular and feared — for herself — to leave the beaten way in prayer. She followed direction and sought assurance; she was faithful to method and used diligent discipline. But one called to be the charismatic guide of hundreds (and through her writings of thousands) of prayer-thirsty hearts needed the freedom to be passive as well as active under the touch of God. She was released by Father Daignault whom she met in 1898. After that she could "follow without anxiety what seems to be the inspiration of grace." She read the mystics.

> I knew then that it was good to wait in silence for the salvation of God .... I heard God's call again. This time it was to break with convention, to seek the liberty of children and live free in his house .... Then gradually the gift of self was simplified for me, and came to consist in greater lowliness of soul and nearness to God, and life became a glorious opportunity to pour myself out in love. [35]

In 1906 another spiritual friend (probably Archbishop Alban Goodier) led her further into the prayer of simplicity. He writes:

> It seemed to make all the difference to her. She at once began living with our Lord in prayer, and her quick sympathy, which made her so easily enter the minds of others, made her no less easily dwell in the mind of our Lord. She became extraordinarily happy in her prayer, like a bird let loose from her cage. [36]

She passed through the purifying darkness that is a call to go on, and then:

> It became easier and easier for her to spend long hours in prayer. After the "dark night" she seemed to sail into the sunlight, became very quiet, and was as one who is certain without troubling any more about doubts. ... She lived a spiritual life in and beneath all her activities; she could with ease make the outer machinery stand still; in a sense, nothing had hold of her, especially after she became Mother General. [37]

Mother Stuart was ready when she was called to Ixelles at the death of Mother Digby and found that she was vicar general. She opened the Seventeenth General Council with the words:

> The time at which the Society is called to elect one of its members to govern is always a moment at which the supernatural touches us very closely. It is under the hand of God; this adorable hand has rested heavily upon it, *manus Domini*

tetigit me. A great silence has been made within souls and within the Society. It is the instinctive preparation for such great actions, for in silence, in the depths of one's consciousness, one hears the voice of God. [38]

The voice spoke her own name; she became the sixth superior general of the Society on August 23, 1911. She was now to extend "the mission given to her: to carry afar a message of hope and of confidence."

The Council met from August 23 to 31. [39] Coming so soon after the last it passed only one decree: the First Saturday of each month was to be kept with the same liturgical observance as the First Friday, in honour of the Immaculate Heart of Mary. Conscious of the fact that she had never known Madeleine Sophie Barat, Mother Stuart wrote to the Society:

> God who has so loved and protected the Society in the past will not abandon it now that it has reached this critical moment . . . . Until now our Mothers General have all known personally, even intimately, our Blessed Foundress. This direct contact has been prolonged for us beyond the usual measure; it is a special grace which has strengthened the basis of our religious existence. The future will test it; may we be strong and faithful. Exterior changes, which are necessary to meet the needs of our times, must not alter its spirit. If it rests upon the foundations which our Holy Mother left us in the Constitutions it can be adapted to anything within the framework of our Institute . . . . Thus, in going ahead along the dangerous paths of a new era, let us keep our souls in the presence of God, nourishing our minds with his truths and his works; let us seek and love him everywhere. "In him is the source of life, and in his light we shall see light." [40]

In the notes of her first retreat after election Mother Stuart wrote: "Sixth superior general of the Society of the Sacred Heart, fifth in line from our Beata! What record will there be before God of my stewardship — of how long? Perhaps very short!" [41] She made a "six-year plan," determined to know the whole Society before the next General Council; she was given three of the six years. She wrote: "My head is full of plans and dreams of what might be done, but I must be patient; people are not ready yet." Would they have been ready in 1917 for new directions given by a creative mind? Mother Stuart was not a revolutionary but she had a sense of evolution, saying: "Uniformity in essentials is good, but we cannot become slaves of this idea." She wrote, for her times, directives for a later time of change:

Epochs of transition must keep us on the alert. They ask us to keep our eyes open upon distant horizons, our minds listening to seize every indication that can enlighten us: reading, reflexion, searching, must never stop; the mind must keep flexible in order to lose nothing, to acquire any knowledge that can aid our mission or serve for our development. We do not try to conform but to be informed. And so, without despising the old or refusing the new methods [of education] we shall reach a new period of consolidation, enlightened and prepared by thoughtful study and ready for true advance. Don't think that we know or ever shall know the last word in these matters; we shall never find anything that does not change. Immobility, arrested movement, bring decadence; a beauty, fully unfolded is ready to perish. So let us not rest in our beautiful past.[42]

She took up the challenge of the law of growth:

Since the frontiers of knowledge are continually advancing, and the demands of both the Church and the Society are calling for fresh adaptations of our principles, it will remain true to the end that (as Cardinal Newman says) "here below to live is to change, and to be perfect is to have changed often."[43]

In this spirit Mother Stuart set out on her widening journeys. Within three years (one hundred days of which were spent at sea) she visited one hundred and one houses; others were familiar to her from earlier travels. She came to know personally almost every member of the Society. Upon each she impressed:

That seal which is the authentic mark of the Institute: an insatiable desire to give ourselves to the utmost for the glory of the Sacred Heart of Jesus, according to the spirit and rules of the Society, a virtue which we call, perhaps in a colloquial sense, devotedness, an uncalculating spirit of sacrifice, and with it a fixed resolve to give and suffer for the sake of love alone.[44]

Between journeys she returned to Ixelles to be with the probanists and to share her reflexions. One of her most penetrating letters is a commentary on the *Cor unum* in which she had experienced "the extent and strength, the purity and sanctity of the love which Christ commands:"[45]

Those who understand the sanctity of the bonds of charity are those who love the most in God. We do not always understand that what we should fear most is not loving too much but loving too little. "This is my commandment, that you love one another as I have loved you." We shall never reach this point; we can never love too much .... So, to enter more deeply into the spirit of our vocation, let us love more. Let us fear indifference, exclusiveness, a local spirit, a national spirit, a spirit of comparisons and criticism. Let us love frankly, loyally, widely, as our Lord has loved us. [46]

November 10, 1913, she set out from Port Said on a journey round the world, with Marie le Bail, the secretary general and Marie de Salm-Salm, [47] whose recent miraculous cure by Blessed Madeleine Sophie she wished to prove authentic. On the deck of the slow steamer she began her book *The Society of the Sacred Heart*, "quite a little book of the sea, planned on the Adriatic, begun on the Red Sea, written on the Indian Ocean and finished on the South Pacific." It summed up her vision of the Society and her desires for it: "It is not the story of its life, it is merely an attempt at a character-sketch." Though some of the points require a new approach today (aspects of government, of training, of "the mixed life," of the division into choir and coadjutrix religious) the sketch remains a living likeness as the study of a spirit.

During the hours on shore in one new house after another she still found time to write. Her letters show her at home in Australia, New Zealand, the Philippines (where there was not yet a house of the Society), Japan, Canada and the United States. They reflect her alert thoughts, her prayer unbroken by contacts with the hundreds of persons who were the better for her passing touch. The last four weeks, spent at Manhattanville, were a culmination of her life-work, with meetings for educators and superiors, and a retreat: "We have come to the very heart of things when we speak of the spiritual life." [48] The Feast of the Sacred Heart was "a heavenly day, scarcely for earth."

By the time Mother Stuart reached Roehampton on June 26, 1914, the physical strain had become too much; her health was broken. But she was happy: "I have found the beatitude of the hunger and thirst for the things of God all through the Society." She herself was tasting union: "When I looked up at the oratory last evening, during recreation on the terrace, I had to turn away quickly; otherwise I would no longer have been free."

She was no sooner at Ixelles than the world war broke out. "I do not bless war but peace," said Pius X sternly just before his death on August 20. Benedict XV came to the helm. Belgium was over-run and the Mother House became a hospital. Mother Stuart wrote:

When all human landmarks are wrenched away and we are sailing, as they have to sail now, with "all lights out," the one thing to which we can thrill is hope in God, an utter trust without understanding, that he will bring the best out of our lives. [49]

Communications were cut with the houses in war-lands, but word came through that the nuns had been driven from Gora, and that at Tournai Adrienne Buhet and Madeleine de Brolac had been killed by a stray bullet through a window. Mother Stuart made her dangerous way back to Roehampton, leaving the Mother House in the hands of gallant Mother Borget. She found all the superiors of Australia, Japan and Egypt gathered for a retreat. It never took place, for Mother Stuart fell ill. Before receiving the last sacraments she wrote to the Society:

> Allow me to use this occasion to ask pardon for the faults that I have committed during my time of government, for all that I have failed to do or done badly, or which could have given pain. But allow me also to assure you of the true affection which I have for each and all, an affection which will lead you all, I know, to forgive your poor mother in the Heart of Jesus. [50]

Her rapturous death came on October 21, 1914: "How he loves me! How he longs for me!" She was buried in the Sacred Heart chapel between Mother Digby and Father Varin.

*   *   *

The Assistants general of this time were a diversified group, ruggedly traditional yet ready for the unexpected. "They devote themselves in perfect harmony", wrote Mother Stuart.

At Ixelles Césarine Borget had a respite from her long struggle with the liquidators, but it was not the final rest of a hard worker aged eighty-five. When the war broke out it was she who scrambled around Brussels, getting passports for refugees by informing astonished officials of her age. "I am the Society's grandmother," she claimed as she entered on a surprising "third career" by crossing still another frontier after the war.

Marthe de Pichon [51] was a contrast, gentle, charming, balanced. Mother Goetz had said to her: "Souls united to our Lord know what to do from hour to hour, from moment to moment." During twenty years as vicar of northern France she lived by Mother Stuart's principle: "To govern is to love." She became assistant general in 1895, and said to the probanists:

To love the Society is not to be attached to one superior, one house, to some children rather than others; it is to be widely, universally ready to serve. It is to seek its interests and its greater good in everything, to enter into its views, to be penetrated with its spirit, to strive to acquire those virtues which make us like the divine Heart that it aims to glorify. [52]

She held that: "The Rule is our framework; don't dream of going beyond it," but added: "Don't be just an 'amen'; you'll do nothing worthwhile like that." To encourage regular observance she edited the *Conferences on the Rule* of Father d'Ahérée. At her death on August 13, 1914, Mother Stuart wrote a character sketch of her in a circular letter: "The memory that she leaves with us is like a ray of soft, white light." The letter took the opportunity to develop a psychological study of the "three ages" of religious life: youth, the mature years, the mounting years. For each: "Let us hope; let us hope each one for herself and also for one another." [53]

Juliette Depret [54] and Sophie du Chélas [55] did not find the mounting road easy. Mother Depret was mistress of novices and superior for many years before going on a visitation of the houses in Canada with Mother Thunder in 1885. Named assistant general in 1893 she suffered from the troubles caused by her own timid and complex nature. Mother du Chélas was a Breton of high, unflinching principles, too straight-forward for her own good. When she became assistant general in 1896 she took Mother Désoudin's place as mistress of probation and formed the probanists roundly. Together with Mother Depret she caused serious misunderstandings. These two, unlike in temperarment and alike in self-caused suffering, retired at the General Council of 1904. The dispersal of French religious was at its height. "In the interests of internationality," said Mother Digby, their places were taken by Mathilde Nérincx, [56] a Belgian, and Jeanne de Lavigerie "who has certainly become Spanish during the twenty-five years of work in our houses of Peru and Mexico."

Mother Nérincx was gay, lively and musical. In charge of the juniorate at Conflans she inspired future teachers by her captivating classes; she was then superior in France and Belgium. As assistant general she lived at Conflans during the brave years when it was the Mother House. In the peaceful interval at Ixelles she prepared the letters of Mother Barat for publication. When the war came she was too ill to leave Brussels where she remained until her death in 1919. It was said of her: "Her soul vibrated to everything touching the

Society; her resources of devotedness were spent for all that is best
in our religious life."

For Mother de Lavigerie the Mother House brought an abrupt
end to a strenuous missionary life on two continents and an island.
"The lion is in her cage," remarked Mother Digby. She settled
down to deskwork under a picture of our Lady of Guadalupe:

> She was in the full strength of her age; her serious air, her deep gaze which
> lighted up when she spoke of the Americas, the stories of her travels overseas,
> sent an apostolic current flowing through us, and she wrote in her notebook the
> names of many future missionaries. [57]

To fill the place left empty by Mother de Pichon's death Mother
Stuart had made a surprising choice: Catherine de Montalembert, [58]
then seventy-two years old:

> She will bring to us, together with her devotedness and the energetic activity
> that is still hers, a very deep love of the Society, and a knowledge of its spirit
> and traditions which go back to the last years of our Blessed Foundress and, in
> active life, to the generalate of our venerated Mother Goetz. You will easily
> understand the importance of prolonging this traditional heritage which links
> our present times with its origins, and the care with which we wish to keep this
> living chain as long as God leaves the links with us. [59]

This link was the daughter of the redoubtable Charles de Montalembert, a leader of Catholic Liberals and a fighter for religious
and intellectual freedom. Catherine was "a womanly edition of her
father" in optimism, daring and fluent speech, with a dash of startling originality. She was vicar of Austria when called to the Mother
House. From there she went often into France to visit the loyal
Children of Mary, unchecked by growing deafness and blindness.
She had found the fountain of youth and was the energetic superior
of the Rue du Grand Cerf as well as assistant general.

Small, precise Marie le Bail [60] was secretary general. "After my
profession no-one knew what to do with me as I was poor at
everything, so I was sent to help Mother Dufour." She never again
left the *secretariat*, where she was good at everything. She first acted
as Mother Lehon's eyes, then took full charge in 1894. For twenty-
five years she was "organ of authority and bond of charity," helped
by an infallible memory. Methodical and kind, she always had a
margin of time for others. During the expulsions she kept the
archives in packing boxes; she unpacked them at Ixelles and packed

them again when the war broke out. She edited the Society newsletter under the title "Echo of the Sacred Heart," then "The Dove" and finally "Echo of the Fortnight." Joy radiated from her office. She had been smothered by Jansenism in her youth; Mother Stuart released her:

> Like many generous and austere persons, you have stopped at one way of using creatures: abstinence. But there are two others, nobler because more in harmony with the purpose of their own creation; use and contemplation. Abstinence maintains balance, but use and contemplation give an impetus for soaring upward. [61]

* * *

Community life stands out with special clarity during this period. To assure its integrity was one reason for Mother Digby's intransigence in leaving France, while Mother Stuart gave it a new dimension. There was no change in life-style, yet the deeply-fixed pattern was more alive. Paradoxically, this came about from both Mother Digby's austerity and Mother Stuart's amenity. The former urged an ever greater stripping of the unnecessary in matters of comfort or even convenience, a curtailing of correspondence, a sharper, separation from the outer world: "Newspapers are always out of place in our community rooms." It was a bracing summons to the independence from "things" that comes of religious dependence. Mother Stuart cultivated the recreational aspects of community life, its power of *détente*, by a development of mind and heart. "There are arts in community life; the art of government, the art of teaching, the art of persuasion, the art of conversation." While superior at Roehampton she had expected all to contribute to "the thought-market":

> This is one of the joys of community life; the strongest, sweetest and most intimate thoughts of others are often flashed upon us unconsciously; or trustfully put into our hands, and we go away richer in mind and heart, "wondering in ourselves at that which has come to pass." I know that also has its comic side when, as Mother N. says: "You bring out your poor little thought, and all the microscopes of the community are turned upon it at the same moment." [62]

This mode of thought-stimulation spread through the English-Irish vicariate and then round the world. It could be formidable if carried too far; a French religious in Dublin marvelled at this

strange holiday pleasure: to write and read aloud a serious essay!
When informal the exchange could be refreshing while reaching a
deep level; some found it tiring to keep up the pace. At the Mother
House Mother Stuart said: "We are so much at home together that
all freely lay their souls on the table for the general benefit." Even
timid Mother le Bail found that:

> To be a ray of joy in community is to think of something to say and to say it
> simply. If we think of nothing we shall say nothing, and if we say nothing the
> community can't enjoy it. [63]

Despite the negative word in the Constitutions concerning "particular friendships, the bane of communities," there have been inspiring friendships throughout Society history. Philippine Duchesne
craved the loved presence of Regis Hamilton;[64] the two "originals,"
Pauline Perdreau and Catherine de Montalembert, complemented
each other; the three Conflans novices, Josephine Augustin,
Marianne Bouterlin and Mary Anne Mahoney,[65] received a
sanction for their friendship from Mother Barat. During this
period of "confirmation" both superior generals encouraged friendships within community life.

When Mabel Digby first went to Marmoutier she found Maria
Zoepffel[66] teaching in the school. The cool-mannered English
woman and the impulsive French woman (each of whom had been
cherished as a friend, despite the generation gap, by Madeleine
Sophie Barat) opened to one another. Maria wrote:

> Mother Digby allowed me to raise the veil of her heart and showed me a
> religious affection which has been one of the greatest graces and sweetest joys
> of my life. God inspired her with a sympathetic love for me which she later
> defined as the perfect kind of love, for, as she said, "in this love there is no
> selfishness." We had permission to talk together and to help each other, and
> we made our holy hours together. [67]

After these silent vigils together they would ask each other:
"Watchman, what of the night?" When Mabel was made superior
Maria promised: "You can count on me for life and for death. I will
be your Cyrenian to help you carry the cross our Lord has laid upon
you." Mother Digby called her "Simon" after that. Maria was an
unquenchable flame, kindling in others love of prayer and of the
Rule; she composed the Novena of Confidence. Mother Digby, as

superior general, always stopped at Chambéry on her way to Rome
to see her friend. When Maria was near death in 1900 Mother
Digby used her full authority:

> Dear, dear Mother, through obedience ask our Mother Barat, who loved you
> so much and took such care of you, to obtain your cure and give you ten more
> years of life, which means ten more years of exile, of suffering, of work for the
> glory of the divine Heart. [68]

Maria obeyed; she died ten years later to the day.

Mother Stuart had a genius for making friends, and both gave
and took from others in "those rare and perfect friendships"
sanctioned by obedience (she was firm on this point) described in
The Society of the Sacred Heart. In the noviceship she exchanged
meditation-thoughts with a fellow novice, which led to a life-long
correspondence. As superior she formed an intimate bond with her
young secretary, Violet Ashton Case, [69] "one of the most beautiful
things God ever made," whom she prepared for an early death.
When elected superior general she jotted in her retreat notes: "Pray
for me, Violet." She knew that:

> We must always be more or less lonely, but sometimes it is given to spirit to
> understand spirit . . . . Then we understand and are understood . . . . Complete
> trust, in which nothing else matters, is the only thing worth calling friendship. [70]

* * *

A salient characteristic of the Society's internationality was ac-
cented by the closing of the French houses: mutual enrichment by a
mingling of cultures. This followed from the sudden large-scale diffusion of personnel and the number of new lands entered. Mother
Digby had literally to re-organize the Society on a world-wide scale.
She wrote in the teeth of dispersal:

> The Society forms one body made up of many families and members; one soul
> must animate it, as the Rule says; one spirit must reign in it despite the diver-
> sities of language and of character among its members. These diversities, far
> from being harmful, add to our religious life a richness, a breadth which we
> must singularly value. The living sap of the Society is too powerful to be held
> in by any frontiers whatsoever; it rises from one spring, from one centre, but it
> flows through every channel, giving vigorous life to its branches in all the
> countries of the world to which we are called. Our dearest duty is to keep this
> breadth, this markedly catholic spirit . . . .

> Let us value the good that is done, the way of thought beyond our im-
> mediate horizon; let us delight in the moral and spiritual beauties found afar.
> Let us believe that God has created on earth a kingdom too universal for one
> continent or race to claim all his gifts as its own .... But all the gifts that he
> pours out so abundantly are for us: beauties of nature and of intelligence, the
> varied gifts of the mind; a richness of native speech marked by these talents;
> treasures of history in which divine Providence is revealed; all is ours for our
> instruction and development. [71]

And so chapel furnishings from France appeared all over the globe
in new sanctuaries. Mother Digby appointed many vicars to countries not their own, and had a way of swinging superiors (without
warning) from land to land, with resulting language problems! As
Mother Stuart wrote:

> The cramping, narrowing, chilling influence of national spirit would be par-
> ticularly out of place in an Institute in which the end and the object are one, the
> nationalities many and changes frequent .... It certainly gives finish to
> religious training to be able to blend freely with those of any other nation ....
> The mingling of nationalities – there have been as many as twelve or more in
> one noviciate – tends to bring out the best in each, to make for mutual un-
> derstanding, for seeing the good in all, for tact, for right reticence. [72]

One effect of the expulsions from France was felt for the next
fifty years: the presence in almost every house of at least one "ma
mère." These gave a dash of *sel gaulois* to the international flavour
of the schools. They brought an "old world" outlook to many young
worlds, at the price of costly adjustments on their part. They
brought a sense of the origins, as seen in the Society's most
tenaciously loyal members. They were an educational asset: native
speakers of the language in honour at the *Sacré Coeur*. The children
used and abused them, teased and loved them. They were not expected to be fluent in their new tongue, hence tragi-comedies. Most of
them died, cherished, on the outposts; then there were no more
"French wars" in the dining rooms where classes had gallantly com-
peted!

At the turn of the century the atmosphere was restive throughout
the world, after the complacencies of the "Victorian Age." Communication was speeded; the telephone, the automobile, and at last
the airplane were dubious novelties. In the uneasy international relations a series of Concordats gave fresh influence to the Papacy. An
astonishing number of houses of the Sacred Heart appeared; for
almost each one closed in France another was opened, not only just

over the border but around the globe. Many of the European houses founded as refuges proved to be temporary, but some took root.

In 1909 the houses in Brussels were formed into a small vicariate of the Mother House. Elsewhere in Belgium four lasting foundations were made in 1904 by Betzy Nieuwland [73] who had the gift of creating stability in the midst of movement (it was said that wherever she appeared "il faisait clair"). These were: La Ramée at Jauchelette, where a free school was opened in an old Cistercian monastery; Lindhout near Brussels which welcomed the exiled boarding school from Lille; Ostende, where *grandes pensionnaires* enjoyed the sea air; and Antwerp where a proposed training college failed at the outset and was replaced by a school. When the war over-ran Belgium many communities were sheltered in England and Holland until they could return, bringing the necessaries of life with them, to their battered homeland.

In England Mother Stuart, as vicar, opened Bonchurch on the Isle of Wight for *grandes pensionnaires* on a bluff overlooking the sea (1904), and Newcastle near the Scottish border where a training college together with boarding and free schools was established (1904). The training college at Wandsworth in London was transferred to Saint Charles Square, leaving the school at West Hill (1905). An interesting experiment was made at Blackheath, a "horrid suburb" of London (1905). It was intended for the formation of pupil-teachers but, say the records, "the Catholic population was not sufficient to support our work, and after two years our Mothers thought it wiser not to renew the lease." The number of small houses opened as refuges was such that a second English vicariate was created, centered at Hammersmith under the government of Philomena Blount, [74] whose large heart opened easily to the distress of the times. This ceased to exist after 1911 when Rose Thunder[75] became vicar at Roehampton. A person of vigour and humour, she launched new apostolic projects.

Marie de Loë, vicar of Italy, made five foundations. The first was at Venice (1896) at the invitation of the Patriarch, Cardinal Sarto, the future Pius X. Naples followed (1899); here there was great need for catechetics among the children of the streets as well as for a boarding school. A small school was opened in the mountainous farmlands of Peschiera near Bergamo (1901); here a young priest named Angelo Roncalli, the future John XXIII, was a frequent visitor. Albano (1903) near the lake of that name in the

Roman countryside was a summer home for the novices of the Villa
Lante; at other seasons a small community worked for the country
people. The Society then entered Sicily with a school overlooking
the harbour at Palermo (1904). In northern Italy there were many
refuges opened, notably Rivoli for the noviceship and juniorate of
France, and from 1907 to 1915 a second Italian vicariate was formed under Caroline Lavialle [76] who governed strictly "in rectitude
and faith."

Marie de Cléry, [77] formed by Madeleine Sophie herself, went to
Spain as vicar in 1897. She opened Godella primarily for village
children (1898); she carried the Society into the Spanish Islands,
founding Palma de Mallorca (1902) and Las Palmas in the
Canaries (1903). San Sebastian (1903) was at first a French school
but soon became Spanish. It was followed by a school on a richly
historic site near Grenada (1905). From 1904 on there were two
Spanish vicariates, under Manuela Vicente (1906) in Sarria and
Carmen Modet [78] in Seville. The latter, called to govern in troubled
times, was gifted with "serene and balanced virtue, founded on
dependence on the Holy Spirit."

Holland became an autonomous vicariate in 1904 under Anna
Bogaers, [79] strong in promoting both studies and social works, who
opened a free school in the Hague, to the surprise of its very Protestant neighbors. A house in Nimegen, begun as a refuge (1903), was
transferred ten years later to Arnhem where the school could grow
more freely. A second house in Poland was opened at Zbilitowska-
Gora (1901) by Marie Anne Schaffgotch, [80] vicar of Austria; she
said of this beautiful property patronized by the Emperor: "For love
of this foundation we must live as do the very poor." She was a
powerful personality, rich in complex contrasts and typical of the
internationalism of this time of rapid turn-over. She, a German,
worked as superior in France, Austria, Hungary, Belgium, Spain,
Holland and her own land with incredible energy and a clarity of
vision that gave her the name of "the Eagle." She said: "The more
we are tossed about to right and to left by the Society, the more we
love her."

Dependent upon Europe but exotically apart were the houses
founded along the southern shore of the Mediterranean. Mustapha
in Algeria, begun by Mother Barat in 1842, had gone on bravely
alone despite grasshoppers and plague. When foundations were
made in Malta and in Cairo in 1903 they formed, together with

Mustapha, a tiny vicariate where sharply clashing cultures met. But by 1909 the French laws reached into Algeria; each religious found at her place in the chapel a note reading: "The Sacred Heart is waiting for you in . . . ." The house furnishings were sent to Malta.

This new vicariate was under the direction of Helen Rumbold. [81] As a child Helen Hopewell was a staunch little Anglican, who, in adventuresome secrecy, was won to the Catholic Church at a school in Belgium. At her confirmation Cardinal Manning said: "Be free as the air and as strong as a rock." She married brilliantly; as wife of the governor of Saint Thomas Island Lady Rumbold travelled and entertained on a lavish scale. The sudden death of her husband and then of her little son changed her life; after a retreat at Roehampton she entered the Society, a fellow-novice of Janet Stuart. Experience of people, originality, unswerving directness in the service of "the dear Lord," served her well as superior and mistress of novices. In August, 1903, she became a missionary in one of the most Catholic countries in the world, and then in one where the cross faced the crescent.

In tiny Malta, where history is cut into every stone, the faith of Saint Paul was lived in the picturesque medieval forms of the Knights of Malta, coloured by folkways. The poorest could lead clean, bright lives. Mother Rumbold began in small Villa Portelli but soon a new convent in Saint Julian's, built of the honey-coloured stone of the country, rose over the harbour. Mother Stuart visited Malta and wrote: "All is simplicity, spontaneity and breezes." The nuns worked to give stamina to the warm, gay piety of the children.

In the meantime Mother Rumbold was raising another school, built of desert-gold brick, in the crowded streets of Cairo, where the community was French-speaking. Among the mosque turrets on all sides were the domes of Christian churches of many rites, Orthodox and Uniate. A country-house was opened on the seacoast near Alexandria (1908), and a house with Moorish lines was built in Heliopolis (1911), "City of the Sun," where once the phoenix had undergone his fiery resurrection every five hundred years. A modern town had risen on the sands covering the temples.

Hélène de Chamerlat [82] was superior at Heliopolis and courageously faced the question of adaptation to non-Christian religions. At first only Christian children were accepted in Cairo. At Heliopolis this rule aroused the Muslim officials who were benefactors of the new school. At a state banquet Sedky Pacha declared:

"Egypt offers hospitality to French religious and they refuse our daughters." By a special Decree of Propaganda Fidei the Society was given permission to admit Muslim and Jewish children, and Sedky Pacha's daughters were enrolled. After a few years Jewish pupils were no longer admitted, as their adaptation to this mixed environment proved too difficult, but the Muslims came in ever greater numbers.

Mother de Chamerlat followed advice: "The time has come to penetrate the world of the crescent. Do not count on conversions but put the leaven in the dough; conversions will come in a hundred years." Unknown to the religious, Charles de Foucauld was then in the neighboring desert, simply to radiate the presence of Christ. So little Muslims became children of the Sacred Heart. They felt the radiation of his love as they learned to bridge the abyss between rich and poor, to raise the level of woman. Mother Stuart began her last journey at Cairo, and said: "The remembrance of Egypt is like a great pageant in my memory, full of consolation on the spiritual side, and a pageant of the ages on the historical side of one's mind."

North America was in the grip of "the big boom" in business, when the first Federations of Labor faced the Corporations and the menace of plutocracy. The agitation of "rights for women" became articulate, making high demands upon education. Yet only three new houses of the Sacred Heart were opened, all in beautiful sites near the Pacific Ocean. Menlo Park (1898) was built in Spanish style in a year-round garden. Forest Ridge in Seattle (1907) and Point Grey in British Columbia (1911) looked upon mountain peaks surrounding a harbour. All three had large parish schools in addition to academies. Menlo Park was all but destroyed by the earthquake of 1906 but was promptly rebuilt, while the house in San Francisco was transferred from Franklin Street to Jackson Street. Because of shifting urban populations other city houses were also transferred; in New York the house on Seventeenth Street moved to Maplehurst, while in Chicago that on North State Street settled on Pine Grove Avenue.

Unity between the vicariates of the United States and of Canada was strengthened by an interchange of vicars. Outstanding among these were Mary Moran, [83] a humorous and far-seeing woman who did much for higher education, and Mary Burke [84] who had a magnetic influence from Saint Louis to the west coast. Both were Irish. Victorine Cooreman, [85] a Belgian, brought her widely varied culture to already cosmopolitan Louisiana. Charlotte Lewis,[86] a strong-principled American, served in many houses in the New York, Canadian and Chicago vicariates. In 1901 the Missouri houses were once more joined to those in Louisiana, while the Chicago vicariate reached westward. Following Mother Digby's visit in 1899 all the noviceships in North America, including the Antilles and Mexico, were merged in the West Wing of Kenwood, Albany, where a common formation made for friendships and unity of outlook throughout a continent.

During the Spanish-American war the houses in the Antilles endured bombardment and isolation while sheltering refugees. Puerto Rico was ceded to the United States; the government forced the house at Santurce to move to a new site at San José. Due to political unrest this house was dependent on the New York vicariate from 1904 to 1911. Cuba became an independent state after the war, and in 1911 the Cuban and Puerto Rican houses were formed into the Vicariate of the Antilles under the government of Hedwige de Cauna.[87] She was French but had spent her religious life in Latin America, described as "very straight and very supernatural." She opened a school at Santiago de Cuba (1911) where catechetical work took on vast proportions. All the houses of the Antilles had vigorous social apostolates.

When Jeanne de Lavigerie was called to the Mother House in 1904 her place as vicar in Mexico was taken by Sophie Lalande. [88] They were old friends, as Sophie had been bridesmaid at Jeanne's wedding. She was fore-armed for trial; her house at Marmoutier had just been taken by the French government and she lived by her probation motto: "I know in whom I have believed."

Her first six years in Mexico were hopeful; under Porforio Diaz the laws against religious schools were not enforced. Mother Lalande learned Spanish quickly, spurred on the Children of Mary, and opened a new house at Monterrey (1908). The building had been an undertaker's establishment; it was emptied of coffins as the living children moved in. A larger house was built, and the bishop, whose opinions she had opposed, said: "She may stand against us all, but she is always inspired by the Holy Spirit." With the withdrawal of the houses in the Antilles Mexico became an autonomous vicariate in 1911.

Diaz resigned in that year, and an anti-clerical revolution raged until 1916; when General Obregon appeared in Guadalajara on

July 9, 1914, the Sacred Heart school was seized and the nuns scattered with their bundles. Sixty gypsy-like figures managed to get onto a packed Chinese boat which ran short of drinking water before bringing them to San Francisco after two months of wandering. On Christmas morning, 1915, the house at Guanajuato was likewise seized, and the nuns made their way in small groups to Louisiana. This house was never recovered, whereas Guadalajara was re-opened in 1923. The other Mexican houses carried on, and eventually the exiles returned to their own country. Mother Lalande stayed in Mexico City, fearless in her faith in God and in the Mexican people.

How was it that the nuns in Mexico were allowed to face prison and gun fire, and keep on with their dangerous mission, while those in France were withdrawn before purely legal measures? Who showed the greater heroism, those who left home without fanfare or those who risked their lives to stay home? At the time no-one questioned Mother Digby's drastic measures in France, but with hindsight they have been questioned. Did she choose (as has been said simplistically) to leave France rather than leave the religious habit? She was well aware (as was Mother Stuart) that the nuns in Mexico put on worldly dress of unworldly style whenever expedient. Situations can only be judged in their context: "secularization" had different meanings in the two countries. Witness to religious life can be given in apparently contradictory ways.

The leading figure in South America's intercultural adventures at this time was Mary Jackson. [89] Of an Anglican family, she was suddenly converted to Catholicism as she impulsively knelt down in the mud at a procession of the Blessed Sacrament. She entered at Roehampton, and Mother Digby formed the ungainly, jovial, downright novice for a mission that would turn on a fulcrum of prayer through a world-arc. "You ground me to powder!" was Mary's expression of gratitude. She sailed with the foundresses for Australia, and was handyman of all crafts at Rose Bay until she became superior at Melbourne. In 1902 a telegram said: "Send Jackson to Paris." When she reached the Mother House Mother Digby met her with: "You are vicar of Chile-Peru-Argentina."

Stopping in Mexico to pick up some Spanish, she reached Santiago and a life made up of the unexpected. Her travels could be measured in round-the-world mileage: back and forth over the Andes, up and down the Atlantic and Pacific coasts, by train, cart, mule-back and shoe-leather. Once her mule refused to let her mount. "Get on from behind," said her guide, "so that he won't see your proportions." The device worked. Six times she went by steamer to Paris, and stopped at Roehampton, begging missionaries. Once, when given an organ, she claimed — and got — an organist. "I'm not at all like you English," she said. She had become meridional in thought and feeling; she changed her name to Maria and greeted all alike with a Latin embrace.

Mother Jackson's first center was Santiago in Chile. The house at Talca burned down in 1907 and was not reopened for fifty years; that in Chillan was closed in 1908. In Peru, Chorillos, a vacation house that later developed into a school, was founded (1903) as well as a city house in Lima, on the Calle Leon de Andrade (1909). In the meantime the vast land of Brazil was opened to the Society, which took up a new language, Portuguese. The arrival in Tijuca was enlived by a revolution. The house was on a hillside overlooking Rio de Janeiro with its magnificent harbour. Here the community was made up of nuns shaken loose from France and the classes were in French (as in many schools founded at this time).

Then Mother Jackson crossed still another frontier into the tiny country of Uruguay, and opened a school at Montevideo (1908). It struggled through an early threat of suppression by the government, and drew the children of anti-clerical families back to the sacraments. The Children of Mary were recruited from the same hostile setting, and took up the Church's work of evangelization in a land of few priests.

This move caused the creation of a new vicariate; Argentina separated from Chile and Peru to join Brazil and Uruguay. From then on Mother Jackson circled through three countries from her new centre in Rio de Janeiro. Her place in Chile was taken by Isabel Batista,[90] a Cuban with wide Latin American experience. A day school was then opened in Rio de Janeiro (1909). It overlooked not only the harbour but "a square where all the tramways cross," a significant thrust into urban life. All along the eastern coast there were too few priests and teaching nuns, while the people were either over-pious with little doctrinal foundation or ignorant of the Christian life altogether. The results were indifference or fanatical opposition to the Church, so the Society took up catechetical work on all levels of the population, stimulated by Mother Jackson until her death in 1926.

The north shore of South America was now calling. In 1907 an international group sailed up the moody Magdalena River to Bogota on the high plateau of Colombia, which boasted of being "the most Catholic State." The superior, Guadalupe Bofarrul, [91] was a Spaniard, firm where tradition was at stake yet quick to seize and adapt to new situations. The community met with a dazzling reception by President Reyes, but when he offered them the elegantly situated house of San Diego an uproar rose in the city: "These are not the Sisters of the Poor but of the Rich." The foundation was blocked for months by popular distrust. When opened it housed a school for the poor as well as the rich, and the Beatification of Madeleine Sophie Barat was celebrated by a *fiesta* given by the newest children of the Sacred Heart to a destitute orphanage. The difficulty lay in forming "model pupils" out of volatile, spoiled children. The mistress general, Maude Dunn, [92] succeeded; in a short time the alumnae of Bogota were leaders of apostolic enterprises throughout the city. This house, too remote to join a South American vicariate, was dependent on the Mother House.

On the other side of the globe an enormous network was forming under the energetic government of Amélie Salmon who began her forty-two year period as vicar of Australia-New Zealand in 1895. She was small, strict, lovable and loving, with a dynamism drawn from prayer. In New Zealand the Society reached up from Timaru in South Island to two new houses in North Island, both on the mountainous shore-line: Island Bay in Wellington (1905) and Baradene in Auckland (1908). The magnificent, wind-blown outlook of both houses formed generations of virile pupils. In Australia a second house was opened on Sydney Harbour at Kincoppal (1903); this was the former home of the Hughes family who had first brought the Society to Australia. A short-lived foundation (1909–1911) was made at Springwood. The tradition of vigorous loyalty grew stronger with the development of these young nations under the Southern Cross.

Then suddenly the Australian vicariate expanded into the Australasian, and stretched from the southern hemisphere into the northern, when Madeleine Sophie's dream of going to the Orient came true in the year of her Beatification. Pius X had appealed to Mother Digby for a foundation in Japan. Mother Salmon with a small group from Australia reached Yokohama on January 1, 1908, and was met on the pier by her priest-brother

whom she had not seen for forty years: "C'est toi, Amélie!"
By cherry blossom time a small foreign school had begun at Azabu
in Tokyo, but in June the community moved into the former home
of a *Daimyo*, a feudal nobleman, on a wooded hill at Sankocho, on
the outskirts of the city. Here a modern building rose for the Japanese and foreign schools. There was no question of "Christians
only"; from the beginning Shinto and Buddhist children crowded
into *Seishin* (Sacred Heart). At first they came in rickshaws, clad in
bright kimonas; soon they came in automobiles, clad in trim navy
blue uniforms (laughed at as "potato-sacks" at home). Madame
Hirata, a Japanese Christian, was the official head-mistress, and the
school could proudly display its native culture to Mother Stuart
when she passed through Japan.

Mother Salmon had gone back to Australia, leaving Sankocho in
the hands of Brigid Heydon, [93] an Irishwoman with wide experience in developing the "popular works" which were the
Society's way of penetrating its milieux. Now her clear judgment
and practical talents, her warmth under reserve, were given for eight
years to adapting the Society to its oriental milieu. Distances were
great, and Mother Stuart said of her: "There were times when
Mother Heydon could consult no-one but God, but he made up by
blessing all that she did."

But Japan was rapidly becoming westernized, and the community was the most international in the Society, Australian-
English-Irish-French-German-American-Canadian. The children
were avid for English, and the missionaries saw no reason – at first
– to master Japanese. When postulants entered, it was they who
went on a "foreign mission" in a community of western life-style.
True intercultural exchange was slow in the beginnings.

*   *   *

A renaissance in Christian scholarship was felt at the turn of the
century; the Vatican archives were open to historians; Catholic universities were founded or re-vitalized; art and literature explored
religious themes. The General Councils held under Mother Digby
and Mother Stuart gave high priority to the Society's educational
mission, as though in response to this challenge. They turned to the
future, in marked contrast to the cautious stability of the preceding

Councils. The two superiors general, so different in their intellectual attitudes, complemented each other. Their common ground was a keen sense of the Society's responsibility to the Church and to civilization at a turning point in history; both insisted on the role of character development.

Mother Digby, despite the powerful intelligence and the resonant command of language shown in her circulars, did not have a "book-mind," and liked to quote her father's remark to her in childhood: "You have a head and so has a pin." She was not interested in art or letters for their own sakes. Mother Stuart wrote:

> She set no limits to the gift of self, and in that gift she saw as great a sacrifice as possible, and therefore to be made without hesitation or recall. It was the renunciation of all intellectual interests that were not directly connected with God. . . . She would never have cared for a long solitary walk or journey, but everything that turned up became living to her in the mind of some companion affected by the sight or the event. [94]

Yet Mother Digby recognized that: "It is ideas that move the world, and ideas acquire their power for action in the milieux where people think." This was her challenge to Sacred Heart schools. She interpreted current movements accurately and moved with them. She said:

> It is specifically for the work of education that we have been approved by the Church; we have to recall the words of the Brief of Leo XIII where he speaks of us as "a religious society devoted to bringing up in piety and in virtue the young people entrusted to its care." We have a grace above all for this work, and just as we find in the devotion stressed in our Constitutions the purest and strongest food for the spiritual life, so the work of education calls for all of our legitimate activity.
>
> Strong studies according to the spirit of our Plan; persevering work demanded of ourselves and of our children; a serious outlook which increases the powers of our mind; sure principles to guide the will and keep the heart for God; this is what is needed for the work of education. [95]

The General Council of 1904 encouraged the work of finishing schools for *grandes pensionnaires*. This had not been undertaken specifically in Saint Madeleine Sophie's time; Mother Goetz had seen it as a natural development called for by the changing times and it was now spreading in the Society. The General Council of

1910 concentrated on education. Mother Digby spoke of the effects of the expulsions from France:

> Driven from the country which was its cradle, which formed its foundress and its first educators and placed it so high in the esteem of those concerned with the education, is the mission of the Society lessened? No, in the eyes of Providence the dispersal of its two thousand five hundred teaching religious is, in the words of the Holy Father [Pius X] a diffusion of the Society in the hospitable countries which have welcomed it, an extension of the cultus of the Sacred Heart, of a deeper awareness of his adorable Person, and a strongly Christian education for a larger number of children. [96]

The Council recognized that the Plan of Studies must be revised by adaptation to different countries, and Mother Digby recalled the value of the traditions to be kept in this greater pluriformity:

> The diversity of languages and of needs makes this a necessity; a single Plan of Studies is not possible. In each country we must take into account the programs and requirements of the government and the desires of the parents who now often ask that their children take state examinations.
>
> Yet how regrettable it would be if the character proper to our education should be lost! What has secured its recognized superiority up to now is the primary end which it has proposed to itself from the beginning: to form for the Church and for the home women of solid faith and attractive virtue, whose good judgments and minds cultivated by all the learning fitted for their situation will give them a strong influence for good. If we wish to remain on this level we must hold strongly to the traditions to which we owe it, not be content with simply useful results but, above all, cultivate the faculties of the children, "bring them up" in the best sense of the term. At a time when the sciences have made such progress we must necessarily give them due importance while still placing upon our studies that literary stamp which is its distinguishing mark. [97]

A Memorial drawn up for this Council by Mother Stuart makes practical applications which, under their quiet tone, were a jolt to established practices:

> It does not seem useful to prescribe books of reference or text books for the classes, as the necessities of country, language and different types of school make uniformity practically impossible. Text books prepared by the religious for the exclusive use of our schools present grave disadvantages. Large quantities accumulate and must be sold, and a worse evil is the stereotyping of teaching for many years when modern discovery and criticism have reached far beyond it. [98]

Through meetings of mistresses general (1897) and mistresses of studies (1899) Mother Digby highlighted strength of character; children must be made independent, courageous and self-disciplined. The ultimate end was stressed: Christian education is to form good Christians:

> We must come back to the basic principle, to the moral side of education, and to that love of souls which must inspire all. For that, an inner life; everything depends upon prayer. The love of our Lord must animate all. "Give me a heart that loves and he will understand," said Saint Augustine. [99]

Her own words will give a reason for a stand that has been held against Mother Digby: her refusal to admit Jewish children to the schools:

> What we must always give is education; we cannot accept children for instruction only; hence we cannot take them without distinction of creed as in the public schools. We may not take Jews, for we must give Catholic education. We cannot dispense them from religious instruction, nor can we water it down to suit prejudice. [100]

It was Mother Stuart who sanctioned the measure adopted in Egypt.

The methods of the superior juniorate had fallen behind. Mother Digby sent for young Marguerite Lesage, [101] put her in a quiet room and gave her ten days in which to rethink the curriculum, "helped by the Holy Spirit alone." Marguerite was ready:

> She was a well-balanced person, gifted with a creative will at the service of an open mind, responsive to new ideas, able to discover them and to profit by suggestions, concerned above all with keeping the spirit of our Holy Mother. It was her task to adapt and to give fresh life to programs and methods, to renew the studies in the schools and the formation of the teachers, according to the Society's traditions. [102]

Mother Lesage was a natural philosopher, "Guardian of truth" was Mother Digby's name for her. For the juniorate she secured the best lecturers in the physical sciences when Mother Digby had supplied the equipment. She was named mistress of studies for the Society, but this office was soon seen as impracticable. Juniorates and councils of studies were set up in each vicariate.

During the expulsions from France the juniorate went first to

Cioché and then to Rivoli under the direction of Marie-Thérèse Duval, [103] famous for her model classes at Conflans, and then of Marguerite's sister, Marie Lesage, [104] who continued the work at Jette.

Mother Stuart had always taken to books with natural zest, aided by an artistic personality. As superior vicar she furthered Mother Digby's undertakings: "Everything says to us: 'Go on! Get in! Go ahead! Seize the land! Don't let the right moment pass!' " She had a keen interest in methods and systems as well as in fundamentals: "Education is the battlefield, not accidentally but essentially." As superior general her influence on the Society was all-pervasive: the self-education of each member through interest, observation, reading, mental discipline and above all personal thought was a life-long responsibility – inescapable. The influence of her ideas passed far beyond the Society through the writings which lived after her.

Mother Digby had died before the adaptation of the Plan of Studies by the General Council of 1910 could be carried out. Mother Stuart clarified the matter:

> Exterior uniformity is no longer possible in all countries, but that unity which is our strength must be kept with regard to the spirit, the principles and the basis of our education, with its religious, philosophical and literary character. Methods of education can and must be constantly bettered. We must take account of the tendencies of modern life which will meet our children when they leave school; we must arm them for a struggle to which they were not formerly exposed, and for this we must keep in the first place as a preparation for life that Sacred Heart education which is the great gift left to the Society by our Holy Mother. The task is not as simple as it was in the first years; we must work harder, think, judge, examine and foresee more than formerly. [105]

Mother Stuart's most direct contribution was her book *The Education of Catholic Girls* published in 1912. This work (fruit of her experiences and of her conferences) concerned the status of Catholic Schools in England at the time, and is in that sense, as it is also with regard to the level of intellectual attainment expected of women, outdated. But the chapters on the various disciplines deal with unchanging elements; those on character (even the one on manners) are timeless. Her most basic thoughts are found in the chapter "The Realities of Life," where this phrase "may stand for all those things which have to be learned in order to live and which lesson books do not teach."

In their travels each of these superiors general shaped the educational work of the Society.

> The visit of Reverend Mother Digby to America in 1898–1899 marked a turning point in the educational policy and program of the religious of the Sacred Heart in the United States. The textual notes of the conference with which she opened the council of studies at Manhattanville show how clearly she had grasped the situation confronting the religious. [106]

For this "still young country" she concluded: "We take the Plan of Studies for our foundation to give us lines and principles, but its elasticity allows it to adapt itself."

Mother Stuart's rapid passage through house after house spurred academic effort in each. It was a turning point for the college of San Pedro, and she afterwards sent an experienced educator from Wandsworth to guide it in a new direction. In Japan she visited the Women's University and several high schools. Dr Mikami the historian asked her to write her impressions, and so her last work, "How Japan Educates Women," appeared in *The Month* for July, 1914, on the theme: "A woman's influence lies at the centre of a nation's life and is the foundation of its strength."

*　　*　　*

The social awareness aroused by *Rerum Novarum* grew keener as the Church confronted the de-Christianization of the working-man's world. Tensions arose between authority and reformers; in France *Le Sillon* was condemned as "social Modernism." Agitation for social justice was widespread but is not traceable in the records of the Society of the Sacred Heart at this time. The failure at Blackheath was perhaps a sign that growth was needed before there could be real insertion into milieux "on the other side of the fence."

Mother Digby's energies were taken up with the anti-clericalism in France, Mother Stuart was concerned with the spiritual well-being of the religious, while both concentrated on the classroom as the chief means of social betterment — at long range. The spirit of cloister forbade the reading of periodicals, except for the mistress of studies who made "coupures" for the benefit of all; a safe distance from current events was inevitable. Yet both superiors general combated an ingrown spirit and urged that the separateness of a religious should make her sensitive to the needs of a larger world. Mother Digby said:

> As it is given to the pure in heart to see God in his creation, so it is given only to the humble and loving of heart to recognize the divine action in human events. [107]

Mother Stuart held that the "inward gaze" should be directed outwards by:

> That habit of attention which keeps our eyes open at all times upon the great resources of the universe where, under the most ordinary appearances, the signs of divine Providence hold instruction and an ever-fresh interest. [108]

In actual fact, concern with social problems took very concrete form in the foundations made at this time. Although the pattern of large houses in beautiful properties (not infrequently the gift of high-placed friends) persisted, and even affected the architecture of buildings in mission countries, many new beginnings took a humble form in simple surroundings. Very large free schools often preceded the select *pensionnats*, and there was an increase in *externats*. In the countries where poor schools had all but disappeared with universal education by the state, other forms of reaching those in need were found. There was a change in emphasis from "helping" to "developing" the poor; in Spain self-supporting *ouvroirs* were founded. Everywhere the traditional "popular works" were changing into well-organized associations such as clubs for business women that reached into the professional world. These groups had their own charitable endeavours, with lending libraries.

The pupils could now take part in missionary and catechetical projects, and even in social service, in a way impossible to the *demoiselles* of crinoline days who had been as much sheltered by cloister as the nuns. Mother Stuart wrote:

> They may acquire a little insight into social problems and the right service of the poor; their minds will be besieged by such questions as soon as they take up their life in the world, and no education is now complete without some preparation for these rapidly growing requirements. Every form of helpfulness which comes before them in school foreshadows claims which will be made upon them afterwards. The Church, the poor, the foreign missions, their own families, all have rights in their lives, and how to give their share of intelligent help, especially how to cooperate and subordinate personal views and gain an

understanding of the ideas of others, is a part of school-training that may not be neglected.[109]

The Children of Mary shared these responsibilities even more demandingly. City houses were sometimes opened expressly to give them a centre from which they could go out into the bleak environments created by industrialization.

The paternalistic attitude sensed (in retrospect) in the Society's earlier charitable work was beginning to fade out, although the "aristocratic" image persisted. The unfortunate name of "the Madames" dogged the steps of the religious who went into countries where it had opprobious connotations. The term was historically justifiable. "Les Dames" was used for "les religieuses" after the French revolution, and was hard to shake off. It enhanced the sense of superiority which had caused such distress to Mother Barat that she had often implored her religious never to speak of themselves or their works, or to make comparisons with other orders. Mother Stuart neatly warned against triumphalism when she said: "Remember that we belong to the Church Militant and don't put on the airs of the Church Triumphant."[110]

* * *

The spiritual atmosphere at the dawn of a new century was freshened. A broader outlook came with the intellectual vigour of Leo XIII and with the call to liturgical prayer of Pius X. Modernism as "the union of all heresies" was condemned, but the modernist attack alerted Catholics to renewal. Ecumenism stirred; reunion with Anglicanism was checked by *Ad Anglos*, but Father Paul Watson launched the Unity Octave. Maryknoll opened new roads to "The Field Afar," while Thérèse of Lisieux opened "the little way" in prayer. It was a hopeful time. "One has to be an optimist to enter into the best spiritual tendencies of our day," said Mother Stuart.

The long shadow of Jansenism paled in the light of the Decrees of Pius X on frequent communion (1905) and early communion for children (1910). Mother Stuart rejoiced:

These Decrees were indeed a new spring, and carried a resistless impulse of fresh vigour to the very soul and centre of religious life for communities of women; and, from the very first months, their influence could be almost measured in "quietness and confidence", in the disappearance of unrest and questionings; in a more perfect unity of spirit . . . . It is important to teach these recent Decrees of Pius X on frequent and daily communion and confession, and also to conform to his teaching and to that of Leo XIII by strengthening the study of Scripture.[111]

No longer was the Bible "to be kept from the hands of young religious." The Biblical Commission had published no less than ten Decrees on the right interpretation of Scripture. The Confraternity of Christian Doctrine was set up and Mother Stuart wrote:

> The teaching of Christian Doctrine was our first *raison d'être* in which our education had its origins, and in which it terminates both for our children and for ourselves. To proportion it to the needs of our times requires not only esteem and application, but love for the subject, to keep it on the one hand from becoming too abstract, as a body of dogma, and on the other from falling into a narrow pietism which is condemned by the Decrees as "an unwise or childish exaltation." The truest apology for faith in these days is an ardent hope, that hope which is the true antecedent of possession.[112]

In the training given in both noviceships and schools the positive rather than the negative note was touched. Discipline was not abandoned but was charged with healthy initiative. There was more room for each one to be a person. "Sister, drop Saint John Berchmans and be yourself," said Mother Stuart. She could show, by an almost imperceptible accent, that some time-honoured attitude was due for evolution. Humility, for example, practiced with such simplicity by Mother Barat, had later taken the form of sometimes spectacular self-abasement, edifying but uncomfortable for others. This had been expected not only of nuns but of school children, and Mother Stuart remarked:

> Humility is not a virtue for children. It is better to inspire them with a sense of their dignity rather than of their unworthiness. With them humility should take the form of frankness and love of truth; they must understand that they should never come down from the high thoughts of the children of God.[113]

Mother Digby said to a young nun who had just discovered that she was "a big sinner": "O no, just a little fool."

Mother Stuart's idea of keeping the Rule was "blending order with freedom." But lest freedom should end by destroying order there was a counterweight in "strict observance." This phrase was popularized by Mother Rumbold when she was superior at Mount Anville:

Her first word had been a call to a very regular life, to the cultus of traditions and of the primitive spirit. She was understood, and it was agreed that Mount Anville would be a house of "Strict Observance." This label, offered with the teasing tone familiar to Mother Rumbold when trying to soften the asperity of some remark, roused genuine enthusiasm. The two words recurred so often that they were called simply by their initials, "S. O." [114]

This cheerful slogan in the cause of exact fidelity spread afar. Novenas of "S. O." were found stimulating. Mother de Lavigerie made Guadalajara "a house of Strict Observance." Be it added that Mother Stuart herself practiced S. O. easily, pleasantly — and always.

Lively discussion was going on among theologians concerning the psychological aspects of devotion to the Sacred Heart, and the relation between the divine and human love in Christ. A synthesis was reached: "The love which Christ has for us in his human nature should be called "theandric rather than human; it is the love of God in the nature that he has taken to himself." It follows that: "There is perhaps no devotion which has so profound and immediate an effect upon the spiritual life." Mother Digby asked: "Who should better understand the fire of this love than those whose whole life is devoted to the study of the divine Heart as it has been revealed through the ages?" Mother Stuart, a born reader of character, saw what devotion to the Sacred Heart could do for the human personality:

It is not to be wondered at that the devotion to the Sacred Heart produces in its disciples a maturity, a spiritual virility of mind and heart difficult for some within the Church to understand and inexplicable to those without. For it presupposes an advanced religious sense which is nothing else than a divinely implanted instinct for the realities of life, and a calm unsusceptibility towards the false realities which are ever being taken for the true . . . . The lover of the Sacred Heart knows that he has not yet believed until he has said his Credo in the midst of doubts, or hoped until he has hoped against all hope when all seemed lost, or loved until he has given all the substance of his house and counted it nothing, or served until he has served in the midst of overwhelming difficulties, or sung to God until he has sung in the night. [115]

Chapter 6

Expansion
1915 – 1946

Never try to suppress the Spirit
or treat the gift of prophecy with
contempt; think before you do anything;
hold on to what is good and
avoid every form of evil.

I Thess. 5:19–20

The life of the Society of the Sacred Heart from 1915 to 1946 is
marked by an expansion of its mission in the face of disturbing
ideologies with the sobriety of Saint Paul's warning to the
Thessalonians.

The period began and ended with a shock to complacency, a
world war, while the League of Nations moved towards the United
Nations in the teeth of revolutions and declarations of independence. Communism and Fascism, already in the atmosphere, took
corporate form in conflicting governments while science speeded
their action; the atom was split in 1918 – with no noise. Pius XI
met these ideologies head on. His action was Catholic Action for
"the peace of Christ in the kingdom of Christ," and he signed the
Lateran Accord. There was no longer an Old World and a New
World, only a globe on which international affairs were becoming
inter-racial.

A teaching order already circling the globe was called upon to
penetrate these shifting, clashing and ambiguous forces. The Society
of the Sacred Heart reached into all the continents, took on new enterprises and entered new fields of education. It expanded while
remaining on the defensive, determined to "hold on to what is
good" in the face of values still uncertain. It met new demands with

"necessary concessions," and the resulting tensions have led to the traumas of today.

Statistics show an imbalance which increased the tensions – and the overwork. The number of schools rose considerably; the enrolments rose enormously while the number of workers rose hardly at all. In 1915 there were 6444 religious in 141 houses in 20 vicariates, while in 1946 there were 6570 religious in 179 houses in 22 vicariates. A lessening in vocations was accompanied by a rise in the age level of the total membership which thus remained almost constant. It was not easy to keep stability while being pulled towards a renewal that could not then be foreseen. Two superiors general guided the Society with surprising smoothness through troubled waters, Marie de Loë (1915–1928) and Manuela Vicente (1928–1946). Despite temperamental differences these two were strikingly similar in outlook; they wanted expansion with no explosion. Under their leadership the Society responded to a very exhilarating form of expansion in the spiritual realm: the Church's increased consciousness of herself as the Mystical Body of Christ whose Heart is the heart of mankind.

*   *   *

Maria von Loë [1] (who in the Society used the French form of her name) was born at Geldern, Germany, on December 9, 1857. (Mother Stuart whom she succeeded was born in that same year.) Her home was typical of the old-time German nobility, with its cultured, chivalric *noblesse oblige*. At the age of three she lost her mother and the Baron von Loë married again. By a misunderstanding the child's sensitive heart closed and she was sent to the Sacred Heart school at Marienthal. She returned home at thirteen, happy and accepted as the centre of the château at Longenburg on the Rhine, and when her step-mother died she mothered her little sisters and brother. When her father married for the third time she went back to school, not at Marienthal, closed by the German government, but at Blumenthal over the Dutch frontier.

Despite her reserve Maria was a natural leader, and the school felt the power of this tall, beautiful girl so serenely balanced, so practical and unselfish. She found her vocation during a pilgrimage to Lourdes and entered at Jette. After her first vows she taught the older children with verve and charm. She was professed at the

Mother House on the day of Mother Lehon's Golden Jubilee, August 25, 1883.

"God made her and brought her into the world to be mistress of novices," declared Mother Désoudin, and Maria returned to Jette to form the white veils, among whom were two of her own sisters. Then and throughout her life, there was something about her that made one think of our Lady, a marian loveliness in person and in manner, a simple, dignified serenity. Others found her "radiant." Her own lucid prayer expressed itself in guiding others.

In May, 1887, Mother de Loë went to Rome where she was to spend the rest of her life. As mistress general she transformed a turbulent school by vigorous old-time methods. In 1891 she crossed the Tiber to the Villa Lante, once more mistress of novices and then superior of the rambling stone palace on the Janiculum. Mother Digby named her vicar of Italy, saying: "The gifts of God have been heaped upon her and she doesn't seem to know it." Soon she was a familiar figure at the Vatican, esteemed by Leo XIII and Pius X, expert at dealing with cardinals and the slow-moving Roman machinery. Each winter she welcomed Mother Digby to the Villa Lante, and in 1908 she was hostess at the Beatification of Madeleine Sophie Barat.

A spiritual intimacy formed between Mother de Loë and Mother Stuart when the latter came to Rome. Pius X said to her at an audience: "Do you know that you have at the Villa Lante a head that could govern three Societies of the Sacred Heart?" When Mother Stuart died a telegram summoned Mother de Loë to Brussels. Thanks to her German passport she got through the firing lines, feeling "like an ant waiting for a mountain to be laid on it." Mother de Montalembert met her at Blumenthal with the dreaded words: "You are vicar general." The Belgian frontier was closed but the unquenchable Mother de Montalembert said to an unknown officer: "I am sure that somewhere you have a mother who is praying for you. For her sake get us a car." He did so, and Mother de Loë brought comfort to the desolate community at the Mother House, and found strength at the shrine of Madeleine Sophie.

The war was spreading. The General Council could not meet in Belgium, so Mother de Loë with Mothers de Lavigerie and Montalembert got back into Holland in a train full of soldiers, leaving Mother Borget to care for Mother Nerincx, too ill to move. Blumenthal, packed with refugees, became the momentary Mother

House. Christmas came, and Mother de Loë heard the carols in her own tongue for the first time in twenty-six years. In this anguishing isolation the Protector of the Society, Cardinal Angelo di Pietri, died. But as she said to the besieged community; "I am not alone, for he that sent me is with me."

Then Holland too was cut off, and Mother de Loë daringly called all the councillors to Rome. By confused and dangerous routes they all got there, even Mother Borget whom no official could resist. On February 22, 1915, the Eighteenth General Council, with members from all the belligerent countries, rose above national feeling and elected Maria von Loë as seventh superior general of the Society of the Sacred Heart.

The Council, which met from February 18 to March 1, 1915, passed a decree (proposed by Mother Borget) that holy communion should be offered every First Saturday for an effective knowledge and practice of poverty in the Society. Faced with the uncertainties of a world at war it returned to the tone of "consolidation": "Let us put in practice the resources of our Institute," for "uniformity maintains unity; we have been formed to this and we must so remain."[2] One decision could only be carried out gradually, the return to France where the government now had other things to think about. Mother de Loë wrote:

> Upon the advice of several French bishops and friends we are now trying to go back into the homeland of our Mother Foundress, not as a teaching order (which would still be impossible) but to take up other works of zeal and to help our Children of Mary .... It is understood that we shall not give up any aspect of our religious life, including the habit. [3]

The councillors went home over battle-fields and mine-strewn oceans, leaving Mother de Loë cut off from most of her houses. She learned that the nuns in the Russian zone had been driven from their homes. "What a moment!" she exclaimed. "Tribulations are such, Lord, that you alone can save me from sinking." In her youth she had made a vow of abandonment to the divine action:

> It is my way more than ever, with all that I now understand of interior solitude, loneliness of heart, and obligations beyond my strength, but also of confidence in which the present difficulties have rootedness. [4]

She looked to the Vatican, visible from the hill above the Villa Lante, and the new pope, Benedict XV, gave the Society his secretary of state, Rafael Merry del Val, [5] as Cardinal Protector. She called all the probanists who could do so to come to Rome, under the guidance of Marie Guibert [6] who had "the gift of penetrating the most diverse mentalities." The novices were sent to Albano.

The Bolshevik Revolution then shook the world, while Italy and America joined the war. Foreign religious were interned but Mother de Loë was spared, due to Vatican intervention. She wrote to the Society:

> Through these grave events our Lord has checked our work with his powerful hand . . . . Happy the religious who can enter fully into the crucifying ways of the divine Master, who centres all her desires on the one thing necessary with a firm resolution to advance greatly in the work of sanctification. Happy is she who believes firmly in the love of her God and sees his Heart through the veils of pain, of uncertainty, of restrictions . . . . The more the war brings about division and hatred the more our charity must become a counterbalance in the divine scales. [7]

The armistice came on November 11, 1918, and while the victors met at Versailles Mother de Loë contacted the whole Society: "The rainbow has risen on our horizon still heavy with clouds, and a new era in history is beginning." The probanists who came to the Villa Lante in 1919 became "the Probation of the Cross," for a contagious disease contracted while crossing the battle sites attacked nearly all, and two died.

With the coming of peace it was seen that Providence had solved the thorny "Roman question" that had vexed the Society since 1833; should not the Mother House of an exempt, world-wide congregation be in the centre of the Church? After the crisis of 1839 it had been ruled that the Mother House should remain in Paris. Mothers Goetz and Lehon had avoided the matter, while Mother Digby had seen the Mother House forcibly uprooted. Then war had shaken it loose and it had fallen like ripe fruit into Rome. The Council of 1915 recognized God's action, and when the Society began its return into France the Mother House stayed where it was. Mother de Loë said:

> I had always loved the Society ardently, but I had not prayed that its centre would be in Rome until, when I became vicar, I saw how advantageous this would be and how much the Vicar of Christ wanted it . . . . After 1915 the will of God seemed to me manifest . . . . I was sure that the Society would

welcome this, but I had not expected the joy and enthusiasm with which the decision was received. [8]

Benedict XV said to the probanists: "You are truly catholic and that is why your Mother House should be in Rome."

In February, 1920, the Society took possession of the Villa Mirafiore on the Via Nomentana, a former home of Victor Emmanuel II which had been a hospital during the war. Its shabby splendour was renovated and simpler wings added. On October 6 the cornerstone of the chapel was blessed, and Mother de Loë recalled the words of Madeleine Sophie Barat at the Paris Mother House in 1857:

> It is a great thing to lay the cornerstone of a religious house and above all of a Mother House. The walls which will rise separating you from the world must recall another building raised upon the chief cornerstone, Jesus Christ. Here will be your first mothers, those who possess most perfectly the spirit of the Society and who perpetuate it by the formation of members able to carry on the work which our Lord in his infinite mercy has entrusted to us. The universe is calling. [9]

Mother de Loë felt that her mission was to answer this call by rooting the Society in the heart of christendom.

Benedict XV died on February 22, 1922, and Mother de Loë said: "His countless works of charity for the children of all nations have preceded him, and to him the sovereign Judge can indeed say 'I was hungry and you gave me to eat'." Pius XI then took on his square shoulders the weight of the kingdom of God on earth. His pontificate opened with a Eucharistic Congress in Rome which filled the Vatican and the Mother House with pilgrims. Mussolini's march on Rome turned Italy into a Fascist state, while Stalin became dictator of a Communist state. Three strong men were facing each other.

In this stirring atmosphere Mother de Loë called the Nineteenth General Council which met from October 16 to November 20, 1922. [10] It examined the Constitutions in the light of the new code of Canon Law drawn up in the time of Pius X and promulgated in 1917. The needed changes were slight; among them were: the postulantship was to be of six months instead of three, superiors were not to remain in office in the same house for more than six years. The Council then considered the efforts made throughout the

Society to meet the call for the higher education of women. At its close Mother de Loë wrote:

> We have sought for ways of keeping the spirit of our Mother Foundress and the characteristic imprint given to her work, despite the concessions necessarily made in different places either to the climate and the mentality of the country or to scholastic demands, or to the new forms of apostolate that local needs require of our zeal. [11]

After the Council central noviceships for the coadjutrix sisters were established in each country: hitherto their formation had been given in many different houses.

From 1920 to 1923 Poitiers was the scene of remarkable events of which the Society at first knew nothing. A Spanish postulant named Josefa Menendez [12] arrived from Madrid on February 4, 1920. She was a simple, ardent little person who had supported her family by dressmaking. Despite her tenacious love for what was most ordinary in religious life she was drawn into extraordinary communications with our Lord who appeared to her almost daily. "From time to time I thirst to make heard a new call to love," he said. She wrote down each word of a gradually unfolded message entrusted through her to the Society and to the world. Marie-Thérèse de Lescure, her superior, summed it up in three words: reparation, confidence, love. It called for a "Work of Love," a conscious and active sharing in the redemptive mission of Christ. It was to be: "A new light thrown in our time upon the unfathomable riches of the Heart of Christ." Madeleine Sophie Barat, who also was seen by Josefa in the corridors of Poitiers that she had known so well, said:

> I only want to tell you that all during my life I sought nothing but the glory of the divine Heart, and now that I live in him and by him my only desire is to see his kingdom come. [13]

Mother de Lescure brought Josefa to the Mother House during the superiors' retreat in October, 1923. Mother de Loë and Mother Vicente, the Spanish assistant general, were sympathetic and strengthened the visionary in this crucifying vocation-within-a-vocation. Josefa was professed shortly before her death and Mother de Loë wrote:

A favour has been granted to the Society through the extraordinary graces given to the humble Spanish coadjutrix sister, Josefa Menendez, who died in the odour of sanctity at Poitiers on December 29, 1923. The favours that she received (concerning which we kept silence while she was living) as also the instructions which our Lord gave through her to religious souls and especially to those of our Society, are now the object of minute examination by competent authority. When we have received ecclesiastical approbation we shall make known to you the mercies of the divine Master, and the encouragement that he has given to this little Society of his Heart. [14]

Mother de Loë did not visit distant countries. She said: "Decidedly, it is not my mission to travel; I can form better contacts with my daughters by the pen and by prayer, and by the affection that I have for each one." She did however journey throughout Europe, rebuilding the ruins after the war, material and moral. Her presence brought assurance, serenity, a clearer and more heavenly outlook. From a distance she communicated this peace to countries in distress, such as Mexico and Hungary.

She was not eloquent in speech or in writing, but: "When our Mother says something it is impossible not to understand." In her circular letters unresolved dichotomies are felt. By temperament she leaned to a defensive rather than a cooperative attitude towards current challenges, often seen as threats. The official statements of the Society in the early twentieth century ring counter to the mentality of today, and a sense of semantic change is again needed. The word "criticism" stood for a want of religious submission rather than for evaluation. "We must guard against the spirit of criticism with which the air of this twentieth century is saturated." Neither nuns nor children must criticize the decisions of authority in any sphere. The idea that such criticism could be validly constructive was difficult to grasp. The word "independence" stood for aloofness from the body rather than responsibility for one's own actions within the body. The phrase "the world" was still used for something incompatible with Christian living; there was a consequent emphasis upon "separation." There were warnings against the "easy-going spirit" fostered by modern inventions, with a certain fear of "progress."

On the positive side is the call to savour the life of prayer, "the obligation to unite the active life to the contemplative, to dedicate long moments to prayer, to recollection, to reflection." This gives joy to fidelity and power to the apostolate.

It is through the heart of Jesus that the regeneration of modern society is to be brought about, and who can fail to see the part that falls to us in this divine work? . . . Intimately united to the divine Heart and clothed with its spirit, the religious of the Sacred Heart sees before her at this hour an apostolic field ready to receive the good seed. Once more the world has wandered from the right way and its followers must say: "We have gone astray." It has sought for happiness in well-being and in the inventions of the human mind, in pleasures of all sorts, far from God and from the Church. Loss of fortune and the more painful loss of loved ones [after the war], checks to pleasure everywhere, are a call back to the Christian spirit, and bring souls to the crib of Jesus and to the foot of his cross. [15]

The process for the Canonization of Blessed Madeleine Sophie had been going steadily on. The *Antepreparatoria* session was held in 1923, two sessions for the examinations of miracles the following year. The cures accepted where those of Marie de Salm-Salm at Jette in 1913 and Rose Coyne at Manhattanville in 1919. [16] The session *De Tuto* took place on February 12, 1924. Mother de Loë announced the coming Canonization:

> The thought of it must fill with joy every religious of the Sacred Heart, and I cannot urge you strongly enough to give to this joy those strong and super-natural bases which will make it the dominant disposition of your souls from now on. The joy of which I speak is the fruit of love "which runs, which flies, which exults." It is the fruit of the Holy Spirit who produces it by his presence and maintains it when nothing is refused to him . . . . It runs like a vibrant note throughout our Constitutions . . . . And so I wish that our Holy Mother, when she looks upon us from her home in glory, will not see one of us, not one, who is satisfied with a watered-down, mediocre religious life, but that all will be true daughters of such a mother and serve the Sacred Heart with a joyous and generous heart. [17]

On May 24, 1925, a pageant moved down the basilica of Saint Peter to the papal altar, with music and cheering. The banner of Madeleine Sophie Barat was carried by a guard of honour of sixteen Jesuits, its streamers held by four members of the Barat family. It was followed by the banner of Marie Madeleine Postel, her contemporary, foundress of the Sisters of the Christian Schools. The papal mass, the symbolic gifts, the swords and silver trumpets, led to the pronouncement by Pius XI of the sanctity of these two, "in the name of the holy and undivided Trinity, for the exaltation of the Catholic faith and the growth of the Christian religion." The basilica was filled with witnesses: the two *miraculées*, nuns, students and friends from the world over.

Mother de Loë's generalate was marked by significant centenaries. That of the Children of Mary in the schools came in 1916 and Mother de Loë wrote a letter to the pupils, asking for "self-forgetfulness, devotedness, and above all a true and solid piety needed more than ever in the calamitous times through which we are passing.'[18] On May 28, 1918, the centenary of the arrival of Philippine Duchesne in North America was celebrated. Mother de Loë could not be present in Saint Charles, but she asked for a renewal in "the double spirit of prayer and poverty"[19] of the rugged missionary. On December 22, 1926, the Society quietly kept the centenary of the approbation of the Constitutions. Mother de Loë called for reflection on "the way in which we keep our Rule in letter and in spirit," and as preparation: "Three months of entire fidelity to these holy rules, such as Mother Rumbold liked to establish in her foundations by the name of Strict Observance."[20] In that year the *Histoire Abrégée de la Sociéte du Sacré Coeur* by Marie Duval was published; its keynote was fidelity to the primitive spirit.

The Twentieth General Council met on October 16, 1928, and discussed new educational opportunities. The councillors were filled with a joyous urgency: "It is not only union, it is unity." Mother de Loë seemed rejuvenated. On the feast of All Saints mass was celebrated in the oratory of Saint Madeleine Sophie. That evening she felt unwell and sent apologies to the Councillors for staying in her room. On the afternoon of November 3 came a sudden thunder storm and the infirmarian offered to close the blinds. "No," said Mother de Loë, "we are in God's hands." Within half an hour she was in his presence.

After the funeral the vicar general, Manuela Vicente, sent a letter to the stunned Society:

> She who was the soul and joy of the Society has left us, but everything has not gone with her; we have a rich and precious heritage which we must make fructify: her teachings, filled with sure and lofty doctrine, her great virtues, her beautiful example, that touch of the supernatural that marked her whole person.[21]

Under these unusual circumstances permission was given to hold the Twenty-first General Council at once, and on November 21, 1928, Manuela Vicente became the eighth superior general of the Society of the Sacred Heart.

Maria Manuela Vicente [22] was born into a Spanish family living in Puerto Rico on August 6, 1862. At the age of two she lost her mother, and her father returned to Aragon. Manolita's childhood was lonely and austere, despite the affection of older sisters. She spent two happy years as a boarder at the Sacred Heart school at Saragossa, then her father also died and she finished her education at home by reading. She was an excellent horse-woman and house-keeper, while devoting herself to parish work. She was serious and aloof, but: "When I was young I had many friends, I don't know why."

She put off following her secret call to religious life. "What would I be good for? I don't like children, I can't do anything, though perhaps I could be an infirmarian." When she fell dangerously ill she was cured during a novena to Madeleine Sophie Barat who brought light for the way ahead. She entered at Chamartin at the age of twenty-eight. A calm, hard-working, unselfish novice, she followed her liking for "being lost in the crowd, drowned in the crowd," and her voice was rarely heard in community.

Inspired by the sermon at her first vows she took as symbol of herself the Palm Sunday donkey, chosen because "the Lord has need of it." During five years at Sarria she learned to like children, and, to her surprise: "How much the community loves me!" In probation Mother Digby's mandate to her was: "Smile!" After her profession on February 7, 1899, she returned to Sarria as mistress general. She was too honest to imitate her exuberant predecessor, saying: "I don't stimulate children; I calm them down." Soon it was the children who stimulated her; she enjoyed teaching the higher classes and the school felt her unfolding powers.

In 1903 she went to San Sebastian opened for the children from France. After a year at "Miracielo, house of welcome," she returned to Sarria as superior. By this time her gay, warm humour was free to sparkle through her quiet manner. When Mother Digby came to Sarria in 1906 she showed Mother Vincente some figurines, all donkeys. "You and I like donkeys; choose one." This was Mother Digby's way of telling her that she was in charge of a new vicariate with Sarria as its centre. From then on the donkey kept his place on Mother Vicente's desk.

She now had nine houses to care for and she brought to her work "a very clear mind with wide avenues through which truth could walk as queen." Every choice, every action was open to the Spirit. For the next twelve years she grew in dynamism, through industrial riots that drove the religious into shelters outside their convents, through dark war years, through constructive enterprises. She often said at a change of occupation: "Now let's go and do the will of God somewhere else." In this spirit she left Spain for the Mother House in January, 1918. She had been chosen as assistant general at the death of Mother Borget.

Mother Vicente was mistress of probation for the next ten years. The grave black eyes lighted up as the gifts of a natural psychologist came into play. "I enjoy observing." "Mimi" appeared on the scene. She was the "Peanuts" of twenty probations, a caricature of the egotist that hides in everyone, "leaping out from behind the door when thought dead." Mimi in pink, Mimi in purple, Mimi in the inkwell, Mimi the dethroned queen, pouting. "Give no role to Mimi in your inner world, in tragedy, in comedy, in mystic drama."

With virile simplicity Mother Vicente brought the probanists face to face with "Jésus Hostie"; her direction was along the straight line, "le seul regard." When they went home after profession she placed the Society in their hands: "On entering you found it fervent, united, generous; it must always be so." The other assistants general would say to persons seeking solutions: "Why don't you ask Mother Vicente about that? She is one of those who best possess the spirit of the Society." "She is so near to God, so near," added Mother de Loë.

When Mother Vicente so suddenly became superior general on November 21, 1928, she faced her task as "the will of God that is our strength and our joy." The Twenty-first General Council took up the unfinished business of the Twentieth from November 17 to 28, and completed a revision of the Decrees. [23] In January, 1929, the Society took part in the great missionary exhibition at the Vatican. On February 11 the Lateran Accord was signed between Mussolini and Pius XI and the Papal States were re-created as Vatican City, while the Encyclical on church and state, *Ubi Arcano Dei*, showed the Pope's powerful vision reaching abroad with new freedom. Mother Vicente wrote, echoing Madeleine Sophie Barat: "May the little barque of the Society be always more firmly attached to the barque of Peter from which come light, strength and peace of conscience." [24] Following the death of Cardinal Merry del Val in March, 1930, the Pope gave his secretary of state, Cardinal Eugenio Pacelli,[25] to the Society as Protector.

Then agitation began in Mother Vicente's native land. Sensing danger, she was suddenly inspired to write to Mother Carmen Modet: "If there is trouble send the novices to Avigliana." The letter reached Chamartin on the morning of May 11, 1931. Mother Modet put it in her pocket unread, for at that moment noises from the street demanded action. She evacuated the house and that evening it went up in flames. She then read the letter and knew where to send the novices. As they were boarding the train a young girl climbed on just in time, the first postulant for Avigliana. Vocations in time of trouble were strong and numerous. Spain became a republic, violence died down for the moment, and Chamartin was rebuilt. The statue of the Sacred Heart had remained erect through the fire.

On September 12, 1932, a rare ceremony took place in Saint Peter's basilica; a statue of Saint Madeleine Sophie was unveiled. It stood in the upper row of the niches reserved for the founders of religious orders, the first to the right. She who in life would not allow herself to be pictured appeared sculptured in white marble. The figure, designed by Quattrini, has the energy of the baroque style, even in the wind-blown veil. With her hand she points to the open book of the Constitutions, a child looks up at her and an angel holds the seal of the Society.

The attitude of Mother Vicente towards adaptation to modern life shown in her circular letters is similar to that of her predecessor. She wrote:

> The situation in the world at the present time asks us to keep our hearts and our hands on high in an attitude of supplication; hell seems let loose against all that is good, all that is holy, spiritual, elevated, religious. To parry the attack we need many fervent, faithful, interior souls who will draw down graces on this perverted world, overwhelmed by the terrible struggle against God and his saints that seems to want to change the life of the nations. Modern ideas develop selfishness, sensuality, easy-going ways. We as religious have more need than ever to watch over our spirit, our religious customs, our traditions. Above all we need to strengthen our interior life; the basis of our religious spirit, in order to do some good to those who come to us looking for the knowledge and love of the Heart of Jesus Christ. [26]

The means to this are faith, humility, charity; these can overcome the chief obstacle which is discouragement. Warnings are given against "interior opposition expressed openly," the spirit of criticism. "We must always keep that simplicity that has no idea of disapproving or of rationalizing." "People are unhappy if they think that they are prevented from developing their personal initiatives." The remedy is "the life of faith that keeps us in the truth." [27]

When summoning the Twenty-second General Council Mother Vicente struck its keynote:

> Its work will consist especially in revising the Ceremonial; in looking at several points concerning poverty and dependence; in adapting ourselves to the needs of the times without touching, as far as possible, any of our traditions; in examining the rule of cloister, so little understood at the present time. We will also speak of the requirements for university examinations. Our religious will understand that it is for us a sacred obligation to determine just how far we can go in the way of concessions and where it is necessary to stop. [28]

The Council, which met from February 25th to March 16, 1935, kept to this road. While making broad "concessions" in educational matters it again checked the free use of communications media such as the newly invented radio, for "not all modern discoveries are for us." [29] It may be that this stance of reluctant adaptation, this cautious balancing, were inevitable at the time. But they were signals of the need of change which could not then be recognized as such.

On the positive side, Mother Vicente's circular letters have a distinctive fire and energy that come from the dominance of one idea, one spiritual passion that gives them an energizing unity; she was possessed by love of the Eucharist and a sense of its transforming power. "Jésus Hostie" was the centre of her own life and of her teaching. It was love of Jesus in the stillness of the tabernacle, in the dynamism of the eucharistic sacrifice, in the charity of intercommunion.

> The eucharistic soul finds her delight in the tabernacle; she draws her light from Jesus in her soul. She wants to be a host consecrated by Jesus and transformed by him. [30]

Love, peace, union, all start from the same point in "the sacrament of life because it is the sacrament of union." She thought of the host under a triple form: the host of the Eucharist, the host of suffering, the host of the present moment. To meet God in the present moment leads to "sacrifice, the response of love to love, the indispensable condition of collaboration in the work of redemption." [31] Mother Vicente found that her mission was to confront world forces and new demands by a deepening of union with the Redeemer.

The road became overshadowed after 1936. Mother Vicente had visited Spain and seen the new Chamartin, but trouble flared into civil war as General Franco fought for liberation. All the houses of the Sacred Heart in the Red Zone were damaged; the communities took shelter in the homes of friends courageous enough to welcome them, and in the houses of England, France and Italy. Maria Galindo, [32] author of *La Glorificadora del Sagrado Corazon*, a life of Saint Madeleine Sophie, died in her sister's home, where a priest had smuggled in a sacred host. Gloria Elio [33] spent weeks in a communist prison, with all the indignity implied. Pilar Alcibar and Maria Verges were carried into the hills to be shot and were mysteriously spared at the last moment. Mother Vicente never lost confidence:

> Graces are pouring down on the Society, sacrifices also. Our Holy Mother said that the latter are a source of the former. Despite the suffering and uncertainty of the present time the Society is moving on and our works are prospering. [34]

She had finished the circle of visits in Europe, she had seen the Society enter Black Africa and India by the dawn of the earth-shaking year, 1939. Pius XI died on February 11 and Cardinal Pacelli took his place as Pope Pius XII on March 2, while Cardinal Luigi Maglioni [35] became Protector of the Society. General Franco entered Madrid in June and the novices could return to Chamartin the following year. July 12 was the centenary of Saint Madeleine Sophie's act of consecration of the Society to our Lady of Sorrows; Mother Vicente renewed the act at the Villa Lante where it had first been made, asking our Lady for "that courage, that firmness which gave her the strength to remain calm at the foot of the cross." She did not know the magnitude of the trial ahead. Hitler had been rising to power; the Nazi threat was as deadly as that of Communism. The Sacred Heart schools in Germany, Austria and Hungary felt the strangle-hold. The second world war broke out in September.

Then the paradox of triumph through the cross was brought home to the Society as the Process for the Beatification of Philippine Duchesne drew to a close. Her body had been exhumed in 1896 and placed in a garden chapel at Saint Charles. Philippine's civic greatness was recognized when her name headed the "Pioneer Roll of Fame" of women who had served the public welfare of the State of Missouri. The Decree of the Heroicity of Virtue was proclaimed in March, 1935. In 1938 the session *Preparatoria* took place in March and the *Coram Sanctissimo* in December. Then, despite the advance of total war, the final session *De Tuto* was held on February 12, 1940.

Mother Vicente had the courage to summon all the vicars to Rome. Zofia Gunther from Poland and Anna Konsted from Austria could not leave their besieged countries. Elizabeth Zurstrassen from Belgium learned of the invasion while in Rome and left before the ceremony. Earthly agony and heavenly glory were superimposed on Pentecost Sunday, May 12, 1940, when Philippine Duchesne was declared blessed by Pius XII in Saint Peter's basilica. The two *miraculés* were present, Señor Bahamonde[36] from Puerto Rico and Mother Carolina Indelli [37] from Italy. At an audience given to the few alumnae who could come the Pope penetrated the theology of the devotion to the Sacred Heart, the mystery of love that had sent Philippine overseas:

> Zeal is an ardent desire to make God reign everywhere, the active clinging of the will to God, that essential will of the Creator that can have no other end than himself. The Lord has made all things for his own sake. The Divine Word, in taking flesh, felt in his own heart, reaction to all those movements that stir the soul .... From this interior movement there sprang like a flame the burning wish: "Father, thy kingdom come, thy will be done." .... It is not too bold to see a link between the wonderful missionary impulse that marks the last two centuries and the spread of the devotion to the Sacred Heart. [38]

The vicars then left hurriedly, taking their probanists with them. Marguerite Nagant from Holland spent four months buffeted between frontiers before reaching home. Then all communications with the Mother House were cut for the next four years.

Mother Vicente became a victim for the Society. In December she fell and broke her hip; immobilized, she gradually lost mental contact with what was going on. On April 19, 1941, Giulia Datti [39] was appointed by the Sacred Congregation of Religious to govern the Society as vicar general. She was Roman of the Romans; her family belonged to the Noble Guard in every sense. Already she had served the Society for long years as superior at Santa Rufina, vicar of Italy, then assistant general and mistress of probation. The sight of her recalled a painting by Fra Angelico; she inspired the "beata pacis visio" of the New Jerusalem. She guided the Society through five years of endurance.

News came fitfully: Roehampton bombed, with the Sacred Heart chapel intact; other houses in Europe and Japan in ruins; Elfriede Buch and Felicitas Schroder crushed to death under the ruins of Saint Adelheid; all foreign nuns interned in Tokyo. In 1943 the death planes flew over Rome. While Pius XII strove to have it declared an open city the attacks went on. They reached the Via Nomentana, shattering the Mother House windows. Mother Vicente did not know why she was carried to shelter in the middle of the night. In August, 1945, the atom bomb stunned the world into peace. Mother Datti wrote at last to the whole Society:

> Our religious family has received much: graces beyond number, a marvellous protection over the lives of ours in the midst of dangers of every sort, graces of religious spirit, of strength and of abandonment which kept up our courage in suffering, difficulties and privations, graces of the *Cor Unum* maintained in all its splendid integrity; and now the grace to take up our works again . . . . Our Lord wills to make use of us to cooperate in the work of redemption and to make known his merciful love. Let us renew our consecration as religious of the Sacred Heart, and may it be the reality of our days. May "thy kingdom come" be our habitual aspiration this year, so that his reign may be extended and established through the whole universe. [40]

Mother Vicente died on January 21, 1946. The roads were open and the Twenty-third General Council could meet. On September 29 Marie-Thérèse de Lescure became the ninth superior general of the Society of the Sacred Heart.

* * *

The assistants in government at this epoch all brought to their post long and adventuresome experience of the expanding Society.

Jeanne de Lavigerie now claimed the title once held by Mother Borget, "grandmother of the Society." "Just to look at her," said the probanists, "calms us down; she inspires tranquillity of heart." At her death on December 6, 1932, Mother Vicente wrote:

She has left us a very dear memory of the past. She walked through the troubles of life with undisturbed calm and serenity drawn from her deep spirit of mortification and detachment. From this came her peaceful attitude towards difficult or painful events, her kindness, that mark of selfless persons who understand, share and relieve the sufferings of others . . . . With her departure for heaven our links with a past era seem broken; she was assistant general for twenty-seven years and was present at the election of three superiors general. [41]

In 1922 Mother de Montalembert retired, to pass gaily through "the little grey corridor" of her last years at the Trinita. Her place was taken by another attractive image of "the good old days," Jeanne Dupont.[42] She had spent many years in the United States as superior of Eden Hall, Pine Grove Avenue and Seattle; in all she initiated guilds for professional women. She was mistress of novices at Jette during the first world war; the formation she gave was marked by the stable complacency of an earlier age:

It is not for us to innovate on our own initiative; those who look to the future with wisdom do not take adventuresome risks . . . . We must love the Society above all else, such as she is. We have received everything from her and we do not realize what a treasure is ours . . . . Undoubtedly we shall see weaknesses and defects in her as in everything that is of this earth. She did not come down straight from heaven but she leads us to it. [43]

When the Society returned to France Mother Dupont became vicar at Lille until called to the Mother House. Simplicity was the keynote to her character and the years went by in "calmness, serenity, confidence, dignity." She kept her Golden Jubilee and then her Diamond, dying in the isolation of the war years on February 21, 1945.

In the void that her death has left, her example is a store-house from which we can draw, to keep the traditions so evident in her and to grow in that union of charity which is the hall-mark of the Society. [44]

In striking contrast to the sobriety of these two was the sparkling, forward-looking spirit of Marie Symon. [45] The lively child from Ostend, "always haunted by the sea," danced her way through school at Jette until grief at her father's death led to surrender to Christ and to "his own joy which has always been the centre of my life." Irresistible *joie de vivre* was her gift to the Society; it came from "the love of wonder; I could die for his beauty." She was joy-giver as mistress general at Jette, as superior at Bois l'Evêque during the hunger of the first war when she was imprisoned for six weeks without knowing why, as educator in Brussels. When she became vicar of Belgium in 1924 she said:

> I am very sure of God. I know that I can lean invincibly upon him no matter what happens. I feel free and joyous, held by no desires save that of the Psalmist: *nisi te, Deus meus*. This desire is burning within me in a form always more apostolic, more catholic. I feel, by his grace, full of courage, full of enthusiasm, of ambition for his work. I wish, as far as he allows, to work unrelentingly in my own humble sphere. [46]

Her hour came when she opened Black Africa to the Society, as will be seen later. She became assistant general in 1933 and travelled widely through Europe and Latin America as Mother Vicente's delegate. These journeys were for her "a film of the glory of God," for "I have always loved the universe." At the Mother House she was "the anonymous helper of the universe" by her intense prayer. She died as her own country was overwhelmed by war on August 12, 1941. Père Charles, theologian of the missions and her director for thirty years, said of her:

> She gave herself to God as one leaping from a cliff, without hesitation and in a single bound .... She had received from him a remarkable capacity for being interested in everything. She kept her eyes wide open, courageously open, on the works of the Creator and the doings of men .... She was at the service of the Church universal, sharing the cares of the Redeemer, looking boldly to the future, adapting ceaselessly to changing situations .... Nothing in her was dull, everything was in full flower. To her, religious life was an enrichment .... She realized in her own person and in her life the essential theology of the devotion to the Sacred Heart. [47]

Helen Rumbold came to Rome as assistant general in 1915, and continued to guide the affairs of Egypt during the war. She died at Roehampton on September 17, 1921; the telegram simply said: "Radiant death." Her place was taken by Elizabeth Lamb. [48] When "Bessie the Tomboy" entered the noviceship her mother said apologetically: "For want of better gifts she is an excellent housekeeper." "But what a precious gift!" countered Mother Digby. She used this gift in England and Ireland, and then in Egypt where she was vicar. Almost crushed by the climate, by calumnies and by wartime hazards she governed lightly, firmly. She was timid but strong as steel, and "came into the room like sunshine."

When named assistant general she said: "This is a situation in which I am really in my element: to organize within a short time and under difficult circumstances some big and unexpected work." This meant the installation of the new Mother House on the Via Nomentana where she became a true home-maker. She still met adventures while visiting Egypt and Malta, and even the Holy Land in search of a summer shelter. "It's all worth while" was her motto, even when, drained by illness, she resigned at the Council of 1928. She died at Roehampton on May 2, 1929.

Mary Guerin, [49] vicar in Chicago, was elected to fill Mother Lamb's place, but after two years she offered her resignation due to frail health. She had never actually taken office. Constance Perry [50] then became assistant general. For twenty-three years she had been mistress of discipline at the Teacher Training College at Saint Charles Square in London. Straightforward and strong for duty, she trained virile teachers. As vicar of England after 1923 she revealed the warm heart known to her students through her austere, reserved manner. She lived by conviction, and "it is by prayer that we stand on the bedrock of faith." At the Mother House she could forget her shyness; probanists and visitors found in her not only a knowledgeable guide to the art treasures of Rome but a friend. Her breadth of mind was felt in some important decisions regarding the Society's adaptation to changing social conditions. In 1946 she resigned and returned to England where she died on November 14, 1950.

Before becoming vicar general Giulia Datti had been in charge of the probation for twenty-two years. Serenity, simplicity, largeness of heart were her gifts to the probanists. "Stay in your joy, sing running on your way. Prayer is more love than thought." By the fall of 1932 the numbers in probation had become so great that all could not live at the Via Nomentana, and for the next eight years a group went to the Villa Lante under the guidance of Jeanne de Traverse. [51] She resembled Mother Datti in her faith touching vision, and the sister probations were closely united.

Mother Borget celebrated her Diamond Jubilee, and died at the Villa Lante on September 20, 1917. For the next thirty-eight years a small figure under a large umbrella could be seen walking beside the superior general in the Mother House gardens at one o'clock daily, discussing the finances of the Society. Henriette de Montlivault [52] had begun her work in the treasury at Annonay until the closing of that house in 1903. She then went to Malta and from there to Egypt until called to Ixelles to help Mother Borget.

As treasurer general Mother de Montlivault rebuilt damaged convents after one war and saw them destroyed in another. During the interval she aided in building many new ones the world over. At the Via Nomentana she organized the *cours pratique* for the probanists; they learned the difficult balance between economy and charity while keeping accounts and handling supplies. She herself lived intensely behind her unassuming manner. Mother Stuart had channelled her energies into patient love: "Peace and joy are the best gifts of the Lord, and he has given them to you." She died on February 1, 1949.

> She was loyal and trustworthy always, broad-minded and comprehending, as her letters and her actions show, with that touch of interest and religious affection which rises above mere business affairs, since she herself saw them in prayer from the lofty point of view that comes from the spirit of love of the Society. [53]

Marie le Bail died on February 18, 1920, having kept the twenty-fifth anniversary of her "silver pen." Her place as secretary general was taken by one who had aided her since 1894, Juliette Clerc de Landresse. [54] "Petit cadavre" is the untranslatable name given to her slight person by Matthieu, gardener at the Rue de Varenne (and *confidant* of five mothers general). She set up the archives at the Via Nomentana and continued Mother le Bail's friendly role as *trait-d'union* between the Society's centre and its far rim. After her retirement in 1935 she was as busy as ever with the printing press, and went about "trotting like a little mouse in search of its hole, the witness of another generation strayed into our own." She died on January 24, 1949. Germaine Mignot [55] had taken up the work of secretary general, a quiet, self-spending person well known already at the Via Nomentana as surveillance of the probation. She died on July 31, 1947.

Another scribe widely known through the Society was Antoinette du Passage. [56] She had gone in 1903 to the school at Brighton as mistress general, and failed completely. She sent a versified account of her woes to Mother Digby: two mice (herself and her superior) were struggling to keep afloat in a jug of cream. One (her superior) had energetically made a pat of butter from which she dominated the situation; the other was drowning. Mother Digby took the hint, and Mother du Passage became private secretary to four superiors general. She also compiled *Counsels for the Time of Retreat* drawn from the writings of Madeleine Sophie Barat, and edited the *Echo of the Month*, with accent on "Roma Felix" that she loved so much. She died on April 17, 1946.

To these dynamic desk-workers, living for so long in the unchanging centre, any change in the Society's way of life would have been unthinkable. Their sentiments (and those of many) were expressed in lyric fashion (and with innocent triumphalism) by Mother de Landresse:

> How much I love it! In the long years of my religious life I have seen the Society in all its phases: troubled, persecuted, glorious, in apostolic expansion. I have always seen it as beautiful, great, noble, always at the height of every situation. The Lord rules it. I have become identified with the Society, in a sense, living at its centre. . . . May God keep it as it is, without spot or wrinkle, until the end of the world, keep its spirit, its union, its traditions, its cloister — and preserve it from the breath of modern times! [57]

* * *

The domestic life of the Society — that of its community relationships — went on tranquilly between the world wars, with extraordinary uniformity in a time of extraordinary expansion. It responded cautiously to ever louder demands from outside. Newspapers were banished from community rooms on the grounds that "they make us lose our peace" (this was said in wartime of international communities), but the Council of 1922 admitted "serious journals for cultural purposes." Cloister was accentuated in this outgoing time, in the face of persistent criticism from without. Yet even from within a growing sense that cloister would soon no longer be viable in the modern world was becoming articulate.

The Council of 1915 stressed "the perfection of common life," and paid tribute to the continuing influence of Mother Stuart in raising it to joyous freedom of spirit:

> A great *élan* was given to prayer and the spiritual life by Mother Stuart. The obstacle is agitation of mind; except for that there has been a real upward flight towards spiritual things, and the recreations have felt the effect of this. [58]

Mother Vicente placed the local community in a larger framework, that of the whole Society, the international community:

Let us not forget that we are the Society of the Sacred Heart of Jesus. A society is more than a fellowship, more than a contact, more than a binding force. It is an intimate association so deep-reaching that it becomes compenetration. [59] . . . . A community is the love of a group united in order to love better. [60]

* * *

The international character of the Society stood out in sharper relief after its centre had shifted to Rome. The reputation for being "a French order" that had gone ahead of it into the most remote countries began to fade out (though it was still expected to teach French with a finish!) By 1939 it had become interwoven with the cultures of five continents and many islands, and its internationality became a sign of its catholicity in the full sense.

The return of the Society to the land of its origin began in 1915. It was organized by Marthe de Lavergne [61] who then took charge of a new vicariate centered at Avigliana which included some houses in northern Italy and those re-opened in France. She had been mistress of novices since 1893 in Conflans, Rivoli, Chamartin and Jette, aiming to form "living and vibrant members of the Society," in a blend of nationalities.

Lyons was the first city to be re-entered, then Nantes, Amiens, Poitiers, Marmoutier, Paris, Marseilles, Lille, Toulouse, Metz, Montpellier and Bordeaux. A heartfelt welcome greeted the religious everywhere. The Children of Mary, called "Guardians of the Past," were on hand to help: old pupils brought their little girls as new pupils. Beginnings were often made in crowded, temporary houses with discreet "private lessons" and a few *grandes pensionnaires*, but regular classes were soon in vigour. Some of the original buildings with their priceless memories, scarred by war, were recovered, notably the *Berçeau* at Amiens, but most were irretrievable. Today the Hotel Biron with its chapel is a Rodin Museum, a place of peaceful beauty open to the public; the Mother House on the Boulevard des Invalides is a government Lycée. The new beginning in Paris was a day school on the Rue Saint Dominique (1919).

In 1920 a French vicariate was formed, and under the government of Louise de Neuville, [62] marked by her own constructive energy and clarity, the work of rebuilding was speeded. There were three vicariates by 1929, and by 1946 the houses in France numbered twenty, of which four were new foundations. The novices were gathered at Marmoutier, and a small neighboring foundation was opened for the juniorate at Rougemont (1917). The boarding school at La Croix Blanche at Bondues was called an "oasis of peace" among industrial centres (1929). It was found impossible to recover Conflans, and so a boarding school for Parisian children was opened at Saint Maur (1929). Fontanil was a small school in the mountains of Savoy near Chambéry (1945); it was to have only five years of life.

New vicariates were formed elsewhere in Europe as the self-consciousness of nations sharpened between the wars. The houses of Ireland and Scotland joined in a single vicariate in 1918, with its own noviceship at Mount Anville; "the Celts were together." Northern Ireland and the Irish Free State first confronted each other; the agitation of the Black and Tan led to lively developments during the long government of Margaret Walsh [63] as vicar. She was "a person of limitless hope," alert to educational trends. She opened a Teacher Training College on the strong "craig" of Craiglockhart in Edinburgh (1918), a rural boarding school at Kilgraston (1930), and a high school, Monkstown, in Dublin (1945). In Germany the tenacious Children of Mary had been pressing for the return of the Society, and when Saint Adelheid was opened in Bonn (1920) it became the centre of a German-Dutch vicariate under Mathilde de Capitain. [64] She had served the Society in many countries and through many trials with radiant and energetic charity. She opened a student hostel in Munich (1930). Her successor, Marguerite Nagant, [65] founded a school in Berlin and governed daringly, with communicative vision, through the following war tensions.

Despite civil war no houses were permanently lost in Spain under the government of Ana Maria Cavanillas [66] and Pilar Alcibar [67] in the vicariate of Sarria, and of Carmen Modet [68] and Maria de la Cavada [69] in that of Seville. All faced the troubles of their land with the chivalric courage and ardour that marked the Society in Spain. Five diversified centres of zeal were gained. Algorta (1916) was a quiet boarding school; Pontevedra in Galicia began for the children of the fisherfolk (1918), while Santa Maria de Huerta near Madrid (1930) was also opened for a village apostolate. At Barcelona a Teacher Training College (1925) continued work begun at Sarria which needed to expand. A school at Pamplona (1939) was a sign of new vigour after the civil war.

In 1928 the vicariate of Egypt-Malta was dissolved; Egypt became dependent upon southern France and Malta upon the Mother House for one year, then upon England. Italy once more became a single vicariate under Laura Theodoli [70] who expanded its mission. A second house was opened in Sicily at Catania (1927), while the Society returned to two cities from which it had been driven by the revolution of 1848: a day school at Genoa (1917) and a house of studies connected with the new University of the Sacred Heart in Milan (1935). The latter was opened by Eleanora Boncompagni [71] who, as vicar, encouraged classical studies. Two other houses were opened in university centers, Oxford (1929) and Louvain (1943). England also gained a new school at Tunbridge Wells (1915) which replaced temporary Leamington. In the English vicariate Winifred Archer-Shee, [72] blending gentleness with strength, was a point of stability in difficult times; she literally spent herself for others during the second world war.

In Central Europe peace did not return with the armistice of 1918; there was restiveness in the Red Zone. The Austrian vicariate lost Prague which was forced to close (1919). But magnanimous Maria de Waldstein, [73] the vicar, had the courage to open a second house in Budapest, Sophianum (1918), which was a centre of higher studies. Ana Komstedt [74] confronted the resulting problems with the same virility during the war of 1939. In Poland, despite the Red menace, the Society was welcomed back to Polska Wies in Posen (1921) which had been closed in 1874, and another school was opened in Poznan (1933). The Polish vicariate was re-created in 1936 under the strong government of Zofia Gunther [75] who founded a house in Warsaw, a city soon engulfed in flames. From then on the houses in Poland were painfully isolated from the rest of the Society.

It was a time of uneasy extremes in the United States: Big Business and the Depression, Prohibition and the New Deal, Cardinal Pacelli's visit and Myron Taylor at the Vatican, finally Pearl Harbor. The Society entered the national centre with a foundation at Washington, D. C. on Massachusetts Avenue (1923). Other beginnings followed the thrust for higher education that was sending the Society to university campuses in Europe. Independent Liberal Arts colleges, even if administered by religious orders, were empowered by the state to give degrees. The vicars, strong, enterprising and clear-visioned educators, were alive to the call. In the southern vicariate Mary Reid [76] began Clifton College in Cincinnati (1915) and Maryville College in Saint Louis (1923); her government was "a remarkable blend of severity and kindness." Mathilde Mouton,[77] who "wherever she passed left a touch of beauty," strengthened the Teacher Training College at Grand Coteau. In the western vicariate Jane Fox, [78] of pioneer spirit, founded Barat College at Lake Forest (1922) while Rosalie Hill [79] transferred the beginnings made at Menlo Park to Lone Mountain College in San Francisco (1930), and founded another college in San Diego (1945) when the centre of the vicariate moved to the west coast. Her far-seeing, energizing influence was felt from one seaboard to another. In the eastern vicariate Mary Moran, wise and dauntless, began Manhattanville College in New York (1916).

As the colleges grew some of the schools in the same quarters found new sites: Noroton-on-the-Sound (1925) opened for the academy of Manhattanville, and Villa Duchesne (1928) for that of Maryville. The shifting of houses in urban areas accelerated: Jefferson Avenue to Lawrence Avenue in Detroit (1918), Arch Street to Overbrook in Philadelphia (1921), Pine Grove Avenue to Sheridan Road in Chicago (1927), Jackson Street to Broadway in San Francisco (1934), Madison Avenue to Ninety-first Street in New York (1934) and Maplehurst to Greenwich, Connecticut (1945).

In Canada the continent-wide stretch between houses was shortened when Corinne Clapin, [80] a French Canadian of quiet influence, made a foundation at Winnipeg in the central lake-region (1935). In Montreal the city house on Alexander Street was transferred to a lofty site on Atwater Avenue (1928). The school at the Sault, with its rich history, was destroyed by fire in 1929, but soon rebuilt. Under the government of Bertha Padberg [81] studies and school life were invigorated from coast to coast.

At the antipodes a noviceship was opened at Rose Bay for the novices of Australia and New Zealand who had hitherto gone to England. Timaru was closed in 1935, but the fervently loyal alumnae kept a centre in South Island to which the Society would later return. The schools to the north were expanding to meet the social needs of New Zealand. In Australia a school was opened in subtropical Brisbane on a beautiful property called Stuartholme (1920) which had belonged to the family of Janet Stuart. The Society entered the university life of this country too when Sancta Sophia College (1925) was founded on the campus of the University of

Sydney. When war threatened the Australian coast the junior school of Rose Bay took refuge in the hills, and this led to the foundation of Kerever Park (1944), a garden paradise. It was named for Alix de Keréver,[82] a French woman who succeeded Amélie de Salmon. She loved and understood her adopted country, the largeness of its horizon. "Mother de Keréver was intensely preoccupied with helping the whole Church, for the divine interests were the mainspring of her life; hence the apostolic spirit that radiated from Rose Bay."

Pan-American movements were gaining force in the early twentieth century; social restiveness was calling for radical change for which the Society of the Sacred Heart would be ready only later on. In the meantime it was spreading quietly in most of the southern countries, with energetic "popular works."

The vicariate of the Antilles stretched out to include Colombia after 1916. Here the growth was rapid; three new schools, welcoming both boarding and day scholars and with extended social work, were founded, Medellin (1930), Manizales (1936) and Cali (1946). All were on the central plateau of Colombia where the ancestral Spanish tradition was strong, and where "force, fertility, exuberance and color inspire joy." Mathilde Moreyra, [83]the vicar, was a Cuban who lived according to the patroness of her land, our Lady of Charity. In Puerto Rico a second school was opened at Ponce (1916) among the mountainous tobacco plantations. In Cuba the flourishing day school in Santiago was moved to a suburban site at Vista Alegre (1925). The Cuban houses suffered from the earthquake shocks of 1932, and still more from a political "reign of terror' a few years later, but they went on unchecked under the progressive government of Maria Tamariz. [84] She began a Liberal Arts College at Santurce in additon to the school.

Conflict was more deadly in Mexico where Calles set up his own schismatic church. The scene was that of Graham Green's *The Power and the Glory*; the young *cristoferos* were shot with "Viva Cristo Rey!" on their lips. Convents were being seized, so Mother Lalande looked over the frontier to Texas. The nuns and children from Monterrey and San Luis Potosi went to Laredo, those from Mexico City to San Antonio and then to Saint Michael's in Louisiana. The house there had been evacuated after a cyclone, but Mother·Reid had it repaired and offered it to the Mexican school; the cheerful and courageous children filled it with new life. Then in 1931 Mexico paradoxically celebrated the fourth centenary of the apparitions of our Lady of Guadalupe, and at this signal the refugees returned, to live in hope and risk.

Mother Lalande kept her Golden Jubilee in 1934 in Mexico City where, despite the menacing atmosphere, the Mexican alumnae paid open tribute to her long valour. She died on November 18, 1938, and her place was taken by Concepcion Paredo. [85] A strong teacher, she had lifted school standards high, and after the return to Monterrey she kept the school in existence by changing it into an Academy of Fine Arts. A woman of high contemplative gifts, she was cured of a severe illness through the intercession of Josefa Menendez. As vicar she looked confidently into a dangerous future, finding a new house in the capital city and reopening Guadalajara.

The two far-flung vicariates of South America remained very stable in work and in spirit. In Chile-Peru Mathilde Bouscayrol [86] from France governed "à l'antique." The house at Talca was wrecked by an earthquake and was closed (1928), while under Carmen Cubero [87] a new school began at Vina del Mar (1936). Las Rosas was opened in Santiago (1942); it was a house of studies and noviceship. In Lima the school on Calle Leon de Andrade was transferred to Salaverry (1941). In Brazil-Argentine-Uruguay Mother Jackson's place was taken by Ana Maria Cavanillas who had already been superior vicar in Spain. She founded a school at Castelar in Argentina (1935) where a noviceship was established, and a Teacher Training College at Valença in Brazil (1936).

As for the foreign missions, the period between the wars can be compared to the great missionary decade in which Philippine had set sail; her influence was felt as the process for her Beatification went ahead. The impetus came from two "Popes of the missions." Benedict XV, in *Maximum Illud*, urged the adaptation of native customs, for: "The Church is Catholic; in no country and among no people is she foreign." Pius XI consecrated the first oriental bishops and asked in *Rerum Ecclesiae*: "Why should not native clergy govern their own people?" The laity became mission-minded; Mission Sundays, mission crusades, mission clubs and magazines arose, all sponsored by enthusiastic school children. Soon after her canonization Mother Barat, from heaven, could see the Society established in cities where she had refused foundations "for now." The Society entered three new mission lands. More religious volunteered than could be sent, and Mother Vicente gave the needed qualifications:

I want persons of good health. They should have strength enough to pass through every obstacle and tread down all fears, devoted persons who will not hold back from giving their all to the Society, with a detached spirit that clings to nothing. They should be somewhat optimistic, for pessimism is the affliction of weak hearts. They should not consider their own suffering, but turn to the Heart of Jesus who loves us and asks for souls. In other words, I want apostles filled with God, givers of God and lovers of prayer, since only such will have an educational influence on their environment. [88]

At the General Council of 1928 mission protectorates were set up; established vicariates adopted those in mission lands.

In Japan, Mary Sheldon [89] became superior of Sankocho in 1917. She was an Australian, educated at Rose Bay where she entered the Society. She was later sent to Auckland as mistress general and superior. "Go on, get to know her, she's grand," said one child to another when they had lost their fright at her cool dignity. During the war a telegram sent her across the dangerous seas into Japan, and for the next forty years the government of the Society in the Far East was in her strong hands. She had the gifts of the builder, calm, decisive courage, practical vision and a heart that grew wider with the horizon. When asked to choose a motto with the initials of her own name she answered: "Mount steadily." Her co-worker was Hermanna Meyer: [90]

In temperament they were a contrast: Mother Sheldon reserved and serene, at home in the things of the mind with a deep philosophical bent, Mother Meyer with a gift for helping women in their home lives; Mother Sheldon with an understanding twinkle in her eyes, Mother Meyer laughing at difficulties and guiding others through them; Mother Sheldon a soul of ivory, Mother Meyer a soul of fire. [91]

Mother Meyer became superior of a house in Kobe near Osaka; it began in a little villa at Sumiyoshi and in 1923 moved to a hilltop in Obayashi. In that same year the school in Tokyo was literally thrown to the ground by the earthquake that set the whole city ablaze on September 1. For six weeks the community camped among the ruins while helping the homeless as best they could. Help poured in from Australia and America, and by October enough had been rebuilt to house three hundred children. Soon there were a thousand, while Obayshi kept pace. Japanese vocations began; at first the novices went overseas to Rose Bay or Kenwood, but by 1939 there was a noviceship at Obayshi. The integration of

Japanese culture with Christianity was speeded by the Church's approval of Shinto Rites such as bowing before the picture of the Emperor. Pius XI declared:

> It is well known that in the Far East certain ceremonies connected with pagan rites have today, owing to modern changes in ideas and customs, no meaning other than a civil respect for ancestors, love of country, and courtesy in social life. [92]

The Society at last reached China in 1926. The foundation was made from Japan, and the houses of the Far East were then formed into a vicariate under Mother Sheldon's guidance. She sailed for Shanghai with Conchita Nourry, [93] a French woman born in Spain. They waded under umbrellas through the water covering their new property on the Avenue Joffre in the French concession, tracing the buildings-to-be. These rose rapidly under Mother Nourry's impetus: an international school followed by elementary then secondary Chinese schools and finally Aurora College for Women, affiliated with the Jesuit University. All this was carried out with the help of the Franciscan Missionaries of Mary whose superior, Mother Carla, was an old child of Riedenburg. Chinese vocations began.

War broke out between China and Japan in 1937; the first university students wrote their entrance examinations to the sound of guns. When fighting became world-wide in 1941 the Sacred Heart compound became a concentration camp for interned nuns, and Mother Nourry was the cheerful, competent and loved hostess of ten communities who shared work, suffering and joy for two years. The schools kept going somehow. Then Japanese authorities took over the college for a Red Cross hospital. The camp was left desolate by the sudden death of Mother Nourry on May 31, 1945, but after August 15 roll-call was taken no more. The officers handed back the keys saying: "We have not won the war." All the works on Avenue Joffre flourished again — for a while.

Things went worse in Japan. Mother Sheldon and Mother Meyer had changed places in 1937; they were cut off from each other by the war. The nuns of nations hostile to Japan were interned, but Mother Sheldon was spared to care for a British invalid. The internees refused to return to their homelands when given a choice, as the bishop had pleaded that their help would be vital when peace came. They were hurried from place to place as bombs fell, carrying their bundles through the streets under flakes of fire. Sankocho again burned to the ground.

Obayashi was claimed by the government; the community took refuge in the mountains, at Karawizara. A nun in a concentration camp near Nagazaki was gathering grass in the fields on August 9, 1945. Hearing a plane she began to run, but: "I had only gone a few steps when there was a fearful explosion and everything turned golden yellow. It seemed as though the sun had burst." The atom bomb had fallen. When life began again all realized from experience that:

> Men and women who go through troublous times together are conscious of so close a bond with one another that they themselves are amazed at times at their sheer exhilaration of spirit. Gladly sharing the little they have, faced with the same uncertainties, they tend in thought and feeling and action to lose hold of the lesser things and hold fast to the greater. . . . In the concentration camps, on the hill of Obayashi, in the half ruined Sankocho, these things were a reality and a joy.[94]

The penetration of Black Africa by the Society of the Sacred Heart offers a study in the evolving concept of "missions" in the early twentieth century. At first it followed the pattern set in the days when countries of the Old World raced for colonial power. Pius XI urged the missioner, in Xavier-like terms, "to advance ever further in extending the reign of Christ." But a development was taking place, and Pius XII said:

> In former times the Church deployed its forces in the countries of ancient Europe, whence they flowed like a majestic river, to what might be called the fringes of the world. Today, on the contrary, she promotes an interchange of life and energy among all the members of the Mystical Body on earth. [95]

"Missions" were coming to be understood as penetration rather than conquest, as confrontation, exchange and inter-relationships based upon understanding.

Marie Symon was vicar of Belgium when a call came from the Congo. She shared the "holy impatience" of Philippine Duchesne and carried the day over Mother de Loë's prudence. She brought Fanny Braun[96] and her companions to Leopoldville in November, 1927. They were wearing white habits, the Society's first concession in dress. A large, handsomely built school at Kalina (now Gombe-Kinshasa) was opened for European children who soon numbered one thousand. But Mother Symon was looking towards the bush, and she did not wait as long as Philippine before finding her "natives." She soon returned to the Congo for a foundation at Kipako in the thickly wooded and all but roadless hills. People poured from the villages by the thousand for the first mass, celebrated outdoors with tom-toms, dancing, and a primordial tribal welcome. The children fought for sleeping places on the brick platforms that served as beds in the new school, and did their own cooking over an outdoor fire. By 1939 there was a second elementary school in the bush at Mbansa-Mboma. These schools aimed at forming Christian mothers in mud-floor village huts. But many African girls were looking beyond to the towns and to marriage with educated men, and in 1946 a boarding school at Mbansa-Mboma for these *évoluées* carried education to the secondary level. The children were predominantly Christian.

The life of the clan determines the customs of the African people who, instinctively religious, meet God silently in creation then sing and dance to express communion. Mother Symon seized the basic principle of pre-evangelization when she wrote:

> The esssential thing in our dealings with the Congolese is reverence for the human personality. Those whom we are trying to raise to be free men and Christians we must treat as such. The message of Christ is a supernatural message; it is the good news of sharing in God's life. It is not enough to devote ourselves, even if we were to kill ourselves in the effort; we must first of all have reverence .... For this we must know and study the region, the people, the village, the customs of the country and the reactions of the Congolese .... We must know them in order to use all those things in their traditions and natural character that can be used for raising them to the level of Christianity. It is the whole man who has to be made Christian and his whole life that has to be lived on a Christian level. [97]

In the spring of 1939 Catherine Andersson [98] led the Society into India. Her breezy, independent personality, rich yet all-of-a-piece, held many strands: English, Irish, Scottish and Norwegian, and she studied in Belgian, Dutch, German and Italian schools. She was an experienced educator before entering at Roehampton at the age of thirty-nine; now she was ready to learn from still another culture. In May, 1940, Sophia College for women, affiliated the following year with the University of Bombay, welcomed its first students: Hindu, Parsee, Mohammedan, Buddhist and Christian, with a mingling of castes, languages and customs. The Indians, a people in search of God, say: "Prayer is the key to the morning and the lock of the evening." The crest chosen for Sophia College shows the legendary Indian tree growing downwards from heaven; its motto is: "Roots upward." As a student put it: "Let it never be said of us, 'because they had no roots they withered away'." [99]

Indians are tolerant of all religious ideas and intolerant of conversion. The college had scarcely begun when it was nearly wrecked by a storm over the conversion of two students. The University threatened to disenfranchise it, but Mother Andersson's courageous stand saved the principle of liberty of conscience; the college continued its work, helping to create the climate of understanding essential for the growth of the Church in India. The students were in the movement known as "Bharda Bhakti" with the goal: "Love India, believe in her destiny, understand her well, be proud of her."

An interesting facet of the Society's internationalism is the fact that it was called upon in three different places to help in the formation of new religious orders, each with a missionary thrust. The first was at San Sebastian in Spain where Marie-Thérèse Dupuoy [100] formed an association for altar boys with the aim of fostering missionary vocations for the priesthood. The work reached surprising proportions in a building on the convent grounds. Mother Dupuoy was an "Easter soul," with sparkling energy and a gift of deep prayer. In 1925 she felt called to form among the young women who helped her a new order. Mother de Loë approved, and in 1930 Mother Dupuoy became the superior general of the Missionary Religious of the Sacred Hearts of Jesus and Mary. Yet she remained a true religious of the Sacred Heart, faithful to rule and to common life in her own convent. She resigned her office in 1950, and by that time her order had spread to many parts of Europe and overseas into China. When driven from China her nuns sought shelter as by right at the Via Nomentana.

The second such order was entrusted to Mother Andersson who was asked by the Archbishop of Bombay to train the first members of the Poor Sisters of Our Lady, an Indian congregation given to social welfare. For three years they lived with the Sacred Heart community, and on March 27, 1942, made their vows in the college chapel. They soon had several houses of their own in Bombay and beyond where they now carry on their apostolate in the spirit of Saint Madeleine Sophie whom they call "Grandmother."

The third began in 1930 when the Fathers of the Foreign Mis-

sions sent three young Japanese to the noviceship at Marmoutier to
be trained in religious life. Marthe de Sieyes, [101] a gifted guide in
spiritual ways, prepared them to return to Nagasaki to form a
Japanese order devoted to education. One of the three remained in
the Society of the Sacred Heart, the others established Junshin Kai
which now does excellent work in thirty-five houses.

*   *   *

The expansion of the Society at this time was more than
geographic; it was most marked in the field of education. In the
mission countries just considered adaptation of the Plan of Studies
to alien environments was made unhesitatingly. But teaching and
curriculum were on a western pattern, for all these lands were moving rapidly towards westernization; the riches of Oriental, African
or Indian cultures were scarcely explored. The way of life
traditional in Sacred Heart schools was followed with amazing
fidelity; this resulted in generations of intensely loyal alumnae of
many races. Even where the majority of students were non-
Christian and so remained, the sense that education is a work of
faith never lessened. It was recognized that "the Society must
educate for Christ before it can educate for Christianity." As Pius
XI put it in *Divini Illius Magistri*: "Education consists essentially in
the formation of man, training him to know what he must be and
how he must live in order to reach his end." [102]

In every country the mainspring to this expansion was "higher
education" under different aspects. Madeleine Sophie Barat had intended that students should leave school ready for life, and life was
now making higher demands. The original Plan of Studies
provided, together with book learning, "whatever may be needed
for the right ordering of life and the requirements of cultivated
society" [103] for girls who are "generally destined in the course of
Providence to be wives and mothers." [104] These wives and mothers
were now responsible citizens, involved in politics and in social service. Women's vote had become something to be reckoned with. By
the nineteen-thirties nuns were seen at the polls; they made a difference in the elections in Spain. Alumnae of convent schools were
not only voting but running for office and fighting their way into
the professions. This presumed their presence in the universities; the
Society would follow them there.

Both superiors general of this epoch faced feminine involvement in public issues with caution, another case of "necessary concessions." Mother de Loë wrote:

> Our Mother Foundress was forced, it is true, to follow masculine studies; she managed to do so, thanks to her superior intelligence as well as the presence at her side of a brother who was both priest and professor. She wanted strong studies as our method of education, in order to form accomplished wives and mothers, not political women as feminism of today aims to do. Without remaining behind, let us not follow that line; it will lead us into paths very dangerous for the faith and the way of life of many. Our children must take part in social service, but they must understand that its primary form is in the family. [105]

Mother Vicente added:

> Today there is much talk of learning, of university examinations, of careers for women. I am not opposed to this; we must keep up with the times, we must work to make our studies strong so that the Society may keep the place that it has always had among the teaching orders. But let us not forget that we have our role as educators, and that the first science that we must teach is the knowledge of Jesus Christ. [106]

The Plan of Studies must be brought up to date. The last major revision had been made by Mother d'Avenas in 1852; the editions of 1889 and 1894 had simplified the detailed descriptions of programs and stressed pedagogy. Through the first world war the experiments begun by Mothers Digby and Stuart had been carried on under a mistress general of studies in each country. In 1922 a new version of the Plan appeared. It was largely the work of Marie Lesage who had organized the advanced juniorate at Jette and put the studies on a solid footing in the French houses as they reopened. Clear and flexible, it had three sections: General Principles, Organization of Studies, and Practical Directives. It was confined to the secondary level, although higher education in the Society was now a reality. The General Council held in that same year examined the handbooks of the new university colleges already established.

There were signs that this growth was inevitable. In the nineteenth century the touchstone for success in education was too often "piety," taken presumably in its best sense. A crisis in the life of a child or of a school had to do with "good spirit" and with submissiveness. Now a new type of crisis had to be met across a generation gap caused by war, and the curriculum had lagged behind. Darwinian evolution had entered the popular imagination and children were questioning the relation of faith to science. One child, troubled about the act of creation, was advised "to take a tonic and make an act of faith." From now on teachers must meet the young mind on the intellectual level and respect the independence of the young will. "They *need* independence," said Gertrude Bodkin.

The original Plan of Studies offered a spring-board for the plunge. The two highest grades, the "first class" and "superior class" were already in advance of the normal secondary curriculum, and could be developed in a variety of ways, independently of the lower grades.

One form was the *Cours Supérieur*, a two-year cycle of humanistic studies not leading to a degree. The one at Ixelles, begun in 1926, drew students from many countries, directed by Hélène de Burlet. [107] She had been imprisoned for fourteen months as "a secret agent of Cardinal Mercier" in war time, and spent the bleak days sharing her optimism with fellow prisoners and embroidering her prayers in tiny coloured stitches onto a huge handkerchief. She was, like all strong personalities, diversely appreciated, but no student was left untouched. She described the *Cours Supérieur*:

> Ixelles is not in the least like a university centre. We are an expression of an intense and special mode of education, the general culture given by the Sacred Heart. We face young girls with their immediate mission, and as they are very homogeneous in age, background and culture, the task can be most fruitful. [108]

Classroom studies rayed out into mission enterprises, and the heart of life at Ixelles was the glowing spirituality that made Christ a reality in the modern world. Mother de Burlet kept the flame burning by letters to her world-wide alumnae. During the second war she was again imprisoned for three months in an airless, newsless cell, and "the experience of 1918 was like a refreshing dew compared to that of 1944. I had never before understood Gethsemane."

Two-year study cycles for *grandes pensionnaires* could be freely adapted to the needs of differing localities, ranging from languages acquired in a refreshing rural scene like Bonchurch to artistic experiences found in the museums and concert halls of a city, as at the Duchesne Finishing School in New York. More rigid was the Junior College department added to the school at Forest Ridge. All these programs, opened in great numbers at this time, met the need for cultural development of girls who did not wish to enter the universities. They became fewer as time passed.

The houses of study opened on university campuses were both communities for student nuns and hostels where other students could find guidance and a home-like atmosphere. These old university towns, Oxford, Louvain, Munich, Milan, filled with young students, were palimpsests of history and battle-grounds of ideas, expressing the dignity and beauty of the life of the mind. The mutual search for truth by men and women, the stimulus of its conflcting aspects, the rich and restless leisure of research, all this brought new life to the Society's teaching through these houses of study. In some places, as in Australia, the Society could take an official place in university life, through teaching and administration. At Sophia College in Bombay, and Aurora College in Shanghai degrees were given by the university but the college was administered by the Society.

The independent Liberal Arts Colleges in the United States and Puerto Rico tested the Society's powers of adaptation in unforeseen ways. The changes were startling: uniforms abandoned, discipline in the hands of the students, enlargement of "permissions" — where would it stop? "O yes," remarked Sarah Brownson, the always stimulating dean of studies,[109] "someday there will be smoking at Manhattanville." "When?" demanded the students. "When it no longer means what it does today."

The growth of the Society's educational principles, both intellectual and moral, along the paths opened by higher education can be seen in the work of Grace Dammann [110] who became president of Manhattanville College in 1932. She is representative of many prophetic and courageously loyal educators at this time of rapid development of the Society's mission. Her aim was Christian leaders among the women of tomorrow; her motto was Paul's "Doing the truth in charity." Students would look through her open door, then enter to talk of music, philosophy, their own tangles, God. Professors brought their best ideas into harmony or clash with their challenging president. All left with "a big ideal, a big spiritual scheme, a big idea or a big book." Her own big dreams took many shapes, such as the National Federation of Catholic College Students. Nowhere was her vision more daring and decisive than in the field of interracial justice. When a storm broke out over the admission of the first black students to the college, her address to the alumnae, "Principles versus Prejudice," shook complacent minds into thinking with the Church. At her sudden death on February 13, 1945, she was found with the *Summa* in one hand and *Prayer in the Modern World* within reach of the other. She had said:

> It is one of the basic characteristics of the education given at the Sacred Heart that it has its roots and its fruitage in *Eternity*. This establishes the special form and colour, the mass and line of its development in *Time*. It is a related thing, not something isolated, apart from the whole of life or from life in its wholeness — human and divine. Thus it is essentially a humanistic education in the best and Christian sense of the term. "God saw all things that he had made and they were very good." The Society strives to introduce her children to these good things of the natural order and especially to those studies which give an understanding of that microcosm which is the masterpiece of his creation, man in his totality and oneness, in his activities and accomplishments, to those studies which tend to develop the faculties which are specifically "human," to those which give a grasp of the underlying and immutable principles by which life must be directed . . . . This education fits the student for the life of an educated Catholic woman called upon to meet problems of the most searching nature, either in a professional career or in the more hidden work of a finely organized home. [111]

The teacher training colleges had entered higher education in their own way long before this time; now new ones were begun and the old ones strengthened. San Pedro in Lima became the Pedagogical Institute giving diplomas for secondary as well as primary education. After the second war the Training College at Saint Charles Square was transferred to Roehampton and became the Digby-Stuart College. The training colleges and university colleges were drawing closer together as the former enlarged their programs and the latter developed education departments offering teaching practice and state diplomas. One highly specialized venture was a response to the Motu Proprio of Pius X on Sacred Music, calling for a revival of Gregorian chant. The Pius X School of Liturgical Music was established at Manhattanville in 1916, under the direction of an enthusiast, Georgia Stevens. [112] For fifty years the school prepared experts who worked for liturgical renewal in schools and parishes.

One novel enterprise was the education of boys. Madeleine Sophie Barat had counted *les gamins* among her friends, beginning with the altar boy with whom she shared her breakfast tray across a window sill — together with an equally palatable catechism lesson. Such as these had their own classes at Jette and at Marmoutier where Thérèse Maillucheau was Latin professor for potential priests.

When Mother Stuart travelled with Mother Digby in 1898 she wrote:

> Yesterday our Mother had the nicest reception she has yet had. This house is almost the only one, I think, that has a *demi-pensionnat* for boys. Of course they are quite separate . . . . These heroes were drawn up in a semi-circle, heels rigidly together, heads erect, very tight knickerbockers, very large white favours, spotless kid gloves. . . . Each boy came up to offer his flowers, looking at our Mother with a respect and awe that I hardly thought young America capable of.[113]

This was at North State Street in Chicago; in time there were fully developed preparatory schools for boys, Hardey Prep at Sheridan Road, Barat Hall in St Louis and Stuart Hall in San Francisco as well as boys' sections in several parochial schools. High-principled men boasted of being Sacred Heart alumni long before the coming of co-education in the Society.

All these rapid developments, together with an enormous increase in school enrolments in every land (and with no increase in the number of nuns teaching) caused an unforeseen factor to enter the Society's educational work: the collaboration of large numbers of lay teachers. On the university level the enrichment coming from specialization and from the masculine mind was obvious. Otherwise the situation was at first looked upon as a regrettable necessity, but gradually the assets of teamwork of variety of training, of the dedicated contribution of lay teachers at every level came to be realized. Cooperation with wider educational efforts gave further enrichment, with the Society's participation in intercongregational groups such as the Association of Convent Schools in England (now the Association of Teaching Religious).

The Society has always kept in touch with its former pupils. Mother Barat invited them back to the Hotel Biron every year to celebrate *la Madeleine*, her feast day on July 22, when there were fireworks, games, songs, a picnic and Benediction. The alumnae returned for retreats and meetings (at which their high heels and silk dresses provided relieving distraction to the uniformed children). Local Alumnae Associations were formed under different names in the late nineteenth and early twentieth centuries, so that the former students of each house might keep their unity and come together for stronger well-doing. National associations followed. In 1933, for example, representatives of all the local associations in the

United States met in Saint Louis and formed the Associated Alumnae of the Sacred Heart (AASH). From then on biennial conferences met in different cities from coast to coast, so that women with common ideals could pool their thoughts and interprises. In 1942 Hildreth Miere initiated the "International Très-Bien," a little card that would open to any travelling child of the Sacred Heart, teen-ager or octogenarian, the doors of Sacred Heart convents and of alumnae homes the world over. Education is an open-ended process.

*   *   *

The growing social awareness of the Church was articulated by Pius XI, who said at his accession:

> We shall always speak as head of the Catholic Church, but still more and above all as a man of our times, that is, as witness and personal actor in the events which threaten our contemporaries. From a certain point of view we shall be more occupied with purely human social institutions and governments than with the Catholic Church itself. [114]

Quadragesimo Anno appeared in the midst of world depression, declaring that: "The worker must not receive in charity what is due to him in justice." The charter of Catholic Action was *Il Fermo Proposito*. It spoke of:

> ... those chosen groups of Catholics who plan to unite the strength of all their forces to fight by every just and legal method against an anti-christian civilization, to repair the harm that is being done, to restore to Jesus Christ his place in the family, in schools, and in society.

Response was electrifying: *Jeunesse Ouvrière Catholique*; the controverted priest-worker movement; the *Semaines Sociales*. Sociology was being integrated with dogma; students took up both the intellectual and the practical challenge to change society.

The Society of the Sacred Heart reacted far more vigorously to *Quadragesimo Anno* than it had done to *Rerum Novarum*. Teenagers were no longer sheltered boarders. Mission clubs for long-distance action now expanded into missions on the home front. The children learned to speak in public, to take initiative and direct their own activities; they became personally involved in the needs of society.

Possibilities for college students were still wider; their studies passed into action. The "Popular Works" usually stemmed from Study Circles. Typical of such groups was the Barat Association at Eden Hall, begun in 1922 by Mary Spallen. [115] Starting as a retreat movement for professional women, it developed lecture circles, "apostolates of cheer," charitable and missionary enterprises, recreational outings and "Barat-by-the-Sea," a vacation house for its untiring members. Groups of Children of Mary in all countries often began such works on their own initiative.

With a desire to clarify the canonical autonomy of the adult Congregation of the Children of Mary, which had been recognized from the beginning, the Society asked Pius XI to confirm this in a document. The answer was not the expected one, due to misunderstandings. In 1930 the pope issued a Brief extending "privileges" to the Children of Mary of the Sacred Heart. They were to join the Prima Primaria; they were to be centred at the Trinita in Rome; none but former pupils were to be admitted. After difficult attempts to adjust to these conditions while keeping the original character of the congregation, it was decided not to profit by "these so-called privileges." In 1932 the centenary of the Children of Mary was kept in a fervent, world-wide union of spirit.

The celebrations initiated in Lyons, the cradle of the Sodality. Representatives of many groups gathered at the Via Nomentana on March 29, when Mother Vicente wished them a deepening of the love of our Lady "which will show itself in generous impulses stemming from the spirit of faith and charity, and will inspire your actions, thus making you sowers of union wherever you go." [116] At the papal audience Pius XI asked them to be women of prayer and active apostles, answering by deeds rather than words the many demands of the Church, of society and of their own family life. Each group throughout the world held a triduum of thanksgiving.

The centenary had a lasting memorial in the publication of *Children of Mary of the Sacred Heart*, [117] brief biographies of modern types of the "valiant woman" of Scripture. The letter from Lyons had asked: "Would the Children of Mary of 1832 recognize in those of 1932 true sisters and faithful successors?" The book showed the continuity of the ideal. The first sketch was of Madame Thérèse Marie de la Barmondière, a *grande dame* of the Old Order, who collected her scattered fortune for the benefit of the unfortunate after the French Revolution. She was the beneficent friend of

Mother Barat and the awesome protectress of the Rue Boissac in Lyons where the Sodality had begun. Here she had hung a portrait of her severe, silk-clad self, attaching a message to the superior, Mother Geoffroy: "Near you, my incomparable friend, I shall, through this picture, spend my life."

The portrait is reflected, in different poses and shades, in the biographies that follow. They show women of different temperaments and cultures, all remarkably strong-minded, ranging from the high aristocracy to the unpretentious bourgeoisie, with the high-median predominating. All have a common likeness: Lady Bountiful living her *noblesse oblige*; all are cultured and attractive women who lived for others. A few presided in artistic and intellectual *salons*; most were the centres of homes where the Christian life was lived simply in the midst of plenty; all were spiritually in earnest, living prayerfully, even mystically, in the midst of too much to do. "Yesterday," said Madame Théodule de Goffinet in Brussels, "while busy all the time with my grandchildren, I was truly penetrated with the presence of God, and so happy." And Madame Annie de Samassa in Budapest: "I cannot describe the face of Christ, it is a mystery, but the light of his eyes goes through me."

There were Lady Cecil Lothian and Lady Georgiana Fullerton, converts of the Oxford Movement and leaders of the Catholic revival in England. There was the lavish Dionisia, Duchess of Pastrana, who literally established the Society in palaces, her own palaces, in Spain. There was Mrs Elizabeth Hughes who gave her family home in Sydney to the Society. There was Mrs Madeleine de Lauréal, a Bostonian who had gone to school at the Hotel Biron and after her marriage in Saint Louis helped Mother Duchesne to establish the first Children of Mary in America. She was still in Saint Louis, almost a centenarian, when Mother Digby passed through. There were two doctors' wives, Mrs Annie Gavin in Boston and Dona Adela de Solanet in Buenos Aires, both giving themselves away to others in money, service and love. There was Masako Yamamoto in the Orient, one of the first pupils of Sankocho. She was baptized at the time of her marriage, and in her home fused the culture of the Land of the Rising Sun with the flowering of her faith. The book closed too soon to include Children of Mary like Lilian Anderson in New York who devoted her Christ-filled life to the slum children in Barat Settlement.

* * *

"I sometimes wonder," said an elderly nun in the nineteen-thirties, "what my life would be like if I had been fed on this doctrine of the Mystical Body in my youth." The same doctrine that was fostering the spirit of Catholic Action was also fostering a wider spirit of prayer. An enlarged range of spiritual reading in community gave a strong doctrinal basis to the prayer of the Society.

Pius XI established the feast of Christ the King on Christmas Day, 1925, in answer to the requests of the faithful gathered by Georges and Marthe de Nouailles, apostles of the social reign of Christ. This marked a fusion of the trends of the day that created its spiritual climate. An article entitled "The Mystical Body and the devotion to the Sacred Heart" developed "the three great concepts inspiring the spiritual life of the faithful: the Mystical Body, the Sacred Heart and Christ the King."

> Here we clearly see the importance of the devotion to the Sacred Heart in the life of the Mystical Body. It is the great means of our age, provided by Christ himself and fostered by his vicars, to bring the members to perform, out of love for Christ, those actions which produce growth in their own spiritual life, and through which they reap benefits which membership in the Mystical Body can bring to themselves, to the whole body and to society at large. [118]

In 1928 the Encyclical *Miserentissimus Deus* urged the Church "to fill up what is wanting in the passion of Christ" by reparation, and the feast of the Sacred Heart was raised to the first class with a new mass, *Cogitationes Cordis Ejus*, "the thoughts of his Heart." The Society adopted this mass, despite the privilege of using the mass *Egredimini* loved by Madeleine Sophie Barat, in order to be more at one with the thinking of the universal Church.

For at this time of expansion, this time of transition from looking back to looking for things to come, the Society was growing in awareness of solidarity with the Church. As Gertrude Bodkin [119] put it:

> Let us be as wide as the world. We have the interests of the Church all over the world in our hearts and that increases our desire. As our desires increase in fervour they spread themselves out all over God's creation, until not one person is excluded from our prayer. [120]

Her own life was a bridge from the early Society to the present (she was born ten years after the death of Madeleine Sophie Barat and was to die during Vatican Council II). She had foreseen a challenge and said; "The Society is only beginning; we scarcely know its possibilities yet."

What is the Society to me? A loved thing must enter into our daily lives. Christian life and religious life become beautiful in the living. We both live and give their beauty. We must show the Society as lovable in its simplicity. Its fate is in our hands, in the hands of those who have taken Saint Madeleine Sophie's thought and assimilated it, who have brought it again into action in new circumstances, in a new age, when things are very different externally from what they were in her day. [121]

Chapter 7

Challenge
1946 – 1958

I have come to bring fire
to the earth, and how I wish
it were blazing already.

Luke 12:49

The years from the end of World War II to the death of Pius XII
were charged with dynamism as the global age moved towards the
space age, through the confused forties and the "fabulous fifties."
The United States issued a "Universal Declaration of Human
Rights," implemented non-politically by UNESCO. New nations
came into being: the Philippines, Israel, South Korea. A Third
World emerged behind the opposing worlds of Communism and
Capitalism. Behind the Iron Curtain violent upheavals took place,
while in the Orient the Bamboo Curtain fell. Pius XII strove for
"Peace, the work of justice."

For the Society of the Sacred Heart these were years of transition
when tradition was challenged by renewal. The Aggiornamento had
not begun; it was prepared for, without realization of all that it
would mean, under the leadership of Marie-Thérèse de Lescure, a
superior general as dynamic as her times. Her sense of mission was
drawn from beyond herself: "I have come to bring fire to the
earth."

A challenge may be a threat or a stimulus. If the one challenged
feels threatened he may defend himself, attack in return, compromise
or go his own way. If he feels stimulated he becomes concerned, involved; he will move with his challenger along parallel lines with his
own goal in clearer view. In the preceding period of expansion the
Society had attempted to meet current challenges in both ways at
once, with resulting tensions. While answering a manifest call to

progress it had been on the defensive; while reaching out it had remained stable and worked by its own pattern.

But after 1946 concession and caution gave way to a more determined stance. The number of communities grew slightly; in 1946 there were 6560 religious in 175 houses in 24 vicariates; in 1958 there were 6852 religious in 183 houses in 35 vicariates. These steady figures are once again deceptive. Vocations were waning while the age level was rising; the pyramid was becoming inverted. New teaching programs and the number of those taught increased far out of proportion to personnel; overwork menaced both efficiency and prayer. Yet, as problems became more complex, a clearer "yes" or "no" was returned to louder demands. Tensions did not vanish; they were confronted. While no radical changes were made in structures or way of life, both were revivified. Old values were re-expressed in "the language of today," as Mother de Lescure put it. She saw horizons, had the courage to move and do, while remaining utterly intransigent to both compromise and basic change.

Yet signs that such change was needed — and was coming — surfaced unmistakably. Renewal was foreseen, but it must await a sign that it came from God. "We must do as we have been doing," said Gertrude Bodkin, "until light comes to change, light from the right source." John XXIII became vicar of Jesus Christ a year after the death of Mother de Lescure, and the light came.

*   *   *

Marie Thérèse de Lescure[1] was born in Paray-le-Monial on December 4, 1884. From her window she could look down into the gardens of the old Visitation monastery where Margaret Mary Alacoque had minded her donkey; she could see the red lamp in the chapel where the Great Revelations of the devotion to the Sacred Heart had been made. The child's very name called the devotion to mind; a General de Lescure, "the Saint of Poitou," had taken part in the Vendean uprising of 1792 in which peasant soldiers died with badges of the Sacred Heart on their blouses.

This unpredictable little girl, intelligent, lively, petulant, with hours of stormy retreat into herself, was one of nine children in a home of the old régime where God and God-loving parents were first-served, in a musical, artistic and intellectual atmosphere. She sensed her vocation early and thought of entering with her first teachers, the Sisters of the Blessed Sacrament, but a passion for prayer pulled her towards Carmel. Although her mother was an old pupil of La Ferrandière and two of her great-aunts, Constantine and Sophie, had been religious of the Sacred Heart, "Zezé" was prejudiced against the Society. She grudgingly consented to read the life of Madeleine Sophie Barat and surrendered when she came to the passage speaking of the spirit of the Society as "generosity – a strong and generous love for Jesus Christ." She entered at La Ferrandière in 1904, and plunged so deep in her new life that Mother de Lavergne sometimes said: "Sister de Lescure, come out of your little chapel."

Events shook her out. The expulsions from France sent the novice to Rivoli, and here she clarified her ideals in the lengthy note-taking at which she was already adept:

> Religious life is Jesus alone in the soul, covering, changing, absorbing all into himself. Jesus has life in such abundance that it overflows. It is this superabundance of God in the soul that makes her an apostle. [2]

After her first vows she went to Avigliana for five trying years. Her mood was too serious, her teaching too lofty, for the taste of the children who kept things lively in other ways. Exhaustion pulled her down. It was a relief to go to the juniorate at Rivoli and study the philosophy of education under Marie Lesage. Steadied, she went to Ixelles for her probation, guided by Marie Guibert. Mother Stuart gave the probanists their name: "Probation of the life of Nazareth" with the motto "My life is hidden with Christ in God." During her long retreat Sister de Lescure was completely in the dark and clung to the one thing necessary, the divine will, when she was professed on February 19, 1912.

She was then given charge of the juniorate at Jette and was just beginning to show her powers as an educator when her health broke down. She was sent to Brighton, but was not helped by the sea air and returned to Rivoli for complete rest. From then on daily headaches were her lot, "my own crown of thorns." Then the war broke out, frontiers were closed, and a year of lonely anxiety prepared her for an unexpected role.

The Society was returning to France in the teeth of war and Sister de Lescure came to Poitiers in 1915 as mistress of studies and then mistress general. Her gifts came into full play, spurred by the energy, insight and unrelenting ardour that consumed her own life. She would take no nonsense; she was omniscient and seemed omnipresent. Creative and intuitive, she could demand much. In her first retreat as mistress general she found "the master-light of my life:"

> Our Lord living within me. Let all contact with the souls of others be a call from him and allow him alone to reach them, giving to them an idea of Jesus Christ, of his Heart and of his Spirit. [3]

Direct work with the school ended when Mother de Lescure became superior at Poitiers in August, 1921. She then learned from the assistant, Antoinette de Girval, [4] of the manifestations of our Lord made to the Spanish novice, Josefa Menendez. What happened from then until the death of Sister Josefa on December 29, 1923, has already been told. Here it will be considered as a shaping force upon the life of Mother de Lescure who had the responsibility of handing on the Message to the world.

By nature she was not attracted to such phenomena, and felt keenly, painfully, this unsought role as guide of a visionary. For more than two years she lived in close intimacy with the simple, obedient novice whom she controlled with unflinching wisdom. She suffered from doubts despite her growing faith in these revelations of which she kept a minute day-by-day account. She informed the Mother House and the bishop of Poitiers of each development and consulted theologians. She knew that she was personally involved in visions that she never shared. "I shall make use of her to accomplish my work," said our Lord to Josefa. When the latter died Mother de Lescure went straight ahead on "this dark and hard road along which it pleases our Lord that I should walk," for "from now on my prayer is turned to this end, that his work may be done and his design of love fulfilled." [5] A booklet of extracts from our Lord's words, *Josefa Menendez à l'Ecole de Coeur de Jésus* was printed for the use of the Society in 1933.

In 1927 Mother de Lescure left Poitiers for Toulouse. Two years later she was placed in charge of the new vicariate formed in southern France with Montpellier as centre; here she remained for thirteen years. Things began quietly enough in this big and busy house, and there were other houses to be visited, including those in Egypt where Mother de Lescure spoke as openly to the Muslim children of the Heart of Christ as she did to the Christian.

For the Message lay on her like a burning weight, and she compiled another booklet, *Un Appel à l'Amour*, of which Cardinal Pacelli approved. "The Message has at last reached beyond the Society," said Mother de Lescure on the day when it went to press. Within six years fifty thousand copies in many languages carried it around the world.

When the civil war in Spain broke out in July, 1936, Montpellier flung its doors wide open, and they stayed open for the next ten years. First came the French nuns driven from Spain, then the Spanish coadjutrix novices. An adjoining house was turned into a noviceship as the times became more grim. The old and ill Spanish nuns followed, then children to be taken into the school and Children of Mary with complete families to be helped to find a livelihood. When Franco triumphed in the spring of 1939 all the refugees went home and Montpellier enjoyed one uncrowded summer.

But in September it turned into a military hospital with the coming of World War II, without ceasing to be a school. Soldiers filled the school quarters; the children filled the community quarters; the community hid in corners. At night desks and chairs went into the corridors to make room for beds. Christmas brought fusioning of all the groups in the courageous atmosphere of joy created by Mother de Lescure as she moved from one to the other. Then twenty-two Carmelites appeared and remained for a year. Just when it seemed hopeless to keep the school, the government evacuated the hospital and the children kept on coming. The centenary of the house was celebrated cheerfully in May, 1941.

In the meantime the entire French noviceship from Marmoutier had been installed in the space left by the Spanish novices, and the entire French juniorate followed them. But the mistress of novices fell ill and Mother de Lescure took charge for many months. French probanists arrived every six months and Mother de Lescure prepared each group for profession, fifty young religious in all. Her way of formation lost nothing of its probing, affectionate severity in this austere setting.

By now there was no fuel and not enough blankets in winter, until one day an enormous truck filled with bedding arrived just after another group of refugees had been taken in on faith. There was less and less food at any season, and the whole household worked outdoors, cutting wood, growing vegetables, hunting for roots and berries. Where work was hardest there was Mother de Lescure:

> One could always recognize her by her way of doing things; when cutting branches she would study each one with care and love before giving the final blow; one could see that she was careful for the well-being of the bush itself. [6]

With all this Mother de Lescure had added another labour of love to her burden; it meant rising long before dawn to find time. She gave those dark hours in an unheated house to writing a fuller version of *Un Appel a l'Amour*, in which the Message was set into the chronology of Josefa's own life. In the summer of 1942 she received the encouragement that she badly needed when François Charmot, S. J. gave a retreat at Montpellier. He upheld her faith in the Message and became her own spiritual guide. The book was ready for publication in 1944, but paper was lacking. Despite war hazard the convents in New York sent a supply and the book appeared. On its frontispiece was the autograph letter of Pius XII written for the earlier edition:

> May these pages contribute effectively to strengthening in many souls an ever fuller and more loving confidence in the mercy of the divine Heart for the poor sinners that we all are. [7]

When the frontiers opened again Montpellier slowly returned to normal life. After the death of Mother Vicente in January, 1946, Mother de Lescure visited the houses in Egypt, presided at a Council of Studies in Paris, then said goodbye to her community "for a few weeks" and left for the General Council in Rome. On September 29, 1946, Marie-Thérèse de Lescure was elected ninth superior general of the Society of the Sacred Heart.

The news went round with the effect of an Easter sunrise after the long night of the war. The name caused no surprise, though unexpected; it was widely known because of the Message. This was the first time that a superior general had been elected without having first served as vicar general named by her predecessor, since Mother Datti had been appointed to that office by the Holy See during Mother Vicente's illness. At the general council no ballot made out by Mother Vicente naming a vicar general could be found and the elections took place uninfluenced by her choice. Only after the event was the ballot found; it bore the name of Marie-Thérèse de Lescure! The stunned superior general wrote to the Society:

In this poor world of ours, torn, off-balance, even hopeless, the work of the Society seems to be more and more needed, and the Heart of Jesus wills to make use of us to bring about a moral reconstruction through the extension of the reign of peace and of charity. [8]

A new atmosphere was felt in this Council, which met from September 29 to October 19, 1946.[9] Adaptations which earlier Councils had barely tolerated were now urged with "the breadth needed in our days." Now it was "less a question of cases to be resolved than of orientations to be given." Choices were to be made "on the spot, not imposed," leaving to different countries "all the latitude necessary." The word *élargir* was a key to many important areas: books for community libraries "chosen from among the best modern authors"; the studies of the young nuns together with apostolic work "which satisfies their need for self-broadening"; more flexible activities for the novices; the development of the coadjutrix sisters. However, a strongly negative stand was taken on a most urgent question:

Despite opinions to the contrary, and the apparent demands of a greater good, we have, resting on the words of the Holy Father whom we consulted, maintained the principle of cloister as the rampart which must keep safe the very source of our religious spirit and of the interior life. [10]

At the close of the Council:

There is unanimity in our decision to keep the Society moving along the lines of its own spirit, more strongly rooted than ever in those religious principles which are its very life and which alone can assure its advance through the adaptation to the needs of souls, to our times, to different countries without fear of deviation." [11]

Mother Zurstrassen, recently appointed assistant general, summed up her impressions of the Council in a letter which reveals how clearly the direction of things to come was felt thirty years ago:

My idea of a more democratic form of government is not very clear for I have not thought much about it. But it would be something like this: for example, a delegate from each country together with the vicar [at the General Councils]; wisely, to pay more attention to what the religious are saying; to tend to liberate those in responsible positions, keeping them respectful and submissive but not passive — that is, avoiding thinking for themselves, and to encourage them to express their ideas with a certain independence until the moment when a contrary decision is given .... Many decisions have been left to the judgment of the vicars in their own vicariates, for more and more differences are emerging among ourselves.

I am sorry that a clearer and more straightforward line of conduct in the matter of cloister was not indicated. It remains a hybrid matter, difficult to defend. But the time was not ripe. How many conditions, such as climate, mentality, government, degrees of openness and of airing one's views, make us want and even ask for different things, things which were accorded at the assembly with great breadth. All the more reason to maintain and strengthen the great structural lines: the primacy of the interior life, the devotion to the Sacred Heart, the vows, the selfless apostolate for "souls," the primacy of education over instruction, concern for an "élite." [12]

On December 12 Clemente Micara [13] was installed as Cardinal Protector; actually he had held the post since the death of Cardinal Maglione two years earlier. In January, 1947, Mother de Lescure wrote:

The fact remains that the Society has rounded an important turning point in its history. In face of the future it must choose its direction. To each of us, no matter who we are, our Holy Mother repeats; "Its fate is in our hands." It is therefore important that all, no matter who we are, should become more aware of the responsibilities now facing us, not in order to fulfil them individually according to our own ideas, but to embrace them in a strong common love for the Society. [14]

After the war-ridden experience of "open house" at Montpellier Mother de Lescure became hostess of the larger "house of welcome" that the Mother House had always been. She found it too small for its role; a wing was lengthened and a storey added. The chapel was remodelled with luminous simplicity. All manner of people came singly or in groups. A new apostolate was formed, called simply "the work of the Mother House"; Italian priests whose churches needed refurnishing knew where to come.

Mother de Lescure was extremely fluent both in writing and in speech. She wrote rapidly, copiously, "from the memory of the heart" that she kept of each correspondent. A few moments spent with her seemed timeless, overflowing. Like Mother Stuart she not only formed close personal contacts but wished to visit every house of the Society. She reached one hundred and three in eighteen countries, with no need of her predecessor's "one hundred days at sea," for between dawn and dark an airplane carried her to the antipodes. During her travels she was often called "our present Holy Mother."

Her circuits began with a visit to Spain and widened throughout Europe. When she stopped at shrines like those at Jette or Grenoble she would send a message to the whole Society. In 1953 she went to the United States, with the centenary of Kenwood as her focal point. Two years later she went through South America. Everywhere, what she had to say passed the language barrier with look and gesture. Some feared her powers of penetration, her severity in correction, her rock-like decision, but few could resist her deep-reaching influence. Even defensive youth, already in revolt against symbols of authority, opened to her. She said to college students:

> You must carry light and warmth and love to the whole world, to all the multitudes who have neither light nor love. You, all of you, are walking on that luminous road and the flame is love. And love is the gift of self; we must give ourselves, give of our riches, to souls and to many souls. This is the message from the Heart of Jesus that I bring to you: lead the world to love by the road of truth. [15]

Gradually the whole Society came to know her paradoxical qualities:

> It was the antinomies of her character that made her so human: a sureness of decision which carried power, together with a self-diffidence that led her to seek supporting counsel in the smallest matters; a rock-like faith that made her dare anything, together with a constant need to struggle against fear, disquiet, anguish; firm to the point of severity in correcting others, and tender as a mother to soothe and heal; wholly recollected while seeing everything; entirely consecrated, reserved and set apart, while nearer to others than anything around them. All these qualities were surprisingly blended, harmonized in a simplicity which attracted all from the greatest to the least. What was her secret? It could be guessed from that childlike look which she sometimes raised to heaven under the crushing weight of her charge. [16]

Encouraging events took place in Rome. The Cause for the Beatification of Janet Stuart was introduced in 1948, and that of Josefa Menendez the next year. The Holy Year of 1950 coincided with the Sesquicentennial of the Society, and Pius XII sent an autograph letter:

> It is not without an inspiration from on high that Saint Madeleine Sophie placed her Society under the sign of the Sacred Heart, the *Labarum* of modern times.... She whose contemplative soul plunged into the abyss of divine love

in order to shine out around her, thus showed that a profound interior life is the condition of any true apostolate. [17]

On November 21 the prayer composed by Mother Desmarquest for the Golden Jubilee of 1850 was said in every house of the Society. In her letter Mother de Lescure quoted long passages from the writings of the Foundress, to recall her continued presence in "her little Society such as she desired it to be, 'consummated in unity' in Christ." The centenary of the death of Philippine Duchesne was kept on November 17, 1852, and Mother de Lescure commented on the prayer of the mass: "Her soul clung to thee by earnest prayer and by self-sacrifice."

In government Mother de Lescure's principle was: "self-effacement, detachment, that the Heart of Jesus alone may govern and that the spirit of the Society alone may give direction." Every act or decision must be preceded by "a moment of intense prayer," for "God will make us hear his word for resolving all questions in his own way." People must be put before things, for: "Each person has necessarily her mentality, her character, her soul, all of which must be harmonized or sacrificed along the lines of the Society's unity of spirit." She wanted "nothing administrative," for: "The Society is not governed like a machine but ruled in love and confidence as a religious family." [18]

The major issues of Mother de Lescure's generalate focused in the Twenty-fourth General Council that met from September 29 to October 20, 1952. [19] When announcing it she wrote:

> Each of our General Congregations, sometimes under difficult circumstances, has marked not so much a sudden turning to new ideas as a unanimous and more generous *élan* in a strengthened understanding by the Society of its own basic nature, conscious of its own spirit and resolute in its fidelity, and by that very fact open to the contemporary interests of the Heart of Jesus as he does his work in succeeding epochs. [20]

Pius XII blessed "this fidelity to dear and venerable traditions re-expressed with prudent openness to the new needs of the hour." At the opening session Mother de Lescure recalled that "the Heart of Jesus is for the Society its way, its truth and its life." Then:

> Turning always to the rich source of our Constitutions, we can stand firm and at the same time be open in the face of all the present needs which call for effort and for adaptation. The same source will keep the Society in religious and

supernatural equilibrium. This equilibrium is quite different from both the isolationism so opposed to the immense charity of the Heart of Jesus which urges us on, and the impulsive acceptance of the solutions offered by modernization which are usually temporary and often risky. [21]

The Council was concerned with rewriting fundamental Society documents, apart from the Constitutions. The first was the Custom Book, "the guardian of uniformity and the bond of unity."

It is necessary to rejuvenate certain expressions, modify and eliminate details that are too concrete or localized, and suppress some decisions that have become outmoded because the conditions of life are in evolution. [22]

The revision, completed the following year, was far from radical. The Decrees of the General Councils were streamlined and organized. They were amplified by a series of *Directives* which brought out the underlying principles of formation, temporal administration, education and enclosure, freeing them from rigid details. (The revision of the *Plan of Studies* will be considered later.) On the whole, this Council was more restrained than that of 1946.

The rule of enclosure was strongly re-affirmed; at the same time the dispensations needed in modern life were enlarged and delimited. Three cases were recognized: care of health, business matters, and apostolic work which implied university studies and educational meetings. No dispensations were given for family visits or for recreational and cultural projects. The most cogent reason for maintaining cloister rested upon the canonical status of the Society:

When, in 1826, our Holy Mother obtained from the Holy See the approbation of the Constitutions, she was compelled, regretfully, to renounce solemn vows, since papal enclosure, which is their condition, is incompatible with the apostolic work of the Society. In compensation for this keenly felt sacrifice, Pope Leo XII accorded to our Mother Foundress the favour of the vow of stability and of the complete renunciation of goods at our profession. But in return the Sacred Congregation of Bishops and Regulars required that cloister (non-papal or semi-cloister) should be established and defined as strictly as possible. It was then that the Fourth General Congregation formulated for the first time the Decrees determining the nature of the cloister proper to the Society. To realize its major importance, we may put the matter thus: the Society's cloister is in direct dependence upon the vow of stability as papal enclosure is upon solemn vows. Since then we have appreciated cloister for its intangible value as a constitutive element of the Society, not simply as a safeguard for recollection and interior life. [23]

The argument appeared unanswerable. What could not be foreseen in 1952 was that within ten years the Church itself would
judge the matter otherwise. For the moment this canonical reasoning
seemed conclusive. But Mother de Lescure did not wish to rest
upon legalism. Characteristically, she moved from an administrative
principle to one which would always be valid, one which would in
time become, in the light of the Church's new attitude, a motive for
penetration into the contemporary world:

> What should go out, escape and radiate from our cloisters, is not religious com-
> ing and going but the immense charity of the Heart of Jesus, overflowing
> among ourselves and upon all those who surround and approach us. [24]

*   *   *

Those who lived at the Mother House at this time formed a
varied group. Mother Datti remained assistant general, charged
with "Roman affairs" and supporting others with gentle strength.
Her Golden Jubilee was kept on July 31, 1948, when the oratory
of Saint Madeleine Sophie was remodelled as a thank-offering for
her valour. She died on November 19, 1954, and Mother de
Lescure wrote:

> She will root us in the love of Holy Mother Church and of her Head; her
> Catholic and Roman soul made her look upon the interests of the Church as
> the only ones which count here below. Above all, she will always be for us an
> unforgettable example of fidelity in the widest sense of the term [25]

Elizabeth Zurstrassen [26] had been mistress of novices and vicar of
Belgium; she came to the Mother House in 1945 to take charge of
the probation and held the post for nineteen years. Her way of formation was "open, supple, facilitating the adaptation to change that
was to come later." Her message was confidence, abandonment,
which she expressed by the English word "surrender," and she combated fear as youth's worst enemy. She retired in 1964 and was
able to say not long before her death on February 2, 1971: "I see
coming a new type of religious of the Sacred Heart and I am filled
with confidence."

Ursula Benziger, [27] who had been mistress of novices at
Kenwood and superior of Manhattanville, was called to the Mother
House by the Council of 1946. She was a dominant, forthright per-

son, generous and wide-visioned, with a sometimes piercing insight into the mystery of prayer which was for her "a biting need, a passion." As assistant general she travelled with Mother de Lescure through North and South America and the British Isles. She too retired in 1964 and died on February 5, 1972.

Elena Yturralde [28] was also summoned by the Council of 1946 from her activities as superior in Spain, to be local superior at the Mother House as well as assistant general. Everything in her was vibrant with a simple, chivalric faith, a spirituality centered in "the gaze of God." After a journey to Spain with Mother de Lescure her health weakened, and from then on her luminous influence went out through letter-writing. She scarcely left her room where a small lamp burning at all hours helped her failing sight. She died at the Mother House on January 26, 1958.

Isabelle Doutreleau was secretary general from 1947 to 1949 when her place was taken by Françoise de Lambilly; in that same year Marguerite de James became treasurer general. Throughout the years of challenge all these co-workers at the centre shared actively in Mother de Lescure's desire to "pass on to the world the burning love of the Sacred Heart, by the full strength of our prayer and work, our fidelity and spirit of sacrifice." [29]

* * *

The aspect of community life stressed at this time was "élargissement." Constantly in her letters Mother de Lescure asked that each house, like the Mother House, should be — within the limits of cloister — wide open in welcome. Each community must be (untranslatably) "un foyer d'amour." Each member must manifest on a wider scale than before the mutual love of the family life within the community itself, none other than "the immense charity" of the Lord:

> This love must be active, burning, through the mutual gift of the best of ourselves each to the other, mothers and sisters making one in the unity of our great love. May it overflow from our religious houses upon many: alumnae, visitors of all sorts, workmen, the poor, priests and religious — and upon our students first of all. These must know that we love them, that we love one another, and that we are happy in our common self-giving to the Heart of our Lord. They cannot mistake this visible radiation of the interior presence of which he is the flame. [30]

Mother de Lescure revealed the source of the internationality of
the Society of the Sacred Heart in the speech which she made when
awarded the Medal of the Legion of Honour by the French government on May 10, 1957:

> This Society owes to its Foundress its expansion around the world. Saint
> Madeleine Sophie – whose heart and mind were so very French and whose
> soul was so very Roman – gave to her work a tradition of catholicity. That is
> why all of us, holding strongly by the best of ourselves to our national origins,
> can yet reach beyond them in order to seek everywhere the kingdom of God. [31]

During her generalate the first task on a world-wide scale was
the rebuilding of the devastation caused by international hatred. As
Mother Bodkin had said while the fighting was still going on:

> There has never been such a time of stress as we are in now. And yet there is no
> fear for the future of the Society; it is a peaceful stress for it has come from
> without. There is no internal division as there was in the crises of former times.
> That is what breaks down charity, and charity is the soul of the Society. We
> are more united than ever, in spite of the violent nationalism everywhere. [32]

In Europe and the Orient almost every house had suffered; Malta
had endured 3339 raids on her tiny surface. Now rebuilding began.
Metz, Arnhem and Bois l'Evêque had to be abandoned, but
Budapest, Gratz, Naples and Padua, though badly damaged, were
reconstructed, while Sankocho rose from its ashes for the second
time. Roehampton was rebuilt around a core that escaped burning:
the Sacred Heart chapel holding the graves of Father Varin,
Mother Digby and Mother Stuart.

This was all made possible by mutual aid, one advantage of an international society. It had always been practised in unspectacular
ways, as when after a landslide at Lone Mountain a large check
arrived with the laconic remark: "You may need this," or when
business transactions in needy countries were helped from afar. Now
the countries that had been spared sent aid on a massive scale. From
Australia and North and South America boxes crushed down and
running over went overseas. From San Francisco Miss Olga Rossi
organized the Alumnae Relief Fund which involved school children
and their families. Many pieces of chewing gum, with notes attached, found their way to destitute children in the pockets of small

sweaters. Eight cows made the slow boat journey to Obayshi. When cases came all but miraculously:

> There are no words to tell you and yours of our gratitude, our joy and our surprise in unpacking your wonderful boxes. So many beautiful and useful things! All so wonderfully chosen and just what we need! ... No longer will our charity and sympathy be hindered by the dismal answer: "That doesn't exist!" [33]

In telling of the development of the Society in this period of challenge and in the renewal that followed, at such close range in time, it is not possible to mention by name nor to appraise all of the recent or still living persons who took part in it. Time must give perspective before this can be adequately done. The growth of the Society followed two very different lines during this brief period; there was constructive though slow expansion in most countries, and destructive conflict in a few where opposing ideologies went on struggling after the armistice. Memories of both are a matter of lived experience.

Along the constructive lines were changes within vicariate communities. In some places the number of houses had become too great for one vicar to govern, so many vicariates were divided; this heightened the sense of community within smaller boundaries. In Europe the tendency was to make more vicariates within one country; France was divided into three, Belgium, Italy and England into two (sometimes with scant regard for geography!). Holland and Germany, on the other hand, separated into two vicariates. The same was true in the United States where the eastern vicariate was divided into those of New York and Washington, and the western into those of Chicago and California. In Latin America countries were given independent status; Brazil separated from Argentina and Uruguay which remained together, while Chile, Peru and Colombia became autonomous. On the other side of the world the Far Eastern vicariate, centered in Japan, lost China and gained Korea, while to the south Australia and New Zealand separated.

Great stress was laid on the development of the noviceships, since the shortage of vocations was being acutely felt. New centres were created so that novices need not go afar, while some were divided or transferred to aid recruitment. Aloof places, blessed with beauty and silence, were preferred. In France Saint Maur moved to

Montvillargène (1947) "the new Conflans," holding the juniorate as well as the noviceship. A chapel was erected in the garden for the bodies that had lain near that of Madeleine Sophie Barat in the Conflans crypt: Mothers Goetz, Lehon and Sartorius, and many early assistants general. The novices at the Villa Lante moved to Frascati in the hills near Rome (1949); this meant the closing of Albano. The English novices moved to the beautiful new home of the Roehampton School at Woldingham (1946). A German noviceship was established at Saint Adelheid (1947) and a Polish one at Zblitowska-Gora (1945). In the United States the west coast had its own noviceship at El Cajon, a new school near San Diego (1956).

In Latin America the Brazilian novices who had been first at Tijuca went to the new house at Belo Horizonte (1952), while the Colombian novices moved from Bogota to Manizales (1957). The Chileans returned to Maestranza (1952). Mexico had its own noviceship at San Luis Potosi (1949), while in the Antilles the novices went to the new school near Havana, Marianao, which fused the two former schools of Cerro and Tedajillo (1955). A significant step was the opening of native noviceships in mission lands; that at Obayashi moved to the new house at Susono (1957), while the Indian novices gathered at Bangalore (1958) and the Congolese at Kimuenza (1952).

The new foundations made were surprisingly few, due to some extent to the shortage of personnel in the face of increased demands. In addition to the five named in connection with the noviceships there were fourteen others, balanced by losses and unevenly spaced on the map. The growth was normal in mission countries, whereas in others post-war conditions called for problematical adjustments rather than fresh enterprises. In Belgium Le Sartay rose on a peaceful hillside in Liège (1950) to take the place of ruined Bois Lévêque. In Germany a school was opened at Hamburg (1952) in a Protestant setting. Many of the foundations in other countries answered the continued call for higher education. In the United States Newton College was opened in Boston (1947), Manhattanville College moved from its crowded New York campus to the country spaciousness of Purchase (1951), while San Diego College for Women settled at Alcala Park (1952). In Washington, D. C. the day school on Massachusetts Avenue was transferred to Stone Ridge (1947). The same trend caused the foundation of

Collège Sophie Barat at the Sault (1956), and Mater Admirabilis Training College at Tal Virtu, Malta (1954) and the University of the Sacred Heart in Tokyo (1948). In Egypt the little house at Ramleh in Alexandria was re-opened (1953).

There were three new educational ventures in Australia and New Zealand; Duchesne College was opened on the campus of Brisbane University (1947), and Loreto Hall, a Teacher Training College, in Auckland (1950), while at Braybrook Christ the King Parish School welcomed the children of numerous post-war immigrants. In Latin America expansion was marked by six new schools on the traditional pattern. At Chihuahua in Mexico (1950) the religious were able to appear openly in the habit for the first time since the anti-clerical troubles. In Peru the Society reached out from Lima to Arequipa in the south (1947) and to Trujillo in the north (1952). Carrasco was opened near Montevideo in Uruguay (1947) and Curitiba in the south of Brazil (1956).

Peaceful development was vigorous in most of the non-western cultures. India obtained national independence in 1947 and the trend towards indianization increased. By this time the graduates of Sophia College were shouldering the new tasks that fell to educated women in a Muslim and Hindu environment. As one of them said: "I have learned to look at things, and at life itself, far more profoundly, to serve and above all to love." In the new high school at Bangalore to the south the proportion of Christian students was far less than in the college, but the climate of understanding created there was expressed in the motto chosen by the children: "Truth and universal love." In the Congo a little house for holidays and retreats was opened at Kimuenza among the hills; it soon developed into a primary school for the village children and a secondary school for *évoluées*.

A daring step was taken in Japan where the University of the Sacred Heart, affiliated to the Catholic University in Washington, D.C., grew out of the teacher training program at Sankocho. The new Liberal Arts college was situated at Shibuya in Tokyo, on the landscaped grounds that had belonged to Prince Kuni, and the first students lived in his small palace while the new buildings were rising. Soon the International School was transferred from Sankocho to the same campus. The teaching of English was a prime attraction, but with a strong faculty of Japanese professors the college developed a fully rounded program under the presidency of Mother

Elizabeth Britt, its far-seeing and spiritually dynamic president. Conversions and vocations were many. The new school at Susono was built on an enchanting site dominated by the beauty of Mount Fuji. Mother Sheldon died in 1954, and it was not long before the college students were delighted (and astounded) to hear the new vicar, Brigid Keogh, address them in Japanese.

Only one new country was entered at this time, Korea, "Land of Morning Calm." The tranquil name rested on a land of granite mountains and of rugged warm-hearted people. The war of 1950 cut it along a line of steel into North and South. The foundation, dreamed of as early as 1908, came true on the Feast of Christ the King, 1956, under the leadership of Cora McHardy-Flint. The streets of Seoul were still pitted with shell-holes. The house, a former seminary, overlooked the River Han where the Korean martyrs had been thrown to their death. Food, light and heating were hard to come by; water was carried from the river in pails slung over a woman's shoulders until a water diviner found the place for a well. The two schools, Korean and International, grew rapidly, for the war was followed by a remarkable growth in the Korean Church; there were lines of children against the lilac blossoms when Mother Keogh came for her first visit. Korean postulants arrived, and were sent to Susono or Kenwood for their noviceship.

This peaceable, even-paced expansion of the Society was counterbalanced by violent tensions in places where anti-christian, antidemocratic forces had taken over. In Egypt, a long legal battle against private schools began in 1949. It was due to Muslim nationalism and resulted in classroom control, restraint and distrust. Violence came in 1952 when the house in Cairo hardly survived the attacks that set the whole quarter in a blaze.

A frenzied outbreak of anti-clericalism in Argentina, in July, 1955, attacked churches and convents. The religious in the two houses in Buenos Aires took refuge in the country homes of friends, while a few struggled, from hiding places in the city, to keep the schools going. The novices at Castelar were sent into Uruguay. Violence came to a sudden end with "the victory of Christ" won by General Lonardi, and in November Mother de Lescure could visit the vicariate.

There was no such happy outcome to the troubles in Poland under a communist government. The polytechnical school in the house at Lwow, founded in 1843 and already transferred four times, was seized. The community was sent off in box cars to other Polish houses. Two invalids and volunteers to care for them were allowed to stay. Eventually one, Elzbieta Walchnowska, remained alone behind the iron curtain to help the cardinal in his thankless work until her death in 1973. Mother Gunther managed to get to the General Council of 1946 but not that of 1952. No religious and few letters could leave the country. Poverty, a choking grip on teaching in schools no longer their own, the need to make a living by raising flowers and chickens, called forth the heroism of sheer endurance. Vocations did not stop, though some young nuns had known torture while serving in the Catholic underground before joining the Society.

The houses in Austria gradually returned to normal; not so those in Hungary. The two houses in Budapest stood on opposite sides of the river. Both underwent heavy bombing during the siege of 1944; their cellars, without light or water, held hundreds of children, friends and strangers, including homeless Jews taken in at the risk of death to their hosts. Both houses recovered enough to be filled with children when the communist infiltration into schools began. At Sophianum the new directress had to admit: "This school is a hard nut to crack." The children resisted, vocally, and refused to sign compromising papers. A girl of fourteen was taken by the police for questioning. When she said: "The Church will go on forever, I not only believe it but know it," her jaw was broken by a blow. Mother de Lescure then wrote a letter to the children of the Sacred Heart the world over:

> The hour has come, as you know, when some among you are called upon to give, for their faith and for their fidelity to the Church, the heroic testimony that is ready for every sacrifice, even for that of life itself, if need be . . . None of you, in the times in which we live, can say that she will never be in such circumstances. We have no fear, for the strength of him for whom we give testimony will not fail us. But all of us, in view of such an event, must make our faith more serious, our prayer more personal, our will more strong, our life more open and given to others, our soul more habituated to joyous sacrifice. Above all, we must be more aware of the divine life within us, our true life. [34]

Before the frontiers closed the Hungarian novices had reached Avigliana which had sheltered Spanish novices twelve years earlier. The older religious also left their country, but Mother de Lescure asked a core to remain as long as possible — the limit being deporta-

tion to Russia. There were eleven left at Sophianum when at mid-
night on June 18, 1950, the police forced the door, searched the
house and packed the nuns into a van. They rode through the night,
"singing the Te Deum in our hearts," to a concentration camp. The
Swiss superior, Hildegarde Gutzwiller, [35] was released. In August
the government announced the dissolution of religious orders and
the camp broke up. The seven Hungarian nuns took jobs; they could
not get passports. Mother de Lescure sent them a message:
"Courage, confidence, the prayer of the Society is upholding you."
They tried to escape over the frontier, and four were imprisoned.
Silence fell for the next few years. At last two aspirants reached the
Mother House on February 16, 1957, more than ready for their
probation. After the tragic reversal of the Hungarian counter-
revolution that same year many refugee students were taken into
Sacred Heart schools and colleges in free countries.

Meanwhile the same drama was going on behind the bamboo
curtain. More than eighteen hundred students, from kindergarten to
university, were happily at work on the compound in Shanghai
when, on May 20, 1949, the People's Party came into power to
the sound of guns. Chinese Communists took all the influential posts
in the schools and the infiltration of Soviet thought began. But the
Legion of Mary was strong and the pupils and teachers heroic. One
of the nuns wrote later:

> What an experience it has been for us during the past eighteen months to learn
> from the Catholic youth of Shanghai that the sense of the living Church does
> not depend on time and on tradition but on persecution and the cross. In a
> short time these young people came into full possession of this precious
> heritage. Those who saw their daily lives said: "This is a revelation of the
> primitive church." The first impression is that they are completely given; the
> sense of the supernatural is not only the dominant note of their lives but its
> vital principle. Our Catholics have always been fervent, but now their religion
> has taken possession of them and transformed them not only as individuals but
> in the family unity of the Church. [36]

By February, 1951, the schools had been completely taken
over. The Chinese novices got by dangerous routes into Japan, and
the foreigners were forced to leave, all but a few who stayed at their
heart-breaking task of dismantling the house, untangling red tape
and parting from friends. The last mass was offered on December 9,
and all left Shanghai except Margaret Thornton whose visa was

kept back for six more months. When she at last reached the
Mother House she did not linger; she went straight back to the
Orient via New York where she picked up an honorary Ph. D.
useful for the college in Tokyo. On Avenue Joffre the massive
statue of the Sacred Heart over the entrance proved too heavy for
the Reds to remove. They wrapped it in burlap and it still stands —
waiting?

* * *

The direction in which the Society's educational work was moving at this time can be seen in the documents rewritten after the
General Council of 1952. The Directives concerning education
given in the revised edition of the Decrees are the most traditional in
expression since they reaffirm the principles found in the Constitutions. They stress education as a work of faith:

> All our works — boarding-schools, day-schools, colleges, teacher training
> colleges, schools for the poor, are apostolic works, having for their end the
> salvation of souls .... Our Holy Mother put education before instruction,
> although she herself was so learned .... That is why the Society, without un-
> derestimating any of the disciplines, tries in its teaching to find the educative
> value of each, and will always give priority to such subjects as philosophy,
> literature, history, the social sciences, which of themselves have the power to
> awaken thought, to form good judgment and to establish principles. ... We
> must keep in our teaching the sense of Christian values, which means turning
> all the knowledge offered to the minds of the children, and all the judgments
> which they are led to form, towards their role in the light of Christian values.
> Our superiority lies in that, and we must keep it at all costs. [37]
>
> Children who cannot reach the level of official studies for any reason should
> not be excluded from our schools. Such was not the thought of our Holy
> Mother. Each child entrusted to us has a right to an instruction adapted to her
> capacities and gifts in view of her future life — Christian, family and social. [38]

These basic principles were expanded to meet the demands of
modern life and freed from the misleading language of the past in
the revisions of the School Rule and the Plan of Studies.

When *Life at the Sacred Heart*, the title of the rewritten School
Rule, appeared, Mother de Lescure wrote:

> It will be, in presentation, form and content, more accessible to the children
> who will, I trust, love it and grasp its spirit. This is what we have tried to do:
> keep the educational traditions of our Holy Mother, and sacrifice none of the

principles of this education according to the Heart of Jesus, without which our work would go awry, but to allow its life-sap, always fresh, to flow into the needs and resources of today's children, whom we must accept as they are in order to make of them what the Heart of Jesus wishes them to be: apostles of their times and of their milieux. [39]

The Rule asks that in every school: "The atmosphere be one of mutual affection, of trustful give-and-take, and of joy," to facilitate a four-fold formation. A knowledge of dogma and of the Gospel, as well as a life of prayer, must underlie the formation to Christian living. This is strengthened by moral formation which rests upon fidelity to duty, submission to authority, straightforwardness, uncompromising loyalty, self-giving in service, good manners, willed discipline and teamwork. Intellectual formation "aims above all at forming the ability to think for oneself." Social formation is given greater importance than in earlier documents:

> Its purpose is to make the pupils open-eyed, alert to every need, every joy and every sorrow that call for their interest, service and self-giving. Thus, little by little, they will learn to widen their horizon from their school-centre to their home-centre, from their immediate surroundings to the wider scene of their town or of their region, of their country and of the whole world. [40]

The title of the Plan of Studies was changed to *Spirit and Plan of Studies of the Society of the Sacred Heart*, with emphasis throughout on "spirit." The expanded text drops minutiae and high-lights essentials; it grapples with the future. Quotations from the Constitutions and the writings of Saint Madeleine Sophie are its focal points. It opens with an analysis of three concepts: instruction (the imparting of knowledge), education ("a work of progressive development, the harmonious unfolding of nature which favours the action of grace") and the supernatural end which is the same as that of the Society itself ("the glory of the Heart of Jesus through the salvation of men").

Each of the five parts begins with a quotation from the Encyclicals of Pius XI or Pius XII, relating the whole to the Church in modern times. Part I centres on the students; the progress of each must be sought "in the rhythm proper to each," taking account of "specific aspects of feminine psychology." Part II is concerned with the Christian in the world, for whom a sense of the Church will lead to "an unfolding in charity." Part III deals with the scale of values of the intellectual disciplines. Part IV traces the cycles of study from the elementary to the university levels. For the first time a proportionate place is given to higher studies which will lead the students "to full maturity of mind and character." Again for the first time, the adaptation of the Society's education to non-Christian milieux is noted:

> In mission countries it is important that the program should include aspects of the national civilizations and cultures which are compatible with a Christian view of the world. [41]

Part V focuses upon an intellectual formation at once traditional and adapted to the needs of each epoch, and upon the fusion of the roles of teacher and of religious who have an apostolic sense:

> This calls for an attitude of prudent openness, of interests enlarged to the dimensions of the world, the very interests of the Heart of Jesus. To be open means to have a soul awake, alert to the demands of varied outlooks without surprise or contradiction; a receptive mind, conscious of the unlimited possibilities of benefit to be gained from the most banal realities of daily life; an all-embracing charity which gives tact, self-forgetfulness and the spirit of adaptation. [42]

The thought-lines of the document move together at the end:

> A close union between human and supernatural perspectives, a sense of depth and of life, and an apostolic sense — these are the characteristics of the spirit of the Society.... The pedagogy of the Society thus finds its meaning in a spirituality centred upon devotion to the Sacred Heart. It is a spirituality harmonizing divine and human values in the closest compenetration, since it is based upon the mystery of the Incarnation, the mystery of God-made-man. [43]

A cross-section of the educational programs of this period reveals great diversity between regions. They were extended at both ends of the age-scale; pre-schools and adult education in night courses were initiated. There was a rising number of commercial or technical schools, giving skills in domestic science and secretarial work; in Poland these took the form of agricultural schools. Most of the European countries had hostels for university students offering trained guidance. In some countries the free schools had completely disappeared, while in others they were attached to every "academy" (consistent translation of Society terms has become impossible!) In some countries, such as the United States and Australia, there was no state aid at all, while in others, like England, a grant was given to many private schools. Elementary and secondary education were sometimes carried on in separate institutions. Affiliation with universities raised academic requirements and called for the designing of new courses, as in Mexico. Juniorates for the young religious were frequently replaced by university studies or, as at Kenwood, developed into a Graduate Division leading to the Master's degree. Pluriformity in education was an actuality, and was accepted as a broadening of basic principles. Specialization was also accepted; it was seen no longer as a threat to the harmony of a rounded program but as its needed outgrowth. An address given to the Associated Alumnae in 1949 traced the growth of the student's mind, will and heart through school and college into specialized fields:

> And all the time an open mind is kept on the world around us, to make applications and to note differences in present-day conditions, to distinguish between what is for all time and what is merely passing, and further to note the far-reaching effects of new scientific knowledge on man's way of life, on his thoughts, imagination and figures of speech. This is the field of adaptability without which the knowledge of the past would lie like a dead weight on the human spirit.[44]

Alumnae Associations were spreading throughout the world under Mother de Lescure's direct inspiration. She wrote frequent letters to Alumnae, Children of Mary, college students and children all together, conscious as she was of their united power for good and their responsibility for service "which the grave circumstances of our times call for."

*   *   *

The Society of the Sacred Heart was, in all probability, unaware in 1955 that a sociological convention in Indonesia had just given to mankind a new term: Third World. Two worlds were already confronting each other on our overcrowded planet, the capitalistic and the communistic. To which would the nations struggling into being in the Orient and in Africa belong? Or would this Third World evolve in its own way? Some twenty years later it would be of overwhelming importance:

> Numerically, it is the greater part of mankind, with its immense population in a state of economic and cultural underdevelopment, subject to flagrant injustice

due to the selfish structures of the world. On the other hand, it is also the part of humanity with the most vigorous potential on the spiritual level, capable of giving lessons in faith and hope to the old world with its scepticism and inclination to atheism. [45]

But the Society had become aware of the "social evolution" to which Mother de Lescure so often referred. "Evolution" is a more life-giving word than "revolution" which only occurs when evolution has been thwarted. In the Society this awareness was shown by a gradual change in the enrolment of children in the schools. At the General Council of 1946 it was said that recruitment must be "enlarged," thus quietly blunting the edge of social exclusiveness — that charge held against the Society almost from the beginning. This enlargement included the Children of Mary and the Affiliées, and perhaps most importantly the noviceships:

> The social evolution now in progress allows us to accept more widely than in the past certain vocations which are not now out of place and which can enrich us with real values. [46]

Concern for the interests of the Church had a wider range now that political questions were so closely interwoven with religious. Nuns called to the polls needed information on local and national levels, which meant a freer use of mass media "if we are to fulfil this duty at the call of the Church."

Involvement in Catholic Action had become part of the program in every school and college. Mother de Lescure liked to see enterprises placed on a permanent footing, and in letters written for special occasions she asked for some lasting memorial in the form of social service. For the Marian Year of 1954 she suggested that the Blessed Virgin be the centre of the literary, artistic and musical activities of the year, and added:

> Let each group of Children of Mary or Alumnae, each apostolic organization, each school or college, found an enterprise of a charitable, social or apostolic nature which, under the patronage of the Immaculate Virgin, may remain as a souvenir of the Marian Year, a lasting testimony to charity and love. [47]

She also encouraged interaction between different countries, as when American college students supported the work done for needy children at the Villa Lante. When faced with glaring poverty on her journey through South America she said to the Children of Mary:

"Until now you have given principally of your money. That is good, but now you must do better. What you must give is yourselves, the best of yourselves." [48]

Mother de Lescure would not admit that any form of Catholic Action could replace the Sodality of the Children of Mary; she counted on it for a spiritual renewal in the modern world. She encouraged affiliation with wider Marian associations, but wished it to keep its autonomy. When Pius XII issued *Bis Saecularis* in 1948, she rewrote both the Act of Consecration and the Rule of the Children of Mary of the Sacred Heart. The accent was placed on close union with the life of the Church, and the new Rule ended with a passage from the Pope's document: "This fervent zeal for interior life develops naturally into new apostolic works, responding to new needs and new circumstances." She wrote to the Congregation:

> The demands of apostolic service today call more than ever for the quality of the spiritual life for which you have felt and expressed the need. After much prayer we have sought to revivify your marian life such as our Holy Mother conceived of it. At the sources of her thought, to which you owe your origin, we have found the rich life-sap which is never exhausted. It is not a question of innovation but of deepening. And so it is with great confidence that we place in your hands today the Rule and the Act of Consecration in a renewed form more adapted to the times in which we live. It changes nothing basic but offers to you all, united in the same desire, the grace of a more profound interior life, a more generous ardour in charity and a more widely open zeal. [49]

The Rule of the Affiliées was also rewritten and the nature of the association was clearly stated:

> It is not a Third Order, by the side of and modelled on a religious congregation. It is an affiliation. The Affiliées are thus members, by a special but real title, of the Society of the Sacred Heart, sharing its end and its work, and the merits and graces that it receives. [50]

Two hundred delegates from the Children of Mary of the Sacred Heart were present at the congress of the World Federation of Marian Associations held in Rome on September 9, 1954. They came to the Mother House and Mother de Lescure said to them:

> You share in the missionary and apostolic movements of Holy Church, which are the overflow from the well-spring of the inner life. You will carry away

from Rome the conviction that what counts is not the number but the quality of your membership, that living sense of the Church to which you belong. [51]

The next year, speaking to the Children of Mary in South America, she defined their role: "To be everywhere witnesses to the Christian spirit, to think, speak, dress and live as Christians, according to Jesus Christ and to his Church." [52]

* * *

The atmosphere breathed within the Church in these years was invigorating, if not heady. Brother Roger Schutz and his fellow monks settled quietly at Taizé; ecumenism had reached religious life, although there were as yet no representatives of the Catholic Church at the world associations of Churches. *Provida Mater* gave official status to Secular Institutes. *Communautés de base* were forming, also imperceptibly. Better World Retreats were gaining momentum. The dialogue mass was gaining in popularity – in Latin of course; only extremists were then talking of liturgy in the vernacular. At his death Pierre Teilhard de Chardin left no doubt that science and dogma must move in step, while Cardinal Suhard reminded the Church that she is not only transcendent but immanent in the world that she continuously redeems; she speaks the idiom and is clothed in the mode of each new age. All these movements created a certain uneasiness in religious orders; some members welcomed them enthusiastically, others felt that they contained a latent threat to religious life itself. Where would they end?

The Society of the Sacred Heart took its tone most directly from the circular letters of Mother de Lescure. These were longer and more frequent than those of any of her predecessors. They were written in an impetuous and urgent style, each was unified by a central theme fully developed. Together they formed a sequence, a *corpus* of spirituality. They drew their inspiration from two main sources: the role of devotion to the Sacred Heart in the modern world, and current movements within the Church as expressed in the Encyclicals of Pius XII.

The devotion to the Sacred Heart was in a state of crisis. At the end of the war positive trends were at work: Sacred Heart radio hours, reminding housewives busy with the breakfast dishes of the morning offering; Sacred Heart luncheon clubs for business men;

family consecration to the Sacred Heart which gathered the household before a home-made shrine. Mother de Lescure supported this last movement, begun by Father Mateo Crawley-Bovey, in a special circular. [53] The developing science of missiology enlarged the missionary scope of the devotion. As Father Charmot wrote:

> The apostolate of love will be as effective today as it was in the early days of the Church. If Christians will show Christ's charity to those who walk in darkness and the shadow of death, then the truths of faith will shine in enlightened hearts. But if this charity is to be pure and sincere and brilliant, like the star of the Magi, its strength must be drawn from the Heart of Christ – no other source will do. [54]

But a reaction against the devotion as such was beginning. In a work called *Crisis and Evolution in the Devotion to the Sacred Heart* [55] a statistical study was made of the attitudes of young militants, leaders of Catholic Action in France in 1945. A misunderstanding amounting to positive dislike was found in this group who demanded virility, simplicity and corporateness in the spiritual life. The practices of the devotion no longer appealed; they were an impediment to its reality. For too long both piety and scholarship had rested upon "the forms of Paray." The devotion, to find new life, must take on forms "more scriptural, more liturgical, more theological." The challenge was accepted by spiritual writers, especially Jesuit, Dominican and Carmelite. Spiritual reading in religious communities stimulated both thought and action.

For Mother de Lescure, light came from the Message entrusted to Sister Josefa, for which she was responsible. She knew that a private revelation implying visions of Christ and of his satanic enemy was repugnant to many good Christians, including many good religious of the Sacred Heart. She herself found it hard to accept. So she never forced it upon others; she presented it with burning earnestness and let it make its own way. This was a hard line for one so forthright to follow, but she knew that the Message, like the devotion itself, must rest on scriptural and theological bases. As Father Charmot wrote:

> This message has in itself no element of novelty, nothing foreign to the Gospel of Saint John, to the most assured tradition, to the teaching of the great lovers of Jesus Christ, to the explicit desires of your Holy Foundress. Our Lord asks of you no innovation in your Institute, not even in your spirituality. He only

wishes that the most essential point, the devotion to the Sacred Heart, the soul of your vocation and the deepest desire of the Heart of Jesus, shall not become a dead letter like the ashes of an old fire, but shall break out like a flame that shines always brighter. [56]

Accordingly, Mother de Lescure composed the *Chain of Souls*, [57] a compact application of the Message, to the prayer of the Society, and formed an organization with the same name for its diffusion in wider circles. Her circular letters for the first two years were concerned with: the primary vocation of the Society as wholly consecrated to the Heart of Jesus; [50] the resulting relation to him as "spouses and victims" because of which "our horizons must be as wide as his own"; [59] the difficulty of uniting the active and contemplative lives, to be solved by "the priority of prayer over action." [60] The twenty-fifth anniversary of the Message brought an appeal to live by it as "the normal unfolding of our vocation." [61]

After 1948 her circulars ran parallel to the Encyclicals of Pius XII. Mother de Lescure had an ecclesial mind; her intense devotion to the Church freed her teaching from subjectivism. As she wrote to the Children of Mary after the Holy Year:

> You have understood the meaning of that community of faith and of love, that community of all races, of all nations, of all languages, of humble and great, of rich and poor, of learned and ignorant, which is called the Church, one in the same Credo, the same communion, the same ardent charity. [62]

The coming together of the Society's Sesquicentennial and the Holy Year of 1950 was significant:

> The time has come, now when our Holy Father Pope Pius XII is awakening the world to its redemptive responsibilities and when so many are called to heroism in their faith, for us to respond with a more decided will and a more serious love to all the demands of our consecration. [63]

Her letter of preparation for the Holy Year, on "the grace and responsibility of the name we bear," stressed the right given by this name "to enter and dwell in the depths of his Heart," for "this is the way of prayer of the Society." [64] The Holy Year also brought the definition of the dogma of the Assumption; it was "the year of the great return through Mary," for which a letter developed the triple marian heritage of the Society: the Immaculate Heart, Mater Admirabilis, "the jewel of the Society, treasure of calm and serenity," and our Lady of Sorrows. [65]

One letter was on the need of reparation in the sense of "remaking and rebuilding the world," above all through education. [66] When *Fulgens Corona* proclaimed 1954 as the Marian Year, Mother de Lescure indicated ways of honouring Mary as "the Pilgrim Virgin." [67] She then took up the thoughts expressed in *Sacra Virginitas*, and in one of her most beautiful letters spoke of consecrated virginity as "love for him who has first loved us." [68] She next faced the problem of the falling off of vocations: "Let us seek together the divine solutions." Those searching for Christ's way for them should be confronted with "his Gospel, his Eucharist, his Mother and his Kingdom." [69] This was complemented by a letter on charity as the bond of union in the Society. [70] *Haurietis Aquas*, the Encyclical on devotion to the Sacred Heart, was answered by a letter on faith as confidence in Christ: faith in his love, in his mercy, in his presence and in his action. [71] This closed the series of letters written "to bring fire to the earth." They were upheld by a document from another pen. Father Charmot published his *Commentary on the Constitutions of the Society of the Sacred Heart* in 1950, and Mother de Lescure said:

> The theological bases of the spirituality of the Society are strongly laid, and the whole is filled with the spirit of the Constitutions and the thought of our Holy Mother. It would seem to be a response to the needs of today, and a new flowering of the ever living grace of our vocation. [72]

*　*　*

The world outlook was sombre on New Year's eve, 1957, when Mother de Lescure said to the Mother House community:

> "No man has seen God." Never more than on this night, it seems, have cold, fear, shadows and anguish hung more menacingly over the world. Where is God? He is here. To him alone it belongs to bring salvation through love. [73]

Her share that year was redemptive suffering. On February 14 she broke her hip. From a wheel-chair she gradually took up her work again, but she was being sapped by cancer. On August 22 she sent her last letter to the Society naming Sabine de Valon as vicar general: "She is well known to all of you for her devotedness and for her attachment to the Society of which Jesus has given her the spirit." [74] Mother de Lescure still held the reins, and lingered till the last day of the year, "offering to the very end, loving to the very end."

Only when her biography appeared was it realized that her life of prayer, source of the radiance that was seen in her, had been habitually passed in Gethsemane. It was her part in the Work of Love by which, in the words of the Chapter of 1970, "the Incarnation must be prolonged." [75]

Chapter 8

Renewal
1958 – 1970

Then the One sitting on the throne spoke:
"Now I am making the whole of
creation new," he said.

Rev 21:5

Renewal has gone by many names: Renaissance, Restoration, Second Spring, Aggiornamento, New Pentecost. It may come about by destruction and replacement, as in the razing and rebuilding of a house, or by growth as in the miracle of spring. Replacement is valid only for something beyond repair; growth is a law of life. It may cause a change as startling as the flight of a butterfly from a chrysalis. It is cyclic; something repeats within a larger movement. It implies rhythm, not the senseless self-assertion of a neon light but the ongoing pattern, ending in synthesis, that is basic to art and to the life-process. Such rhythm does not close the circle; it widens the spiral. In an organism the cycle moves towards fulfilment, and when fulfilled loses itself in a larger cycle. The Old Covenant becomes the New, death becomes resurrection. "I am making the whole of creation new."

Pius XII died on October 11, 1958, and Angelo Roncalli became John XXIII, or better, Good Pope John, living his motto: "Obedience and Peace." Vatican Council II startled the Church into her own renewal. Before it closed the vista seen through the window that it had opened reached beyond the curve of the earth; the space-age had begun. On Christmas Eve, 1968, the first men to see "the good earth" from space sent back a message: "In the beginning God . . ." By July men were walking on the moon. Below, the Third World was coming alive in the nations of Africa and Asia, while the Arab lands became storm-centres. The Church and civil society were intermeshed as never before.

Sabine de Valon was born in Cahors, France, on October 16, 1899. She entered the Society of the Sacred Heart at Marmoutier and was professed in Rome on February 24, 1929. In France she served as mistress of studies, mistress general and superior at Grenoble and Toulouse before taking over the government of the Trinita in Rome in 1954. As vicar general she called the Twenty-fifth General Council, and on April 26, 1958, became the tenth superior general of the Society.

The Council met from April 24 to May 12, [1] and Mother de Valon struck the key-note at the opening session: "We must come face to face with the reality of today." She then spoke of the "sense of the Society" as expressed earlier by Mother de Lescure:

> The sense of the Society is the sense of what is human. We must seize this human terrain such as it is, without illusion, without a look fixed lingeringly on the past, without rosy idealism, seize it as it is to christianize it, the human terrain in its entirety. . . .
>
> The sense of the Society is found in the sense of our own times; it cannot be stabilized or fixed in immutability under pain of stagnation. . . . The Society must be for all times and all places while remaining itself. . . .
>
> The sense of the Society is found in the sense of continuity, which means that in order to remain itself it must constantly return to its sources, taking its point of departure from those sources. . . .
>
> The sense of the Society is found in the sense of its final end: the glory of the Heart of Jesus.
>
> The sense of the Society is the sense of love. [2]

The call to renewal was inescapable from the beginning of Mother de Valon's generalate, five years before *Perfectae Caritatis*, and the three Councils which she summoned were increasingly concerned with it. But before considering their Decrees, or the actual renewal of religious life, it will be well to look at the growth of the Society's work, educational, missionary and social, on an international scale. For Mother de Valon not only encouraged experiments in education but started a powerful missionary thrust resulting from her vision of the Church in a global world. This thrust was connected with an accelerating awareness of the cry for social justice, a force in Christian as well as non-Christian cultures. These three interwoven movements vitalized the whole Society and speeded the concomitant renewal of religious life itself.

* * *

In the educational field sudden wrenches in aims and methods were causing some alarm but more hope. As Mother de Valon went through Europe she studied the "new breed" of students, themselves the product of social and scientific shock. She wrote to the Society:

> Just now, when the evolution of all things is so rapid and when, so easily and under the pretext of progress, all things are questioned, it is good to seek together the way that we must follow. Are we going to run blindly after every novelty? Are we going to immobilize ourselves in the possession of a legacy from the past as if, by this effort, we could stop the too rapid movement of our times? Before such alternatives it is not the changeable world which must guide us but the light of the Church, of the Church always herself and always young, the Church which is "the kingdom of God on the move." [3]

She then quoted Pius XII who had said to the vicars of the Society shortly before his death: "The education of young girls today requires an updating of methods with a deepening of the principles that inspire them."

The Society's response is seen in the Directives of the Councils of 1958 and 1964. The former faced the question (and the implied reproach) of social exclusiveness:

> We must recognize the rise of the social class which in former days was the *milieu* of our free schools for the poor [*écoles*]. So the text of the Constitutions dealing with the "poor classes" is no longer relevant. . . . But the spirit remains: the aim of christianizing this social class which is now rising in status and which will, perhaps, someday be the class of greatest influence [*classe dirigeante*]. We cannot at this moment face a brusque and total assimilation of classes which in some countries would meet with opposition, but a slow assimilation can be made. Perhaps a solution can be reached by diversifying the curriculum, which would be a good thing: some of the students, either in the academies [*pensionnats*] or in the free schools can be prepared for a technical career, some for a career in the liberal arts. In any case we must value our *externats* [day-schools for children of less social standing than those in the *demi-pensionnats*]. . . . We must avoid stressing social distinctions; above all, we must do our best, by our charity, to bring social classes together. [4]

The Chapter of 1964 (the first to use that name instead of "Council") faced today's students. "They are the product of a century which has lost the sense of God." Richly endowed, they are in search of liberty. They must be educated to liberty by a deepening of faith. For this, the entire human personality must be formed to responsibility, to a social sense and social openness, to serious intellectual work. In conclusion:

> The total formation of the children, a synthesis of both the human and the supernatural formation which we owe them, is brought about little by little through the collaboration of all. More than ever we have teamwork with the lay professors, with the teachers of religion, with the parents, for there must be concerted action. A fruitful field is opened in this drawing together in mutual collaboration in our apostolate with the laity. This harmony, wholly in the spirit of the [Vatican] Council, is excellent for us, and the children will benefit greatly by this teamwork in charity and joy. [5]

The sense of teamwork was immensely strengthened at this critical time by world-wide collaboration among the alumnae. The first World Assembly of Alumnae was held in Rome in 1960. Another at Brussels in 1965 developed into AMASC (*Association Mondiale des Anciennes du Sacré Coeur*). The first president, Madame Coppé of Belgium, died after two years; her place was taken by Maria Ignacia Areyzaga of Spain under whose impulsion the Association faced the challenges thrown down to women claiming their liberation. Her work passed into the hands of Patricia Horsley of Australia, elected at the meeting in Mexico City in 1974. The AMASC Charter gives its goals:

> AMASC, as part of the Pilgrim Church, aims to help its members:
> 1. to place themselves at the service of today's world in order to create a more just and fraternal society, with increased awareness of their social responsibilities and in the name of a faith which is both living and lived in its personal and communitarian dimensions;
> 2. to create and maintain friendship and unity between all National Associations and Federations so as to achieve a truly international collaboration;
> 3. to co-operate actively and effectively with the Society of the Sacred Heart in its various undertakings and options;
> 4. to be represented in the international organizations with an attitude of constant openness and discernment. [6]

Broadening outlooks brought their own problems. Mother de Valon wrote at the beginning of 1960:

> In many parts of the world arms are reaching out to us, begging for the benefit of the strong education more necessary than ever now that, little by little, faith is wavering and the sense of God is being lost. We answer these calls to the utmost of our possibilities. . . . Almost everywhere our schools, colleges and training colleges are so crowded that we have to stretch the walls and put up new

buildings. In these houses, which we must modernize to meet today's needs, activity is increasing and the work of our religious becomes more and more intense.[7]

Despite this urgency the foundations in Europe, North America and Australia-New Zealand were not numerous, and some apparently flourishing houses were closed. The obvious reason was lack of personnel but the causes went deeper: the changing concept, content and form of education itself. The few new houses, in most cases, reflect these changes.

The trends were clearly seen in France. The needs of the juniorate called for a centre in the city, so a style of convent new to the Society was opened in Paris (1965): one floor of an apartment house on Avenue Lowendal became a centre for student nuns and for the alumnae. The school on the Rue Saint Dominique was transferred to Chatenay Malabry (1967); it became the "Groupe Scolaire Sophie Barat," which included students of a greater social range in larger numbers and with a wider program. There was a similar broadening in other French schools, some of which undertook co-education in collaboration with Jesuit schools.

The first real penetration into a slum area took place at Besos in Barcelona (1963). This was the spearhead of a thrust soon to be felt throughout the whole Society. Mother de Valon said: "This will give some of our religious the privilege of living among the people and of bringing to them a knowledge of the love of the Heart of Jesus." [8] The exuberance of the pioneer community witnessed to this love as they joined in the games and lessons of their pupils – noisy, lovable, and of no age limit. In Madrid a large modern school named for Pius XII rose near Chamartin (1960); its studies led to advanced teaching diplomas. The year 1966 was prolific. In Bilbao a night school and technical courses were begun at Recaldeberri; on the Canary Islands a *Patronato* was opened at Fuertevantura; in Madrid a *Colegio Mayor* offered advanced courses at Romera Robledo. In that same year the Society entered a new country; a student hostel at Coimbra in Portugal broadened its internationality.

In Italy the school at Naples widened its scope when it was transferred to a new site on the Corso Europa (1963), but the hostel for university students in Venice was closed. The Italian noviceship at Frascati became international in 1964 when novices representing countries from all over the world were fused in one group. No other foundations were made in Europe, while Brighton, (Hove) in England and Leeson Street in Ireland were closed (1966).

In the United States the new houses were of the traditional type for the most part, but experimentation was vigorous everywhere. El Cajon opened the Saint Madeleine Sophie School for mentally retarded children. In Texas the Society at last accepted the invitation given a century earlier by Sam Houston when it entered the city of his name (1960). Maryville College moved to a new site where it could freely expand (1961). Lake Forest could no longer hold the growing college together with the school, and the latter moved across a ravine to a site fittingly named Woodlands (1961). It inherited furnishing from the school at Saint Joseph, Missouri, which had just been closed.

The Society returned to Buffalo, where an earlier foundation had been forced to close, when a school was opened at Nottingham Terrace (1961). The school on Lawrence Avenue in Detroit moved to Bloomfield Hills where there was room to experiment (1958). At Princeton, New Jersey, a daring architect integrated a modernistic building into its setting of woods and boulders, the Stuart Country Day School (1963). Carrollton was opened at Miami, Florida (1961). Here nuns and students together sought out the migrant workers in their camps, to evangelize the grassroots workers of America, themselves rootless. In New York City the Harlem Preparatory School, sponsored by Manhattanville College in collaboration with negro educators, helped drop-outs from school to find their way into universities.

In New Zealand there had been no house of the Sacred Heart in South Island since the closing of Timaru. But loyal alumnae called for a return, and the religious were welcomed back into Christchurch (1959) where they opened a secondary and an elementary school. In Australia a parish school was opened at Sadleir near Sydney (1966) among industrial workers living in clean, sturdy houses. In these two Pacific countries poverty is not marked as in many lands by sub-human squalour. In the same year a new community called Barat Burn was established on the grounds of Rose Bay.

* * *

In the meantime energetic developments had been taking place in the mission lands. In February, 1961, Mother de Valon wrote to the Society:

> The harvest is whitening in the Far East; vocations are numerous, many openings are offered to the Society which can make manifest the love of the Heart of Jesus and carry his message. I must have first-hand knowledge of these possibilities and of the directions that they may take. [9]

She set out with Ursula Benziger and Alice Mallet in cherry blossom time. Taiwan was the first stop. As the car curved up the road to the new school at Taipei through lines of wondering Chinese children Mother de Valon experienced a penetrating insight into the meaning of "mission" which clarified during the rest of her journey.

This foundation had been made only the year before by Marian Kent and four Chinese religious driven from Shanghai ten years earlier. Many alumnae from China had taken refuge in Taiwan, and the new school, with its red columns, its moon-door, its roof of gilded tile, was soon standing on the slopes of Goddess Mountain overlooking the river. This rapid rise was due to an inspiration of Mother Benziger who had written to the children of the Sacred Heart of every nation, appealing for their "mighty mites." At the laying of the corner stone the Chinese Minister of Education had said:

> I noticed on the stone that we have just sealed that this building is the gift of the Children of the Sacred Heart the world over. This is a manifestation of the universal charity that reigns in the Catholic Church. Such a spirit harmonizes well with that of our country which has a proverb: "The whole of humanity is one great family." [10]

Already the school was overcrowded with children from the city, but at the foot of the hill a village called for "pre-evangelization"; soon there was a primary school for the bare-foots. For years both schools were helped by Mother Benziger's letters to far-away children beginning: "Dear Founders and Foundresses."

The travellers went next to Seoul where the war-scars were healing. It was a stimulating moment for the Korean Church, freed from oppression and challenged by the North Koreans over the border. New wings had to be added to the Sacred Heart school, and higher education for women was needed. Bishop Quinlan, survivor of the Death March, found property for the Society among the granite mountains circling Chun Cheon not far from the No Man's Land cutting North from South Korea. By 1964 Songsim College for Women would be built on a plateau cut from the mountain side.

Japan was the next stop, a country racing with the West in prosperity. Mother de Valon was received with art festivals in Obayashi, Susono, Sankocho and Seishin University, where the high moments were the baptismal ceremonies at which Christians and non-Christians rejoiced together. She found the novices from all three countries gathered at Susono where Mount Fuji signed their lives with her own mystery. The route then curved up to the northern island of Hokkaido to visit the site, again mountain-girt, of a new school to be opened the following year at Sapporo.

The communities were filling with young oriental nuns who soon outnumbered the foreign missionaries; many went abroad to study. Closer work with the Japanese population came in 1967 when a small community settled next to a parish church at Amakusa, not far from where the martyrs of Nagasaki had given their lives, and opened a kindergarten.

Back at the Mother House, Mother de Valon shared her inspiration with the Society:

> My experience during this journey urges me to tell you of a thought that I have pondered for a long time. . . . Has the moment come for us to do still more to invigorate the missionary thrust of the Society? You know to what extent there is now awakening among all peoples the desire to know, the desire for social advancement, the urge to reach the degree of cultivation needed for this advance. Let us heed the desires of Pius XII [in *Evangelium Praecones*]: "Young people today, above all those trained by higher studies and the liberal arts, will be the leaders of tomorrow; we all know the importance to be given to the teaching in schools and colleges." Does this not mean that missionary life so envisaged opens to the Society a work that is truly its own? . . . Workers are few, but will not the vocations that we so much desire come in greater numbers when the Society broadens its field still more and officially takes its place in missionary life? [11]

The letter outlined the spiritual, intellectual and material preparation needed, and suggested means: a Mission Procurate at the Mother House for information and exchange, a mission fund to be supplied by a mission tax in the schools, a bulletin, "serious in tone,

to give news of our already existing missions and to confront the
questions of missiology."

All this was carried out with speed. The tireless Mother Benziger
set up art displays at the Mother House; Marguerite du Merle
became mission secretary for the Society; enthusiasm spread (only
the mission tax was found unacceptable by parents struggling to pay
tuition). The new journal was entitled *Mitte Me*, the answer of
Isaiah to the call of Yahweh, echoed by Philippine Duchesne to
Madeleine Sophie Barat: "Here I am, send me!" In the first
editorial:

> Doctrine and principles being of the greatest importance, the Review will deal
> in the first place with points of missiology, and then, passing on to the level of
> news, achievements, needs and desires, it will show the missions of the Society
> within the framework of the great missionary plan of the Church. . . . Mis-
> sionary spirit calls for generosity of soul, a complete break with selfishness, the
> reversal of certain traditional views. It is a whole mentality, a whole new at-
> titude to be adopted, one which is disinterested and looks to the future. . . . It
> is an acid test of all our ways of judging things and of our spiritual values
> themselves. [12]

Mitte Me appeared twice a year in French, English and Spanish, until 1966. Each issue, with artistic photography, presented one country, or one group of countries, in the light of the Church's unfolding
concept of what it means to be sent.

The third issue announced still another form of the *élan
missionaire*:

> Among the missionary movements of the past months we find a very happy in-
> itiative: the institution of the Mission Volunteers of the Sacred Heart. It ap-
> plies to young girls who wish to give one or two years to the missions. This
> apostolate is a response to the appeal made by the Church to the laity. There is
> a double advantage for those who offer themselves: security, since they will
> live in a convent of the Sacred Heart, and the fullest flowering of their best
> qualities in the Lord's harvest field. [13]

Formation centres were set up at the Mother House, at Barat
College in the United States, at Melbourne in Australia. The fifth
issue pictured the first group of Volunteers at the feet of John
XXIII who said to them: "Live always in joy." An article quoted
letters from Brazil, Tokyo, Taiwan, the Congo, telling of the adventures of teaching, playing, praying, cleaning house, of exhilaration
and of bracing cultural shocks.

On the last day of that stimulating year, 1961, Mother de Valon wrote:

> Among the signs of our Lord's love I must point out the unanimous eagerness, joy and confidence with which all have responded to the missionary appeal that I made some months ago. And I was deeply moved when, a few days later, our Lord himself seemed to ratify it by offering us a small place in the heart of Black Africa where there is so much to be done. [14]

This "small place" was in Uganda. The foundresses from Ireland, Scotland and Australia, led by Winifred Killeen, arrived at Nkozi in January, 1962, and accepted a Teacher Training College given to them by the White Sisters. The equator ran across the garden, Lake Victoria glinted in the distance. The students arrived by the cartload, all singing, with bags of banana paste for their meals. They were noisy and devout, for "to an African adoration is as natural as swallowing." Soon the nuns were teaching as best they could in Luganda, for although these girls studied in English they did practice teaching in an elementary school where children crowded in from the bush. The task was gigantic, to educate through teachers-to-be as many as possible of the women of Uganda-to-be.

When the national elections took place in February the community passed breathless nights and days behind barricades, hearing the Muslim drums threatening attack. The danger passed and in October the nation declared independence. The Christians in Uganda had been morally strengthened, and the bishops asked in their Pastoral Letter: "May they make their voices heard in every sector of social life." Accordingly, the Society opened a secondary school at Kalisizo in 1964, where some two hundred out of the thousands struggling for admission could be educated to liberty.

In the meantime another African land had reached nationhood in 1960, Chad, hot and flat, where the village folk still hunted in prehistoric fashion. To the north lay a stronghold of the Muslim religion, to the south a stronghold of native animism. "We want to learn" was the cry, and a community of religious of the Sacred Heart — French, Dutch, Spanish and Polish under the leadership of Simone de la Hitte — opened a school at Chagwa in 1964. Classes met on the river bank among fishing nets until a secondary school was built where Chadian and European children mingled.

In the Congo a turning point was reached under the shock of violence when the country became Zaire in 1960. There were only seventy Africans among sixteen hundred children at Kalina, but a training college for black teachers had been opened in 1958. The other houses were overflowing with African children. On July 6, 1960, armed men appeared at Mbansa-Mboma at two in the morning. They beat the guards and broke into the chapel, where they lined up along the communion rail and insulted the household that had gathered to pray. When they left, the community made their way to Kalina which had opened its doors to everyone:

> Many in distress came for shelter; numbers of Belgians arrived destitute and at the limit of their endurance. Our nuns made themselves all things to all men, showing the way to some, getting food for others, when as many as five relays of meals would follow in rapid succession, providing what was needed in the dormitories. A linen room was organized where baby clothes were made; the children were kept amused. . . . Days and nights were spent thus, and only after two weeks were the nuns able to go to bed at night. Finally, on August 15, the last communities returned to their convents (250 nuns of different orders), and Kalina, as in other years at the same date, prepared for the opening of school. [15]

But this "reopening as usual" was different; all the children were African, and radical adaptations were in demand. In November, 1961, the first general assembly of the bishops of the Congo held its meetings in the Sacred Heart school; their presence was "a pledge that the numerous problems to be studied will be seen from the African point of view." The Sacred Heart vicariate of Zaire became autonomous in 1963, and an upsurge of native Catholic Action began in the schools. "Educational work in all its facets, human and religious, wide hospitality, these functions are essential to the apostolic work of the Society." An Apostolic School for "Bernadettes," African girls aspiring to religious life, was opened at Kimuenza.

The Indian vicariate also became autonomous, in 1964. In December Paul VI continued his "dialogue with all religions" by flying to Bombay for a Eucharistic Congress. India's few Catholics were joined by Protestants, Muslims, Hindus, Jains, Sikhs, Zoroastrians and Jews thronging to gaze at the *burra-guru*, the "great holy man," who prayed before a quarter of a million worshippers: "May God make of us one family of his children." Sophia College helped to prepare the Liturgy.

In both the college and the high school at Bangalore service through understanding of "the other" was breaking down the fatalistic attitude of the higher castes towards the poor. The Society reached the villagers in 1961 when a school was opened in a Jesuit parish in Harigaon. As the nuns jolted along the mud roads through sugarcane fields they heard an orchestra of drums and flutes coming to meet them. The children, nearly all Catholics, thronged into the school. Mother Andersson could not come as she had desired to this house of simplicity; she died on August 18, 1961. Adoration and inner silence were at the core of her service of India where it is easy to speak of the Heart of Christ; the phrase "Heart of God" is frequent in Indian prayer.

The whole Society was involved in one Indian enterprise. When Madeleine Sophie was canonized, a Belgian Jesuit in Gangutoli asked help of the mother house; a mission post was set up in honour of the new saint. The *Echo of the Month* kept the Society informed of his struggles; if a new motor-bike was needed it was soon supplied by far-off students who supported his school run by Indian nuns. In 1954 the church of Saint Madeleine Sophie was blessed; from this centre chapels were opened in twenty-five villages, and seventeen more schools sprang up. In 1961 the Belgian missionaries handed over the church to Indian priests; Saint Madeleine Sophie was at home.

The mainspring of the *élan* started by Mother de Valon is found in the Decree of Vatican II, *Ad Gentes*:

> Christ is the source and model of that renewed humanity, penetrated with brotherly love, sincerity and a peaceful spirit, to which all aspire. Christ and the Church which bears witness to him by preaching the Gospel, transcend every particular race and nation, and therefore cannot be considered foreign anywhere or by anyone. [16]

The Chapter of 1964 made this concrete for the Society of the Sacred Heart:

> The Council has reminded us: the Church is by essence wholly missionary. Today more than ever she is seen as a whole, charged with evangelizing a world which is also a whole. . . . The missions must no longer be looked upon as an avant-garde of the Church, nor the missionary enterprise as an "expedition" or a "conquest." Rather than conquest we speak today of presence or of witness. . . . Similarly, the missionary work of the Society is not something apart. It is integral to the work of the Society which is inserted into that of the Church. We do not go to the "pagans" to "conquer" them — which implies domination — but we go very humbly and respectfully to open the way for an

encounter of their culture and even of their religion with the Church, and to open to them the love of Christ which awaits them in the proclamation of the Good News and the testimony of our lives. We must realize that conversions are not the only fruit of the missions. [17]

Three phases of the Society's mission in a non-Christian land are outlined in these Directives:

> The Society is established such as she is; she becomes loved, she studies the situation, she gains experience by living. The first native vocations appear. . . . Then vocations become more numerous, though the mission still has need of foreign personnel. . . . Finally, the Society, while remaining herself, has become Indian, Oriental, African. [18]

The recognition of this had been slow in coming; uniformity, especially in community life, had for too long been equated with unity. After 1964 the ideal was seen, and followed at an uneven pace in different lands.

* * *

The note of social awareness was sounded in the fall issue of *Mitte Me*, 1965, which was devoted to South America; the editorial asked:

> Latin America a missionary country? With a higher percentage of baptized Catholics than any other continent? Can this really be true? Such a question is like an accusing finger pointed at us all. It is a reminder to every Catholic the world over that the conversion of the human race must begin with that of the baptized Catholic. A movement in this direction has been set on foot in Latin America, and it is one of the great hopes of the Church today. For if the word "Catholic" points to the transcendence of the Kingdom of God which Christ came on earth to found and which the Church endeavors to spread throughout the world, the same word indicates that she permeates like leaven, like a supernatural force of energy, every soul and every culture which gives her welcome. [19]

The bold words of Archbishop Helder Camara of Brazil were then quoted, a sign that the Society no longer felt, as it had a century earlier, that "every innovation is a danger."

> Let no-one be scandalized to see me with people generally held to be dangerous or compromising, of the left or of the right, in office or in opposition, reformers

or their opponents, revolutionaries or anti-revolutionaries, in good or bad faith. Let no-one try to classify me in any particular group or tie me to any particular party. I keep open house and open heart for all without exception. . . . No missionary effort on behalf of Latin America will be of such value to our African and Asian brothers as the achievement of the true spirit of brotherhood within our continent, a fraternal dialogue with the world of underdeveloped peoples. [20]

This implied that the religious problem was inseparable from the social problem, as John XXIII had stated in *Mater and Magistra*:

> Though Holy Church has the special task of sanctifying souls and making them partake of supernatural goods, she is also solicitous for the needs of men's daily life, not merely with those having to do with bodily nourishment and the material side of life, but also those that concern prosperity and culture in all its many aspects and historical stages.

The phenomenal awakening of the social consciousness — and conscience — of the Latin American Church began in 1955 when the first Continental Congress of Bishops met in Rio de Janeiro, with the Sacred Heart convent of Morro de Gracia as hostess. Vision and courage reached out from that assembly like the arms of the gigantic Christ watching over the harbour. A hopeful image emerged: bishops at one with their people. Organizations were formed: CELAM (Episcopal Council of Latin America), CLAR (Latin American Conference of Religious) and CAL (Pontifical Commission for Latin America). The aims of CAL were largely educational, for education alone could exorcise "folk-lore Christianity."

The Society of the Sacred Heart moved into line. It was high time to confront — with hindsight and contrition — the image of social privilege by crossing social frontiers.

One problem was common to all South American countries: the slums clinging to the skirts of the luxurious homes of the "established": *barrios, favellas, callamparas*. Already the Society had plenty of free schools and "popular works"; already the alumnae were extremely active in social service. They had set up meeting places for catechism and sewing classes, then small dispensaries, then associations with trained workers capable of transforming a whole neighbourhood, with such names as "Madeleine Sophie Social Centre" or "Mater Admirabilis Guild." Here they were joined by the students in Sacred Heart Schools who learned to meet Christ in the down-trodden.

When, following the Chapter of 1964, the religious were no longer bound by cloister and appeared on the front lines, the effect was electrifying. Typical was a threeweek mission in a slum area of Santiago, Chile, where the nuns joined the laity in a parish undertaking. At its close the pastor said at the breakfast party given for the workers by the poor:

> There is no need to thank us; we are all brothers, those who live in the seminary or in the convent and those who live in this district. It is natural that brothers and sisters should love and visit one another. [21]

This movement ran parallel to that of the Priest Workers, checked for so long and now approved. Gradually the religious of the Sacred Heart moved into the pastoral ministry needed in "no priest land."

A noticeable change of tone in the *Echo of the Month* was heard; its accounts were no longer solely intramural but told of this penetration into wider areas. Stable works grew out of these adventures in sharing: classes for illiterate adults at Rio de Janeiro, a radio school in Colombia in collaboration with "Radio Sutatenza," a Providence Bank at Curitiba, commercial and technical courses added in many schools. Five suburban centres for basic instruction were opened in as many years in Cali, Lima, Buenos Aires and Montevideo. Chorillos, near Lima, developed into INIF (Instituto Nacional Industrial Feminino).

When Mother de Valon journeyed through South America in 1965 she felt that others should learn the lesson of the *barrios*. From Lima she wrote a letter to the Sacred Heart alumnae the world over:

> Today for the first time I turn to all of you, to whatever continent you live in, since I want to share with you my anxiety and to pass on to you an appeal from Our Lord. . . . I would like to let you share, in some measure, the thoughts and feelings that come to me at the sight of so many material and spiritual needs among the poor. . . . To the end of my life I shall remember the sad sight of the *barrios*, those multitudes of huts clinging to the mountain side where human beings live like the beasts with whom they often share their habitations. . . . Their bodily hunger is not the worst aspect of this situation. Illiteracy is something that evokes pity in our era. Inability to read, ignorance of all that enables one to think, are terrible evils. . . . Yes, they are Christians, but rather by habit, rather by way of a mysterious call to something unknown, something better, something towards which they aspire and which very few people help them to discover. God's longing cries out from these hovels, and

this cry reaches us; it spreads all over the earth. We must hear it, heed it, even if it is inconvenient, even if it upsets our ordinary well-ordered lives. [22]

She had put her finger unerringly on the point most significant for the Society's mission: illiteracy. This was an aspect of the social problem to which the Society had a special call.

But no educational work today can stop at "alphabetization," the first step of a long ladder which even the poorest set out to climb. CELAM ambitioned higher education, essential for the full growth of a culture, and advanced study cannot be divorced from social responsibility. The Society of the Sacred Heart must take its part. A new school was opened in Cordoba, in the interior of Argentina (1958). The long-standing teacher training college of San Pedro moved to a new site at Monterrico where the wings of the building reached out "like the rays of a monstrance," said Mother de Valon when she saw it from an airplane. Reaching out still further was the influence of the "Sampedranas" trained to go into "regions as varied as our climate," in fetid slums or on the lonesome fringes of civilisation, forming thousands of more than literate citizens. Another teacher training college developed at Curitiba. Soon there were university colleges at Carrasco and Lima, while Montivideo had its Institute of Philosophy and Letters, and Medellin had its Faculty of Arts and Decoration and its Faculty of Modern Humanities, both dependent on the Pontifical University of Bolivia. The young people who benefited faced the change needed in their own outlook:

It is young girls and women who have had the least preparation for the present situation. . . . One might be tempted to look back somewhat wistfully upon the romantic days when woman's place in the home was one of sweetness and beauty, but the alarm has sounded and young people must meet it with generosity and the ready sacrifice called for by this time of transition. Woman must often renounce her lawful claims, expose herself to danger, measure up to reality. She must hold her own in education, in politics, in the professions, and in particular concentrate upon a solution to the problems of today. [23]

Long ago the Society had found a Third World when Mother Duchesne had sought out a submerged minority, the North American Indians. In 1965 the Society reached the South American Indians, at Jaen on the far slope of the Peruvian Andes. The inhabitants are descendants of the Incas, all Catholics, all in need of book learning. The Society took over a government high school, working in poverty, simplicity and tropical heat. Across the river lay Amazonia where the Ahuarunas, still primitive, were still waiting for the Good News. There is no end to it.

In the meantime trouble had been mounting in one Latin American land where outright Communism was solving social problems in its own way. The seizure of power by Fidel Castro in Cuba had almost started a third world war in 1961. The two Sacred Heart schools were closed, and the Cuban nuns had to leave at the moment when they felt most needed. Some went to Puerto Rico and some to Carrollton in Miami where exiled Cuban children could study side by side with American children.

Some went to Venezuela. This foundation in still another country had been asked for by the many Venezuelan women educated in Sacred Heart schools elsewhere; it was made possible by the events in Cuba. A large school was opened at Carracas. It flourished at first, then paid the price for its clear stand on social justice. Resulting difficulties led later to the withdrawal of the religious, who found other ways of being a leaven in a land where youth forms half of the population.

"Egypt is a crucible. Most of the problems which confront the Church today are found there, and are smelted by fire." [24] It is the meeting place of three continents, and the unity in diversity envisaged by the Chapter of 1964 could be lived in this narrow strip of land with a richness found nowhere else. There was an acute need for ecumenism in its Christian community of Catholics of seven different rites, Orthodox Copts, and Protestants, and the dialogue with Islam was at last beginning. Intensifying these religious differences were the social. Egypt was loved by Mother de Valon who visited it twice during her generalate, in 1959 and in 1965. Vatican II and the Chapter of 1964 had made a difference in the interval, and an experienced missionary saw what the Society was facing:

> In the recent past there were places where limited and chosen Catholic forces were grouped to serve a small clientele. This was the accepted order. But the sudden awakening of the country, hitherto considered to be as static as the pyramids, at first left the missionaries at a loss. Some followed those Catholics who emigrated, others lost courage; but there were those who took up the challenge in faith and hope, changed their ways and their methods, and renewed the ancient Church of Egypt. Certainly the new ways are more difficult.... At this moment our Lord is in the villages, in the overcrowded slums, in those girls of the new social class who are taking the place of the old

ones, more rare and more refined but who belong to yesterday. . . . We feel and know that the Society of the Sacred Heart has put itself on the map at the bidding of the Council. . . . This youthful eagerness to fit into new conditions and to use them despite so many obstacles, calls for a miracle. It will happen. [25]

Already in 1940 Father Henry Ahib Ayrout, S. J. had founded an association of "Responsibles," with a training centre in Cairo, to serve Christian minorities in the villages of Upper Egypt, home of the Fellahs, peasants who ploughed as in the days of the Pharaohs. He made a network of small schools, dispensaries and catechetical centers. Here Sacred Heart alumnae and students put on white aprons and braved the dirty huts where flies clung in clumps to the faces of little children. "With all my heart and soul I want to help them, for I love them with my whole being," wrote a school-girl.

After 1964 the nuns who had prepared such students could join them on their rounds. In Cairo, a few minutes from the convent, was Charabeya where Fellahs looking for work lived one family in a room and spilled into alley-ways. Mass was said in these rooms. Further off was Meduit-Masser, a Christian quarter with neither church nor school but abounding in children. Nuns, alumnae and children worked there together, and Mother de Valon came with them on her second visit to Egypt. She said:

At the Council we learned to love better. And the role of the laity was stressed in this splendid business of loving. But if we are to love better there must be a break-through in our lives, for we are bound hand and foot by our selfishness. . . . It is true that Egypt is in difficulties, but you do not have to be rich in order to help. What is needed is to give oneself. Those people with such good faces, those children who ran out to you, were not asking for money; they were asking for love. [26]

In Heliopolis the religious went to Matarieh where, says legend, the Holy Family rested in the shade of a great tree (still seen) on their "flight into Egypt," and set up a class outdoors. In 1966 the Society at last settled in Upper Egypt and became at home with the Fellahs at Samalout where all the works started by the Responsables became its lasting apostolate. The next year the Encyclical *Populorum Progressio* of Paul VI declared that "development is the new name for peace."

* * *

This thrust into the human situation was a sign of the New Pentecost, the blowing of a purposeful wind, in which the Society of the Sacred Heart would undergo the changes in structure and in way of life that renewal demands. Would its charism be lost — or itself renewed? If "Yahweh's plans hold good forever," are changes part of "the intentions of his heart from age to age?" [27]

Matters were precipitated in the nineteen-sixties by two forces working in the same direction and in opposition — real or apparent: the Church and "the world." The latter is an ambivalent entity; there is the world for which Christ would not pray, and the world which God so loved that he sent it his only Son. It may be risky for the Church and the world to be in alliance. But the word "risk" has undergone conversion: "Be brave, I have conquered the world." [28] In religious life two signs of urgency appeared. One was negative, disturbing, turned against itself, and yet valid: restive criticism, sometimes with discontent, even revolt. The other was wholly positive: a clear call, involving both the Hierarchy and the whole People of God: a mandate for the renewal of religious life given by a Church Council.

John XXIII had scarcely begun his pontificate when he suddenly proposed Vatican Council II:

> I was the first to be surprised at the proposal, which was entirely my own idea. . . . This is the mystery of my life; we do not look for other explanations. I have always repeated Gregory of Nazianzen's words: "God's will is our peace." [29]

The Council was announced to the dumb-founded Cardinals, and commissions began to work just as the Third General Assembly of Churches reaffirmed that "Jesus Christ is the light of the world." The Council was convoked in *Humanae Salutis*: "to bring the modern world into contact with the vivifying and perennial energies of the Gospel." [30] The first session began on October 11, 1962, with a "Message to Humanity." It emphasized: "Whatever concerns the dignity of man; whatever contributes to the genuine community of peoples." [31]

Almost one hundred years earlier Vatican Council I had held its one unfinished session, and Mother Goetz had been in Rome at the time. The Society then shared its mentality. At the third session of Vatican II Mother de Valon was among the official observers. In the intervening century the pendulum of thought had swung through a wide arc, and the Society recognized, with *Gaudium et Spes*, that: "The human race has passed from a rather static concept of reality to a more dynamic, evolutionary one." [32] The Church was discovering her own powers of evolution, in order to be the leaven in such a world:

> To carry out such a task the Church has always had the duty of scrutinizing the signs of the times and of interpreting them in the light of the Gospel. Thus, in language intelligible to each generation she can respond to the perennial questions which man asks about this present life and the life to come, and about the relationship between them. [33]

At the end of the first session of the Council John XXIII declared: "There will be a new Pentecost indeed." As he lay dying on the following Pentecost Sunday he said over and over: "May they all be one!" His offering was consummated the next day, June 3, 1963.

Giovanni Battista Montini became Paul VI on June 21, and the Council reconvened in September. A reign of violence was intensifying; John F. Kennedy was assassinated on November 22. As a sign of the search for peace and unity the Pope set out for the Holy Land in January, 1964.

> In one of the holiest but most hate-ridden corners of the earth the Pontiff mingled with the people, literally rubbing elbows with the Jordanian royalty and the poorest Arabs, with Christians, Moslems and Jews. [34]

In April Pedro Arrupe became superior general of the Society of Jesus, and Paul VI outlined, in his "Discourse to General Chapters," the reform of religious life that would soon begin.

Mother de Valon prepared the Society of the Sacred Heart for its Twenty-sixth General Chapter by letters stressing the connection between the renewal of the Church and that of the religious orders:

> The Church is Jesus Christ. The Church is ourselves. . . . To take upon ourselves the life of Jesus is our first responsibility. The second lies in carrying out with full ardour the task which is ours in the Mystical Body of Christ. We see our mission in the opening lines of the Constitutions: "This little Society is wholly consecrated to the glory of the Sacred Heart of Jesus and to the propagation of its worship." [35]

And as the time drew near:

> I know that there are some in the Society, and they are the greatest number, who look for the coming of tomorrow as a messenger of the great, the beautiful work which the Holy Spirit carries on constantly in the Church; they are waiting with hearts overflowing with hope. [36]
>
> Hope is indeed the virtue of the present moment; we look to God, we look to the future. Something is awakening in the world under the impulsion of grace; a star burns in the night, the dawn is coming. We await a tomorrow prepared by love; tomorrow God will show his marvellous mercy and the eternal youth of his Church. It is the atmosphere of the Council that brings this hope over the horizon. . . . May our Society become more and more conscious of her own nature, of what Jesus Christ asks of her, of what she can and must be to today's world. [37]

The two Council documents concerning religious life in the modern world were still under discussion during the Chapter of 1964, and were only promulgated later. But their contents were known and the Society drew its light from them. Chapter VI of *Lumen Gentium* declared that religious life is a symbol of the unbreakable bond between Christ and his spouse, the Church; that it is a sign to all men, attracting to the Christian vocation and foretelling the resurrection; that although it does not belong to the hierarchical structure of the Church, it does belong inseparably to its life and holiness, and the hierarchy approves and controls it; that through religious the Church wishes to give to believers and non-believers alike an increasingly clear revelation of Christ; that the evangelical councils are based on the example and words of our Lord. It stressed that religious life does not impede the development of personality for the counsels contribute to purification of heart and spiritual liberty, nor does it withdraw a person from the service of his fellow men, since even strict contemplatives are united to them in the Heart of Christ and cooperate with them spiritually. [38]

Perfectae Caritatis gave the lines for the renewal which each order must undertake on its own responsibility. Its capital principles are found at the beginning:

> The pursuit of perfect charity serves as a blazing sign of the heavenly kingdom. . . . Renewal involves two simultaneous processes: 1) continuous return to the sources of all Christian life and to the original inspiration behind a given community, 2) an adjustment of the community to the changed conditions of the times. [39]

Five guide-lines are given: the norm is the following of Christ as proposed by the Gospel; it best serves the Church for each community to have its own character and purpose, as seen in the spirit of their founders and in their heritage; all communities should share in the life of the Church; all members should be aware of contemporary human conditions; renewal of spirit alone gives life to external renewal.

The Twenty-Sixth General Chapter met from October 12 to November 15, 1964, one of the most significant in the history of the Society. Though composed of the same *ex officio* members as before, with no elected delegates, it was given the name of Chapter. It was carried on "in an atmosphere of joy, of confidence, of openness, of entire liberty and of intimate union," and all adaptations were made "in the luminous wake of the Church," [40] and in the spirit of the Encyclical *Ecclesiam Suam* which had just appeared, stressing the role of dialogue in renewal. As Mother Zurstrassen wrote:

> I hope and I believe that, when the Society has been "aired," and let us say "aggiornamentée," our young religious will have a deeper sense of their personal responsibility and will become more and more strongly attached to the essentials which will have been brought into relief by the suppression of accretions which have become too heavy and unacceptable.... Certainly, our assembly is "progressive"! What an abyss between this and the last Council! [41]

With regard to formation, the question of vocations was approached in the light of "the desires and fears of youth, and of the image of itself given by the Society." Greater emphasis was placed on human values in the noviceship, on the positive rather than the negative aspects of commitment. First vows were to be temporary, "a measure which will enable the novices to become conscious of their engagement and leave them greater liberty." [42] The five years of aspirantship would, ideally, be given entirely to doctrinal and professional study. Greater simplicity and flexibility in the customs of community life at all levels were encouraged.

One question long under consideration was brought to a head by "the desire of the Church expressed through Vatican II that in Institutes of religious women there should be only one category of religious." [43] The social evolution and the general rise in the level of education made it undesirable to keep the distinction between choir religious and coadjutrix sisters. Janet Stuart had defended it in *The*

Society of the Sacred Heart: "Seen from within there are reasons which give great value to the distinction." [44] These values were now outweighed. Already in 1961 the coadjutrix sisters had adopted the habit of the choir religious, and the Chapter decided for the integration of the two categories. Although, as in all sudden adjustments, there were difficulties in carrying it out (in some countries more than in others) these could be solved by time and generous effort, and the fact of the fusion was welcomed:

> How our large religious family will now grow in the splendour of charity in the eyes of God and the world! We shall find in this measure new joy and new possibilities for good. [45]

The most far-reaching decision, perhaps, was the abrogation of cloister. Currents of thought and feeling both within and without the Society had been rising for many years, but these had not generally been recognized as "signs of the times" in the sense of John XXIII but rather as signs of a failure to seize the values for which cloister had always stood. In this dilemma a directive came from Vatican II, and Mother de Valon said to the Chapter:

> The Church has spoken, or is about to speak, since the schema on religious life has not yet been voted, but certainly there will be no difficulty on the article of cloister which says: "It is fitting that other religious orders (meaning those not monastic) dedicated to apostolic work should be exempt from cloister." We accept the word of the Church in full obedience, and I believe that if she speaks thus she does well. [46]

To the whole Society she wrote:

> The present great renewal of religious life consists in becoming conscious of the duty which every religious has of becoming an authentic apostle, an authentic witness to Jesus Christ. Is this necessity not still more urgent at this hour when the Church asks that for religious leading an active life the limits of cloister should no longer present an obstacle?... It is the Holy Spirit himself who wishes to show to the world this being whom God has chosen for himself, this volunteer who seeks below only the Kingdom of God, not only because she has come to serve and the tasks of the apostolate are numberless, but also and above all because she brings into the world, plunged in materialism, the luminous testimony to a life beyond. [47]

The principle was clear, but during the next three years certain practical controls, difficult to apply consistently, caused ambiguity.

At the close of the Chapter five instead of four assistants general were elected: Emilia Lurani, Maribeth Tobin, Magdalena Melia, Gabrielle Paradeis and Josefa Bultó. Françoise de Lambilly remained secretary general and Gisela Posada became treasurer general. When the vicars returned home they were wearing silver rings, and soon all were doing likewise in sign of the greater simplicity that religious should manifest. The gold rings received at profession were given to the Holy Father for his charities.

Mother de Valon pin-pointed the principle of greater flexibility in community life which followed the Chapter:

> It is time to recall the difference between traditions and tradition. There are undoubtedly certain traditions that should be left behind because they no longer hold the spirit that once gave them reason for being, and the young generation that comes to us now cannot find this spirit. A purely exterior observance is no observance; the young are right in wanting to know the reason for things. When there is no meaning things should and must change. So much for traditions. But the tradition of a religious family is the patrimony of which the values must be kept, defended and enriched. [48]

These values are: respect, prayer, the silence and regularity that make the beauty of the house of God, renouncement that fosters generosity, and family spirit.

A refreshing moment in this time of "letting go" was the centenary of the death of Saint Madeleine Sophie, May 25, 1965. Mother de Valon called for a year of preparation:

> A centenary marks a completed stage, a halt on the road of time, a stopping to look back along the way covered and to give thanks, a pause for taking breath and looking courageously to the future. We shall make this pause under the eyes of our holy Foundress, guided by the light of her example and of her teaching. [49]

This could be assured by a strengthening of prayer, obedience and charity in the Society. A memorial was drawn up in the form of a study entitled *Statistics*. With the help of detailed maps and diagrams it studied each vicariate under the headings: scholastic establishments, associations, social works, the religion of pupils and professors, the nationality of the religious, new "openings upon the world," and the academic preparation of the teachers. The whole spoke of a surge of vitality ready to go forward. The day itself was celebrated with quiet intensity. A search into the writings of Madeleine Sophie was stimulated. As Mother Zurstrassen had said:

I am convinced that our spirit can penetrate into any "formula," and that we must take into account those things, good in themselves, which have sprung up spontaneously from the soil of present needs. Moreover, is it not her [Madeleine Sophie] broad-minded directives that have made it possible for the Society to take root in every country, and to carry on its work of education in each? Yes – there is our tradition. [50]

Vatican Council II closed on December 8, 1965. One passage in Paul VI's closing address, "Message to Human Beings," had special significance for the Society:

The hour is coming, in fact has come, when the vocation of woman is to be achieved in all its fulness, the hour in which woman acquires in the world an influence, an effect and a power never hitherto achieved. [51]

In January Mother de Valon commented on *Perfectae Caritatis*: the call to renewal is the call of the Church to love, the love heard in the desire of Christ "that they all may be one." "If our charity is open to this desire we shall have understood the lesson of the Council." [52] At Christmas time, 1966, all RSCJs appeared in a simplified habit, and in the following April Mother de Valon announced the Special Chapter for implementing *Perfectae Carritatis* required of all religious orders.

The preparation was searching. In the past any religious had been free to send suggestions to the General Councils and a few had done so; now all were urged to contribute their *desiderata*. A commission was needed to edit the overwhelming response. Delegates were elected in addition to the *ex-officio* members. This measure had been rejected in 1874 because "all innovation is a danger." Now innovation with its attendant risk was welcomed. Eighty-six capitulants met for the most arduous Chapter ever held – and the longest, October 1 to December 14, 1967. In the chapter room a simultaneous translation system did its best in French, English and Spanish. Over the chairman's place was a symbol to which all eyes could turn: Fra Angelico's picture of the piercing of the Heart of Christ. That was the hour which Madeleine Sophie had seen as the birth of the Society; the present hour was rebirth. In her opening address Mother de Valon said:

Is it not urgent to confirm by our witness – since religious life is a sign – that the spirit of the Gospel is always new, that it can solve all problems and that it will never be out of date? I think that our Chapter must consider the world today through the Heart of Christ, in order to bring to it more faith, more hope, more love. [53]

The road ahead was not clear. Tensions, polarization, misunderstanding among those with mutual desires and aims were inevitable. The Chapter was a crucible, purifying, testing, forging the future. On November 7 Mother de Valon gave her resignation as superior general, "for the good of you all." In this impasse Cardinal Antoniutti, Prefect of the Sacred Congregation of Religious, presided at a plenary session. On the grounds that "a special and post-conciliar Chapter" did not have the right to refuse or accept the resignation (a right given in the Constitutions to an ordinary General Council) he accepted it in the name of the Church.

Painfully, trustfully, prayerfully, the Chapter went on under Maria Josefa Bultó as vicar general. Born at Barcelona in 1905, professed on February 28, 1932, she had served as superior in Spain until becoming assistant general in 1958. Already she had acted as vicar general for a short time in 1966. On December 5, 1967, she became the eleventh superior general of the Society of the Sacred Heart. The assistants general were Maribeth Tobin, Magdalena Melia, Barbara Nicholls, Caterina Barcherini, Madeleine Drujon and Kiyoko Wakamatsu, with Gisela Posada as treasurer general and Andrée Meylan as secretary general. In her closing address to the Chapter Mother Bultó called on all:

> We must strengthen and make more authentic our Cor Unum. The basis for this will no longer be uniformity but confidence, love, and the sole desire of working together in the apostolic task given us by the Church. [54]

The results of the difficult, often anguishing, always faith-guided deliberations were embodied in *Orientations for a Time of Experimentation*, a serene, urgent and luminous document to guide the Society through the next three years. The preface, written retrospectively at the end of the Chapter, echoed its beginning:

> The Society, like the Church, is a part of living history; it does not wish to — in fact it cannot — renew itself according to a rigid framework decided beforehand. Consequently, the Chapter has not tried to define the old but still-new realities of Saint Madeleine Sophie, but rather to make them live through human and religious experience. It has kept its eyes fixed on the world of today, in order to bring to it, through the Heart of Christ, more faith, more hope, more love. [55]

The Society of the Sacred Heart, "an apostolic institute in the
Church and the world today," is aiming to renew itself "in a spirit
of union and conformity with the Heart of Jesus expressed in the
language of today," and "Christ is present in an evolving world. . . .
Where he is there must be the Church." If the Society is to be a
witness to love, a first duty is to remove obstacles to this:

> Identification with a particular social class, triumphalism, an air of self-
> satisfaction, a tendency to stress structures rather than persons, and a certain
> lack of charity among ourselves. [56]

The norms for government are subsidiarity, decentralization and
participation of all members. Vicariates have become provinces;
those in government have a limited term and are to be assisted by
councils and commissions. The foundation of the consecrated life is
prayer seen as the source and expression of charity, and the vows
seen as commitments of love. Community life is fraternal charity at
the service of the world. The work of education is to be confronted
in the light of reality:

> In a world where man is becoming more and more conscious of his own worth,
> education acquires fundamental importance since by it man becomes man;
>
> — in a world where interpersonal relations are increasingly important one of the
> first roles of education is to enable man to dialogue;
>
> — in a world of scientific and technical progress it is more and more necessary
> that Christian educators do not create a parallel world but, by taking part in
> this progress, contribute to the building up of the Body of Christ;
>
> — in a world which longs for the universal brotherhood of man . . . the Society
> should do all in its power to bring about the fusion of classes and the equality
> of races;
>
> — in a world which is working towards the unity of the human family, we must
> go beyond local and national spirit and help developing nations;
>
> — in a world where hunger and ignorance can be overcome only by education,
> we should ask ourselves if our pupils leave us with a determination to change
> the world . . . and if we ourselves educate the children who have the greatest
> need of us;
>
> — in a world where the Church calls us to new tasks we must give to education
> its full present-day dimension;

— in a world which is moving towards socialization of education we must read the signs of the times. [57]

Mother Bultó assured the Chapter at its close: "The pierced Heart of Jesus will be an inexhaustible source and stimulus for this."

* * *

The following years were a bridge that carried the Society from a long-built-up security into a future-on-faith, a bridge not unlike those swaying rope-constructions that span chasms — safe for the confident. Mother Bultó serenely created such confidence as she went from one province to another. Her first concern was the healing of misunderstanding, and she wrote to the Society:

These few lines will reach you from Egypt, from the desert, where I have had the immense grace of meeting Mother de Valon. . . . You know, or you must have guessed, that the departure of our Mother whom we loved, whom we still love so much, who had spent herself without sparing any effort in the service of the Society, was painful. . . . Our Mother felt that some of the capitulants did not have confidence in her and, wishing at any cost to keep union in the Society, she gave her resignation. [58]

Mother de Valon added a postscript:

Our mother general has given you the real reason for my resignation; you have the right to know it. Now I repeat what I have written to so many among you since December 5: guided by the new mother general, in whom I have full confidence, let us be very united and keep the Society strong in that union drawn from the Heart of Our Lord. [59]

Helpful events gave new points of departure. The sesquicentennial of the mission of Philippine Duchesne was celebrated in June, 1968, at Saint Charles; where the shrine holding her body (in the transept of an unfinished basilica) summoned pilgrims in the spirit of Philippine: bold, bare, strong, blending light and colour in rugged harmony. A booklet written for the event brought that spirit into the Society's mission today:

The earth looks now for frontier-seekers: men and women, visited by anguish, who can yet step gently over despair to fashion a resurrection-realm, a joy-burst country, a hope-hallowed world. The paradoxes will remain:
— our individual efforts in a work beyond the grasp of any single mind;

– our living for the future which is not yet ours while working in a now that is
ours;
– an underlying joy despite abiding grief;
– responsible striving for a world which we cannot explain;
– being part of the Body of One who is Beginning and End;
– risking our lives that we may find them;
– challenging social patterns in which we find false comfort;
– sharing restlessness in the Spirit yet being instruments of peace. [60]

Coordination with other groups gave fresh strength, as the
Society worked with the International Union of Superiors General,
and with SEDOS, an association of missionary orders. The *Echo of
the Month* undertook dialogues between the provinces of the Society
on crucial issues. Some provinces shared their educational efforts, as
in the Stuart Conferences which drew together all the schools in the
United States. A central Educational Secretariat was formed. The
thorny problem of social integration in the classroom was faced
squarely, especially in South America where fusions were made between poor and well-to-do students. Many new ventures sprang up,
for the *Orientations* said that in addition to the institutions already
existing:

> Many other means are in our power today: teaching in the parishes, in the
> inner-city, catechetical centres, classes in adult education, centres for the han-
> dicapped and for the abandoned, visits to families according to apostolic need,
> vacation camps, participation in missionary teams, finally, every work of
> education as need arises. [61]

One painful aspect of this multiplication was the closing of old
and loved houses: in Canada, the Sault-au-Recollet; in the United
States Duchesne College, the city house in Saint Louis, Rochester,
Eden Hall; Louvain, San Sebastian, and Cabellero de Gracias in
Madrid. In some cases, both at this time and later, the administration of the school passed into secular hands while a few religious
remained on the teaching staff. It is hard to find the causes at work
in this sometimes too sudden process, and misunderstandings arise.
The most obvious causes are alarming – want of funds and of personnel. But deeper causes bring a challenging hope; they are found
in the documents of Vatican Council II: Christ's need to be present
through his Church at the heart of the present crisis. The
evolutionary process brings wrenches and false moves, but goes in
the right direction. As *Populorum Progressio* says:

Development demands bold transformation, innovations that go deep. Urgent reforms should be undertaken without delay. It is for each one to take his share in them with generosity, particularly those whose education, position and opportunities afford them wide scope for action.

While many large schools and colleges were kept and strengthened, the need for new apostolates became imperative, despite the feared "splintering". The two forms of education should help each other. Reality is a teacher; children in school learn from it. As but one example: should a religious needed in the classroom go off to work in a women's prison, alone? She is not alone, she has the support of her community and what she is doing feeds back into the classroom. More educated women will be ready to remove the causes of crime. Such long-range results are costly. The Society realizes that a more open communication with alumnae, parents and friends could have spared much misunderstanding; it too is learning.

Despite these hazards the Society continued to spread at this time and in the years following. It entered three new countries with very different enterprises: at Goteburg in Sweden a kindergarten and work for adults was begun (1969); in Manila a community of young Philippino nuns began a work of infiltration into student and diocesan life, serving the native Church (1969); while a foundation in the countryside in Bolivia brought the Society into contact with indigenous people living close to the soil (1973). In Europe there were foundations in France at Chantilly, Francheville and Bordeaux (all in 1970), in Belgium in Beloeil (1969), and at Innsbruck in Austria (1970). At Nagoya a small community moved into a settlement of Japanese workers (1971), while at Poona an Ashram, or Indian house of prayer was opened (1973). [62] Uganda became an autonomous province, and soon included Chad and several small communities in Kenya working in native schools and seminaries.

It would be impossible to name all the smaller houses — or better communities — that began in these years. [63] Their number rose prodigiously; many were experimental and often temporary. There were provincial houses; small houses connected with larger ones; division of communities within the latter; apartments in cities, especially in poorer areas, where the religious could do needed local work or teach in Society schools while living as "presences" in a different milieu; centres of "second career" activities. As the Church is gradually changing her image from an institutionalized Church to a Pilgrim Church, so too the religious orders.

Statistics for this period are complex and shed a light both rosy and sombre. Society membership was on the increase at first; it reached a peak when it rose above the plateau of the six thousands where it had rested since 1891: in 1963 there were 7074 religious in 195 houses. A sharp decline then began; ten years later there were 6136 religious in a proliferation of 446 houses (some very small). The number of novices, however, had been declining for many years while the age-level was still rising. The pyramid was inverted.

Disturbing factors were evident during the years of experimentation. They had been at work in all religious orders, largely unperceived; now they suddenly surfaced. Each was, in its own way, a "sign of the times" to be heeded.

The lessening of vocations could, at its worst, be interpreted to mean that religious life was no longer viable in the modern world. Vatican II had said otherwise:

> The more ardently religious unite themselves to Christ through a self-surrender involving their entire lives, the more vigorous becomes the Church and the more abundantly her apostolate bears fruit. A life consecrated by the profession of the counsels is of surpassing value. Such a life has a necessary role to play in the circumstances of the present day. [64]

This implies that renewal would be in itself a source of future vocations. Formation in keeping with the idealism and potentialities of modern youth would be the condition. Mother de Loë had said in 1928:

> The mould of our religious life has not been broken. Vocations of the twentieth century must enter into it and adapt to it as did the young people who gathered around our Mother Foundress. [65]

Certainly generations of young people had done just that with the utmost generosity, but perhaps the mould had not always done its work because each generation was different from the last. The letter had perhaps moulded the spirit; now it was time for the spirit to mould the letter as in the beginning.

The adaptation of formation begun after the Chapter of 1964 accelerated after that of 1967:

This formation, like all that is vital, must be adapted to the person just as she is, with her human possibilities and her spiritual charisms; to the times, the signs of which one must read as they reveal the presence of God and his plan for the world; to the spirit of the Institute: the love of Christ lived in a consecration of one's whole being to his service and to the service of all men. It must be integral: attentive to the harmonious development of physical, moral and intellectual aptitudes; uniting to a profound spiritual and apostolic formation, a rich human one; achieving the maturity of a balanced personality, fully conserious of belonging to Church and to the service of the Church. [66]

The most dismaying factor was the number of committed religious who left their orders. This aroused searching auto-criticism in the religious orders themselves. Can it be that renewal was not only due, but overdue? Can it be that structures once effective had become not only ineffective but harmful? In a search for true freedom good and bad tendencies can run along strangely parallel lines, and in the effort for the valid development of personality it is likely that some selfishness, unseen as such under the long security of rule, would surface. Admitting the truth is part of the purification needed in all renewal. Constructive criticism on the part of individuals and the order is a sign of the thirst for integrity that causes restlessness. A religious order, like the Church itself, is a "community of sinners" in constant need of the same regeneration that it brings to the world.

These discoveries caused keen tensions in community life. Mother de Valon had written in 1959:

The quality of our work derives from the quality of our love. May this love find good soil in our community life so favourable for its growth; our prayer above all, and then the mutual help which each brings to the other. [67]

Her letter on prayer showed where help is always to be found:

In facing the human solutions that we must seek I feel the need of saying to you in the name of our Lord: grow more and more in the spirit of prayer, be souls of prayer. . . . Prayer is not an exchange of thoughts: God has no need of our thoughts, he asks for our presence. Prayer is a meeting of two loves that seek each other. [68]

* * *

Father Pedro Arrupe, speaking for the Jesuits in 1969, said:

The Society [of Jesus] cannot take up an attitude of introversion and passivity which would make it useless and condemn it to a slow death. Neither can it allow itself to be carried along helplessly by the torrent of events or by "accomplished facts." Nor can it let each individual follow his personal charism and go his own way without any relation to the entire body of which he is a member by free choice. The Society has only one real option; to serve the Church it has to adapt itself in an apostolic spirit to the modern world, following Christ's norms and taking into account the guidelines of Vatican II. [69]

This basic option had already been made by the Society of the Sacred Heart; it must now be implemented, allowing for the personal charism of individuals "in relation to the entire body." In preparation for the Chapter of 1970 each community acquired, not without struggle, the techniques of group dynamics, so that each member could take her part. As Mother Bultó said:

This profound renewal, based upon the "follow me" of Christ and upon our primitive spirit, involves us personally. This means a sincere and deep "conversion of heart." Each of us is called by Christ to be more gospel-hearted, striving generously to follow Christ more nearly by a share in his life — chaste, poor and obedient. [70]

The most probing measure was a questionnaire sent out from the Mother House and prepared by an international team; its aim was "to gather information on the general trends of ideas and on personal opinion on certain important points." It asked sixty-five questions concerning the Society's understanding of its own charism, nature and mission, and the needed adaptations. On November 21, 1969, 93.8% of its members responded. The answers were tabulated by Father C. Spruit, C. P., representative of KASKI, Institute of Socio-Religious Research at the Hague, who worked at the Mother House. When sending the results to the Society Mother Bultó said:

I want to ask all those who read this work to do so in a spirit that goes beyond all differences of age, of province, of nationality, of mentality. Let us read it, let us sound its depths, simply as religious of the Sacred Heart having but one heart and one mind. . . . Let us think *Society*. [71]

The Questionnaire was followed by a Self-Survey made by each province. These complemented the first study by high-lighting local differences. Pluriformity within unity was emerging as an accepted ideal. Father Spruit then compared the Self-Surveys to the answers to the Questionnaire and made a synthetic interpretation. Again Mother Bultó wrote:

> Our present task is the search, both individual and communal, of the truth concerning our religious life. . . . Let us read this study with tranquillity and objectivity, with the desire to be enlightened, knowing full well that we do not possess the whole truth, knowing too that we are conditioned by our past, by our mentality, by our desires and fears. If we are truly haunted by the desire to live in our time the evangelical mission of Saint Madeleine Sophie through a meaningful apostolate, if we have her concern for "littleness" and poverty, her thirst to make the love of Christ present among men, then Father Spruit's study cannot fail to meet a real need. A strong desire to be faithful to the Gospel and to the spirit of the Society is in itself the assurance of our hope. [72]

The conlcluding section of the synthesis reflected the realities of a time of transition: traumas, uncertainties, courage, faith in the New Pentecost. It looked at "the evangelical community of the Society" from three standpoints in time. At the origins:

> The personal experiences of the Foundress in her life of faith, the charismatic touch of the redemptive mystery of God's purpose, are expressed in her relationship with others and with the world. . . . Through her the Church witnessed to that love of God which transcends its own concrete and temporal structures. [73]

At the present moment:

> The surveys lead us to think that the original charism has become rigid by institutionalism in which it is hard to recognize the dynamic confrontation and vital involvement of the beginnings. [74]

In the future:

> If, beginning with the evangelical inspiration of the Foundress and of the charismatic service that she rendered to the Church and to the world, we wish to give renewed value to the concrete meaning and actuality of the Society of the Sacred Heart, we find the fundamental elements and guidelines for realizing them in a radical accentuation of the tendencies manifest in the post-Conciliar Church, tendencies which are in line with the original inspiration of the Society. [75]

To do just this the Twenty-eighth General Chapter met from October 3 to November 16, 1970. Forty-eight elected delegates joined the twenty-nine provincials at the Mother House, and a new

element was introduced by five young religious who had not yet
made their final profession; they had voice – a lively one – without
vote. The Chapter met, as Mother Bultó said:

> ... to affirm again our determination to centre our lives on Christ and on his
> love, that love of which the Heart pierced on the cross is a permanently effec-
> tive symbol; to deepen our fidelity to our religious consecration and to the
> vocation proper to us, diluting its demands in no way, and convinced that the
> Society's ideal will prove suited to any age so long as it keeps contact with the
> Gospel and so long as it can combine total fidelity with a constant willingness
> to adapt and to grow. ... This fidelity to Jesus will make it try with gospel
> daring to live forcefully, effectively and dynamically our unity in diversity. [76]

Each provincial then spoke. These frank reports of the efforts,
hopes and – not seldom – anguish of the past three years bared the
problems of each province and the varying speeds of renewal.
Almost everywhere there had been some conflict with the *status quo*,
cooperation with other groups, and new ministries. Some countries
admitted to a non-democratic mentality, a heritage of history, that
blocked communal discernment; others proclaimed "a theology of
liberation and of secularization." One report spoke for all:

> Every expression of our religious life should reproduce in its members the
> features of Saint Madeleine Sophie, the features of an apostle formed in the
> austere school of Christ humble, poor and crucified, fully given over to the will
> of the Father, an apostle animated by a living faith, by zeal for souls, whose
> homeland is the whole world and whose love reaches to the ends of the
> earth. ... Each province must understand the *aggiornamento* as the demands of
> love which, far from taking from religious life the possibility of living the
> paschal mystery in all its fulness, will give a new vitality to this marvellous
> possibility, so that each religious can share with greater intensity in the richness
> of Christ, and become, through intimate union with him, the authentic expres-
> sion of his features shining with light from the Father, his eyes fixed lovingly
> on his brothers who thirst for him. [77]

The intense debates were crystallized in a document remarkable
for quintessential brevity. The Society, "determined to live today,
according to the charism of Saint Madeleine Sophie, its mission of
showing forth the love of God-made-man," saw that:

> It is more than ever essential that the movement of the Incarnation be
> prolonged and the love of Jesus be revealed – Jesus who lived as a brother
> among men and who freely gave his life for them. In this perspective the
> Society faces a serious choice: either we live our fellowship authentically, in the

spirit of the Beatitudes, or our life ceases to have meaning. Renewed in depth, this life must remain rooted in prayer. [78]

This will require "nothing less than a conversion," and for this "may Mary, Mother of the Church, help us to live today in faith. open to the Spirit."

The Chapter then chose, from among the overwhelming number of points to be considered, five essentials upon which to focus:

"May they be so completely one that the world will realize that it was you who sent me and that I have loved them." This prayer of lasting power, the ground of unity in diversity, has moved us to take several fundamental options which converge on a single centre: the Heart of Christ. [79]

These options have already been considered in this book as principles inherent in the Society from the beginning. Here they will be given in the order of the Chapter Document, to show their interrelationship.

An international community, one and necessarily pluriform, we want to live our new awareness of this communion and to accept the practical consequences of coresponsibility and sharing at the international level. [80]

At a time when the integral development of man is a task of special urgency, we reaffirm our educational mission in the Church. [81]

In the light of the Gospel and of our social context, we wish to stand in solidarity with the poor. [82]

At this time when man hungers and thirsts for justice, our attitude must be one of solidarity with the Third World which suffers poverty and oppression. [83]

We commit ourselves to the renewal, at depth, of our life as a community, convinced that this is the one condition essential to the future of our religious life and to a genuine response to the summons of the Church. [84]

In the development of each Option, and through the following sections, the basic assumption is that "this new life is to be renewed in depth and rooted in prayer." [85]

With regard to formation: "In response to God's call, community and candidate together seek the means of living the Gospel in the Society of the Sacred Heart." [86] After her first commitment, in the form of a promise, the formation of the young professed "must take into account not only the religious herself but also her country and its needs." [87] The preparation leads to "the reciprocal, definitive commitment between the young religious and the Society as an international community." [88] But this is only a beginning; "continuing formation" is a life-long process involving: education for relationships, discernment of the values of secularization, the effort to live our commitments in their communal dimensions, and personal formation.

The section on government shows that each religious belongs at one and the same time to three communities, the local, the provincial and the international, and:

> This true co-responsibility for the building of community in order to accomplish the ecclesiastical mission of the Society in a dynamic fidelity to its charism becomes operative by: dialogue, communication, subsidiarity, experimentation and evaluation. [89]

The local community is "a plan for life in common which grows each day in prayer and interpersonal relationships." [90] The provincial community is responsible for "determining and attaining common goals that will permit the Society to serve the Church as national or regional needs demand." [91] At the centre is the General Team made up of the superior general and her four councillors, while the General Chapter is a "legislative body which represents all the members of the Society and assures their union in one spirit." [92] The Society will strive to live:

> Along the lines marked out by Vatican II: return to the Gospel in the spirit of the Foundress, to respond to the needs of the world. This triple exigency is summed up in the central theme of our Constitutions: union and conformity with the Heart of Jesus. [93]

On November 6, 1970, Maria de la Concepcion Camacho was elected twelfth superior general of the Society of the Sacred Heart. Born in Seville in 1927, professed on February 11, 1955, she had served in the university college in Madrid and then as superior at Pamplona and provincial of northern Spain. The first members of the Central Team were Doreen Boland, Françoise Cassiers, Mary Catherine McKay and Maria Luiza Saade. Geneviève de Thélin became secretary general and Gisela Posada remained treasurer general.

Sister Camacho communicated the results of the Chapter to the

Society as a call "to live today with renewed fidelity the spirit of our Constitutions," for "we all share the responsibility to go deeper into the Heart of Christ, bearing the fate of the Society in our hands." [94] The Chapter had given assurance:

> As religious of the Sacred Heart, ours is the heritage of Saint Madeline Sophie, passed down to us through generations of our sisters who have gone before us preparing the way. Her spirit lives in us and urges us forward on that same path into the unkown. [95]

PART THREE

LIFE-SAP

1779–1976

Jesus stood there and cried out: "If any
man is thirsty let him come to me. Let
that man drink who believes in me!" As
Scripture says: "From his breast shall
flow fountains of living water." He was
speaking of the Spirit which those who
believed in him were to receive.

Jn 7:37–39

Inwardness For The Outgoing

"There are no true Christians in the world and no true religious without the habit of prayer," said Madeleine Sophie Barat. Religious life, like Christian life itself, is unthinkable without the prayer that places God at the centre of consciousness, of choice of act, "through Christ our Lord," from whose heart rise the living waters of the Spirit. Mother de Valon called prayer "the life-sap which bears fruit through a close union with God." [1] This is what assures the continued identity of the Society of the Sacred Heart in the growth of its charism through time.

In this field terminology is, once again, far more than "a new name for the same old thing," and semantic understanding is needed. New insights into old truths cause a fresh development of the concept itself, calling for a renewal of expression. "Evaluation" is a more creative process than "a chapter of faults"; "examination of consciousness" is more exhilarating than a five-pointed "examen of conscience." Today there is a significant swing away from the word "soul" as used for a human being to be saved, Each "soul" is now seen as a person in the biblical sense, a psycho-somatic whole to be saved in his totality, now and hereafter.

Spirituality is "the synthesis of human factors transformed by faith," [2] or "the unique experience of Christ which transforms the men and women of a certain age and culture. It is thus inevitably bound up with events of the times." [3] Gradually it is formulated into "schools of prayer," while each religious order develops prayer of a distinctive quality. That of the Society of Sacred Heart might be described as "inwardness for the outgoing." This distinctive spirituality, this life-sap drawn from the origins and rising throughout the historical development just traced, is a heritage rooted in tradition and now expanding with the spirituality of the post-conciliar Church. It is classic contemplation correlated with this morning's headlines.

Chapter 9

Rooted in Prayer

Jesus said: "Mary!" She knew
him then and said in Hebrew:
"Rabboni!" which means "Master."
Jesus said to her: "Do not cling
to me, because I have not yet
ascended to the Father. But go
and find the brothers and tell
them: 'I am ascending to my Father
and your Father, to my God and
your God'."

Jn 20:16–17

Every year on July 22 the feast of "la Madeleine" was celebrated as
Mother Barat's name-day, and she once told the novices what the
Easter dawn encounter between Mary Magdalene and Christ meant
to her:

> There is the spirit of the Society. Our first movement is to linger at the feet of
> the Master; that is the contemplative life, that is what we must do in prayer.
> But it is then that Jesus says to us: "Go, tell my brothers." Mary becomes an
> apostle. Why can we not say to the whole universe: "Know his Heart?" [1]

Many years earlier Father de Tournély had caught the essence of
this gospel scene when he saw what the charism of the Society of
the Sacred Heart was to be:

> It is destined to be devoted to the Heart of Jesus, to awaken the love of Jesus
> in souls and the light of his teaching in minds. For this it will enter into the
> sentiments and interior dispositions of that divine Heart and will reveal them
> to others by means of education. [2]

A correlation of the two passages reveals the way of prayer of the
Society.

Each religious order shares corporately in the prayer of the Church, a public act, the liturgy by which Christ prays in his total Body to the Father through the Spirit. At the same time each religious finds a personal prayer-road to God. Is there also a spirituality proper to each religious order?

History answers; the classic schools of Christian spirituality are the gift of the religious orders to the Church. The charism of each community found a mode of prayer in keeping with its mission and life-style, and this passed beyond the group as a heritage to all who pray. There are: the unstructured prayer of the desert hermits, silent, radical, "a fire in the bones"; the rhythmed prayer in common of the monks which grew into the Divine Office; the singing freedom of the Franciscans; the scripture-based wisdom of the Dominicans; the inward stripping and illumination offered for the world of the Carmelites; the unbounded overflow into act of Jesuit contemplation, energized by the "methods" and patterned on the Spiritual Exercises; the contact with Christ-in-the-other of the Sisters of Charity. Many orders, such as the Passionists, focus upon some central devotion. Today there are returns to the beginning in a contemporary setting, as when the Little Brothers and Sisters inspired by Charles de Foucauld keep to their desert-in-the crowd.

Each school had its doctors, saints and disciples through whom the tradition of the older religious orders passed into those founded after the French Revolution. The Society of the Sacred Heart drew upon many currents of thought and practice from the past, and interacted with contemporary religious trends as it grew; all the time its own charism moulded these into a spirituality in harmony with its apostolate and its way of life. This spirituality can be traced in the writings of Madeleine Sophie Barat.[3]

The times into which she was born were unpromising, yet she somehow defied both their Jansenistic moralism and their floridly sentimental romanticism. Undoubtedly her thought and still more her use of language and imagery reflect these outlooks, but she kept her grip on essentials: patristic teaching, classic authors and a direct approach to Scripture. In the steady piety of her little home in Joigny she had escaped the deadly atmosphere of the late eighteenth century when Deism all but choked the sense of God's loving intervention in his world. In the spiritual writings of the nineteenth century there is something akin to First Empire drapes and Second Empire crinolines (Mother Barat's symbol for "our puffed-up cen-

tury"). Theology was rigid, piety effusive, and "the cloister" was
unduly suspicious of "the world." But Sophie went straight from
Joigny into the mission-minded Catholic restoration, and followed
the powerful orientations of Lacordaire in whose sermons:

> Christ, true God and true man, was rediscovered as the central reality of
> Christianity and the incarnation of the love of God. . . . Many influences gave
> back to Catholic piety a characteristic orientation of which the eucharistic
> developments and the extraordinary success of the cultus of the Sacred Heart
> were the most marked expression. [4]

Under the influence of Father de Tournély (whom Madeleine
Sophie had never seen) and Father Varin (who was her guide for
fifty years), Berullian spirituality became all-pervasive in the way of
prayer of the Society, as the wording of the Constitutions shows. It
was both trinitarian and incarnational in outlook. As the Son adores
the Father in the Holy Spirit, so the Christian is drawn into the
divine life by loving adoration; by self-emptying he is freed to rise
to transforming union through the death of the Incarnate Word.
Mother Barat here found the poles around which the spiritual life
revolves:

> You have seen in the lives of all the saints about whom you read that they
> never wearied of studying and meditating upon Jesus incarnate and Jesus dy-
> ing. . . . This is what fills all souls with the love of God, for although the Holy
> Spirit leads persons in different ways according to their age, character, tem-
> perament and position, he thus guides all who burn with the love of God. For
> his action, even when it varies on some points, is always the same in what con-
> cerns the incarnation and the death of God. [5]

For Mother Barat the cross was more than a sign of suffering, a call
to penance; it was the source of life, of redemptive love, of joy itself.
"All good things come to us through the cross," and a lover of
Christ "must know nothing but the cross, if she seeks her happiness
elsewhere, *errat, errat*!" [6]

For Bérulle, prayer was centred in the "interiority" of the God-
man in whom the divine and human elements are in hypostatic union. The praying Christian enters the depths of the praying Christ,
surrendered to the inner mystery of his love, source of the outward
mysteries of his mortal life and of his life prolonged in the Church.
Madeleine Sophie wrote:

You must not only know the mysteries of our Lord but reproduce them in yourself. . . . Through this knowledge of his mysteries and the reproduction of his virtues Jesus wishes to bring about an intimate and perfect union between himself and us. What is needed is to leave the way open for the free action of God, to die to ourselves and let him live in us. [7]

In 1853 she became acquainted with the mass *Egredimini* which expresses this form of the devotion to the Sacred Heart, and obtained permission to use it in the Society instead of the mass *Miserebitur* which expresses the passion-centred form of the devotion as revealed at Paray-le-Monial. Mother Stuart says of *Egredimini*:

It honours and celebrates the love of Christ as manifested in his whole life on earth: the inward life of the Sacred Heart with all its expressions of itself, with its tenderness, its splendours, and the glow of its sanctuary fire. . . . It is not to be wondered at that the Blessed Foundress hailed with delight the discovery of this Office and mass and set it before the members of the Society as a form of the devotion which was to be specially theirs, as already set forth in every page of the Rule. This meditative, imitative, penetrating and inward manner of the devotion, which imposes no set form, and admits of endless diversity of assimilation, was exactly what she sought; and it is rooted in the Society which she founded.[8]

The mass *Cogitationes* and those composed in recent years also return to the spirit of *Egredimini*.

The early directors of the Society formed its way of prayer according to the Spiritual Exercises and methods of Saint Ignatius. The salient points of Jesuit spirituality all brought their dynamism: the following of Jesus of the Gospels, generosity in the service of the Kingdom, the *agere contra*, the passing of contemplation into action. The aim "For the greater glory of God" was made specific: "For the greater glory of the Sacred Heart of Jesus." Underlying all was the First Principle and Foundation: "Man was created to praise, reverence and serve God, and by this means to save his soul; and everything else on the face of the earth is for the sake of man and to help him to attain this end." Madeleine Sophie said:

Interior spirit is nothing more than this truth understood in its full height, depth and breadth. .. An interior person, concentrated on the object of her love, makes God her life, her good, her all. As soon as the Holy Spirit seizes upon such a soul his first work is to strip it of attachment to itself and to creatures. Let us put no limit to the action of the divine Spirit. [9]

Of Saint Ignatius she said: "A characteristic virtue was his union with God in prayer; it is from this union, the fruit of true prayer, that light and strength are drawn." [10] She saw the Society as sharing in his gift and mission:

> Let us become more and more penetrated with the importance of the gift of prayer, and let us ask it for each other from the Lord, unceasingly. In the century of Saint Teresa the Church had need of two orders, one which would offer to God fervent prayer to move him and obtain the salvation of men, and another which would combat valiantly under the standard of Jesus Christ. . . . One was the order of the reformed Carmel, the other the Company of Jesus formed by the companions of Saint Ignatius. One was like Moses praying on the mountain, the other like Aaron fighting on the plain. And they both had great need of prayer, as their founders recognized so well. Our Society which is made for both these works – the practice of prayer and the salvation of men – must draw its strength from contemplation. [11]

The Carmelite elements in the spirituality of the Society reflect Madeleine Sophie's own attraction. As a child she made her doll's house into a Carmelite cell, and as a young girl:

> This was her ideal of religious life: to live in God, to adore him, to love him in the Blessed Sacrament, to live a life of genuine hard-working poverty in solitude and forgetfulness of the world, to recite the Divine Office in union with the Church. [12]

At twenty she took on the demands of total service without letting go those of total prayer. Later, in the high tide of administrative work, she wrote:

> Let us agree that we must often give up our tastes, especially those of us who once thought of entering Carmel. You are in the same case and I congratulate you; you would never have had as many opportunities to mortify your self-will as at the Sacred Heart. When we understand the redemption we never say "enough," since souls are to be the reward of all this abnegation. The essential thing is to keep interior spirit in the midst of this fracas. . . . Carmel should be planted in the Sacred Heart as the most beautiful tree in that fair garden. [13] . . . I love to find among my daughters souls who have thought for a time of joining Carmel, because they have the foundation of interior life which, united to the apostolic life, makes them excellent religious. [14]

Mother Barat herself became known as "the Saint Teresa of our century" and shared with her forerunner a masculine virility (urged on her by Father Varin's "Esto vir!") together with womanly warmth and humour. She composed no treatises on the interior castle but spoke of the reality with the same experiential insight and often the same metaphors, such as the living water that rises in wells and falls in rain, for: "Without prayer, without recollection, which is the water of the Holy Spirit; everything withers and dries up." [15]

> From where did Teresa draw her graces? From prayer, from her union with God. . . . From the depths of her solitary cell she took in the entire world in her desire to win it for Jesus Christ. Our hearts must be no less vast than her own. [16]

She frequently echoes John of the Cross in her interpretation of the Song of Songs. "Give all that you may find all," and:

> When, after whole years passed in dryness one can obtain a quarter of an hour of union with our Lord one should feel amply rewarded. After so many trials and combats, followed by a painful illness in which all the senses had to suffer, you can at last cry out with Saint John of the Cross: "O happy lot! On a dark night I went out unperceived." Now it only remains to keep with the greatest care that peace which is a gift of the Heart of Jesus. [17]

John's doctrine that progressive purification is brought about by prayer itself is echoed in the Constitutions:

> Let all then apply themselves lovingly to prayer which will lead them to the Heart of their divine Spouse and unfold to them its adorable perfections and especially its immense charity; let them place their happiness as much as possible in this holy exercise which, by purifying their hearts, will unite them closely to the Heart of Jesus by conformity of sentiments, of affections and of will. [18]

Since the Society exists to glorify the Heart of Christ, its prayer too seeks his glory. That word is radiant with biblical significance; it has the weightiness (*kabod*) of God's own being and the power of his presence, the shining out of his inner excellence. Christ asked that all men might see "the glory you have given me because you loved me before the foundation of the world." [19] The prayer of a Society living to reveal the love of God who became man must be the prayer of Christ's own Heart, turned to the Father, turned to his brothers with "the Love with which you have loved me," the Holy Spirit. Such prayer is adoration and petition in one; it is fused with the service of men. The Constitutions demand this profound inwardness:

The spirit of this Society is essentially based upon prayer and the interior life, since we cannot glorify the Heart of Jesus worthily save inasmuch as we apply ourselves to study its interior dispositions in order to unite and conform ourselves to them. [20]

And they add: "The surest way of having access to the Heart of Jesus is a tender devotion to the Immaculate Heart of Mary," [21] that heart "so perfectly conformed in all things to the adorable Heart of Jesus, her divine Son." [22]

Such a spirituality has a built-in polarity between the pulls to withdraw and to be "busy about many things," a polarity acutely felt by Madeleine Sophie and in varying degrees by all who have followed her. It is a condition of that "overflow of contemplation into action" described by Thomas Aquinas, [23] the price for something priceless. The tension comes largely from problems of time and place which bring the two elements into conflict. When both are grasped with generosity they move towards fusion in the simplicity of love. Traditionally, religious life of this form has been called "the mixed life," a term no longer in favour precisely because it suggests duality. Using it in its best sense, Janet Stuart said:

The mixed life is blessed with a specially intimate likeness to the manner of living of our Lord during his life on earth. No gift of self, however active, could equal the entire devotion with which he was at the service of every class of persons or individual need. No contemplative rule could measure itself against his nights of prayer after such days of work. . . . Here the great difficulty of the mixed life is felt. It must consist not of two separate parts but of an inward spirit of consecration which has two movements, like the vital act of breathing, and the outward and inward movements are each incomplete without the other. The deep intaken breath of prayer is given back again as the sound of a voice carrying its gift from God. [24]

In Madeleine Sophie's time such a life for women was in the experimental stage. "So!" said a bishop, "You want to be contemplatives while doing the work of educators! That is risky!" She knew that it was risky but was sure that it was possible:

An order which unites the active and the contemplative life has a powerful grace which wonderfully supports its action. That is what I feel called to establish in our Society before our Lord calls me to himself. . . . I ask the Heart of Jesus to draw to it many who have an attraction to prayer. Then I shall say my *nunc dimittis*, for it is thus that I have always conceived of the Society of voice carrying its gift from God. [24]

* * *

As Madeleine Sophie disclaimed being a foundress so she would disclaim being a model of prayer, yet in her are found the sources of the Society's spirituality. She spoke very little of her own prayer; any records that she may have kept were destroyed. Yet her letters, her conferences, her advice to others, and above all her own life are revelations of God's way with her and with the Society that was just beginning.

She began to pray so young that she had gone far before receiving guidance or method. The child at Joigny was sensitive to God by intuition, while her exceptional powers were being disciplined by Louis. The four lonely years in Paris gave her the intellectual basis needed by one who was to guide others. Louis opened the whole Bible to her at a time when only the Psalms, Gospel and Epistles were reading matter for ordinary Catholics; the rest was forbidden. Sophie savoured the Prophets, the Song of Songs, the Apocalypse, and "the extraordinary gift of understanding Scripture" received on her first communion day came into play. Scripture soaked into her thought and expression; her writings are saturated with quotations, usually indirect and allusive, the stuff of her own prayer.

> Her contact with Scripture forged in her what was most personal and most pure in her inspiration regarding the Heart of Christ, and assured a sound doctrinal dimension to the thought and the distinctive orientation of her spirituality. [26]

Of the Fathers of the Church her favourite was Saint Augustine, and of the Doctors, Saint Bernard.

In her youth Madeleine Sophie shrank from treatises on mystical theology, saying: "What's the use of reading all this when I can't live it?" But Louis did not yield, and she ended by both reading and living. "The works of the great mystics all passed through my hands," [27] she said. The medieval contemplatives drew her; the *Revelations* of Saint Gertrude lay at hand on her desk, while her letters are redolent of "the two Catherines," of Francis of Assisi and of Tauler. She sought not theory but experience. Once, when commenting on the words of Saint Augustine: "We shall see, praise and love God," she developed the first two words but stopped at the third, saying that she feared to weaken it, for: "Only he who loves can speak of love." [28]

She knew from experience how to discern the charismatic touch of God in the depths of a human personality, for she passed very young through the darkness that reaches into the roots of consciousness. Scruples and doubts led to limpidity and utter trust, to illumination on her spiritual road: "Humility is the way in which I shall become like the saints. That's the way I shall prove to God that I love him." [29] When Father Varin's liberating "Courage and confidence!" replaced Louis' conscience-searching, she saw that: "We have everything with humility. This virtue known and practiced draws into the soul that is captivated by its beauty all the Gifts of the Holy Spirit." [30] These seven Gifts operated in her life in no ordinary way. Wisdom (Sophia) was dominant throughout, and shaped not only her own growth but that of the Society in accordance with its charism, for: "Since Wisdom attains to God by a kind of union of the soul with him, it is able to direct it not only in contemplation but in action." [31]

Fear of the Lord, which Sophie called "the chaste fear of displeasing him," forged her youth, when she knew the things most feared by the human heart: war, change, separation, loneliness. Her shy sensitiveness and inner suffering held her in a crucible. In her early religious life these yielded to passionate purpose, although she took initiative only with painful self-distrust. Her balance and warm humour shook off what was merely servile in a fear that chastened her prayer and kept her humbled in her own nothingness. She was always aware of what she called "the terrible truths of religion," of "the two eternities" between which every man must choose, of the punitive action of God's Providence in events such as war or the cholera, of the responsibility of his elect to stay his public anger. One shadow of Jansenism that clung to her was the haunting fear that the number of those lost might be very great. Most of all she feared her own responsibility for the Society: "If only I do not wreck it through my fault!"

Father Varin sternly urged his "perpetual trembler" to open up, and after 1802 when she was placed in authority she was freed to pour herself out in love. The years at Grenoble and Poitiers overflowed with the attractive Piety that is a sign of God's child at home. It was seen in the flushed cheeks, even tears, with which she spoke of God. Sometimes she was breathless, even speechless, before some mystery. Then gestures betrayed her; one day she dropped on her knees to kiss a paving stone where a cross was engraved, exclaiming: "Spes unica" (words later engraved on the profession cross of the Society). In time sobriety tempered her, but she kept for sixty years this childlike freshness of devotion to the things that helped her to pray: flowers, sunsets, animals, *chéri* (the crucifix on her desk), the statue of our Lady whose small ivory hands she touched to her own forehead in blessing every night.

In these years she gave full vent to her love for the Song of Songs. She had a famous "little blue book," *Meditations on the Canticle by the Fathers of the Church*, which she shared with like-minded friends, talking or even singing over its pages at the far end of the garden. Her favourite themes glint through her letters: "Arise, my love, and come," or "Catch us the little foxes," or "the hole in the rock" that is the Heart of Christ.

Her buoyancy was sorely tried after 1816 in the overwork of exacting administration in Paris where: "The desert is opening before me!"

I am like the secretary of some minister; I have no time to breathe. When business and visits crowd in, is Jesus there in the midst of chaos? Yes, but is he pleased? Can he be there in peace? I doubt it, and how painful are these doubts to a soul that seeks him and finds everything but him! Pray for such a one if you know her.[32]

In this dilemma the gift of Counsel came into play:

We should do as few stupid things as possible, but to wait for a time when we would do none would be the stupidest thing of all. It is sure that the way to avoid them is to draw near to God by recollection, prayer, abandonment to his good pleasure. The counsel of the Holy Spirit changes our nature and gives us that prudence and wisdom which are the virtues of God himself.[33]

It was at this time that she felt most torn between prayer and work. When driving one day through the empty countryside she dreamed of jumping from the carriage and hiding for good in the forest, "but then we reached the next town, and goodbye to my day-dreams!" This tension gave an astringent, realistic tone to her prayer. She was, perhaps, inclined by nature to pessimism, and the sense of the fleetingness of all things took hold of her. She wrote in the strain of "vanity of vanities" found in Ecclesiastes:

O God, what a life! How our poor hearts must suffer until they rest only in God and until he is our only support! In looking upon all that surrounds me I

gladly say with a saint of the past century: "No, you are not my God!" ...
But at least this God for whom I am made and towards whom I throw myself
without the power of taking hold of him, who then is he? Oh, my God – he is
truly a hidden God.[34]

The gift of Counsel not only guided her practical choices but
"changed her nature" until she could accept tensions as a purifying
element in the deepest prayer. The letters of this period are filled
with references to the mystics, to "the Catherines, the Gertrudes
and so many others that you know."

> Believe that this great God who so loves to communicate himself would still
> do the same if he found hearts well disposed. And where should he find them if
> not in the Society of Jesus and in that of his Heart?[35]

She was willing to pay in her person:

> Without doubt it is in counting yourself *pro nihilo* that you will find happiness.
> That is the source of the river of peace. From afar we see it flowing, but few
> have the courage to go to this precious fountain-head.[36]

The next period was a time of searing trial for herself and for the
Society. She said on the eve of Pentecost, 1827, "Tomorrow I shall
ask for you the gift of Fortitude; you must ask it for me and for the
whole society."[37] She knew that: "This gift is necessary in order to
fulfil our vocation to its whole extent."[38] Her fortitude took the
lovable form of patient endurance: No-one could outwait or outpray
the gentle Mother Barat. But it also roused her: "Only the
violent will carry off the kingdom of God! That word 'violent'
says so much to me!"[39] And warningly: "You know what I'm like
when I'm angry!"[40] The letters of this time are urgent. War,
cholera, anti-clerical attacks called for vigour; "If we are faithful
and generous nothing can harm us; we will be strong with the
strength of Christ."[41] In her retreats:

> When the Lord makes his presence felt it is not always a time of rest for the
> soul. When he makes known to her what she is before him it is sometimes a
> burden hard to bear. ... The Lord is gentle but he is also strong, and so when
> Scripture says to us: "Wait for the Lord with patience" it adds: "Act with
> courage and let your heart take new strength."[42]

Under "the searching eye of God" she put on divine strength by giving away all that was left to her of self-determination; she made a private vow of obedience in all that concerned her personal conduct. Her prayer was intense in these years. Mother de Limminghe, her monitor, testifies that she was drawn swiftly through the alternations that mark a mystic ascent:

> Favoured at certain times with most intimate communications from our Lord during the long hours that she passed before the Blessed Sacrament, Mother Barat felt herself set on fire with so great a love that she could hardly bear its ardours. In this state, always so full of sweetness even in its vehemence, she expressed with candour and humility the ineffable delight that she felt in the union of her heart with that of God. Our Lord truly nourished her with his love; she found it hard to take any other food. More than once I had to rouse her from her contemplation. Then, absorbed and carried out of herself, she would stammer: "He was uniting himself to me with so much goodness!"
>
> The moment came when these consolations disappeared to give way to a kind of dryness of exile. Our venerated Mother suffered from this all the more keenly because she attributed it – very mistakenly – to her infidelities. All that was painful in this state could not, however, make her relax her fervour which seemed, on the contrary, to increase. She only felt a stronger desire to serve the God of goodness who hid himself from her eyes. This zeal devoured her; the gentleness with which it was tempered made it all the more efficacious. [43]

As the crisis of 1839 gripped the Society Mother Barat herself was passing through personal conflicts. Letters from her spiritual director accused her of over-activity, even of a tinge of worldly ambition. On a deeper level she entered the Dark Night. A piece of paper marked "Souvenir at the end of my resolutions, 1839," reads:

> I ask insistently of the Sacred Heart of Jesus, through our Lady of Seven Sorrows, to recover the way of prayer that I once had and that I have lost through my long infidelities. [44]

After 1844 there was peace within the Society in the midst of persecutions from without, and Mother Barat wrote: "We are made to suffer from all sides but I fear nothing at all." [45] Through suffering she came to say: "I thank God for the knowledge that he is giving me of persons and of things." [46] This was sublimated into the gift of Knowledge, and one who watched her wrote:

> Her elevated soul dwelt habitually in a simple contemplation, never letting itself be preoccupied with merely secondary causes without rising to the principle of all things. [47]

Her letters point along one line, simplicity leading to the prayer of quiet. To one to whom she could say: "I believe that your spiritual state is like my own," she wrote:

> Be in peace about the state of your soul and your manner of prayer; only love and do what you please. The essential thing, the proof of true love, is forgetfulness of self and of one's own interests, to think only of the one loved. . . . So what difference does it make how you pray, provided that your heart is seeking the one you love?[48]

And again:

> I see that Jesus is working in your soul and that your will is leaning towards that divine centre. Continue to be like the sunflower and turn always towards the rays of the divine Sun of Justice. Then, dear Justine, you will enter more and more into the way of simplicity.[49]

Mother Barat had seen this peace-giving truth even in the year of anguish, 1842, and expressed it in a letter which is like a concentrate of the theology of prayer, her own prayer:

> Be reassured. I understand silence better than words, especially your silence, dear Eulalie. I know the feelings that cause it and I appreciate it the more. For our Lord above all I want that intimate, profound silence. Who will give us to love him thus, in the abstraction of our whole being that passes into his – if I may so speak! Let us pray like that and we shall love. That is true simplicity, and from that point this lovable virtue will pervade all our actions, and then one is very near perfection.[50]

These were her eucharistic years: "If we could only understand what one communion can do for us! It should make each of us into another Jesus Christ."[51] Her favourite place for prayer was a tribune overlooking the altar.

> Go to the tabernacle. The golden door will remain closed, everything will go on as usual, but we can stay there without ecstasy, forgetting everything else in the peace that surpasses understanding. One is silent, resigned. Soon nothing is felt from without. A trouble becomes nothing; it passes into God. One feels a delicious well-being that strengthens and purifies. For a religious everything is there in her eucharistic contacts. . . . Empty yourself before plenitude.[52]

Plenitude could now flow into her because of earlier self-stripping. She could enlarge her gesture: "Say to all creatures, 'No, you are not my God but you help me to possess him more and more'."[53] Her profound solitude in God alone became ever more peopled: in "my long sleepless nights" as well as in the long day-hours of contemplation, she wrestled with the woes of the world:

> My soul is filled with grief at the sight of the pain — the anguish even — of the Holy Father, as I learn each day of the evils tearing at the Church. Can we think of anything else? We should be set on fire with zeal to try to bring back a few souls and to strengthen a great number of others in the faith. [54]

After the Jubilee of the Society in 1850 old age came on her with no lessening of work. She was free from tensions by then and lived quietly in the light of the gift of Understanding, the vision given by Revelation:

> I relish with you and for you the profound and moving wisdom held in Sacred Scripture; it alone contains the good, the true, the beautiful and the sublime. A pure soul who is drawing near to her God with her will by suffering is worthy to understand this wholly divine language since it flows from the same God from whom the Prophets drew it. . . . There is nothing more efficacious for launching a soul into the mysteries and anchoring her there. [55]

By now the gift of Wisdom possessed her wholly:

> I see time flowing by. Soon I shall pass into eternity, and I see the value of grace that corresponds to each moment that is lived supernaturally. . . . I scarcely need faith any more; I see so much of the divine realities in the light of eternity that all the rest is becoming merely a magic lantern show. [56]

Did Mother Barat know the mystical states that lie over the border of the prayer of quiet? Mother Stuart asked:

> May it be supposed that having sacrificed her strong drawing to a life of solitude and silence, she sacrificed with it the special favours to which her soul seemed so well attuned? . . . It may be that the higher paths of prayer had to be renounced for the sake of other needs; or it may be that she was led in them far higher than we know. [57]

She leaves the question open, but Mother Barat's contemporaries were in no doubt; they had seen too many betrayals of mystic experience beyond her control. The first to be recorded occurred under a walnut tree on the morning of her profession, the last at her desk not long before her death. But ecstatic states are not the only sign of such experience. There is a self-portrait of Mother Barat drawn in a conference for Pentecost in 1827. The scribe who took down her words added a footnote; "It was herself that she was sketching without knowing it":

> O if it were given to me, if I were not unworthy to speak to you of the happiness of one who surrenders to the Holy Spirit fully and with no reserves! If I could tell you what goes on in her, if I could picture for you her joy! It is not she who acts, it is God; she only moves, only walks, by his inspiration. Everything becomes easy to her. She knows no more difficulties, she meets no more obstacles. The Holy Spirit enchains such a person. She is his, he binds her to himself. . . . The one of whom I have been speaking finds the secret of penetrating hearts; as it is no longer she who acts there is no turning back upon self. She does not know that she is doing good; in one sense she does not even want to. Rather, she has only one desire: to follow the impulse of the Spirit and obey him in all. [58]

* * *

Madeleine Sophie knew that each member of a religious order is called to a personal way of prayer in harmony with the spirituality of the whole body, a vocation within a vocation. She herself was extraordinarly gifted as the charismatic guide whom each one needs to find and follow her way. Spiritual guidance was her uninterrupted occupation, for she used every possible contact to draw others to "the one thing necessary." She never failed in a letter, no matter what the subject, to speak of "the things we most care about," and her pen moved under the Spirit: "Goodbye. I intended to write something quite different but I had to follow my impulse and say what I never thought of." Still more she sought the hours of exchange of which there is no record: "I shall keep your intimate avowals to talk over face to face when it shall please the Lord to give us that joy." Even when alone: "I am always occupied with you before the Lord." In her guidance she followed the advice given to Mother Goetz:

> The less there is of your own action the more will the good Master supply with his own, and despite the number [of novices] and the shortcomings of each everything will move ahead with ease. For when there is question of directing souls the action of God is needed. All the elements obey man, so to speak, but the Creator and Redeemer has kept the realm of souls for his own. He wants to make use of us, certainly, but only as instruments and not as prime movers.

Let us allow him to act. Let us be no more than a gardener who cultivates the soil; he turns it over and pulls out the weeds, but once the seed has been sown he has nothing more to do than water it and drive away the insects and other enemies of the plant. [59]

The Ignation methods of prayer had been in honour in the Society from the beginning, but their use in formation was only decreed at the General Council of 1833. The first reaction was a cry of dismay from Mother Duchesne overseas, already "the woman who prays always":

These new regulations and directives frighten me. . . . My heart is so dry that I can scarcely think through all these rules and methods, so it will be far worse for me to try to carry them out. . . . I have never been able to reflect on a subject; I see it as a whole, and what I have once seen I shall see for ten years without change or addition. . . . In that state of soul all methods and all considerations become mere distractions for me. [60]

Mother Barat herself had guided Philippine along this stark way. The methods are a help, but even a beginner may go beyond them when they prove unhelpful. To a young religious she wrote:

As to your way of prayer, it seems to me that you can rest in it tranquilly and not force yourself to meditate since you have no attraction for it. Be content to stay before God in a quiet submission to all that he wills to work in you. If, however, you are aware that dryness or boredom are taking from you the presence of God, then say a few passages from the Psalms or other parts of Scripture, just to draw yourself back. [61]

Individuality is respected: "Philippine and Thérèse go by very different roads." Temperament, the right moment, the unique call are all recognized. And "because I know by experience how few understand true spirituality," she warned against illusion:

Mistrust your own imagination and a certain subtle and refined pride which hides easily under the veil of great sanctity when we seek it more for pleasure than for pleasing God. [62]

And common sense made short work of self-made difficulties:

Don't make such a fuss! Turn all that to our Lord by a calm and simple look, and let people talk. Don't think about it; forget yourself, forget even your own perfection, so to speak, in order to see only Jesus and his glory. None of this self-absorption that checks the action of the Holy Spirit who wishes you to be all his in prayer, in work and in intention. That is what God wants of you and that should be your attraction. Your fault is found in Chapter V of the Song of Songs where the bride fears to rise to open to the Bridegroom who knocks. Read it.[63]

She brought virile reassurance to those at each stage of the spiritual combat; her understanding was compassionate, her demands unflinching. To one floundering in overwork:

As to your difficulty in keeping recollected and in union with our Lord in the midst of such distracting occupations that are too much for you, do not be uneasy. It is for God that you must put up with them.... Without effort and without straining your mind, tend gently towards union with Jesus Christ at the high point of your soul, through the practice of recollection to which you must grow accustomed, restraining natural activity as soon as you become aware of it.[64]

To one passing from active to passive prayer:

Jesus has already purified your senses; now his healing hand is trying to purify the powers of your soul, if I may say so. Let that hand act upon you and do not be troubled by this purifying operation. Rest in your nothingness, in your powerlessness before him, before souls, before yourself. Only make acts of acceptance.... By your inward suffering you will do more for others than all methods could do, for perhaps these would not be free from self-seeking and a certain reliance upon your own resources. Besides all this, I believe that bodily fatigue counts for much, and also your hard work. When you get a week of rest and of solitude this powerlessness and this withering dryness will lessen if they do not go away altogether.[65]

Mother Barat truly "accompanied" those whom she guided within sight of the City of Peace:

The calm and tranquillity which you have enjoyed in your solitude and which still fill you have passed into my own soul.... You have suffered so much and for so long a time, for so many years, that I am happy in the peace that floods your heart. That peace is more divine when less emotional. Do not regret this; it is all the purer and our Lord acts more freely apart from natural causes.... Crosses that come, the dryness, the sense of absence, cleanse the soul and prepare it for closer and more complete union with the Beloved.[66]

Sometimes Mother Barat intervened in the sufferings of others by heroic identification, as one young person testified:

After some months of constant struggle I went to our Mother and told her about the state of my soul, saying that I could no longer go on like that. "Give me a few days to arrange this matter with our Lord," she said. "I will pray for you and then we shall see." Some time later she sent for me and said: "At a moment when our Lord was communicating himself to me in a special way, I begged him to relieve you, and I offered myself to him in order to bear in your place these trials through which you are passing. His answer was a positive 'no' despite my insistence, and then he added: 'My will is that she should come to me by that road of pain'." [67]

She had a sovereign respect for the rights of God over others. One day when she visited Conflans the novices crowded round her and she paid great attention to the delighted few who were to make their first vows the next day. She paid no attention at all to the one probanist who was to be professed. Mother de Limminghe intervened: "Aren't you going to say something to our future professed?" Mother Barat turned with a deep look to the young religious: "There is no need for me to speak to her; already she is tasting God."

Madeleine Sophie's over-all name for the life of prayer was "interior spirit." One passage in a conference given in 1844 is a mini-treatise on its essence, principles, development and fruit:

What is interior spirit? It is the entire sacrifice of ourselves by the mortification of our senses by the immolation of our passions, by the ceaselessly renewed recollection of the presence of him for whom we act. Interior spirit is, then, an intimate union of our soul with God, a chaste fear of displeasing him, an immediate dependence upon his grace, upon the touch of the Holy Spirit. It is a fine and sensitive tact of the soul in recognizing in herself the operations of God that she may give herself over to them. Interior spirit is the complete stripping off of self and of one's own interests. Picture to yourself an interior soul; what peace, what calm, what gentleness, what dependence, what humility! How devoted she is; how gracious, easy and pleasant are her dealings with everyone! Her charity and her zeal equal her love of God.... Interior persons are generally the gayest and the most lovable. [68]

* * *

It is evident that the keystone of Madeleine Sophie's spiritual doctrine is awareness of the action of the Holy Spirit. In this she was ahead of her times and markedly in touch with our own. Because of this she formed a Society which she wished to be, like herself, given to the Spirit. She wrote in the last year of her life some words that are like an open letter to the future:

> Your love of the Society has brought you light; as you have understood that its driving force comes from the Heart of Jesus and that all that we are and have must be spent for his glory, so also you understand that his grace, his Spirit, must be the source and the end of all that we do. [69]

The core of this doctrine is not a theorem but a vital act: surrender to the Paraclete. Passivity (as that word is used in classic spirituality: an intensely alive *fiat* to divine initiative) was the basic attitude of Madeleine Sophie's being. She admitted this, in her own self-effacing way, when she wrote:

> I was pleased with your retreat and with your resolutions, especially the tendency towards that simplicity which suits you through and through: a simple gaze at God, dependence upon every movement of his divine Spirit as far as you perceive it, tranquillity when you fail. In this way you will grow strong in abandonment to God. There, without searching afar, is the true source of sanctity, working noiselessly, without show, scarcely felt. I hardly dare say that this attraction is very much like what God gives to your Mother. [70]

She asked of others what she knew that God was asking of them as of herself, her own habitual gesture of surrender. To one who hesitated:

> Few give themselves over to the Holy Spirit, and what a mistake we make in not being among the privileged few! Believe me, it costs much more to stay in a miserable mediocrity in which one belongs neither to God nor to oneself. It is swimming between two currents, difficult and dangerous. Hurry up and plunge into mid-stream. The Holy Spirit will then carry you and you will get to port more quickly. [71]

To one ready to take the plunge:

> If you give yourself over once and for all to the leading of the Holy Spirit, as you have begun to do, everything will prosper in your hands. . . . Since our guide is God our actions will be divinized, if that is possible. [72]

And again:

> Far as you are from help in these matters, I marvel to see how our good Master supplies for it by putting into your heart what you should seek and what you

should avoid. Give yourself over to the direction of the Spirit of God when your inspiration tends to hold you united to Jesus Christ by the imitation of his virtues. . . .[73] When the Spirit of Jesus has taken possession of a heart that corresponds to his operations he becomes master. Then one is happy, for he always brings peace and true liberty. [74]

To one asking how:

It is for you to answer this question. And if you answer that you have not the means, I tell you that if you lean upon God who made all things from nothing and give yourself over to the Holy Spirit by letting yourself be his instrument, he will work this marvel in you. . . . And to get to the bottom of my thought, which is almost a conviction, our Lord wants you to enter on this way of perfection and of love for him and for souls by giving yourself over to the Holy Spirit by being a victim offered to his love and to his good pleasure. [75]

To be aware of the Spirit: "Let your heart be more attentive than your head, for the Holy Spirit is love, and to seize hold of him it is more needful to love than to understand." [76]

One of Mother Barat's symbols for her century was steam-power for which, at first, she had little use: "We do everything by steam and I don't know whether the Holy Spirit can work at that pace." But after travelling — "at ten miles an hour!" — by steam locomotion she was converted.

Forget all that is past and even your own inner depth; drop everything into God and believe that he will do all through you if you have this confidence. Let go of a self-centred spirit so as to empty the place and give it over to the Spirit of Jesus. Once this is done everything goes like a steamboat, without your own impulsion. That is truly the breath of the Holy Spirit. [77]

This abandonment is the price of transforming union.

More than ever turn your eyes away from your self. Lose yourself in the nothingness of your being, or better still in the immensity of the Heart of Jesus. Give him your life; he will give you his own. As soon as you are nothing he will create a new being. It will be himself, and you will be all but changed into him.[78]

Madeleine Sophie speaks constantly, sometimes in a casual and surprising context, of "the Spirit of Jesus." Often *esprit* is not capitalized and would seem to be a generic term. But she means it in a very specific sense: this Spirit is the Sanctifier, the Third Person of the Trinity. The phrase is found in the Acts of the Apostles where the equivalence is clear:

> They travelled through Phrygia and the Galatian country, having been told by the Holy Spirit not to preach the word in Asia. When they reached the frontier of Mysia they thought to cross into Bithynia, but as the Spirit of Jesus would not allow them, they went through Mysia and came down into Troas. [79]

When Madeleine Sophie said: "Substitute the Spirit of Jesus for your own," she was linking the Paraclete with the Heart of the God-man, the Third Person of the Trinity with the Second. Her awareness of the Holy Spirit is Christo-centric; surrender to him means entry into the Heart of Christ: "The Spirit of Jesus who lives always in an interior person united to the divine Heart will know at the right moment what to do, to decide, to counsel." [80]

She thus focused upon the role of the Holy Spirit in the devotion to the Sacred Heart. Father Varin once said:

> I have no doubt that when, nine hundred years before Jesus Christ, God placed in the mouth of the Prophet Isaiah these beautiful words: "You shall draw waters with joy from the Saviour's fountains," he had your Society in mind. Those words are, I think, the first and most perfect revelation of the devotion to the Sacred Heart. [81]

John the Evangelist saw the source of those waters:

> On the last and greatest day of the festival, Jesus stood there and cried out: "If any man thirst let him come to me. Let that man drink who believes in me." As Scripture says: "From his breast shall flow fountains of living water." He was speaking of the Spirit which those who believed in him were to receive. [82]

The fullest scriptural revelation of the prayer of Christ is the discourse after the Last Supper and the priestly prayer at its close. As Father Charmot said: "The light from the Heart of Christ which illumined the mind of Saint Madeleine Sophie became radiantly incisive in the gleaming pages with which Saint John ends his Gospel." [83] She was led into the trinitarian prayer of "the Word of the Father breathing Love." [84] She met the Trinity in looking at the Son of Man, and said in a conversation one day as though anyone could follow her there:

> When are you going to say: "Today at last I understand the divine life"? If

you could have one moment of union with the divine Trinity! You would then taste such joy in heavenly things that you would no longer hesitate. Nothing would be capable of distracting you from the love of our Lord. You would find nothing costly if for one second you had understood this life of union. [85]

In the approach to this union lies the "glory" that Jesus Christ came among men to give to his Father, the "glory" that the Society of the Sacred Heart is called to give to him through its mission to men. The Heart of Christ is, said Madeleine Sophie, "the sacrament of trinitarian love."

Now I understand the need that we have of the Heart of Jesus, and how, in mercy, the august Trinity kept the knowledge of that Heart for these evil days. You cannot do too much to make known the devotion to the Sacred Heart. [86]

It was necessary that the Son of God come into the world to reveal the Holy Trinity and to glorify it. To continue this divine mission he chose twelve apostles. He has now called us to this divine apostolate; he has made us his representatives, his disciples. [87]

Barely a year before her death Mother Barat wrote to Mother Goetz who was to succeed her, a letter that is a legacy. She began by consoling Josephine who felt crushed by her responsibilities, and then challenged her:

You must be convinced that Jesus will supply for all that is wanting to you, provided that you lean upon him and strip yourself of all your self-determined action as soon as you are aware of it. Jesus will then give you his divine Spirit and will act upon you as he did upon his disciples. . . . Deep calls upon deep, that nothingness that draws without hindrance the sovereign Good, the august Trinity that animates nothingness by the divine Spirit in giving us the Heart of Jesus to be our model, our saviour and our merciful pardon. [88]

She then remembered a detail: "You forgot to tell me whether you found in the envelope of letters that I sent you Saturday the 125 francs that I gave you for the third-semester tuition of that little girl whose name I forget." She did not take separate sheets of paper for the Trinity and for the francs; life had become one whole.

* * *

For the next one hundred years the spiritual traditions of the Society upon which Madeleine Sophie had set her seal were followed with emphasis upon fidelity rather than creativity. Their growth has already been traced in connection with the spiritual climate of successive epochs, from slow "consolidation" to sudden "renewal." The means by which they were transmitted are a strong factor in the Society's continuity.

The ideal expressed in the Constitutions of having one noviceship for all candidates was soon found to be impossible. As centres of formation multiplied unity was assured by the fact that the "Exercise" drawn up by Mother Goetz was followed in every country and in every culture, together with unchanging customs. Yet a shift in psychological method occurred early. Janet Stuart saw that:

> At one time, not under the rule of the Blessed Foundress but under some of her companions, who had themselves been trained in hard discipline, the method of training by severity was in honour. . . . But this was not the true spirit of the Sacred Heart.[89]

Gentle, unspectacular and all-demanding, in the Ignatian spirit of "the Two Standards" and of unquestioning obedience, the training "has taken everything; self-love has nothing left, not even the last satisfaction of feeling that it has done much and handsomely."[90] Each novice gives her all, while:

> The Society stakes its honour and its happiness on the quality of its members; on their understanding and faithfulness and love of their vocation. For their safe-guarding no sacrifice is counted great; long training, long patience, changes at great cost to the success of work, indefinite postponement of what is called usefulness to wait a riper perfection; these are some of the outward signs of the value set on the members as individuals.[91]

Initiation into prayer used the Ignatian methods, even in non-western cultures. It used disciplines as old as monastic life itself, symbols and exercises of the humility, mortification and recollection that are the ramparts of the interior castle. Love of prayer, desire for the experience of God, was a strong — often the strongest — drawing force of vocations; this assured the light-hearted acceptance of discipline.

The inwardness won at such cost was sorely tried when the aspirant was thrown into active life — to sink or swim. The discipline was then often administered by undisciplined children. But probation came at last, a time when the young adult could find her personal way, helped by the "long retreat." This experience, so deep-reaching for the individual, was also a force for centralization when young people of many nations were moulded by a single spiritual guide, often over decades.

Unity of outlook deepened in the life of the professed. The annual eight-day retreat, focal point of personal renewal, always followed the Spiritual Exercises of Saint Ignatius, though the frequent *tridua* might explore other schools of spirituality. The year followed the liturgical cycle with its heart-warming feasts, each with its preparation, its colours and customs and para-liturgical fun behind the scenes in a holyday-holiday mood, its priedieux before the lighted altar of the Blessed Sacrament. The Little Office was offered as a "tribute of love to our Lady." Yet its recitation had meant difficulties even in the early years; few people were free at busy times, with consequent loss of dignity and devotion.

Spiritual reading, as a common exercise, again fostered a shared viewpoint while leading to vigorous confrontations of thought. Part of the time was given to reading the life-accounts of past members of the Society from all over the world which created a strong sense of solidarity. At first long-approved books of somewhat moralistic tone were preferred. Gradually current books were encouraged, and these kept the communities open to theological trends and to their impact upon the apostolate.

The rhythm of personal prayer — length of time, hour of day, even place — was set by rule and settled by custom. This, the most precious of the day's occupations, was secure. The rule of silence protected recollection, the rule of cloister protected the way of life. The individual had no responsibility regarding these observances, but she was wholly responsible for the use made of this large liberty to be in the presence of God. She alone could make the difference between fruitful fervour and the routine which threatens all too-well-regulated things. Because of this control by rule and custom the spiritual life ran the risk of becoming part of the structures that were imperceptibly hardening. And because of the close connection between prayer and outward observance, it was hard to know at what point the precise laws which once assured freedom *for* prayer came to inhibit freedom *in* prayer — perhaps even prayer itself.

Guidance was sought from those in authority, and followed the vertical line of obedience. The office of superior implied government, the mother-daughter relationship at the heart of community life, and the direction in prayer of each individual. The love, gratitude and devotedness normally felt for superiors testify to the extent to which this difficult ideal was realized. The danger lay in the exclusiveness of such direction, and there were, inevitably, times when the guide was unequal to her task for want of the needed gifts and training. Yet the history of the Society shows that, at each stage of its growth, the personalities, the rich endowments and the sanctity of great charismatic leaders, both in formation and in government, have vivified the whole body. They communicated their insights and their way of prayer through the gift of themselves to others; through them the primitive charism was transmitted. As guides of others, each held firmly to the spiritual traditions of the Society, yet each exploited its richness in a highly distinctive way. In general they respected the inviolable freedom of a searcher after God, and fidelity to their direction did not form stereotypes.

Given the Society's busy apostolate, and its stress on common life, are exceptional mystic graces compatible with its spirituality? Madeleine Sophie Barat experienced them, and she did not think of herself as a person apart. She took care to clarify the distinction between authentic mystical experience and the phenomena that sometimes accompany them. Of visions and ecstasies she said:

> To tell you the truth, I do not think that our Lord will confide these extraordinary gifts to us. He would find few souls humble enough to be led in this way. I ask them for no-one, for they can be abused. It is a loss, it is true, but I prefer humility.[92]

She would tolerate no illusion, and believed that "true ecstasy is that which carries us out of ourselves."[93] Yet she received into the Society a young girl known to have visions. These ceased as soon as Marie Lataste[94] passed the noviceship door, and she went on to transforming union without them. Of Thérèse Maillucheau, Madeleine Sophie said:

> She is in the ways of prayer that are called extraordinary. Alas, why *extra*? All elderly religious should come to be like Mother Maillucheau, living for the Eucharist, before the Blessed Sacrament if possible. And how rare it is to reach that point![95]

The Message later given to Josefa Menendez was officially accepted by the Society, but never imposed on individuals. It was manifested in an extraordinary way, but: "This Message in itself contains all the fruitfulness of the Constitutions." [96]

With wisdom, with common sense, with experience, Madeleine Sophie Barat had urged each religious to go the full way along her own road to the point where all roads converge, and in this she has been followed by the many spiritual guides who have drawn their inspiration from her. As one among many of them said:

> Only put your soul in contact with Jesus Christ and there is nothing that you cannot become and do. We should pray in any way that we find easiest, easiest and most reasonable, which means based on faith and on a realization of our nothingness before God. The way we want to pray, the way we like to pray, is the way we should pray. So pray in any way that puts you into contact with God. Careful preparation is what God wants; what he does with us in prayer is his affair. . . . And the heights are not reached until we have attained union. [97]

Chapter 10

The Contemplative Outlook

With me in them and you in me,
may they be so completely one that
the world may realize that it was
you who sent me, and that I have
loved them as much as you have loved me.

Jn 17:23

It was this "prayer of lasting power" that inspired the options that are the core of the Society's renewal. The options themselves are thus a recognition that "Renewed in depth, our life must remain rooted in prayer."[1] Religious orders are asked to catch the rhythm of a spiritual evolution, and: "Nothing less than a conversion is required of us," in order to be a presence "declaring that communion with the Father has already begun."[2] The air is stirred by wind and fire, disturbing pentecostal signs that work not despite but through the insecurity of change.

The undercurrents of "the new spirituality" surfaced at Vatican Council II, all moving towards the "opening on the world" seen by John XXIII. Religious orders are seeking to follow their own way of prayer in the same direction. The Church is the People of God, spreading the eucharistic meal for brothers who pray together, rise and walk on together – a Pilgrim Church. Former ramparts of safety are seen as walls of separation, as communion reaches out into inter-communion. The Society is both working and praying in closer collaboration with other groups, with dioceses, parishes, religious congregations and the laity. It prays: "May Mary, Mother of the Church, help us to live today in faith, open to the Spirit."[3]

Signposts can be read: The current trends among the People of God to which a religious order must find an authentic relationship. One of the most compelling is the rediscovery of the biblical basis of prayer. The two foci of renewal, continual return to the Gospel and return to the Founder, are one and the same in the case of the Church; the Christ of Scripture is the same Christ who is the Church, Christian prayer is "through him, with him and in him." With scholarship leading the way, the Gospel is taking profound possession of the inward life of religious and laity alike. "If a new Christianity is to come about, it will be an age when men will read and meditate the Gospel as never before. It will become 'fire in their bones'," [4] said Jacques Loew, founder of *communautés de base* and of *Ecoles de Foi*, movements that find Christ alive and at work in the twentieth century. Established religious orders are opening to such movements, and Mother Bultó urged exposure to the dynamism of the Gospel on the part of the whole Society:

> We must interpret in the light of the Gospel various situations as they arise. This presupposes not only being aware of but accepting what is new. Is the Gospel not always — does it not ever remain — the great innovation that upsets our routine, shows up our laziness, and jolts our apathy? [5]

Another pointer is the thought of Pierre Teilhard de Chardin, priest, scientist, philosopher, poet and seer, that runs through many of the documents of Vatican II, especially *Gaudium et Spes* which says: "The pivotal point of our total presentation will be man himself, whole and entire, body and soul, heart, conscience, mind and will." [6] Teilhard declared: "I love matter!" This jolts the time-honoured stand of asceticism which saw matter as at war with spirit. But Teilhard saw the entire cosmos in unbroken evolution up through matter, mind and spirit to the Omega-point, Christ. In the Chinese desert, without bread or wine, he offered his "mass over the world" at dawn: "My chalice and my paten are the depths of a soul wide open to all those forces which, in a moment, will rise from all parts of the globe and converge towards the Spirit." [7]

This incarnational view of the sanctification of the universe was extremely significant for the spirituality of religious life, as it highlighted positive values rather than the negative ones which had traditionally been stressed. It was not contradictory but complementary to the authentic "negative way" of John of the Cross. Teilhard too knew "the dark night" and called it "the diminishment," one with the *kenosis*, the obedience unto death of the cross. His stress on the human as assumed by the divine in the Incarnation denied the dichotomy between nature and grace. Mortification is less a denial of the good things of life than a joyous — and costly — availability through love, a celebration of life. Contemplation lies at the heart of an abounding vitality:

> Some, seeing the mystic motionless and crucified, will think that his activity has left this earth. Not so. Nothing acts more intensely upon the world than purity and prayer. These hang like an inviolable light between the world and God, and through their serene transparency pass the waves of creative energy and of grace. What else is the Virgin Mary? [8]

This synthetic view opens the way to that problematical "secularization" that is visibly altering the religious orders. Secularization as a recognition of the divine in the human is far from that "secularism" which is "the world thinking about itself." The Society of the Sacred Heart had, from the first, aimed at a way of life and of dress that, as the Constitutions said, would be "simple and without singularity, as becomes persons consecrated to God who keep with the world those relationships necessary for its purpose." [9] Time moved on, leaving styles behind, and what was once "simple and free from singularity" ceased to be so. As the Chapter of 1970 said:

> The phenomenon of secularization is a universal fact, a current in our civilization which nonetheless takes various forms from one country to another. It involves a progressive "desacralization" of certain aspects of our life — our houses, for instance, and our clothing — which were formerly identified with religious life itself and which accentuated our separation from the world. Religious must enter the present situation intelligently, with integrity. And that this may be so, we must recognize the inherent values of the world. "By virtue of their very creation, all things have been established in their nature, their truth, their own excellence" [to quote *Gaudium et Spes*]. [10]

The leadership of youth is a "sign of the times" which is often uncomfortable, always exhilarating. A teaching order learns from those it teaches, and of late the Society has been baffled, alarmed and inspired in its classrooms. Speaking of student insurrection, Pierre Bockel has said:

> These events have let loose an insatiable thirst to live beyond the constraints of present-day society, and that brings a promise. . . . To refuse "having" is to search for "Being." . . . All this constitutes a "spiritual revolution," and always

in the desert, that is, on the margin of established society. . . . It is a symbolic and significant expression of a vast movement of thirst and of spiritual search among young people the world over. . . . And in it I perceive the breath of the Spirit.[11]

The power of youth appears at both ends of the spectrum of thought-in-action, from the Symbionese Army of Liberation to the Easter crowds at Taizé. The Taizé movement is ecumenical, evangelical, monastic and wide open. There the young find what they seek and give what they find — an ideal for all education. It is prayer-centred: They want:

> To set out like people on the march, to explore all the dimensions of the People of God; along the way to create words and gestures that will become signs of contradiction in the gospel sense. This leads us to become at the same time un-wearied seekers for communion. This communion holds within itself a dynamism which crosses all frontiers of age, of culture, of race. Seekers for communion with God are led into the tension between combat and contempla-tion, two attitudes which seem opposed but which are revealed as being at the heart of each other. [12]

This sounds like the pull between contemplation and action so familiar to many in the Society, but the word "combat" (*lutte*) adds an aggressive note: a call to radicality. At the Council of Youth in August, 1974, thousands of young people from the ends of the earth wrote "A Letter to the People of God" calling on them to become a "People of the Beatitudes."

> For today we have one certitude: the risen Christ is preparing his people to become at the same time a contemplative people thirsting for God, and a peo-ple of justice in a vital combat for men and for nations who are exploited, a people in communion where the unbeliever will find his creative role. [13]

Brother Roger answered: "You are at the gates of contemplation. There you will find energy for new beginnings, for boldness of com-mitment." Will vocations for the established religious orders be found among such young people? One of them writes:

> For me, today, to give my life means to lose it by passing from a very active student life to a religious life more contemplative, apparently useless, hidden. It is infinitely beyond my own power to thus remain still before God for a people from whom I come, who have made me what I am, to the very fibres of my being, especially the student world, the world of youth. I know that in me

there are the same polarities as in them: hope and disgust, atheism and living faith, richness and poverty. And my life is to stay in church before God, certain that to work marvels and to change the face of the earth, he has need only of our "yes," radical and unreserved. [Signed: a young religious.] [14]

Charismatic liberty to follow the Spirit, a sense of his action in public and private events is now "blowing in the wind." "It is a great art to act only according to the Spirit of Jesus," said Madeleine Sophie Barat. To learn the art is now imperative, when the Society is experiencing, with the whole Church, an increased tension between fidelity and creativity, between the hierarchy and the people, between legalism and the law of love, between the establishment and the prophets. Many religious join Pentecostal meetings, many convents play host to them. Here, in a cenacle-quiet waiting, or in a commotion of tongues, faith-sharing with all sorts of people enriches conventual prayer. Contacts are made with loosely constructed and extremely vibrant new communities, parochial, *de base* or underground. It is good for a Society with long traditions to be refreshed by marginal currents that will someday be mainstream.

The exchange being made between Christianity and other world religions is cross-fertilizing prayer. Cyril Martindale once said that the gospel of Saint John would not be fully understood until India had brought her philosophy into the Church. Now there is a startling search for the values found in oriental prayer among young occidentals who practice "transcendental meditation" sitting cross-legged on the floor. Buddhist and Hindu masters come half-way round the world to offer retreats and prayer-guidance to machine-driven disciples looking for inward Reality.

> They flock into the International Society for Krishna Consciousness. They find the immediate joy and energy of communion with the Transcendent Being. The experience is so powerful that they are soon prepared to spend hours in prayer. . . . They are chaste, they are fanatic, they are happy. [15]

This places an important responsibility upon a Society which not only educates the youth of non-christian cultures but draws members from among them. Its internationalism has much to do with prayer. At first Oriental and African novices were formed by traditional western theology; practices interwoven with the religion of their native culture, together with its Sacred Books, were left out as "pagan." Now reciprocal studies are finding common values. But more important than the content of learned treatises or animist mythology is the way of prayer native to the Oriental or African mentality. Mystical experience is the deepest meeting point of the races; Zen Buddhism parallels John of the Cross, Sankara and Meister Eckhart are akin. [16]

In the Society the spiritual assets of internationality are now being developed. In the Far East Christian-Zen retreats are open; in India the liturgy is beginning to be indianized and an Ashram offers Indian prayer-experience; in Kenya the teaching of doctrine begins with tribal customs and legends and moves from there into the Gospel parables; in Egypt, where prayer to Allah calls from the minarets, friendliness in school and mutual works of mercy are breaking down the walls between Christianity and Islam.

All these characteristics of post-Vatican II spirituality have one thing in common: a compelling sense of its social dimension. Prayer is transcendent, reaching beyond the here and now; Jacob's ladder leans on the edge of heaven. Prayer is immanent, for God is within. Prayer is incarnational; the Son of God became man. The vertical line is cut by the horizontal, with the heart of the Son of Man at the center of this cross. The Other is found in the other. Many young people, burning to better conditions on this overcrowded planet, first meet Christ in his misfit brothers. The ache of brotherhood felt around the world compels communication through prayer. The Chapter of 1970 found that:

> At the deepest level of our vocation this call resounds today, to contemplate the Heart of Christ through the pierced heart of humanity. This union and conformity to Jesus makes us determined to be present in the world as he was, close to his brothers and available to them. "Let this mind be in you which was also in Christ Jesus." [17]

* * *

From these "signs of the times" it would seem that the original charism of a Society "essentially based upon prayer and the interior life" [18] and "consecrated to the sanctification of others as the work dearest to the Heart of Jesus," [19] will find its full potential in today's world by a simpler, more intense and more constant unity of prayer and service in love. By this charism religious of the Sacred Heart are placed at the meeting point of the vertical and horizontal lines, at the point of departure of the inward and outward movements. A committed prayer, *prière engagée*, centres in the Heart of God who became man. "And it is up to mankind, whose fears, solitude and love Christ shared, to manifest his glory." [20]

The conditions of modern life are a formidable and inescapable challenge to this total prayer. How pray under the clamorous tensions of speed, pressure, crowding and noise — and without the former safeguards? An article called "The Prayer of Speed" [21] claims that these obstacles must serve rather than hinder prayer; they make it effective in a world that craves solitude, leisure and serenity, despite itself. The article opens with the familiar "O God make haste to help me!" and closes with the statement that deep contemplation goes on in the subways. The building of the Kingdom of God is urgent, and urgency compels to inwardness if God is to be the Builder. "The charity of Christ urges us — and so do the times," [22] said Madeleine Sophie Barat. One must look deep, reflect, create interiority under the drives of need. What she called "the ever-renewed recollection of the presence of God for whom we act" [23] will become continuous if adverse circumstances are made to deepen recollection till it bears fruit.

It is still more demanding to be without a rule of silence, even at home. Many voices speak — some of them electronic. Prayer listens for one voice that "speaks by silences." [24] The role of silence is — and always will be — of the essence. Yet silence itself is for the sake of the word that we keep silent to hear, and prayer's social dimension heightens the role of speech. Sympathetic listening, discussion fed by thought, sharing of what is heard in silence, alertness to mass media, drive us into the mystery of God's will-at-work. Both speaking and listening create a need, a need that cannot be denied, for times of absolute stillness — generous times. Retreat, withdrawing, renewal are the conditions for Paul's "Pray always, praying in the Spirit on every possible occasion." [25]

"You know that I have never finished praying," said Madeleine Sophie who never let go of her long hours of solitude while denying herself to no-one. She would allow of no division: "To give ourselves exclusively to contemplation or to action would not be in the spirit of our vocation which has for its aim the glory of God and the salvation of men." [26]

*   *   *

For prayer to be creative in post-conciliar times it must follow the pilgrim way of the Church. A change in structured patterns, in the habits that gave it a settled place, assures this freedom. The time, place, rhythm, form and length of personal prayer are determined by serious and generous choices saying "yes" to the Spirit, who may speak as forcibly in the garden as in the chapel. Cherished devotions — rosary, stations, novenas — may be modified, abandoned or more widely spaced, while new ones are evolving.

Madeleine Sophie had seen eucharistic adoration as bound up with the call to glorify the Heart of Jesus, and even with the mission of education. The half-hour of prayer in the afternoon was called "adoration"; it was thought of as representative prayer for the needs of the Church and of the world. The Custom Book said:

> It seems that the religious of the Sacred Heart, consecrated to him as spouses and victims, can do nothing more agreeable to him than to unite themselves to the sacrifice of the altar. [27]

Madeleine Sophie united adoration closely to the eucharistic sacrifice, saying: "I want it to be the act to which we bring the most preparation, after Holy Communion." [28]

During the century after her death the accent fell upon silent prayer, alone before the tabernacle. Today it falls upon the eucharistic meal which prolongs Christ's presence in the fellowship of his members, the bond which unites all men to him. And so there is a constant stimulus to creativity in the liturgical service which is the heart of community life. Michel Jean of the Blessed Sacrament Fathers said to the assembly of Sacred Heart provincials in 1975:

> Today Christ's presence is conceived of as something much more vast than formerly. The Eucharist is one of the ways God gives us to perceive his all-pervading, continuous presence which is independent of the Eucharist. . . . When we pray before the Eucharist we recall one whole aspect of the life of Christ and of our own life: our prayer is for the Passover of humanity. We can contemplate and interiorize the whole wealth of significance of the Eucharist which John XXIII called "the synthesis of the Christian Credo." [29]

Formation for prayer aims to give stability that supports freedom. In the noviceship the right atmosphere for the discernment of the word of God in Scripture, in relationships, in events and in personal prayer is created. After their first promise the young

professed deepen their prayer by the scriptural and theological study
"which alone can nourish an apostolic spiritual life in our secularized
world."[30] Probation as an international experience is a stronger unifying force than ever; it is held in such different settings as Susono
near Mount Fuji and Assisi near Mount Alverno. At profession each
young religious signs her act of perpetual commitment on the altar.

The need for enlightened spiritual help during ongoing formation
(the lack of which has obscured the way for many) is being met by
the training of more religious for this ministry. The Society of Jesus
has released the dynamism of the Spiritual Exercises in a modern
context. There are directed retreats, a deepened reliving of the long
retreat made earlier, group renewal sessions. Most essential is community life itself for which each religious is responsible:

> Some elements are fundamental: a serious prayer life, centred in the
> Eucharist and the Word of God, a contemplative outlook on the world, which
> presupposes times of deep prayer both solitary and shared, and an atmosphere
> conducive to the experience of God both for ourselves and for those about us. [31]

Between the patterned liturgy in public and the wordless prayer
in solitude another form is emerging: communal prayer with its free,
unstructured sharing. Each community must work out its own form.
As Paul Molinari says:

> Whereas in the past relationship with the Lord was normally considered to be
> a purely private affair, presently there is a growing tendency to feel that one's
> insights and inspirations should be shared with one's brothers and sisters. . . .
> What is being shared is the love of Christ which has gathered us together.
> Whenever it is undertaken with seriousness, charity and discernment, com-
> munities move rapidly from discussion to dialogue, to communal reflections on
> the Scriptures or other spiritual writings; there follows the sharing of personal
> insights, leading to spoken prayer in which people verbalize spontaneously
> what is found in their hearts. . . . Normally, such shared prayer gives rise to a
> deeply felt need on the part of the group for silence; and in this atmosphere
> quiet contemplation rapidly develops. [32]

Sharing has opened a new apostolate: helping others to pray. A
religious was called to the parlour by an unknown visitor. "I have
come because I want to learn to pray; please take me to the chapel
and pray with me." The surprised nun found herself praying out
loud with a stranger. In a mud-brick house in a poor quarter of
Kinshasha a small community welcomes Zairois students who come

to read the Bible, talk of God and pray together. In Ephpheta House near Detroit young suburban parents do the same, thinking of their children whom they must teach to pray. In many countries religious of the Sacred Heart are working with intercongregational or ecumenical retreat teams and workshops.

> This new form of prayer is also creative of a new attitude towards God and the world. The sharing of aspirations and inspirations, of experiences and anxieties, results in a prayer that is intimately attuned to the realities of life. . . . It also intensifies the deeply felt need for closer union with Christ and the desire to share his values and thus leads us back to the contemplation of Christ himself in his mysteries. [33]

The challenge to devotion to the Sacred Heart which first appeared in the nineteen-forties is now throwing light on the significance of the devotion for prayer. The devotion itself is undergoing renewal together with religious life and with the Church by a "return to origins and the spirit of the Founder." A recent study[34] made to discover whether devotion to the Sacred Heart is in a state of decline, survival or progress concludes that it has become more than ever the integrating principle of Christian life, even without benefit of sign or title. Its essence is high-lighted: recognition of Jesus' divine-human love, the focal point of his own life of prayer.

Réné Voillaume, speaking for the Little Brothers of Jesus, sees that:

> Only in the Heart of Christ who is both God and man — who adores the Father and loves man to the point of laying down his life for each of us — can this union be realized, a union otherwise unobtainable, between created and non-created, the world and eternity. The Heart of Christ may be thought of as a point in infinity at which two seemingly divergent or parallel lines meet: that of the world which is God's creation entrusted to the labour of men — the image of which passes — and that of the eternal kingdom already initiated here on earth. [35]

On the back of a holy card showing the Heart of Christ Teilhard de Chardin wrote: "The God of the Gospel," and he spoke of the devotion as: "That spark by which my universe was finally to centre itself by transformation into love in the Heart of Christ." [36] Madeleine Sophie Barat, in her own simple way, had synthesized these truths:

It is not a question of a heart of flesh, but the heart is the centre of the affective phenomena; in this sense the divine Heart is worthy of our adoration and our love. [37]

Yet she often spoke of the Heart of Jesus open upon the Cross.

The prayer of the Church has always been directed to the Father "through Jesus Christ your Son, our Lord, who lives and reigns with you in the unity of the Holy Spirit." The liturgy is trinitarian prayer. Awareness of the mystery of the Three-in-One as the basis of human life is now overflowing from liturgical formulas into social and personal life. At Vatican Council II Cardinal Wyszynski, primate of Poland, faced the College of Bishops: "I ask that the Church be defined by what lies deepest in her being — God in Trinity." The Council responded by focusing upon the Church as the People of God, "a people which draws its unity from the unity of Father, Son and Holy Spirit."

> This people is holy with the holiness of the Trinity. Its marks of unity and of catholicity are a reflection of the unity of the Trinity in the distinction of the divine Persons and their inseparability. The Church is a reflection of the Trinity, a projection outward of the mystery of the three divine Persons united in a single life of light in the Word and a single life of love in the Holy Spirit, communing in the same beatitude in an indivisible unity. [38]

The sense of the social nature of the Church and of her relation to the needs of a society in evolution is paralleled in theology and in morality by a sense of God as community:

> The real standard ultimately of what is right and good is the love-life, the community-life, of the divine Persons. Imitating the divine Persons in their total communion with each other is the fundamental law of God for which other law is designed. [39]

The Trinity, then, is the pattern of shared life — the group, the family, the religious community, the People of God. The 1967 Chapter of the Society of the Sacred Heart says:

> Community life can be thought of as "a likeness to and a share in the life of the Trinity in the mutual gift of love and service, in unity of action and distinction of function." [40]

The "prayer of God" in which Christ spent his nights on the mountain top is nothing less than the very life of God, the mutual communication of Being-Knowledge-Love, which became human prayer through the Heart of the Word. Madeleine Sophie said:

> This was the intention of the divine Master, the goal of our vocation: union with the Heart of Jesus and through him with the Trinity, the beginning for us of heaven on earth. ... Our vocation consists in nothing else than cooperating with the Trinity in the work of the salvation of the world. [41]

Chapter 11

Mission for Justice

What is good has been explained to you man;
this is what Yahweh asks of you:
only this, to act justly, to love tenderly
and to walk humbly with your God.

Micah 6:8

The prophet's word strikes three key-notes of renewal; it also gives a three-stroke character sketch of Madeleine Sophie Barat. The collect of her mass speaks of her as "marvellously endowed with humility and charity," and she, follower of Jesus meek and humble of heart, shared his hunger and thirst for justice:

"Blessed are those who hunger and thirst for justice." These words come from the Word who is truth — the divine Word. But what is this justice for which we must hunger and thirst? It is God, justice and holiness supreme, he whom we long for as our goal. . . . We must become like those who really hunger. Starving creatures throw themselves upon whatever can fill them; they must be held back lest they harm themselves. Give me those who hunger and thirst like that for justice. [1]

Biblical justice is sanctity which gives to both God and man their full rights.

At an assembly of provincials in December 1972, Sister Camacho gave the text from Micah as a watchword for the Society of the Sacred Heart as it seeks to clarify its present mission:

To act justly. This is not being done in our unjust world and Jesus came to fulfil all justice. It is for us to do so now, but it is a work which he began and we must be aware of its evangelical dimension.
To love tenderly. This expression brings us to the very heart of our vocation. If we live in depth the unity of our five options we will act justly, we will live justly, and hence will effect a change in structures. But we will achieve this

only in the measure that we love tenderly, for this is the work of justice in the true evangelical sense, a fulfilment of that justice which is Jesus living and active in us.

To walk humbly with your God. Discernment in its most profound sense means just that, to walk humbly with our God, to let ourselves be formed by him constantly. When we are deeply aware that our religious life is a constant search for God, for the Transcendent, then we walk humbly. [2]

A circular letter from the Central Community at the close of the assembly said:

The meaning of mission came to be our focus, . . . mission, the call of Jesus in the power of the Spirit. At the heart of the mystery of the Incarnation is the mystery of mission. . . . Jesus alone can give us the strength to be open to the Spirit who enables us to struggle against injustice and who "makes all things new." [3]

"I think," said Sister Camacho, "that we are going to return to 'little ways,' and I hope that we shall rediscover 'the little Society' desired by our Holy Mother." [4]

In September, 1973, the Communications Team compiled a brochure, called *Mission and Justice*. The research was done by literally the whole Society; individuals, communities, provinces sent in the relevant texts which were woven together into a study of the commitment to justice inherent in the charism of Saint Madeleine Sophie and now brought sharply into focus by the call of the Church in today's world. It brought her attitude to her own times into relation to the present scene under the headings: justice in the biblical sense, the relation between mission and justice, the fulfilment of mission with justice, and "today."

The Chapter of 1970 was explored and began gradually to reach down into the consciousness of the Society during the hope-filled years that followed. As in the beginning, it was found that a spirit must become incarnate in life before it can be articulated; the search for ways and words continued. As throughout its history, the Society looked to new lands, now with a broadened sense of what education asks. In 1973 a hostel for the students from mountain districts was opened by the Egyptian vicariate in the core of racial and religious tension: Beyrouth in Lebanon. In 1974 Mary Braganza of India joined the central community. In January, 1975, the Mother House left the Via Nomentana for a simpler setting in an apartment complex on the Via Gandiglio in Rome. In the course of that year the central community completed its far-flung journeys to gain mutual understanding of all the provinces, and then regional meetings of provincial teams, in which the central team took part, were held on five continents: Asia, Europe, North America, South America and Africa. November 21 marked the one hundred and seventy-fifth year of the life of the Society.

Now, as preparations for the Chapter of 1976 are advancing, the Society is looking back to its origins in the light of the present as it takes a new direction into the future. Questions are pressing, but pat answers are not accepted, for "to go forward is to go deeper."[5] Mother Stuart saw that this would always be so, as she looked ahead at the dawn of our century to an age of risk:

> Things do not clear up in this world; they are not definite, finished, explained and accounted for. So long as we seek such definite assurance and clear explanations we have not truly learned the religious life. It is tested by the uncertain and the inexplicable; its greatest certainties come of taking for granted things which cannot be verified in this life. [6]

Among the matters not cleared up for which existential solutions are being sought are: how to form "evangelical communities"; how to penetrate the "global village" of our planet; how to counter by gospel living the pressures of nationalism, racism, power structures, social stratification, a consumer society, injustice; how to answer the cry of the deprived. In the forefront stands the question of how best to implement the Society's educative mission, re-affirmed as it goes into the byways as well as the highways:

> We think of education as the integral development of the person which sets him free and opens to him an attitude of service which will make him actively involved and responsible in the transformation of the society in which he lives, and in this way brings him to a personal encounter with Christ and with all men in faith and hope. [7]

It is found that work in solidarity with the poor is sometimes in tension with the established forms of education, but they are two sides of the same coin:

> Today our brothers and sisters of the Third World tell us insistently: if you live in the First World, the affluent world, the developed world, your duty is to change the values of that world. . . . For many of us, our solidarity with the poor and the Third World can be best expressed by taking responsibility for

the First World. This means bearing the burden of guilt, the guilt of conquest and oppression. [8]

Intellectual excellence and the power of thought placed at the service of love can best effect radical change.

It is "the contemplative outlook on the world" that is, as Sister Camacho has said, "the strength of our call, helping us to unify prayer and life, prayer and the struggle for justice." [9] More than ever prayer is "the life-sap that bears fruit through a close union with God." [10] We look to it for the fruits of justice, the fruits of the tree of life which are "for the healing of the nations." [11] This means satisfying the hunger and thirst for prayer, for prolonged prayer, depth prayer, prayer that is lived, committed, involved – and total. Madeleine Sophie Barat put it very simply:

> Ask Saint Joseph for a love of the interior life – at least for the desire of it, for the Society will do no good, you yourselves will do no good, unless you enter on this way. You will be blessed if you have this hunger and thirst, for it is in the interior life that we find the security of justice. [12]

Can it be done? She thought so:

> With what faith and perseverance we should pray! We have so much to win from the Heart of Jesus! Within and without everything is limited, and we should have no other limits than the horizon. Where shall we find such spaciousness? In the Heart of Jesus, who, placing our nothingness in his immensity, will renew its life and give it his own essence, like iron in the fire. We shall then act without check or limit; everything will be possible, even the impossible. [13]

Notes

Foreword

1 The principal biographies of Saint Madeleine Sophie are:

Alcover, Catalina, RSCJ. *Caminos de Ayer al Paso de Hoy, Santa Magdalena Sofia*. Madrid, 1965.

Baunard, Louis. *Histoire de Madame Barat*, 2 vols. Paris: Poussièlgue, 1876. See bibliography for subsequent editions.

Cahier, Adèle, RSCJ. *Vie de la Vénérable Mère Barat*, 2 vols. Paris: de Soyes, 1884.

de Charry, Jeanne, RSCJ. *Sainte Madeleine Sophie*; Tournai: Casterman, 1965.

Galindo, Maria Luisa, RSCJ. *La Glorificadora del Sagrado Corazon de Jesus*. Barcelona: Tipografia Casals, 1934.

Jarmai, Edith, RSCJ. *Tuzben Izzo Elet*. Budapest: Varitas, 1944.
    Magdalena Sophia Barat. Vienna: Herder, 1963. (A translation into German.)

Latge, Maria Tereza, RSCJ. *Sob o Signo do Fogo*. Paulinas, 1965.

Maguire, Catherine, RSCJ. *Saint Madeleine Sophie Barat*. New York: Sheed and Ward, 1960.

Poncelet, Geneviève, RSCJ. *Qui Est-Elle?* Rome: Apulia, 1965.

Richardson, M. K., *Heaven on Thursday*. London: Burns and Oates, 1948.

de Schaffgotch, Marie Anne, RSCJ. *Die Halige Magdalena Sophia Barat und ire Stiftung*. Frieburg: Herder, 1925.

Vermehren, Isa, RSCJ, and Smith, Eileen, RSCJ, *Mutter Barat*. Berlin: Morus Verlag, 1966.

Vita della Santa Maddelena Sofia Barat. Florence, 1925.

Ward, Margaret, RSCJ. *Life of Blessed Madeleine Sophie Barat*. Roehampton, 1911.

Williams, Margaret, RSCJ. *Saint Madeleine Sophie: her Life and Letters*. New York: Herder and Herder, 1965.

2 *Documents of Vatican II* (New York: America Press, 1966), p. 467. Referred to hereafter as *Documents*.

3 Mabel Digby, RSCJ. *Lettres Circulaires de Notre Vénérée Mère Josephine Mabel Digby, pour toutes les Religieuses de la Société* (Rome: Maison Mère, 1960), p. 72. Referred to hereafter as *Circulaires–Digby*.

1 Ps 104:30. Unless otherwise indicated all quotations from Scripture are taken from the Jerusalem Bible.

2 A definition of renewal given by the women religious who were auditors at Vatican Council II, quoted by J. M. R. Tillard in "Les Grandes Lois de la Rénovation Religieuse," *L'Adaptation et la Rénovation de la Vie Religieuse*. Unam Sanctam Series, 62 (Paris: le Cerf, 1967), p. 105.

3 June 10, 1857. *Conférences de la Vénérable Mère Madeleine Sophie Barat* (Roehamptom, 1900), 2 vols. II:333. Referred to hereafter as *Conférences*.

4 Sept. 5, 1848. *Lettres Choisies de notre Bienheureuse Mère pour les Seules Supérieures* (Rome: Maison Mère, 1922–1965), 5 vols. I:271. Referred to hereafter as *Let. Sup.*

5 *Chapter 1970*, American version, p. 6.

6 Title of an address given by Pedro Arrupe, Superior General of the Society of Jesus, at an International Seminar, Rome, Nov. 19, 1970.

Chapter 1, *Design*

1 June 4, 1844. *Lettres Choisies de Notre Sainte Mère, addressées aux Religieuses* (Rome: Maison Mère, 1928–1957), 5 vols I:111. Referred to hereafter as *Let. Ch.* The original text, misquoted in the printed version, reads: "S'il m'etait donné de revivre, ce serait pour ne plus obéir qu'à l'Esprit Saint et pour n'agir que par lui. Vains regrets! Il ne nous est plus permis de rentrer dans le sein de notre Mère; mais au moins ne pouvons-nous commencer à vivre aujourd'hui de cette vie divine et surhumaine?"

2 Nov. 20, 1857. *Conférences* II:348.

3 *The Sacred Wood*, "Tradition and the Individual Talent" (London: Methuen, 1920), p. 49, 59.

4 *Documents*, p. 468.

5 I Cor 12:4–7.

6 A saying of Max Weber.

7 Sept. 11, 1904, *Circulaires*-Digby, p. 185.

8 Jan. 18, 1909, *Ibid.* p. 295.

9 Oct. 28, 1840. *Conférences* I:309.

10 *Chapter 1970*, p. 44.

11 Adèle Cahier, RSCJ. *Vie de la Vénérable Mère Barat* (Paris: de Soyes, 1884), 2 vols. II:254. For the primary sources of the early history of the Society see the bibliography in Jeanne de Charry, RSCJ, *Histoire des Constitutions de la Société du Sacré Coeur*, vol. I, *La Formation de l'Institut* (privately printed, 1975).

Subsequent volumes are in preparation. Referred to hereafter as *Histoire des Constitutions*.

12 1845. *Conférences* I:400.

13 "In Joannis Evangelium," *P. L.* XXXV:1463.

14 March 27, 1852. *Conférences* II:229.

15 June 10, 1857. *Ibid.* p. 333.

16 C. A. de Grandmaison. *La Bienheureuse Mère Barat* (Paris, 1909), p. 141, n.

17 Aug. 11, 1826. *Lettres Circulaires de Notre Bienheureuse Mère* (Roehampton, 1904, 1917), 2 vols. I:15. Referred to hereafter as *Circulaires-Barat*.

18 Janet Stuart, RSCJ. *The Society of the Sacred Heart* (Roehampton, 1923), p. 17.

19 *Ibid.* p. 18, 19.

20 *Chapter 1970*, p. 26.

21 *The Society of the Sacred Heart*, p. 115, 116.

22 Cahier I:518.

23 Cahier II:437.

24 *Archives Générales de la Société du Sacré Coeur*, referred to hereafter as AGSC. These General Archives are at the Villa Lante in Rome. As they are at present being reclassified references will be given only to the series in which each document is found. This quotation is from *Série: Papiers Barat*.

25 *Documents*, p. 73.

26 *Ibid.*

27 *Ibid.*

28 Mark 3:13.

29 Rev. 2:22, Douai version.

30 Acts 2:42.

31 St Jerome, "Life of Saint Paul" in *The Desert Fathers*, tr. by Helen Waddell (New York: Holt, 1936), p. 48.

32 Madeleine Sophie Barat referred to St Pachomius as the source of religious discipline and also honoured a legend when she said: "The greater number of our rules come from Saint Pachomius to whom they were brought by an angel." *Conférences* I:402.

33 *Dialogues of St Gregory*, Bk. II, *P. L.* LXVI: 196.

34 Ecclesiasticus 44:6.

35 "Canticle of the Sun."

36 *Histoire des Constitutions*, p. 5.

37 Louis Baunard. *Histoire de la Bienheureuse Madeleine Sophie Barat* (Paris: Gigord, 1910), 2 vols. II:16.

38 *Constitutions et Règles de la Société du Sacré Coeur* (Lyon: Pelagaud, 1852). The revised edition of 1922 bears this same imprint. The English version (Roehampton, 1890, revised 1922) will here be used. Referred to hereafter as *Constitutions*. "Abridged Plan of the Institute," par. II.

39 Jer 30:24.

40 *Oeuvres Complètes de Bossuet* (Paris, 1862), VI:271.

41 *Haurietis Aquas*.

42 Matt 11:29.

43 John 7:38.

44 Cant 2:14.

45 Bede the Venerable, "In Cantico," *P. L.* CXI:1139.

46 "Sermo in Cantico LXI," *P. L.* CLVII:761.

47 *Life and Revelations of St Gertrude* (London, 1870), p. 315.

48 See volume III of *Histoire Littéraire du Sentiment Religieux en France* (Paris, 1929).

49 Quoted in Jean Bainvel, *Devotion to the Sacred Heart, its Doctrine and History*, tr. by E. Leahy (London, 1924), p. 200.

50 Quoted in G. Hamon, *Histoire de la Dévotion au Sacré Coeur*, 5 vols. (Paris, 1923–1929), I:140.

51 Her niece and several great-nieces later became religious of the Sacred Heart.

52 L. V. Bougaud, *Revelations of the Sacred Heart to Blessed Margaret Mary* (New York: Benziger, 1890), p. 148.

53 Cahier II:323.

Chapter 2, *Vision 1779 – 1800*

1 *Mission and Justice* (Rome: Mother House, 1973), p. 111.

2 I Pet 2:5.

3 *Chapter 1970*, p. 33.

4 *Notice sur le Révérend Père Léonor-François de Tournély* (Vienna, 1886). He was born January 20, 1769, and educated in a château home in Laval. A younger brother, Xavier, joined him in the Seminary of Saint-Sulpice.

5 Achille Guidée, *Vie du Père Joseph Varin* (Paris, Poussièlgue, 1854). He was born February 7, 1769, and educated in a château home in Besançon.

6 *Léonor-François de Tournély*, p. 29.

7 *Ibid.* p. 34.

8 Acts 4:32, Douai version.

9 Marie Duval, RSCJ, *Histoire Abrégée de la Société du Sacré Coeur* (Rome: Maison Mère, 1926), p. 16.

10 Adelaide Elizabeth Le Noir, *Vie de son Altesse Sérénissime Madame la Princesse Louise-Adelaide de Bourbon-Condé*, 3 vols. (Paris: Dufour, 1843).

11 *Histoire des Constitutions*, p. 135.

12 *Léonor-François de Tournély*, p. 119.

13 From a conference given July 31, 1851, quoted in *Histoire des Constitutions*, p. 119.

14 Achille Guidée, *Notices Historiques sur les Pères du Sacré Coeur* (Paris, 1860), p. 45.

15 Marie-Anne of Austria was born in 1770 and died in 1809.

16 Louise and Léopoldine Naudet were born in Florence in 1772 and 1773 respectively. After the dissolution of the Dilette di Gesù Léopoldine founded the Sisters of the Holy Family in Verona. The cause for her beatification is now in progress.

17 *Histoire des Constitutions*, p. 238.

18 The baptismal register gives evidence that Madeleine Sophie was born during the night of December 11, but she herself kept December 12 as her birthday.

19 Guidée, *Notices Historiques sur les Pères du Sacré Coeur*. Louis Barat joined the Fathers of the Sacred Heart, later known as the Fathers of the Faith, all of whom joined the Jesuits after the reconstruction of the order in 1814. He became a noted professor in Paris and died in 1845.

20 Cahier I:3.

21 *Vita della B. Maddelina Sofia Barat* (Florence, 1908), p. 5.

22 Cahier I:9.

23 Pauline Perdrau, RSCJ, *Les Loisirs de l'Abbaye*, 2 vols. (Rome: Maison Mère, 1934), I:77.

24 Baunard I:12.

25 Perdrau I:167.

26 *Ibid.* 169.

27 Octavie Bailly was born in 1773, and helped imprisoned priests during the Revolution. She was later sent to the Roman house of the Dilette and upon its dissolution returned to Amiens as mistress of novices. But she left the Society of the Sacred Heart to become a Carmelite, and as Sister Beatrice of the Conception died in Paris in 1825.

28 Marie-Françoise Loquet was born in 1770; she directed a professional school for working girls in Paris.

29 Baunard I:28.

30 Cahier I:25.

31 *Ibid.*p. 23.

32 *Ibid.* p. 21.

33 *Ibid.* p. 29.

34 *Histoire des Constitutions*, pp. 178–181, 246–257. See p. 180 for the formula of consecration of the Dilette di Gesù.

35 Cahier I:31.

36 *Ibid.* p. 30.

37 *Information*, monthly bulletin of the Society of the Sacred Heart sent from the Mother House, Sept. 30, 1972. A character sketch of Madeleine Sophie Barat drawn by Dominique Sadoux, RSCJ.

Chapter 3, *Realization 1800 – 1864*

1 Lesson for Matins, May 25.

2 Perdrau II:107.

3 *Histoire des Constitutions*, p. 339.

4 *Conferences of our Very Reverend Mother Janet Stuart*, given at the Superiors' Retreat, Manhattanville, 1914 (Roehampton, 1914), p. 58.

5 Cahier I:43.

6 Perdrau I:167.

7 *Chapter 1970*, p. 44.

8 *Society of the Sacred Heart*, p. 22 ff.

9 Perdrau I:131 f.

10 Vincent J. O'Flaherty, SJ, "Renewal, Call and Response," *Studies in the Spirituality of the Jesuits*, vol. 5, nos. 1 and 2 (Jan and March, 1973), p. 20.

11 Baunard I:51.

12 *Ibid.*

13 Perdrau I:422 ff.

14 *Histoire des Constitutions*, p. 121.

15 In this conference to the community at Amiens in 1815 Father Varin summed up the ideals of Father de Tournély for the women's order which he hoped to found. *Histoire des Constitutions*, p. 122.

16 *Vie de Madame Suzanne Geoffroy* (Poitiers: Oudin, 1854), "Mère Suzanne Geoffroy" in *Religieuses du Sacré Coeur*, 2 vols. (Paris: Gigord, 1924). Vol. I, *Quelques Contemporaines de la Fondatrice*, will be referred to hereafter as *Contemporaines*. Suzanne Geoffroy was born in 1761 and died in 1845.

17 *Histoire des Consitutions*, p. 19 f.

18 Geneviève Deshayes was born in 1767 and died in 1849. Her journal is a valuable account of the first years of the Society.

19 Henriette Grosier was born in 1775 and died in 1842.

20 Baunard I:64.

21 Cahier I:37.

22 *Ibid.* p. 36.

23 Marie Dufour, RSCJ, *Vie de la Révérende Mère de Charbonnel* (Paris, n, d,), and *Contemporaines*. Emilie (Catherine) de Charbonnel was born in 1774 and died in 1856.

24 *Vie de la Révérende Mère Félicité Desmarquest* (Paris n. d.). She was born in 1780 and died in 1869.

25 *Histoire des Constitutions*, p. 122.

26 Louis Baunard, *Histoire de Madame Duchesne* (Paris: Poussièlgue, 1873; Marian Bascom, RSCJ, *Blessed Philippine Duchesne* (Manhattanville College, 1946); Louise Callan, RSCJ, *Philippine Duchesne: Frontier Missionary of the Sacred Heart* (Westminster: Newman Press, 1957, abridged edition 1965); and Marjorie Erskine, RSCJ, *Mother Philippine Duchesne* (New York: Longmans, 1926). She was born on August 29, 1769, and died at St Charles, Missouri, on November 18, 1852.

27 *Histoire des Constitutions*, Texts to Chapter 3, p. 134.

28 *Histoire des Constutitons*, p. 384.

29 *Ibid.* p. 385.

30 *Ibid.* p. 366.

31 Subsequent General Councils (or General Congregations) until that of 1967 were made up of *ex-officio* members and hence were not called Chapters, as this canonical term implies representative delegates from all the provinces.

32 The commemorative plaque in the room where the election took place states erroneously that Mother Barat was elected by unanimity.

33 *Vita della Beata Maddelina Sofia Barat*, p. 106.

34 Baunard I:143.

35 Josephine Bigeu was born in 1779 and died in 1827.

36 *Contemporaines*. Thérèse Maillucheau was born in 1779 and died in 1857.

37 See *Souvenirs du premier Noviciat de Poitiers* (Roehampton, 1898). This is an abridged edition of the manuscript Journal.

38 Cahier I:146.

39 Margaret Ward, RSCJ. *Life of Blessed Madeleine Sophie Barat* (Roehampton, 1911), p. 115.

40 Grandmaison, p. 43.

41 *Ibid.*, p. 42.

42 Baunard I:246.

43 *Ibid.* p. 273.

44 Cahier I:201.

45 After becoming a Jesuit Father Varin assisted in the foundation of several other religious orders, notably the Sisters of Notre Dame de Namur founded by Blessed Julie Billiart, and fostered the missionary movements in France. He died on April 19, 1850.

46 Later nineteen members of this community returned to the Society of the Sacred Heart. The separated branch received papal approbation on August 10, 1827, and still continues under the original name of Religieuses de l'Instruction Chrétienne, with its Mother House at Flône. Despite the misunderstandings at the time of the rupture the two are sister congregations, each venerating Madeleine Sophie Barat.

47 *Histoire des Constitutions*, Texts, p. 175.

48 The house of Saint-Denys opened on October 9, 1815. Mothers de Sambucy and Copina were later joined by Mother Baudemont. In 1832 Mother Barat visited Saint-Denys and brought reconciliation. In April of that year the struggling community was united to a branch of the Ursulines.

49 Henriette Girard was born in 1764 and died in 1842.

50 A source for the biographies of religious of the Sacred Heart named from now on, as well as for the history of houses and of vicariates, is *Lettres Annuelles de la Société du Sacré Coeur*, referred to hereafter as *Let. An.* They began in 1805 in the form of handwritten letters sent directly from each house to every other house and signed by the whole community. After 1836 they were sent in a fuller form to the Mother House from where, polycopied and later printed, they were sent out to the whole Society. The series ceased in 1965. For Emilie Giraud see *Let. An.* 1856–1858. She was born in 1788 and died in 1856.

51 *Let. An.* 1846. Eugénie de Gramont was born in 1788 and died in 1846. She caused difficulties during the crises of 1815 and 1839 but remained loyal to the Society. Very influential at the Hotel Biron, she was largely responsible for its aristocratic reputation.

52 The Council elected as assistants general Josephine Bigeu, Henriette Grosier and Catherine de Charbonnel who was also treasurer general. Philippine Duchesne became secretary general.

53 Manuscript of *Histoire des Constitutions*, Part II; still unpublished in 1976.

54 Cahier I:239.

55 *Circulaires*-Barat I:11.

56 March 2, 1816. *Let. Ch.* I:193.

57 July 10, 1820. *Ibid.* p. 400.

58 July 9, 1820. *Circulaires*-Barat I:13.

59 The Council re-elected Mothers de Charbonnel, Grosier and Bigeu, while Henriette Ducis took Mother Duchesne's place as secretary general.

60 Baunard I:460.

61 Aug. 11, 1826. *Circulaires*-Barat I:15, 17.

62 Carlo Pedicini was Protector of the Society from 1826 until his death in 1844. During the crisis of 1839 he supported the proposed changes in opposition to Cardinal Lambruschini, papal secretary of state.

63 Baunard I:466.

64 The Council elected Mothers de Charbonnel, Bigeu and Desmarquest as assistants general.

65 March 12, 1832. *Let. Sup.* I:78.

66 The Council elected Mothers de Charbonnel, Desmarquest, Eugénie de Gramont and Eugénie Audé as assistants general. Elizabeth Galitzin became secretary general.

67 Eugénie Audé was born in 1795 and died at Rome in 1842.

68 *Circulaires*-Barat I:54.

69 Demetrius Augustus de Galitzin, *Vie d'une Religieuse du Sacré Coeur, Princesse Elizabeth Galitzin* (Paris: Techener, 1869). She was born in 1783. During the crisis which followed the Council of 1839 she saw her mistakes and offered her life for the Society. She died of yellow fever at St Michael's in 1843.

70 *Vie de la Révérende Mère Pauline de Limminghe* (Paris, n. d.). She was born in Belgium in 1792 and was one of the religious of the separated house of Dooresele who returned to the Society. She was provincial of the houses in Italy from 1839 to 1851, and died in 1874.

71 Some of these changes were: the aspirantship was to be of ten years duration; the vow of stability was to be withdrawn from the coadjutrix sisters; the cross and ring were to be given at first vows and the crucifix at profession; the Little Office of our Lady was no longer to be said in choir; the government of local superiors was to be limited to six years; provincial superiors were to assist the superior general in the work of government, and these were to form the General Council; the Mother House was to be in Rome.

72 After July 16, 1839, the Society recited every Friday the beads of the Seven Dolours in thanksgiving for the preservation of unity after the crisis.

73 The council elected as assistants general Mothers de Charbonnel, Desmarquest, de Limminghe and Galitzin. The latter remained secretary general.

74 Marie Thérèse Virnot, RSCJ, *Le Charisme de Sainte Madeleine Sophie* (Poitiers, 1975, privately printed), p. 100.

75 *Summary of the Constitutions*, Part I, par. 1.

76 Aug 1839. Baunard II:187.

77 June 1, 1842. *Circulaires*-Barat II:130.

78 Oct 18, 1842. *Let. Sup.* III:111.

79 Baunard II:216.

80 March 13, 1841. *Ibid.* p. 183.

81 Feb 21, 1842. *Circulaires*-Barat I:101.

82 Cahier II:10–11.

83 *Ibid.* 38.

84 *Vie de la Mère Pauline Perdrau* (no imprint). She was born in 1815 and died in 1895. She was on intimate terms with both Mother Barat and Mother Goetz, and has left valuable memoirs of them in *Les Loisirs de l'Abbaye*, 2 vols. (Rome: Maison Mère, 1935).

85 Despite artistic shortcomings this mural has extraordinary spiritual vitality. The young Mary is sitting alone in the temple; her spindle is still, an open book lies on her work basket. Prayer enfolds the slight figure in the rose-coloured gown and severe white veil which fails to hide a golden curl. The title "Mater Admirabilis" was confirmed by Pope Pius IX.

86 Luigi Lambruschini, born in 1776, was Protector of the Society from 1844 until his death in 1854. He opposed current movements towards liberalism in the Church. He was a friendly support to Mother Barat although he misunderstood the adjustment of the Constitutions made in 1851.

87 Baunard II:338.

88 The Council elected as assistants general Catherine de Charbonnel, Félicité Desmarquest, Elizabeth Prevost and Henriette Coppens who became treasurer general. Adèle Cahier became secretary general.

89 Giusto Recanati was Protector of the Society from 1854 until his death in 1861.

90 Baunard I:291.

91 *Conférences* I:24.

92 *Ibid.* p. 400.

93 Manuscript of *Histoire des Constitutions*, Part II, still unpublished in 1976.

94 Dec 18, 1838. *Circulaires*-Barat I:82.

95 *Society of the Sacred Heart*, p. 112.

96 *Chapter 1970*, p. 13.

97 Cahier I:31.

98 Baunard I:52.

99 Cahier I:42.

100 Perdrau II:103.

101 Perdrau I:409, 411.

102 Cahier I:90.

103 Nov 20, 1812. *Let. Ch.* I:148.

104 *Chapter 1970*, p. 14.

105 Ms *Poitiers Journal*

106 *Souvenirs du Premier Noviciat de Poitiers*, p. 27.

107 *Histoire des Constitutions*, p. 441, 442.

108 Cahier II:467.

109 *Pensées et Maximes de Notre Sainte Mère* (Rome: Maison Mère, 1940), p. 120.

110 Sept 5, 1828, *Let. Sup.* I;34.

111 Oct 27, 1828, *Ibid.* p. 36.

112 Mar 20, 1832, *Ibid.* p. 79.

113 *Mémoires de la Révérende Mère Stanislas Tommasini* (Roehampton, 1918), p. 73.

114 *Summary of the Constitutions*, Part I, par. XIII.

115 *Chapter 1970*, p. 14.

116 *Orientationes ad Experimentum*, p. 67. Quoted from the *Journal* of the

Union of Superiors General, May 16, 1967, p. 34.

117 Baunard I:271.

118 Baunard II:321.

119 Dec 7, 1831, *Let. Ch.* II:293.

120 Apr 17, 1822, *Let. Sup.* II:269.

121 Feb 3, 1806, *Let. Ch.* I:17.

122 July 20, 1837. Louise Callan, RSCJ. *Rose Philippine Duchesne, Frontier Missionary of the Sacred Heart* (Westminster: Newman Press, 1957), p. 606.

123 Aug 24, 1846, *Let. Ch.* III:278.

124 Aug 29, 1818, *Let. Ch.* I:280.

125 Cahier I:436.

126 Apr 5, 1819, *Let. Ch.* I:314.

127 Ward, p. 418.

128 Cahier II:44.

129 Baunard II:292.

30 June 15, 1841, *Let. Sup.* III:84.

131 *Let. An.* 1891–1892. Mathilde Garabis was born in 1810 and died in 1891. As mistress of novices she guided Sister Marie Lataste (q. v.) and was vicar of southwestern France from 1870 to 1878.

132. Oct 2, 1852. *Let. Sup.* III:239.

133 Oct 4, 1852. *Let. Sup.* IV:108.

134 *Chapter 1970*, p. 14.

135 *Constitutions*, Abridged Plan, Par. VI.

136 Baunard I:219.

137 Madeleine Sophie's sister, Marie-Louise Dusaussoy, had eight children: Louis, a priest who served as chaplain in Sacred Heart convents in Louisiana and Chile; Stanislaus, who remained unmarried; Thérèse, Sophie, Eliza and Julie, all of whom became religious of the Sacred Heart; Zoë, who entered but left the noviceship and became Madame Cousin; and Dosithée who died as a child after offering her life for her aunt who was ill at the time. Oscar, the son of Zoe, died young, and there are no direct descendants of the family of Madeleine Sophie Barat. There are however many collateral descendants, and the family tree is recorded in the Sacred Heart convent in Joigny.

138 Perdrau I:90. See also I:67–71 for many such instances.

139 Baunard II:316.

140 Aug 13, 1859, *Conférences* II:417.

141 Feb 20, 1845. *Let. Sup.* I:226.

142 *Chapter 1970*, p. 9.

143 Perdrau I:423.

144 Baunard I:52.

145 Feb 3, 1806. *Let. Ch.* I:15.

146 Octavie Berthold was born in 1887 and died in 1833. She offered to go to America in thanksgiving for her conversion from Calvinism, and formed many of the first American novices.

147 Catherine Lamarre was a coadjutrix sister who served valiantly on the American frontier where she died in 1845.

148 Marguerite Manteau was a coadjutrix sister especially trusted by Mother Duchesne. She died in 1847.

149 Dec 8, 1841. *Let. Ch.* III:86.

150 Cahier II:323.

151 *Chapter 1970*, p. 7.

152 Madeleine d'Ernemont, RSCJ, *La Vie Voyageuse et Missionaire de la Révérende Mère Anna du Rousier* (Paris: Beauchesne, 1932) and Margaret Williams, RSCJ, *Mother Anna du Rousier* (New York: Manhattanville College, 1946). She was born in 1806.

153 AGSC, Série *Papiers Barat.*

154 May 15, 1843. *Let. Sup.* I:190.

155 Nov 1855. *Let. Ch.* IV:219.

156 June, 1829. *Philippine Duchesne, Frontier Missionary of the Sacred Heart*, p. 494.

157 *Vie de la Révérende Mère Aloysia Hardey* (Paris: Maison Mère, 1887); Mary Garvey, RSCJ, *Mary Aloysia Hardey* (New York: Longmans Green, 1925); Margaret Williams, RSCJ, *Second Sowing* (Sheed and Ward, 1942) and *Mother Aloysia Hardey* (New York: Manhattanville College, 1945). She was born in Maryland in 1806.

158 *Contemporaines.* Euphrosyne Jouve was born in 1896 and took the name Aloysia as a novice at Sainte-Marie d'en-Haut. After her vows she became ill, yet Mother Barat gave her a share in government, hoping for her cure. She died in 1821 and many graces were granted at her tomb.

159 Williams, *Second Sowing*, p. 144.

160 Baunard II:233.

161 AGSC, Série *Papiers Barat.*

162 *Let. An.* 1845. Marguerite Chonez was born in 1786 and entered the Dames de la Providence, a small order which became amalgamated with the Society of the Sacred Heart in 1826. She died in Algiers in 1845.

163 Aug 7, 1859. *Let. Sup.* IV:261.

164 Sept 15, 1858. *Conférences* II:377.

165 Grandmaison, p. 193.

166 Perdrau I:142.

167 *Ibid.* p. 270.

168 *Chapter 1970*, p. 10.

169 *Histoire Abrégée*, p. 16.

170 *Perdrau* I:422. The earliest extant formulas of profession show that this vow was made from the beginning.

171 Grandmaison, p. 14, n.

172 Perdrau I:77.

173 *Ibid.* p. 300.

174 *Ibid.* p. 237.

175 Dec 8, 1862. *Let. Ch.* V:229.

176 *Ibid.*

177 *Constitutions*, Part III, Chapter III, par. I.

178 *Spirit and Plan of Studies of the Society of the Sacred Heart* (England, 1958), p. 12.

179 Baunard II:443.

180 Apr 18, 1845. *Let. Sup.* I:228.

181 Oct 10, 1845. *Ibid.* p. 235.

182 Perdrau II:69.
183 *Ibid.* p. 103.
184 Dec 29, 1845. *Circulaires*-Barat I:125.
185 The first printed edition of the Plan: *Réglement des Pensionnats et Plan d'Etudes de la Société du Sacré Coeur de Jésus* (Orleans: Alex Jacob, 1852). See bibliography for subsequent editions and revisions.
186 Henriette Ducis, born in 1774, was an outstanding educator at Amiens, and secretary general from 1820 to 1833. She died in 1844.
187 Grandmaison, p. 155.
188 March 10, 1864. *Circulaires*-Barat I:197.
189 Apr 20, 1845. Baunard II:369.
190 *Let. An.* 1869–1871. Aimée d'Avenas was born in 1804. She organized the first juniorate in 1848 and supervised the revisions of the Plan of Studies from 1826 to 1851. She died in 1871.
191 Feb 12, 1833. *Let. Ch.* II:361.
192 Dec 20, 1845. *Circulaires*-Barat I:127.
193 Perdrau I:68.
194 Perdrau II:257.
195 *Chapter 1970*, p. 10.
196 June 23, 1850. *Conférences* II:195.
197 A large percentage of such children were received gratis.
198 Feb 12, 1856. *Lettres aux Mères en Charge* (Rome: Maison Mère, 1924), p. 136.
199 Baunard II:291.
200 May 5, 1833. *Conférences* I:215.
201 AGSC, Série *Papiers Barat.*
202 Jan 12, 1852. *Let. Sup.* III:200.
203 *Constitutions*, Abridged Plan, Par. VI.
204 Aug 3, 1839. *Let. Sup.* III:46.
205 Cahier I:334.
206 Feb 17, 1818. *Let. Ch.* I:243.
207 July 24, 1852. *Let. Sup.* III:230.
208 *Chapter, 1970*, p. 11, 12.
209 AGSC, Série *Papiers Barat.*
210 Baunard I:440.
211 Perdrau I:101.
212 Baunard II:579.
213 *Ibid.* p. 316.
214 Jan 15, 1862. *Circulaires*-Barat I:227.
215 Baunard II:40.
216 *Ibid.* p. 37.
217 *Ibid.* p. 39.
218 *Rule Book of the Children of Mary*, p. 7.
219 1864. *Let. Sup.* II:304.
220 Dec 17, 1841. *Let. Sup.* I:150.
221 Pentecost, 1834. *Conférences* I:242.
222 Sept 21, 1859. *Circulaires*-Barat II:311.
223 Matt 3:15.

224 Nov 5, 1819. *Let. Ch.* I:366.
225 *Pensées et Maximes de Notre Sainte Mère*, p. 93.
226 Cahier II:482.
227 *Ibid.* p. 661.
228 Mary Quinlan, RSCJ. *The Society of the Sacred Heart: a Microcosm in a Changing World*, an unpublished study, 1973.
229 March 6, 1849. *Let. Ch.* III:332.
230 June 29, 1831. *Let. Ch.* III:275.
231 March 4, 1837. *Let. Sup.* I:98.
232 Aug 4, 1832. Baunard II:58.
233 Nov 10, 1831. *Circulaires*-Barat I:29.
234 Jan 12, 1831. *Let. Ch.* II:241.
235 Baunard II:35.
236 Oct 11, 1853. *Lettres aux Mères en Charge*, p. 186.
237 Cahier II:603.
238 Jan 22, 1855. *Let. Sup.* II:56.
239 Perdrau I:180.
240 *Ibid.* p. 201.
241 Baunard II:310.
242 Perdrau II:309.
243 March 23, 1829. *Lettres aux Mères en Charge*, p. 53.
244 Aug 5, 1863. *Circulaires*-Barat II:316.
245 The Council elected as assistants general Elizabeth Prevost, Gertrude De Brou, Adèle Lehon and Josephine Goetz, as secretary general Adèle Cahier, as treasurer general Josephine Mahé.
246 May 21, 1865. *Let. Sup.* II:260.
247 Cahier II:658.

Fidelity and Creativity

1 July 26, 1852. *Let. Sup.* III:231.
2 Nov 30, 1831. Callan, *Philippine Duchesne*, p. 542.
3 *Chapter 1970*, p. 45.

Chapter 4, *Consolidation 1865 – 1895*

1 *Various Holiday Subjects*, an unpublished compilation.
2 Aug 3, 1839, *Let. Sup.* III:46.

3 Joseph McSorley, *An Outline History of the Church* (St Louis: Herder, 1946), p. 764.

4 Charles Augustus de Reisach was Protector of the Society from 1867 until his death in 1869. He helped to prepare the agenda for Vatican Council I and was an expert in Church-state relations.

5 Rafaele Monaco La Valetta exerted a very conservative influence over the Society as Cardinal Protector from 1870 until his death in 1896.

6 *Conferences given at the Superiors' Retreat, Manhattanville*, p. 43.

7 An analytic study of these statistics is now in process.

8 Marie Barbaren, RSCJ, *Vie de la Révérende Mère Jeanne de Lavigerie* (Rome: Maison Mère, 1935), p. 127.

9 *Chapter 1970*, p. 45.

10 *Vie de la Mère Maria Zaepffel* (Rome: Maison Mère, 1925). She was born in Alsace in 1832. As mistress general and superior she was an ardent "apostle of the Rule." She died at Kientzheim in 1910.

11 *Vie de la Mère Marie Zaepffel*, p. 74.

12 Marie Dufour, RSCJ, *Vie de la Très Révérende Mère Josephine Goetz* (Roehampton, 1895); Pauline Perdrau, RSCJ, *Les Loisirs de l'Abbaye,*, vol. II (Rome: Maison Mère, 1936); M. K. Richardson, RSCJ, *Life of our Venerated Mother Josephine Goetz* (no imprint). Brief quotations without reference are taken from Dufour or Perdrau.

13 See *Contemporaines* and *Let. An.* 1863. Henriette Coppens was a Belgian born in 1785. She was one of the religious of the separated house of Dooresele who returned to the Society in which she served as mistress of novices, provincial of eastern France, assistant general and treasurer general. She died in 1863.

14 Perdrau II:143, 151.

15 *Ibid.* p. 271.

16 *Ibid.* p. 302.

17 *Histoire Abrégée*, p. 257.

18 Perdrau II:168.

19 The Council elected as assistants general Elizabeth Prevost, Adèle Lehon, Adèle Cahier and Juliette Désoudin, as secretary general Amélie de Savonnière, as treasurer general Césarine Bulliat.

20 *Religieuses du Sacré Coeur*, vol. II, and *Let. An.* 1888. Maria Mayer was a German born in 1829. She became vicar of Austria where she died in 1888.

21 Perdrau II:448.

22 *Histoire Abrégée*, p. 258.

23 *Vie de la Révérende Mère Goetz*, p. 179.

24 Apr 19, 1869. *Lettres Circulaires de la Très Révérende Mère Josephine Goetz* (Paris, no imprint), p. 68. Referred to hereafter as *Circulaires*-Goetz.

25 AGSC, Série *Conseils Généraux*.

26 May 9, 1872. *Circulaires*-Goetz, p. 96.

27 p. 306.

28 Marie Dufour, RSCJ. *Vie de la Très Révérende Mère Lehon* (Roehampton, 1895); M. K. Richardson, RSCJ, *Life of our Venerated Mother Adèle Lehon* (no imprint). Brief quotations without reference are taken from Dufour.

29 June 4, 1852. *Let. Sup.* II:35.

30 May 30, 1857. *Let. Sup.* III:411.

31 June 12, 1861. *Let. Sup.* II:183.

32 The Council elected as assistants general Adèle Cahier, Juliette Désoudin, Natalie de Serres and Aloysia Hardey, as secretary general Marie Dufour, as treasurer general Césarine Borget.

33 AGSC, Série *Conseils Généraux.*

34 *Ibid.*

35 *Décrets des Congrégations Genérales de la Société du Sacré Coeur* (Paris: Maison Mère, 1874), p. 75.

36 p. 310.

37 AGSC, Série *Papiers Lehon.*

38 *Ibid.*

39 June 4, 1874. *Lettres Circulaires de notre Très Révérende Mère Adèle Aimée Thérèse Lehon* pour Toutes les Religieuses de la Socité (Roehampton, 1914), p. 28. Referred to hereafter as *Circulaires*-Lehon.

40 *Mémoires de la Révérende Mère Maria Stanislaus Tommasini*, p. 88.

41 Quoted in *Circulaires*-de Sartorius (edition for superiors), p. 248.

42 Apr 7, 1884. *Circulaires*-Lehon, p. 97.

43 In 1884 the assistants general elected were Adèle Cahier, Juliette Désoudin, Aloysia Hardey and Césarine Borget. In 1890, Juliette Désoudin, Césarine Borget, Clémence Fornier and Augusta de Sartorius. Both Councils re-elected Marie Dufour as secretary general and Césarine Borget as treasurer general.

44 Dec 30, 1890. *Circulaires*-Lehon, p. 144.

45 Dec 31, 1892. *Ibid.*, p. 153.

46 *Vie de notre Très Révérende Mère Adèle Lehon*, p. 403.

47 Marie Dufour, RSCJ, *Vie de la Très Révérende Mère Marie-Augusta de Sartorius* (no imprint); M. K. Richardson, RSCJ, *Life of our Venerated Mother de Sartorius* (no imprint). Brief quotations without reference are taken from Dufour.

48 July 27, 1864. *Let. Ch.* V:210.

49 *Vie de notre Très Révérende Mère Marie-Augusta de Sartorius*, p. 74, 224.

50 Aug 19, 1894. *Lettres Circulaires de notre Très Révérende Mère Augusta Huberta de Sartorius*, pour Toutes les Religieuses de la Société (Roehampton, 1914), bound in the same volume as the circular letters of Mother Lehon. Referred to hereafter as *Circulaires*-de Sartorius, p. 216.

51 The Council elected as assistants general Juliette Désoudin, Juliette Depret, Mabel Digby and Césarine Borget who remained treasurer general. Marie le Bail was elected secretary general.

52 June 14, 1895. *Circulaires*-de Sartorius, p. 245.

53 *Vie de la Très Révérende Mère Marie-Augusta de Sartorius*, p. 253f.

54 Apr 19, 1869. *Circulaires*-Goetz, p. 68.

55 *Let. An.* 1870–1872. Marie Elizabeth Prevost was born in Santo Domingo in 1784. She served the Society as provincial of southern France and assistant general, and died at Chambéry in 1871.

56 Williams, *Second Sowing*, p. 398.

57 June 19, 1886. *Circulaires*-Lehon, p. 128.

58 *Let. An.* 1875–1876. Natalie de Serres was born in 1818. Despite physical handicaps she served the Society as vicar of south-eastern France, assistant general and mistress general of studies. She died in 1876.

59 Oct 12, 1876. *Circulaires*-Lehon, p. 42.

60 *Vie de la Mère Clémence Fornier de Mairard* (Roehampton, 1896). She was born in 1818 and died in 1893.

61 March 20, 1893. *Circulaires*-Lehon, p. 159.

62 *Vie de la Révérende Mère Adèle Cahier* (Paris, n. d.). She was born in 1804. She was superior at Santa Rufina in Rome before taking charge of the secretariate.

63 June 12, 1885. *Circulaires*-Lehon, p. 126.

64 *Let. An.* 1866–1867. Amélie de Savonnières was born in 1816 and died in 1867.

65 *Let. An.* 1904–1906. Marie Dufour was born in 1823.

66 Nov 29, 1852. *Let. Sup.* II:44.

67 Apr 17, 1822. *Ibid.* p. 269.

68 *Let. An.* 1898–1900. Josephine Mahé was born in 1816. In the Society she became "treasurer for life" but was treasurer general only from 1864 to 1865. She died in 1899.

69 *Let. An.* 1870–1872. Césarine Bulliat was born in 1805. She became treasurer general in 1865, and in 1870 was sent to Marmoutier to escape the siege of Paris; she died the following year.

70 *Vie de la Révérende Mère Césarine Borget* (Rome: Maison Mère, 1927). She was born in Savoy in 1827. She served as treasurer general from 1872 until her death in 1917.

71 *Vie de la Révérende Mère Juliette Désoudin* (Roehampton, 1904). She was born in 1811.

72 June 19, 1897.*Circulaires*-Digby, p. 34, 39.

73 *Let. An.* 1905–1907. Georgina Lévêque was an Alsation born in 1834.

74 *Chapter 1970*, p. 27.

75 Apr 7, 1884. *Circulaires*-Lehon, p. 108.

76 *Society of the Sacred Heart*, p. 30 f.

77 See Appendix.

78 *Vie de la Révérende Mère Jeanne de Lavigerie*, p. 55.

79 *Let. An.* 1893–1894. Alix de Kérouartz was born in 1812. She was vicar of northern and then of western France and died in 1893.

80.*Let. An.* 1881–1882. Esther d'Oussières was born in 1799. She was vicar of eastern and then of northern France and died in 1881.

81 *Let. An.* 1888–1889. Lucie Merilhou was born in 1807. She made the first foundation in England at Berrymead and in 1858 became the first vicar of the English-Irish vicariate. She was then vicar of Belgium from 1867 until her death in 1888.

82 *Let. An.* 1880–1881. Marcella Goold was born in Brussels of an Irish family in 1820. She was vicar of England-Ireland from 1866 to 1872. She died in 1880.

83 *Let. An.* 1896–1898. Christina Gazelli was born in Turin in 1813. In 1870 she became vicar of southern France and in 1879 vicar of Italy until 1891. She died in 1897.

84 *Let. An.* 1870–1872. Valérie de Bosredont was born in 1806. She became the first vicar of Spain from 1869 until her death in 1887.

85 *Let. An.* 1886–1887. Camille Parmentier was a Belgian born in 1834.

She was vicar of Spain from 1869 until her death in 1887.

86 *Let. An.* 1899–1901. Clementine de Gagern was born in Bonn in 1838. She was vicar of Austria from 1889 to 1897, and died in 1900.

87 *Let. An.* 1881–1882. Victoire Noizet was born at Soissons in 1808. She was sent to the first foundation at Lemberg and became vicar of Poland from 1864 to 1868. She died in 1881.

88 *Let. An.* 1869–1870. Thérèsine Trincano, an Italian, was born in 1809. She went to the United States in 1874, then became the first vicar of Canada from 1864 until her death in 1868.

89 *Let. An.* 1876–1877. Clémence Cornélis, a Belgian, was born in 1823. She went to the United States and then to Canada where she was vicar from 1868–1874. She died the following year.

90 *Let. An.* 1924–1926. Ellen Mahony was born in New Brunswick of an Irish family in 1843. She was vicar of Canada (1881–1888, 1908–1925), of Chicago (1888–1892), of New York (1895–1908). She attended six general councils and died in 1925.

91 *Let. An.* 1909–1911. Amélie Schulten was a German, born in 1841. After working in the United States she was vicar of Canada from 1888 to 1896, then went to Mexico, Peru and Chile where she died in 1907.

92 Aug 22, 1869. *Circular Letters of Very Reverend Mothers Josephine Goetz, Adèle Lehon and Augusta de Sartorius* (Brighton, 1948), p. 16.

93 *Let. An.* 1853–1854. Maria Cutts was an English convert, born in 1781. In 1844 she became the first vicar of Louisiana, and died in 1854.

94 *Let. An.* 1879–1880. Amélie Jouve was born in 1799. At the death of her sister, Aloysia Jouve, she took the name Aloysia. She went to Canada in 1847, and became vicar of Louisiana in 1854. In 1864 she returned to Europe and became vicar general of central and then of western France. She died in 1880.

95 *Vie de la Révérende Mère Anna Josephine Shannon* (Roehampton, 1929). Anna Shannon was born in Ireland in 1810 and went to Louisiana as a child. She became vicar of Louisiana after the Civil War, until 1882. She died in 1896.

96 *Let. An.* 1897–1899. Genevieve Gauci was born in Malta in 1834. In America she was mistress of novices and superior before serving as vicar of the Chicago-Maryville vicariate from 1887 to 1895. She died in 1897.

97 *Let. An.* 1912–1924, and "Sarah Jones" in *God's Middlemen* ed. by Loretta Corcoran, RSCJ (New York: Manhattanville College, 1948). She was born in New York in 1823. She was vicar of New York from 1872 to 1895 and died in 1911.

98 *Let. An.* 1872–1873. Rose Guthreaux, born in New Orleans in 1825, was brought up in the orphanage of the Sacred Heart convent. She was vicar of Chicago from 1869 until her death in 1872.

99 *Let. An.* 1880–1881. Elizabeth Tucker was born in England in 1809. She was superior at Eden Hall and went through the Civil War in St Louis before coming vicar of the Chicago-Maryville vicariate from 1872 to 1876. She died in 1881.

100 *Let. An.* 1909–1911. Margaret Niederkorn was born in Luxembourg in 1828. She entered in the United States and was vicar of the Chicago-Maryville vicariate from 1880 to 1888. She died in 1910.

101 *Let. An.* 1876. Mary Anne Layton was born in Kentucky in 1802. She was the first American religious of the Sacred Heart, a coadjutrix sister serving with heroic courage on the mission to the Indians. She was paralyzed for the last fourteen years of her life and died in 1876.

102 *Contemporaines* and *Let. An.* 1876. Lucille Mathevon was born in France in 1793. As superior of the Indian mission she wrote the vivid Journal that tells of life at Sugar Creek. She died at Saint Mary's in 1876.

103 Louise Callan, RSCJ. *The Society of the Sacred Heart in North America* (Longmans Green, 1937), p. 305.

104 *Ibid.* p. 308 f.

105 *Let. An.* 1880. Suzannah Boudreaux was born in Louisiana in 1823 and was a *protégée* of Mother Duchesne. She became vicar of Louisiana in 1873 and of the Chicago-Maryland vicariate in 1876.

106 Jan 13, 1842. *Let. Sup.* III:99.

107 *Let. An.* 1894–1896. Fébronie Vercruysse was born in Belgium in 1832. She became the first vicar of Australia-New Zealand from 1888 to 1894. She died the following year.

108 *Let. An.* 1942–1945, Supplement. Amélie Salmon was born in France in 1848. She went to Australia in 1885 and became vicar in 1895. She retired in 1936 and died two years later.

109 *Let. An.* 1927–1929. Micaela Fesser was born in Spain of a Cuban family in 1837. She served in Cuba and Puerto Rico, and was mistress of novices for the Mexican noviceship at Grand Coteau. She died in 1927.

110 *Let. An.* 1905–1907. Mary Elizabeth Moran was born in New Orleans in 1836. She became vicar of Louisiana in 1876, of Mexico-Antilles in 1883, and of Spain in 1895, for three years. She died in Belgium in 1905.

111 *Mémoires de la Mère Maria Stanislaus Tommasini* (Roehampton, 1918), and M. K. Richardson, RSCJ, *Tommasini* (London: Sands, 1950). She was born in 1827 and died in 1913.

112 Perdrau I:199, II:68.

113 *Let. An.* 1863–1865, p. 175.

114 *Let. An.* 1888–1889. Angelita Alentado was born in Cuba in 1839 and went to Chile in 1879. She was vicar of Chile-Peru from 1881 until her death in 1888.

115 *Let. An.* 1910–1911. Elizabeth Windhoff was born in Germany in 1837. She went to Chile in 1870 and was vicar of Chile-Peru from 1888 to 1898. She died in 1908.

116 *Vie de la Révérende Mère Jeanne de Lavigerie* (Rome: Maison Mère, 1935).

117 Perdrau II:624.

118 May 13, 1867. *Circulaires*-Goetz, p. 46.

119 Apr 22, 1883. *Circulaires*-Lehon, p. 106.

120 *Let. An.* 1879-1880. Marie-Anne Martin was born in 1818 and died in 1880.

121 *Let. An.* 1877–1878. Maria Dagon was born in 1845 and died in 1878.

122 *Let. An.* 1908–1910. Lucie Durand was born in 1831 and died in 1908.

123 *Let. An.* 1876–1877. p. 338.

124 Margaret Williams, RSCJ. *Mother Anna du Rousier* (New York: Manhattanville College, 1946), p. 36.

125 Jan 3, 1879. *Circulaires*-Lehon, p. 67.

126 *Life of Mother Henrietta Kerr* (Roehampton, 1886) and *Notes of Retreat of Mother Henrietta Kerr* (Roehampton, 1887). She was born in 1842 and spent her early religious life at the Trinita. She was an outstanding mistress general at Roehampton, while fighting chronic illness. She died in 1884.

127 *Religieuses de Sacré Coeur*, vol. II. Josephine Augustin was born in France in 1823. She was an influential mistress general at Beauvais where she died in 1889.

128 *Let An.* 1900–1902. Josephine Errington was born in Dublin in 1853. She had a genius for teaching and became a powerful mistress general at Roehampton and at Manhattanville where she died in 1902.

129 *Let. An.* 1924–1925, Supplement. Pauline de Flaujac was born in France in 1850 and used her musical and artistic gifts as mistress general at Pau. She was later superior in Spain and died in 1925.

130 Mary O'Leary, *Education with a Tradition* (New York: Longmans Green, 1930). p. 193.

131 Oct 1, 1872. *Circulaires*-Goetz, p. 105.

132 Feb 3, 1879. *Circulaires*-Lehon, p. 66.

133 May 4, 1839. *Let. Sup.* I:111.

134 *Conferences given at the Superiors' Retreat*, Manhattanville, 1914, p. 34.

135 Apr 19, 1894. *Circulaires*-de Sartorius, edition for Superiors only, p. 241.

136 *Règle de l'Association des Affiliées de la Société du Sacré Coeur* (Paris, 1869). In the printed editions the word "promise" is used instead of "vow". The group formed by Louise de Montaignac became eventually the Oblates of the Heart of Jesus.

137 *Enfants de Marie du Sacré Coeur*, 2 vols. (Paris: Gigord, 1932), I:178.

138 *Ibid.* p. 202.

Chapter 5, *Confirmation, 1895 – 1914*

1 Ann Pollen, RSCJ. *Mother Mabel Digby* (London: Longmans Green, 1914); Juliette de Landresse, RSCJ. *Vie de la Très Révérende Mère Josephine Digby* (Aix-la-Chapelle, 1915); and M. K. Richardson, RSCJ, *Mabel Digby* (London: Longmans Green, 1956, reprinted as *Sudden Splendour*, 1957). Brief quotations without reference are taken from Pollen.

2 *Mother Mabel Digby*, p. 190.

3 AGSC, Série *Conseils Généraux*.

4 The Council elected as assistants general Juliette Désoudin, Juliette Depret,

Marthe de Pichon and Césarine Borget who remained treasurer general. Marie le Bail remained secretary general.

5 AGSC, Série *Conseils Généraux*.

6 Sept 14, 1895. *Circulaires*-Digby, p. 18.

7 *Ibid.* p. 17.

8 Angelo di Pietri, who had been Nuncio to Spain, was Protector of the Society from 1886 until his death in 1911.

9 Jan 29, 1896. *Circulaires*-Digby, p. 29 ff.

10 Dec 12, 1897. *Ibid.* p. 67.

11 *Ibid.* p. 90.

12 Nov 11, 1898. *Ibid.* p. 96.

13 Maria Droste zu Vichering was born in Munster, Germany, in 1863, and was educated at the Sacred Heart school at Riedenburg. She asked to enter the Society of the Sacred Heart but was refused for reasons of health. She became Mother Mary of the Divine Heart in the Good Shepherd order. It was due to her intervention that Leo XIII consecrated the human race to the Sacred Heart on June 11, 1899. Mother Mary died three days later. She was beatified on November 1, 1973.

14 *Annum Sacrum*.

15 Nov 18, 1899. *Circulaires*-Digby, p. 99 f.

16 Sept 14, 1901. *Ibid.* p. 126.

17 *Let. An.* 1905–1907. Alexandrine Dupautaine was born in France in 1823. She was vicar of northern France from 1875 to 1900. She died in 1906.

18 Jan 6, 1902. *Circulaires*-Digby, p. 130.

19 *Mother Mabel Digby*, p. 293.

20 At this Council Sophie du Chélas and Juliette Depret resigned as assistants general; Mathilde Nérincx and Jeanne de Lavigerie were elected to fill their places. Marthe de Pichon and Césarine Borget were re-elected; the latter remained treasurer general and Marie le Bail remained secretary general.

21 *Let. An.* 1904–1906. Juliette de Lapeyrouse was born in France in 1823, and was superior at the Rue de Varenne during the siege of Paris. She died in 1904.

22 Nancy Bakewell was instantaneously cured of hip disease during a novena to Madeleine Sophie Barat.

23 *Let. An.* 1938–1940. Marie Klippel, as a young religious at Riedenburg, was instantaneously cured of an internal injury through the intercession of Madeleine Sophie Barat, in 1882.

24 Apr 15, 1908. *Circulaires*-Digby, p. 255.

25 Jan 1, 1908. *Ibid.* p. 241.

26 Jan 18, 1909. *Ibid.* p. 294.

27 *Let. An.* 1926–1930. Supplement. Marthe de Lavergne was born in France in 1858. She was mistress of novices at Conflans, Rivoli, Jette and Chamartin, and vicar of the Avigliana-France vicariate from 1915 until her death in 1929.

28 The Council re-elected all the officers of 1904.

29 May 27, 1911. *Lettres Circulaires de notre Très Révérende Mère Janet Erskine Stuart*, pour Toutes les Religieuses de la Société (Rome: Maison Mère, 1963), p. 6. Referred to hereafter as *Circulaires*-Stuart.

30 Maud Monahan, RSCJ. *Life and Letters of Janet Erskine Stuart* (London: Longmans Green, 1922); Juliette de Landresse, RSCJ. *Vie de la Très Révérende Mère Janet Erskine Stuart* (Roehampton, 1921); and Angela Cave, *Janet Stuart* (New York: Manhattanville College, 1946). Brief quotations without reference are taken from Monahan.

31 *Life and Letters*, p. 15, 18.

32 *Ibid.* p. 37, 38.

33 *Ibid.* p. 76.

34 This press undertook the printing of Society literature, including the *Annual Letters*, until its destruction during the war of 1939.

35 *Life and Letters*, p. 172.

36 *Ibid.* p. 313.

37 *Ibid.* p. 315.

38 AGSC, Série *Papiers Stuart*.

39 The Council elected as assistants general Jeanne de Lavigerie, Mathilde Nérincx, Marthe de Pichon, and Césarine Borget who remained treasurer general. Marie le Bail remained secretary general.

40 *Circulaires*-Stuart, p. 14.

41 AGSC. Série *Papiers Stuart*.

42 Aug 13, 1912. *Circulaires*-Stuart, p. 40.

43 AGSC, Série *Conseils Généraux*, unpublished Memorial on Education by Mother Stuart.

44 *The Society of the Sacred Heart*, p. 114.

45 *Summary of the Constitutions*, par. XIII.

46 Jan 3, 1912. *Circulaires*-Stuart, p. 29.

47 Marie de Salm-Salm was born in Austria in 1874. She was cured of a crippling hip disease at the shrine of Blessed Madeleine Sophie at Jette. She was later superior at the Villa Lante at the time of the canonization, and died at Riedenburg in 1965.

48 Conferences given at the Superior's Retreat, Manhattanville, p. 25.

49 *Life and Letters*, p. 458.

50 Sept 12, 1914. *Circulaires*-Stuart, p. 86.

51 *Vie de la Révérende Mère Marthe de Pichon* (Roehampton, 1916). She was born in France in 1840 and was assistant general from 1895 until her death in 1913.

52 *Vie de la Révérende Mère Marthe de Pichon*, p. 205.

53 Nov 1, 1913. *Circulaires*-Stuart, p. 74.

54 *Let. An.* 1911–1913. Juliette Depret was born in Moscow of a French family. She was assistant general from 1893 to 1904, and died in 1913.

55 *Let. An.* 1908–1910. Sophie du Chélas was born in 1829. She was vicar of central France from 1880 until her appointment as assistant general in 1896. She retired in 1904 and died the following year.

56 *Vie de la Révérende Mère Mathilde Nérincx* (Roehampton, 1924). She was born in Belgium in 1845. She was vicar of northern France from 1900 until the expulsions, then assistant general from 1904 until her death in 1919.

57 *Vie de la Révérende Mère Jeanne de Lavigerie*, p. 225.

58 *Vie de la Révérende Mère Catherine de Montalembert* (Roehampton, 1930). She was born in France in 1841. She was vicar of Austria from 1905, then assis-

tant general from 1913 to 1922. She died at the Trinita in 1928.

59 Aug. 1913. *Circulaires*-Stuart, p. 64.

60 Juliette de Landresse, RSCJ. *Vie de la Digne Mère Marie le Bail* (Roehampton, 1904). She was born in France in 1852 and spent her whole religious life in the secretariate, and was secretary general from 1894 until her death in 1920.

61 *Vie de la Digne Mère Marie le Bail*, p. 104.

62 *Life and Letters*, p. 201.

63 *Vie de la Digne Mère Marie le Bail*, p. 112.

64 Eulalie Hamilton was born in St Louis in 1805 and took the name Regis in religious life. She assisted Mother Duchesne on her deathbed. She was superior in many houses and died in 1885.

65 For an account of this trio see "Mère Josephine Augustin" in *Religieuses du Sacré Cœur*, vol. II, p. 219 ff. Mary Mahony died as a novice at the Villa Lante; Madeleine Sophie Barat, then ill herself, climbed a long flight of stairs on her knees to visit her.

66 Maria Zaepffel was one of the very young nuns with whom Mother Barat formed a bond of special friendship in her old age.

67 *Vie de la Digne Mère Maria Zaepffel*, p. 92.

68 *Ibid.* p. 401.

69 *Let. An.* 1908–1910. This account of the life of Violet Ashton-Case was written by Mother Stuart herself.

70 *Life and Letters*, p. 155.

71 Sept 11, 1904. *Circulaires*-Digby, p. 184.

72 *The Society of the Sacred Heart*, p. 47.

73 *Let. An.* 1917–1919. Betzy Nieuwland was born in Antwerp of a Dutch family in 1847. As vicar of Belgium from 1897 to 1915 she not only opened refuges but sent many Belgium nuns to England during the war. She died in 1917.

74 *Let. An.* 1940–1945, Supplement. Philomena Blount was born in England in 1850. After being vicar of the temporary vicariate from 1907 to 1911 she was superior in various houses until 1934. She died in a war refuge in 1945.

75 Maud Monahan, RSCJ. *Life of Reverend Mother Rose Thunder* (Roehampton, 1930; French version of the same date), and *Let. An.* 1926–1930, Supplement. Rose Thunder was born in Ireland in 1852 and was vicar of England-Ireland from 1911 to 1923. She carried out many apostolic enterprises: night classes and educational experiments. She died in 1926.

76 *Let. An.* 1931–1933. Caroline Lavialle was born in France in 1854; she was vicar of northern Italy from 1907 to 1915, then helped with the reopening of the French Houses. She died in 1932.

77 *Let. An.* 1910–1912. Marie de Cléry was born in Metz and brought up in Algiers. She was vicar of Belgium from 1889 to 1897, then of Spain from 1897 to 1906. She gave life to the *oeuvres populaires* and died in 1911.

78 *Let. An.* 1932–1937, Supplement. Carmen Modet was born in Spain in 1865, and was vicar from 1904 until her death in 1935.

79 *Let. An.* 1917–1918. Anna Bogaers was born in 1841 in Holland, where she was vicar from 1904 to 1907. She was alert to the social needs of her country and died in 1919.

80 *Let. An.* 1929–1931. Marie-Anne Schaffgotch was born in Berlin in 1856. She was vicar of Austria from 1897 to 1905, and also served in Hungary, Germany, Spain and France. She worked with the alumnae in Vienna and died in 1930.

81 *Vie de la Révérende Mère Helen Rumbold* (Roehampton, 1925). She was born in England in 1847. After her missionary career she was assistant general from 1915 until her death in 1921.

82 *Let. An.* 1932–1937, Supplement. Hélène de Chamerlat was born in France in 1847. After the expulsions she went to Spain and then to Cairo where she was vicar of Egypt-Malta from 1921 to 1926. The account of her life is a study in the principle of missionary accommodation. She died in 1932.

83 *Let. An.* 1931–1934, Supplement. Mary Moran was born in Dublin in 1851. She was vicar of Canada from 1901 to 1908 and then of New York until 1932. She died in 1934.

84 *Let. An.* 1905–1907. Mary Burke was born in Ireland in 1847. She worked at Buenos Aires, then at Kenwood as mistress of novices. She was vicar of Chicago-Maryville from 1857 to 1902, and was then named vicar of Canada but was too ill to take office. She died in Bilbao in 1904.

85 *Let. An.* 1929–1930. Victorine Cooreman was born in Belgium in 1850. She worked in Italy before going to Louisiana as vicar from 1903 to 1910. She then went to Egypt and back to Belgium where she died in 1926.

86 *Let. An.* 1947–1950, Supplement. Charlotte Lewis was born in Detroit in 1857. She was vicar of the Chicago province from 1901 to 1907, then superior in many Canadian and American houses. She died in 1947.

87 *Let. An.* 1927–1929. Hedwige de Cauna was born in France in 1858. She served in Mexico, Cuba and Peru, and was then vicar of the Antilles from 1911 to 1925. She died in 1928.

88 *Let. An.* 1942–1943, Supplement. Sophie Lalande was born in France in 1854. She was superior in several French houses before the expulsions.

89 *Let. An.* 1924–1926, Supplement. Mary Jackson was born in England in 1853.

90 *Let. An.* 1915–1917. Isabel Batista was born in Cuba in 1862. She was vicar of Chile-Peru from 1908 to 1910. She then worked in Spain, Puerto Rico and Cuba, and died in 1917.

91 *Let. An.* 1932–1937, Supplement. Guadalupe Bofarrul was born in Spain in 1850. She served in Spain, Colombia and Puerto Rico and died in 1932.

92 *Let. An.* 1954–1958. Maud Dunn was born in Canada of an Irish family in 1868 and was educated in England. She served as mistress general and superior in Colombia and the Antilles where she died in 1956.

93 *Let. An.* 1915–1917. Brigid Heydon was born in Ireland in 1862. She served in England, Ireland and Australia before going to Japan where she died in 1916.

94 *Mother Mabel Digby*, p. 358.

95 Jan 13, 1897, *Circulaires*-Digby, p. 57.

96 AGSC, Série *Conseils Généraux*.

97 *Ibid.*

98 *Ibid.*

99 AGSC, Série *Conseils Généraux*.

100 Callan, RSCJ, *The Society of the Sacred Heart in North America*, p. 762.

101 *Let. An.* 1932–1937, Supplement. Marguerite Lesage was born in France in 1862. She was charged with the studies of Conflans and of the probation at Rivoli, was superior in many houses and died in 1935.

102 *Let. An.* 1932–1937, Supplement, p. 99.

103 *Let. An.* 1923–1925, Supplement. Marie-Thérèse Duval was born in France in 1865. She was in charge of the advanced juniorate. She was vicar of Belgium from 1919 until her death in 1924. She wrote *L'Histoire Abrégée de la Société du Sacré Coeur* during the war.

104 *Let. An.* 1931–1934, Supplement. Marie Lesage was born in France in 1866. She was mistress of studies and of the juniorate in many places, and in 1922 supervised the revision of the Plan of Studies. She died as superior of Joigny in 1933.

105 Aug 13, 1912. *Circulaires*-Stuart, p. 38.

106 Callan, *Society of the Sacred Heart in North America*, p. 760.

107 Sept 11, 1904. *Circulaires*-Digby, p. 187.

108 Nov 1, 1913. *Circularies*-Stuart, p. 72.

109 *Society of the Sacred Heart*, p. 51.

110 Unpublished *Conferences for a Time of Vacation*.

111 AGSC, Série *Conseils Généraux*.

112 *Ibid.*

113 *Life and Letters*, p. 65.

114 *Vie de la Révérende Mère Helen Rumbold*, p. 67.

115 Unpublished compilation.

Chapter 6, *Expansion 1915 – 1946*

1 Marie Barbaren, RSCJ, *Vie de la Très Révérende Mère Marie de Loë (Rome: Maison Mère, 1932), and M. K. Richardson, RSCJ, Life of our Venerated Mother Marie dè Loë* (no imprint). Brief quotations without references are taken from Barbaren.

2 AGSC, Série *Conseils Généraux*. The Council elected as assistants general Jeanne de Lavigerie, Catherine de Montalembert, Helen Rumbold and Césarine Borget who remained treasurer general. Marie le Bail remained secretary general.

3 Mar 10, 1915. *Lettres Circulaires de notre Très Révérende Mère Marie de Loë* pour Toutes les Religieuses (Roehampton, 1929), p. 22. Referred to hereafter as *Circulaires*-de Loë.

4 *Vie de la Très Révérende Mère Marie de Loë*, p. 24.

5 Raffael Merry del Val was born in London in 1865. He was secretary of state under Pius X and Protector of the Society from 1914 until his death in 1930.

6 *Let. An.* 1931–1934, Supplement. Marie Guibert was born in France in 1862. She was in charge of the juniorate and the noviceship, then mistress of probation at Jette and Rome from 1909 to 1918. She was then superior in various French houses until her death in 1930.

7 Mar 10, 1915, *Circulaires*-de Loë, p. 25.

8 *Vie de Notre très Révérende Mère Marie de Loë*, p. 389.

9 *Histoire Abrégée*, p. 422.

10 The Council elected as assistants general Jeanne de Lavigerie, Jeanne Dupont, Elizabeth Lamb and Manuela Vicente, as treasurer general Henriette de Montlivault, as secretary general Juliette Clerc de Landresse.

11 Nov 7, 1922. *Circulaires*-de Loë, p. 117.

12 *Un Appel à l'Amour* (Toulouse: Apostolat de la Prière, 1944), English version: *The Way of Divine Love* (Westminster: Newman Press, 1949).

13 *Un Appel à l'Amour*, p. 565.

14 Jan 18, 1924. *Circulaires*-de Loë, p. 145.

15 Dec 1918. *Circulaires*-de Loë, p. 60.

16 Enid Barham, *Some Chosen Sisters* (New York: Manhattanville College, 1947). Rose Coyne, born in Albany in 1887, entered the Society as a coadjutrix sister despite ill health. She spent her religious life at Manhattanville where she developed consumption. She was instantaneously cured during the night of May 24–25, 1919, following a novena made to Blessed Madeleine Sophie on the inspiration of Mother Rosalie Hill. Sister Coyne was an active worker from then until her death in 1945.

17 Jan 18, 1925. *Circulaires*-de Loë, p. 184.

18 Nov 16, 1916. *Ibid.*, p. 328.

19 Nov. 16, 1916, *Ibid*, p. 46.

20 Aug 1926. *Ibid.* p. 294.

21 Nov 9, 1928. *Lettres Circulaires de notre Très Révérende Mère Maria Manuela Vicente*, pour Toutes les Religieuses de la Société (Rome: Maison Mère, 1947), p. 15. Referred to hereafter as *Circulaires*-Vicente.

22 Louise de Morineau, RSCJ, *Vie de la Très Révérende Mère Manuela Vicente* (Rome: Maison Mère, 1950). Brief quotations without references are taken from this source.

23 The Council elected as assistants general Jeanne de Lavigerie, Jeanne Dupont, Giulia Datti and Mary Guerin. Henriette de Montlivault remained treasurer general and Juliette de Landresse secretary general.

24 *Vie de la Très Révérende Mère Manuela Vicente*, p. 32.

25 Eugenio Pacelli was born in Rome in 1876. He served as diplomat in Germany and papal secretary of state. He was Protector of the Society from 1930 until his elevation to the papacy in 1939.

26 Jan 13, 1933. *Circulaires*-Vicente, p. 96.

27 June 29, 1939. *Ibid.* p. 202.

28 July 7, 1934. *Ibid.* p. 231.

29 The Council elected as assistants general Jeanne Dupont, Giulia Datti, Constance Perry and Marie Symon, as secretary general Germaine Mignot, while Henriette de Montlivault remained treasurer general.

30 *Vie de la Très Révérende Mère Manuela Vicente*, p. 349.

31 *Ibid.* See Chapter VI, "Vie Spirituelle," p. 335 ff.

32 *Let. An.* 1932–1937, Supplement. Maria Galindo was born in Spain in 1865. She was in charge of the juniorate and superior in many houses. She died in 1937.

33 *Let. An.* 1956–1961, Supplement. Glorio Elio was born in Spain in 1883. She was mistress of studies and superior, and died in 1960.

34 *Vie de la Très Révérende Mère Manuela Vicente*, p. 315.

35 Luigi Maglioni was born in 1877. He worked for the League of Nations and was Nuncio to Paris, then papal secretary of state. He was protector of the Society from 1939 until his death in 1944.

36 Señor Bahamonde of Puerto Rico was cured of a fatal liver condition as his family prayed to Philippine Duchesne.

37 Carolina Indelli, RSCJ, an Italian, was cured of ear trouble through the intercession of Philippine Duchesne.

38 Margaret Williams, RSCJ. *The Sacred Heart in the Life of the Church* (Sheed and Ward, 1957), p. 192.

39 Louise Vétillard, RSCJ, *Vie de la Révérende Mère Giulia Datti* (Rome: Maison Mère, 1956). She was born in Frascati in 1868.

40 Jan 18, 1946. *Circulaires*-Vicente, p. 236.

41 Dec 8, 1932. *Ibid.* p. 93.

42 *Vie de la Révérende Mère Jeanne Dupont* (Rome: Maison Mère, 1940). She was born in Douai in 1855.

43 *Ibid.* p. 127.

44 Aug 15, 1941. *Circulaires*-Vicente, p. 230.

45 *Vie de la Révérende Mère Marie Symon* (Rome: Maison Mère, 1948). She was born in 1871.

46 *Ibid.* p. 135.

47 *Ibid.* p. 196, 255.

48 Marie Barbaren, RSCJ, *Vie de la Révérende Mère Elizabeth Lamb* (Rome: Maison Mère, 1935). She was born in London in 1871.

49 *Let. An.* 1934–1937, Supplement. Mary Guerin was born in Chicago in 1876. She was vicar of the Chicago vicariate from 1925 to 1929. She died in 1945.

50 *Vie de la Révérende Mère Constance Perry* (Rome: Maison Mère, 1957). She was born in Staffordshire in 1869, and was educated at Jette, and by wide travel.

51 *Let. An.* 1947–1952, Supplement. Jeanne de Traverse was born in France in 1867. She served in the United States, Mexico, France and Italy, and died in 1951.

52 *Vie de la Révérende Mère Henriette de Montlivault* (Rome: Maison Mère, 1953). She was born in France in 1865.

53 Feb 1, 1949. *Lettres Circulaires de la Très Révérende Mère Marie-Thérèse de Lescure* (Rome: Maison Mère, 1958), p. 49. Referred to hereafter as *Circulaires*-de Lescure.

54 *Let. An.* 1947–1952, Supplement. Juliette de Landresse was born in France in 1858 and began her long career in the secretariate immediately after her profession.

55 *Let. An.* 1946–1948. Germaine Mignot was born in France in 1895.

56 *Let. An.* 1946–1948. Antoinette du Passage was born in France in 1872.

57 *Let. An.* 1947–1952, Supplement, p. 177.

58 AGSC, Série *Conseils Généraux.*

59 *Vie de la Très Révérende Mère Manuela Vicente*, p. 260.

60 Jan 20, 1939, *Circulaires*-Vicente, p. 195.

61 *Let. An.* 1926–1930, Supplement. Marthe de Lavergne was born in France in 1858. She was mistress of novices and of probation, then vicar of the Avigliana-France vicariate from 1915 until her death in 1929.

62 *Let. An.* 1947–1950, Supplement. Louise de Neuville was born in France in 1861. She was vicar of northern France from 1922 to 1940, and died in 1951.

63 *Let. An.* 1947–1950, Supplement. Margaret Walsh was born in Ireland in 1864. She was vicar of the Irish-Scottish vicariate from its formation in 1918 until her death in 1946.

64 *Let. An.* 1954–1958, Supplement. Mathilde de Capitain was born in 1867 in Constantinople of a German family. She served in Holland, Austria, Belgium and France, and was then vicar of the new German-Dutch vicariate from 1920 to 1935. She died in 1953.

65 *Let. An.* 1958–1961, Supplement. Marguerite Nagant was born in Holland in 1853 of a Belgian family. She was vicar of the German-Dutch vicariate from 1935 to 1950. She died in 1960.

66 *Let. An.* 1958–1961, Supplement. Ana Maria Cavanillas was born in Spain in 1871. She governed the Sarria vicariate from 1917 to 1926, then went to South America as vicar of Brazil-Argentina-Uruguay until 1953. She died in 1961.

67 Pilar Alcibar was born in Spain in 1877 and governed the Sarria vicariate from 1926 to 1959. During the Civil War she barely escaped execution by guerrillas, and died in 1961.

68 Carmen Modet rebuilt the Chamartin that she had seen burned.

69 Maria de la Cavada was born in Spain in 1886. She was vicar in Seville from 1935 to 1953, then went to Brazil as vicar until her death in 1966.

70 *Let. An.* 1919–1921. Laura Theodoli was born in Rome in 1875. She governed the Italian vicariate from 1915 to 1919 and died the following year.

71 *Let. An.* 1958–1961, Supplement. Eleanora Boncompagni was born in Rome in 1885. She was vicar of Italy from 1928 until her death in 1955.

72 Winifred Archer-Shee was born in 1882 and was vicar of England from 1930 to 1946. She died in 1972.

73 *Let. An.* 1932–1937, Supplement. Maria de Waldstein was born in Austria in 1885. She governed the Austrian vicariate from 1913 until her death in 1934.

74 Anna Komstedt was born in 1880, and was vicar of Austria from 1934 until her death in 1952.

75 Zofia Gunther was born in 1889. She was vicar of Poland from 1936 to 1963. She died in 1966.

76 *Let. An.* 1935–1944, Supplement. Mary Reid was born in St Louis in 1861. She was vicar of St Louis from 1911 until her death in 1937.

77 *Let. An.* 1935–1944, Supplement. Mathilde Mouton was born in Louisiana in 1893. She was vicar of St Louis from 1937 until her death in 1944.

She sponsored the second exhumation of the body of Philippine Duchesne in 1939.

78 *Let. An.* 1939–1947, Supplement. Jane Fox was born in St Louis in 1859. She was vicar of Chicago from 1909 to 1925, and died in 1936.

79 Unpublished manuscript life. Rosalie Hill was born in Maryland in 1878. She became vicar of the Chicago vicariate in 1929 and took charge of the California province when it became autonomous in 1958. She retired in 1961 and died in 1964.

80 *Let. An.* 1954–1958, Supplement. Corinne Clapin, a French Canadian, was born in 1865. She was vicar of Canada from 1925 to 1937 and died in 1956.

81 *Let. An.* 1958–1961, Supplement. Bertha Padberg was born in St Louis in 1882. She was vicar of Canada from 1937 until her death in 1958.

82 *Let. An.* 1935–1945, Supplement. Alix de Kéréver was born in Britanny in 1871. She was vicar of Australia-New Zealand from 1936 until her death in 1942.

83 *Let. An.* 1947–1950, Supplement. Mathilde Jimenez was born in Havana in 1864, and married Señor Moreyra. After his death she entered the Society and became vicar of the Antilles-Colombia vicariate from 1925 to 1935. She died in 1950.

84 *Let An.* 1961–1963, Supplement. Maria Tamariz was born in Mexico in 1878. She was vicar of the Antilles-Colombia vicariate from 1934 to 1954 and died in 1962.

85 *Let. An.* 1961–1963, Supplement. Concepcion Peredo was born in Guadalajara in 1876. She was mistress general in Mexico during the government strangle-hold on education. She was vicar from 1938 to 1954 and died in 1956.

86 *Let. An.* 1939–1947, Supplement. Mathilde Bouscayrol was born in France in 1864. She became vicar of Chile-Peru from 1910 to 1933 and died in 1943.

87 Carmen Cubero was born in Spain in 1882. She was vicar of Chile-Peru from 1933 to 1952; in that year the two countries became separate provinces and she continued to govern Peru until her death in 1965.

88 *Vie de la Révérende Mère Manuela Vicente*, p. 317.

89 Clare Percy-Dove, *Mother Mary Sheldon* (Sydney, n. d.). She was born in Australia in 1876, and was superior at Melbourne and Auckland before going to Japan.

90 *Let. An.* 1954–1958, Supplement. Hermanna Meyer was born in Germany in 1877 and came to Tokyo in 1909. She died in 1955. Her brother Rupert has become known as "the saint of Munich."

91 *Mother Mary Sheldon*, p. 47.

92 *Decree on Pagan Rites.*

93 *Let. An.* 1939–1947, Supplement. Conchita Nourry was born in 1881 of a French family in Spain. She served in Australia and Tokyo before going to Shanghai where she died in 1945.

94 *Mother Mary Sheldon*, p. 102.

95 *Evangelii Praecones.*

96 Fanny Braun was born in Brussels in 1879. She headed the mission to the

Congo where she founded four houses before returning to Jette where she died in 1967.

97 *Vie de la Révérende Mère Marie Symon*, p. 164.

98 Sara Grant, RSCJ, *Life of Mother Catherine Andersson* (Bombay: St Paul's Press, 1962) and *Let. An.* 1958–1961, Supplement. She was born in England in 1887 and received a cosmopolitan education. She became an outstanding educator before making the foundation in Bombay.

99 Silver Jubilee Booklet of Sophia College.

100 *Let. An.* 1953–1955, Maria Theresa Dupouy was born in Spain in 1873. After fulfilling her extraordinary mission she died at San Sebastian in 1953.

101 *Let. An.* 1937–1940, Supplement. Marthe de Sieyes was born in France in 1883, and became mistress of novices at Marmoutier. When the noviceship was evacuated because of the war she died on the way to Montpellier in 1940.

102 Quoted in *Spirit and Plan of Studies*.

103 *Plan of Studies*, 1852.

104 *Constitutions*, Chap. III, par. III.

105 *Vie de la Très Révérende Mère Marie de Loë*, p. 268.

106 *Vie de la Très Révérende Mère Manuela Vicente*, p. 192.

107 Odette Biolley, RSCJ, *Une Ame d'Elite, Mère Hélène de Burlet* (Déclée de Brower, 1964).

108 *Ibid.* p. 88.

109 Sarah Brownson was born in 1870. She directed the growth of the studies at Manhattanville College from 1916 to 1926 and died in 1952.

110 *God's Middlemen*, ed. Loretta Corcoran, RSCJ (New York: Manhattanville College, 1948) and *Let. An.* 1939–1947, Supplement. Grace Dammann was born in Baltimore in 1872. She was president of Manhattanville College from 1933 until her sudden death in 1944.

111 *Tower Postscript*, July, 1933.

112 Bee Hargrove, "Georgia Stevens" in *Two Manhattanville Nuns* (New York: Manhattanville College, n. d.). She was born in 1870. She directed the Pius X School of Liturgical Music from 1916 until her sudden death in 1945.

113 *Life and Letters*, p. 101.

114 Daniel Rops, *Un Combat pour Dieu*, 1870–1939; vol. VI of *Eglise des Révolutions* (Paris: Librairie Arthème Fayard), p. 115.

115 *Let. An.* 1963–1965. Mary Spallen was born in Philadelphia in 1869. She directed the Barat Guild from 1921 to 1953, and died in 1958.

116 *Vie de la Très Révérende Mère Manuela Vicente*, p. 159.

117 *Enfants de Marie du Sacré Coeur*, 2 vols. (Paris: de Gigord, 1932).

118 George Ganss, SJ., "The Mystical Body and Devotion to the Sacred Heart", *Ecclesiastical Review* (XCVII:321).

119 Margaret Williams, RSCJ, *Mother Gertrude Bodkin* (no imprint). She was born in Ireland in 1875. She came to the United States as mistress of novices then as vicar of the New York vicariate from 1933 to 1953, and died in 1966.

120 *Ibid.*, p. 139.

121 *Ibid.* p. 145.

1 Marguerite du Merle, RSCJ, *Vie de la Très Révérende Mère Marie-Thérèse de Lescure* (Rome: Maison Mère, 1961). Brief quotations without reference are taken from this source.

2 *Ibid.* p. 24.

3 *Ibid.* p. 38.

4 *Let. An.* 1940–1942. Antoinette de Girval was born in France in 1865. After the expulsions she went to Spain and came to Poitiers as mistress of novices in 1917. She died in 1940.

5 *Vie de la Très Révérende Mère Marie-Thérèse de Lescure*, p. 95.

6 *Ibid.* p. 143.

7 This book was soon translated into many languages.

8 AGSC, Série *Conseils Généraux.*

9 The Council elected as assistants general Giulia Datti, Elizabeth Zurstrassen, Elena Yturralde and Ursula Benziger. Henriette de Montlivault remained treasurer general and Germaine Mignot secretary general.

10 Oct 29, 1946, *Circulaires*-de Lescure, p. 9.

11 AGSC, Série *Conseils Généraux.*

12 *Mère Elizabeth Zurstrassen, à travers sa Vie, à travers sa Correspondance* (no imprint), p. 23.

13 Clemente Micara was Protector of the Society from 1944 to 1964. The office was then discontinued.

14 Jan 25, 1949, *Circulaires*-de Lescure, p. 13.

15 Notes of Mother de Lescure's visit to Manhattanville College, 1953.

16 *Vie de la Très Révérende Mère Marie-Thérèse de Lescure*, p. 195.

17 Sept 14, 1949, *Circulaires*-de Lescure, p. 67.

18 *Vie de la Très Révérende Mère Marie-Thérèse de Lescure*, p. 252.

19 The Council elected as assistants general Giula Datti, Elizabeth Zurstrassen, Elena Yturralde and Ursula Benziger, as treasurer general Marguerite de James, as secretary general Françoise de Lambilly.

20 June 6, 1952, *Circulaires*-de Lescure, p. 107.

21 AGSC, Série *Conseils Généraux.*

22 Nov 13, 1952, *Circulaires*-de Lescure, p. 114.

23 *Ibid.* p. 120.

24 *Ibid.* p. 121.

25 *Ibid.* p. 161.

26 *Mère Elizabeth Zurstrassen, à travers sa Vie, à travers sa Correspondance.* She was born in Belgium in 1888. She became mistress of novices at Jette in 1926 and vicar of Belgium in 1933. She was assistant general and mistress of probation from 1945 to 1964, and died in 1971.

27 Ursula Benziger was born in New York in 1885. She was superior at Maplehurst and Manhattanville, then assistant general from 1946 to 1965. She died in 1972.

28 Louise Vétillard, RSCJ, *Vie de la Révérende Mère Elena Yturralde* (Rome: Maison Mère, 1933). She was born in Spain in 1897. She was superior of

several Spanish houses and assistant general from 1946 until her death in 1958.

29 Nov 13, 1952, *Circulaires*-de Lescure, p. 122.

30 *Ibid.* p. 121.

31 *Vie de la Très Révérende Mère Marie-Thérèse de Lescure*, p. 316.

32 *Mother Gertrude Bodkin*, p. 91.

33 *Mother Mary Sheldon*, p. 108.

34 Jan 29, 1948. *Circulaires*-de Lescure, p. 220.

35 *Let. An.* 1959–1961, Supplement. Hildegarde Gutzwiller was born in Switzerland in 1897. She upheld the houses in Budapest during the Russian siege until the confiscation in 1950. She died in Germany in 1957.

36 *Mitte Me*, VI:67.

37 *Décrets des Congrégations Générales* (Rome:Maison Mère, 1953), Part II, p. 155.

38 *Ibid.* p. 161.

39 Nov 13, 1952. *Circulaires*-de Lescure, p. 115.

40 *Life at the Sacred Heart* (White Plains, 1953).

41 *Spirit and Plan*, p. 239.

42 *Ibid.* p. 280.

43 *Ibid.*

44 *Mother Gertrude Bodkin*, p. 100.

45 O'Flaherty, *op. cit.* p. 17.

46 AGSC, Série *Conseils Généraux*.

47 Nov 29, 1953. *Circulaires*-de Lescure, p. 132.

48 *Vie de la Très Révérende Mère Marie-Thérèse de Lescure*, p. 228.

49 Oct 29, 1949. *Circulaires*-de Lescure, p. 222.

50 *Règle des Affiliées*, 1953.

51 *Vie de la Très Révérende Mère Marie-Thérèse de Lescure*, p. 268.

52 *Ibid.* p. 228.

53 Mar 5, 1948. *Circulaires*-de Lescure, p. 32.

54 François Charmot, SJ, *The Sacred Heart in Modern Life*, tr. K. Sullivan, RSCJ (New York: Kenedy, 1952), p. 147.

55 *Etudes Carmélitaines* (Desclée, 1950).

56 *Vie de la Très Révérende Mère Marie-Thérèse de Lescure*, p. 290.

57 June 16, 1950. *Circulaires*-de Lescure, p. 69.

58 Jan 2, 1947. *Ibid.* p. 12.

59 Jan 13, 1947. *Ibid.* p. 18.

60 Jan 13, 1948. *Ibid.* p. 24.

61 Apr 16, 1948. *Ibid.* p. 34.

62 Jan 12, 1951. *Ibid.* p. 224.

63 Jan 13, 1949. *Ibid.* p. 40.

64 Nov 10, 1949. *Ibid.* p. 57.

65 July 16, 1949. *Ibid.* p. 52.

66 Dec 8, 1951. *Ibid.* p. 98.

67 Nov 29, 1953. *Ibid.* p. 130.

68 June 25, 1954. *Ibid.* p. 138.

69 Dec 6, 1954. *Ibid.* p. 163.

70 June 17, 1955. *Ibid.* p. 176.

71 May 25, 1956. *Ibid.* p. 187.

72 Nov 1, 1950. *Ibid.* p. 150.
73 *Vie de la Très Révérende Mère Marie-Thérèse de Lescure*, p. 130.
74 Aug 22, 1957. *Circulaires*-de Lescure, p. 215.
75 *Chapter 1970*, p. 7.

Chapter 8, *Renewal 1957 – 1970*

1 The Council elected as assistants general Elizabeth Zurstrassen, Ursula Benziger, Josefa Bultó and Emilia Lurani, as treasurer general Marguerite de James, as secretary general Françoise de Lambilly.
2 AGSC, Série *Conseils Généraux*.
3 June 29, 1959. *Lettres Circulaires de notre Très Révérende Mère Sabine de Valon* (Rome: Maison Mère, 1967), p. 35. Referred to hereafter as *Circulaires*-de Valon.
4 *Directives et Décisions de la 25ième Congrégation Générale* (Rome: Maison Mère, 1958), p. 38.
5 *Directives et Décisions de la 26ième Chapitre Général* (Rome: Maison Mère, 1964), p. 47.
6 AMASC Bulletin, February, 1975.
7 Jan 6, 1960. *Circulaires*-de Valon, p. 45.
8 Jan 10, 1964. *Ibid.* p. 138.
9 Feb 2, 1961. *Ibid.* p. 74.
10 *Mitte Me* VI:28.
11 July 12, 1961. *Circulaires*-de Valon, p. 77.
12 *Mitte Me* I:1.
13 *Ibid.* III:62.
14 Dec 13, 1961. *Circulaires*-de Valon, p. 87.
15 *Mitte Me* II:26.
16 *Documents*, p. 594.
17 *Directives* 1964, p. 49.
18 *Ibid.* p. 50.
19 *Mitte Me* VII:3.
20 *Ibid.*
21 *Ibid.* IX:45.
22 Apr 20, 1969. *Ibid.* IX:57.
23 *Ibid.* p. 54.
24 *Ibid.* X:1.
25 *Ibid.* X:2, by Henry Habid Ayrout, SJ.
26 *Ibid.* X:6.
27 Ps 33:11.
28 Jn 16:33.
29 *Il Giornale Dell'Anima* (Rome: Di Storia et Letteratura, 1964) p. 384.

30 *Documents*, p. 703.

31 *Ibid.* p. 5.

32 *Ibid.* p. 204.

33 *Ibid.* p. 201.

34 *Time* Report, 1965, p. 89.

35 May 15, 1962. *Circulaires*-de Valon, p. 99, 105, 107.

36 July 5, 1963. *Ibid.* p. 123.

37 Jan 10, 1964. *Ibid.* p. 129, 132.

38 *Documents*, p. 73 ff.

39 *Ibid.* p. 468.

40 Dec 15, 1964. *Circulaires*-de Valon, p. 153.

41 *Mère Elizabeth Zurstrassen*, p. 38.

42 *Directives 1964,* p. 16.

43 *Ibid.* p. 24.

44 *Society of the Sacred Heart*, p. 26.

45 Dec 15, 1964. *Circulaires*-de Valon, p. 159.

46 *Directives 1964*, p. 28.

47 Dec 15, 1964. *Circulaires*-de Valon, p. 156.

48 *Directives 1964*, p. 65.

49 May 15, 1964. *Circulaires*-de Valon, p. 140.

50 *Mère Elizabeth Zurstrassen*, p. 26.

51 *Documents*, p. 733.

52 Jan 8, 1966. *Circulaires*-de Valon, p. 185.

53 Special Chapter, 1967. *Orientations ad Experimentum*, p. 9. Referred to hereafter as *Orientations*.

54 *Ibid.* p. 90.

55 *Ibid.* p. 14.

56 *Ibid.* p. 21.

57 *Ibid.* pp. 61–65, abridged.

58 July 7, 1968. Circular Letter, Bultó.

59 *Ibid.*

60 Sharon Karam, RSCJ, Sesquicentennial Booklet, 1818–1968: *Philippine Duchesne, Frontier Missionary*.

61 p. 64.

62 In Poona a community of religious of the Sacred Heart joined with some Anglican Sisters of Saint Mary the Virgin.

63 The term 'fraternity' is often used for small groups within larger ones.

64 *Documents*, p. 467.

65 Jan 2, 1928. *Circulaires*-de Loë, p. 315.

66 *Orientations*, p. 73.

67 June 29, 1959. *Circulaires*-de Valon, p. 42.

68 Jan 6, 1960. *Ibid.* p, 46.

69 O'Flaherty, *op. cit.* p. 11.

70 Sept 28, 1968. Circular Letter, Bultó.

71 Mar 14, 1970. *Ibid.*

72 May 20, 1970. *Ibid.*

73 *Société du Sacré Coeur: Etude sur les Provinces*, p. 196.

74 *Ibid.*

75 *Ibid.* p. 202.
76 *Chapter 1970*, p. 2.
77 AGSC, Série *Conseils Généraux*.
78 *Chapter 1970*, p. 7.
79 *Ibid.* p. 8.
80 *Ibid.* p. 9.
81 *Ibid.* p. 10.
82 *Ibid.* p. 11.
83 *Ibid.* p. 12.
84 *Ibid.* p. 13.
85 *Ibid.* p. 7.
86 *Ibid.* p. 18.
87 *Ibid.* p. 19.
88 *Ibid.* p. 20.
89 *Ibid.* p. 26.
90 *Ibid.* p. 28.
91 *Ibid.* p. 30.
92 *Ibid.* p. 33.
93 *Ibid.* p. 44.
94 *Ibid.* p. 1.
95 *Ibid.* p. 44.

Inwardness for the Outgoing

1 *Conférences* I:260.
2 May 25, 1958. *Circulaires*-de Valon, p. 23.
3 Conference given by Barbara Hogg RSCJ.
4 Joan Timmerman, *Not Yet my Season* (New York: Vantage Press, 1909), p. 47.
5 Margaret Williams, RSCJ, "Inwardness for the Outgoing," *The Way* (Supplement no. 7, Jun, 1969).

Chapter 9, *Rooted in Prayer*

1 Cahier II:323.
2 *Histoire Abrégée*, p. 16.
3 Maria Escartin, RSCJ, *El Misterio de Cristo en la Spiritualidad de Santa Magdalena Sofia Barat* (Regina Mundi, Rome, 1966) and Mary Wolff-Salin,

RSCJ, *Prayer according to Saint Madeleine Sophie Barat* (University of Louvain, 1971) and *A Question in the Theology of Religious Life* (University of Louvain, 1975).

4 R. Aubert, *Histoire de l'Eglise* (Paris, 1912), XXII:463.

5 Dec 2, 1832. *Conférences* I:159.

6 Jan 29, 1815. *Let. Ch.* I:187.

7 AGSC, Série *Papiers Barat.*

8 *Society of the Sacred Heart*, p. 56.

9 Aug 1844, *Conférences* I:368.

10 1834. *Conférences* I:258.

11 Oct 15, 1835. *Conférences* I:270.

12 Perdrau I:75.

13 Alexandre Brou, SJ, *Travail et Prière, Sainte Madeleine Sophie* ((Paris: Beauchesne, 1926), p. 21.

14 Process of Beatification, Congregatione Sacrorum Rituum, *Romae seu Parisien, Beatificationis Servae Dei Magdalena Sophia Barat* (Rome: Typis Fratrum Monaldi, 1879).

15 June 27, 1841, *Let. Ch.* II:143.

16 Oct 1806. *Souvenirs du Premier Noviciat de Poitiers*, p. 3.

17 July 10, 1826. *Let. Ch.* II:143.

18 *Summary of the Constitutions*, par. IV.

19 Jn XVII:24.

20 *Summary of the Constitutions*, par. I.

21 *Constitutions*, Part IV, par. XXXI.

22 *Plan Abrégé*, par. IV.

23 *Summa Theologica* II–2, Q. 182, Art. I ad. 3.

24 *Society of the Sacred Heart*, p. 65.

25 Cahier II:412.

26 Maria Josefa Escartin, RSCJ, *El Misterio de Cristo en la Spiritualidad de Santa Magalena Sofia Barat*, p. 159.

27 Cahier I:17.

28 *Ibid.* p. 195.

29 *Ibid.* p. 25.

30 Mar 22, 1853. *Let. Sup.* II:159.

31 *Summa Theologica*, IIa, IIae, Q. LIV.

32 Cahier II:392.

33 May 3, 1825. *Let. Sup.* I:11.

34 Sept 24, 1816. *Let. Ch.* I:200.

35 Mar 17, 1817. *Let. Ch.* I:215.

36 Nov 15, 1819. *Let. Ch.* I:365.

37 June 2, 1827. *Conférences* I:124.

38 May 22, 1830, *Conférences* I:124.

39 July 14, 1826. *Let. Ch.* II:145.

40 Dec 7, 1830. *Let. Ch.* II:232.

41 Feb 13, 1842. *Let. Sup.* I:158.

42 Cahier II:500.

43 *Ibid.* p. 379.

44 *Ibid.* p. 387.

45 Grandmaison, p. 111.
46 Dec 29, 1839. Baunard II:196.
47 Perdrau I:67.
48 Aug 22, 1847. *Let. Ch.* III:277.
49 Feb 9, 1851. *Let. Ch.* IV:14.
50 Jan 4, 1842. *Let. Sup.* I:151.
51 Apr 12, 1843. *Conférences* I:338.
52 Perdrau I:427.
53 Nov 10, 1850. *Let. Ch.* III:398.
54 Cahier I:646.
55 Brou, p. 137 f
56 Perdrau II:31.
57 *Society of the Sacred Heart*, p. 62.
58 June 2, 1827. *Conférences* I:18.
59 Nov 27, 1850. *Let. Sup.* II:12.
60 Nov 29, 1834. Callan, *Rose Philippine Duchesne*, p. 570.
61 Mar 23, 1823. *Let. Ch.* I:156.
62 Cahier II:568.
63 Mar 29, 1832. *Let. Sup.* I:80.
64 Brou, p. 181.
65 Nov 4, 1854. *Let. Sup.* II:53.
66 Apr 2, 1833. *Let. Sup.* II:295.
67 Cahier II:615.
68 Aug 1844. *Conférences* I:367.
69 June 9, 1864. *Lettres aux Mères en Charge*, p. 166.
70 *Let. An.* 1870–1872, p. XVII.
71 Aug 22, 1832. *Let. Ch.* II:339.
72 June 26, 1852. *Let. Sup.* III:222.
73 Jan 12, 1857. *Let. Sup.* II:112.
74 May 31, 1858. *Let. Sup.* IV:44.
75 Mar 1856. *Let. Ch.* IV:249.
76 AGSC, Série *Papiers Barat*.
77 July 7, 1841. *Let. Sup.* III:84.
78 Oct 18, 1850. *Let. Ch.* III:394.
79 Acts 16:7.
80 Aug 19, 1846. *Let. Sup.* I:252.
81 AGSC, *Commentaire sur la Règle des Soeurs Coadjutrices*.
82 Jn 7:37–39.
83 François Charmot, SJ. *Constitutions of the Society of the Sacred Heart: Commentary* (Vatican City: Typis Poliglottis Vaticanis 1954), p. 27.
84 *Summa Theologica*, I, Q. 43, art. 5, ad. 2.
85 Aug ?, 1847. *Conférences* II:80.
86 Feb 22, 1859. *Let. Sup.* IV:161.
87 1847. *Conférences* II:42.
88 May 16, 1864. *Let. Sup.* V:361.
89 *Society of the Sacred Heart*, p. 38.
90 *Ibid.*
91 *Ibid.* p. 33.

92 Brou, p. 286.

93 Cahier II:388.

94 Pascal Darbins, *Vie et Oeuvres de la Soeur Marie Lataste*, 2 vols. (Paris: Bray, 1862). Marie Lataste was born in Mimbaste into a simple village family. As a young girl she was favoured with extraordinary mystical graces. She entered the Society as a coadjutrix sister in 1844 and the visions ceased. She died after making her first vows in 1847.

95 Perdrau I:243.

96 Apr 16, 1948. *Circulaires-*de Lescure, p. 36.

97 *Mother Gertrude Bodkin*, p. 127.

Chapter 10, *The Contemplative Outlook*

1 *Chapter 1970*, p. 7.

2 *Ibid.*

3 *Ibid.* p. 6.

4 Marie-Paule Préat, *Jacques Loew ou le Défi Evangélique* (Fayard, 1974), p. 103, 96.

5 Opening address, *Chapter 1970,* p. 3.

6 *Documents*, p. 201.

7 *Hymne de l'Univers* (Paris: Editions du Seuil, 1961), p. 21.

8 *Ibid.* p. 244.

9 *Constitutions*, Abridged Plan, par. XII.

10 *Chapter 1970*, p. 22.

11 *L'Enfant du Rire* (Paris: Grasset, 1973), p. 193 f.

12 Brochure from Taizé, 1973.

13 *Documentation Catholique*, Oct 6, 1974.

14 Brochure from Taizé, 1973.

15 C. H. Earle, "The Future of Catholic Schools," *The Way* (Oct 1974, vol. 14, no. 44), p. 300.

16 William Johnson, SJ, *The Still Point* (New York: Harper and Row, 1971) and K. Otto, *Mysticism East and West* (New York: Collier Books, 1962).

17 *Chapter 1970*, p. 45.

18 *Summary of the Constitutions*, par. I.

19 *Constitutions*, Abridged Plan, par. IV.

20 *Chapter 1970*, p. 44.

21 Jean Leclerq, OSB. *Prayer: the Problem of Dialogue with God*; ed. C. F. Mooney (Paulist Press, 1969), p. 23.

22 Nov 10, 1831. *Let. Ch.* I:29.

23 Aug 1844. *Conférences* I:367.

24 Francis Thompson, "The Hound of Heaven."

25 Eph 6:18.

26 June, 1847. *Conférences* II:34.

27 *Coutumier de la Société du Sacré Coeur* (lithographed, 1853), Part I, p. 9.

28 Jeanne de Charry, RSCJ, "Eucharistic Adoration in the Constitutions and spirituality of Saint Madeleine Sophie," *Documentation* for the Assembly of Provincials, May, 1975.

29 *Documentation* for the Assembly of Provincials, May, 1975.

30 *Chapter 1970*, p. 19.

31 *Ibid.* p. 14.

32 *The Way* (Oct. 1974), p. 322.

33 *Ibid.* p. 323.

34 A project for CARA.

35 Réné Voillaume, *The Need for Contemplation* (London: Darton, Longman and Todd, 1971), p. 68.

36 Cited in G. Poncelet, RSCJ, *Qui Est-Elle?* (Paris, 1965), p. 12.

37 *Souvenirs du Premier Noviciat de Poitiers*, p. 30.

38 M. M. Philipon, *Trinité et Peuple de Dieu* (Paris: Editions St Paul, 1968), p. 15.

39 Cyprian Cooney, *Understanding the New Theology* (Bruce, 1969), p. 88.

40 *Orientations*, p. 67. The quotation is from the *Journal* of the Union of Major Superiors. May, 1967, p. 34.

41 AGSC, Série *Papiers Barat*.

Chapter 11, *Mission for Justice*

1 Nov 1, 1845. *Conférences* I:387.

2 *Information*, "Assembly of Provincials," no. 4, Dec 5, 1972.

3 Dec 15, 1972.

4 *Information*, "Assembly of Provincials," no. 4, Dec 5, 1972.

5 Gisèle Schutzenberger, RSCJ.

6 *Society of the Sacred Heart*, p. 116.

7 *Mission and Justice*, p. 42.

8 *Ibid.* p. 43.

9 Letter from the Central Team to the Provincials, Nov 21, 1974.

10 May 25, 1958, *Circulaires*-de Valon, p. 23.

11 Revelations 22:2, Douai version.

12 Mar 19, 1847. *Conférences* II:5.

13 July 16, 1852. *Let. Sup.* III:231.

Appendix

Growth of the Society

A. Countries grouped according to continents, in chronological order of foundation.

    I. *Europe, 1800:*

        France, 1800. All houses closed by legal confiscation between 1902 and 1909; gradual return after 1915.

        Belgium, 1808. Dooresele withdrawn in 1814; new beginning at Jette in 1836.

        Italy, 1823. Houses in Piedmont closed in revolution of 1848; those in Papal States in revolution of 1862.

        Ireland, 1842

        England, 1842

        Austria, 1843   Simultaneous beginning at Lemberg in

        Poland, 1843   Polish Austria.

        Spain, 1846

        Holland, 1848

        Germany, 1851. Houses closed by Kulturkampf in 1873; return in 1920.

        Czechoslovakia, 1872. House closed in 1919.

        Hungary, 1883. Houses closed in Communist revolution of 1950.

        Scotland, 1894

        Malta, 1903

        Portugal, 1966

        Sweden, 1969

        Lebanon, 1971

    II. *North America, 1818:*

        United States, 1818

        Canada, 1842

        Cuba, 1858; Houses closed in Communist revolution of 1961.

        Puerto Rico, 1880

        Mexico, 1883

    III. *Africa, 1842:*

        Algeria, 1842. House closed by legal confiscation in 1909.

        Egypt, 1903

        Congo (Zaire), 1927

        Uganda, 1962

        Chad, 1964

        Kenya, 1973

IV. *South America, 1854:*
Chile, 1854
Peru, 1874
Argentina, 1880
Brazil, 1904
Colombia, 1907
Uruguay, 1908
Venezuela, 1961
Bolivia, 1973
V. *Oceania, 1880:*
New Zealand, 1880
Australia, 1882
VI. *Asia, 1908:*
Japan, 1908
China, 1926. House closed by Communist revolution of 1951.
India, 1939
Korea, 1956
Taiwan (Free China), 1962
Philippines, 1969

B. Evolution of Provinces
1839. Provinces established by the Sixth General Council.
1851. Existence of provinces approved by the Holy See, with the title changed to vicariate. Established provinces reorganized at the Seventh General Council.

In the following table the provinces as of 1976 are grouped according to the geographical-cultural regions of the assemblies of 1975-1976, in chronological order of foundation, with date of provincial autonomy.

I. *Europe, 1800:*
1. France: number of provinces varied; fused into one in 1970.
2. Belgium, 1851
3. Italy, 1839
4. England-Malta, 1858
5. Ireland-Scotland, 1918
6. Austria, 1851
7. Poland, 1864-1868, 1936
   Spain, 1864:
8. Northern Spain with Bolivia, 1976
9. South-central Spain with Portugal, 1976
10. Holland, 1904
11. Germany-Sweden, 1946

II. *North America, 1818, and Oceania, 1880:*
United States: 12. St. Louis, 1844
                 13. New York, 1844
                 14. Washington, 1950
                 15. Chicago, 1958
                 16. San Francisco, 1958
17. Canada, 1864
18. Australia-New Zealand, 1888.

III. *Latin America 1854:*
    Northern: 19. Puerto Rico, 1911
                20. Mexico, 1911
    Southern: 21. Chile, 1854
                22. Peru, 1952
                23. Argentina-Uruguay, 1953
                24. Brazil, 1953
                25. Colombia, 1950-1960, 1969
                26. Venezuela, 1973
IV. *Africa, 1903:*
    27. Egypt, 1904-1926, 1970
    28. Zaire, 1963
    29. Uganda-Chad-Kenya, 1973
 V. *Asia, 1908*
    30. Japan-Korea-Taiwan-Philippines, 1926
    31. India, 1964
    32. Korea, 1976

Bibliography

Only selected books in English, French and Spanish (with a few unprinted works and titles in other languages) are here given. A complete bibliography of the literature of the Society of the Sacred Heart, including some archive material and unpublished studies, is in process of compilation at the Mother House.

Alcovar, Catalina, RSCJ. *Alma de Fuego, la Beata Filipina Duchesne*. Barcelona, 1941.
  Caminos de Ayer al Paso de Hoy: Santa Magdalena Sofia. Madrid: Grafias, 1965.
  Cien Años de Educacion Cristiana, 1845–1945. Saragossa, 1946.
Barat, Madeleine Sophie, RSCJ *Conférences de la Vénérable Mère Madeleine Sophie Barat*. 2 vols. Roehampton, 1900.
  Conseils pour le Temps de Retraite. Rome: Maison Mère, 1933.
  Letters to our Religious. 2 vols. No imprint. (translation of other volumes in process.)
  Lettres Choisies de notre Bienheureuse Mère.
  vol. 1(1804–1822), Roehampton, 1920
  vol. 2 (1823–1837), Rome: Maison Mère, 1928
  vol. 3 (1838–1850), Rome, 1940
  vol. 4 (1851–1859), Rome, 1955
  vol. 5 (1860–1865), Rome, 1957
  Lettres Choisies de notre Bienheureuse Mère aux Mères en Charge.
  Rome. Maison Mère, 1924.
  Lettres Choisies de notre Bienheureuse Mère Fondatrice pour les Seules Supérieures.
  vol. 1 (1816–1850) Roehampton, 1922
  vol. 2 (1850–1865), Rome: Maison Mère, 1923
  vol. 3 (1826–1857), Rome, 1954
  vol. 4 (1858–1860) Rome, 1957
  vol. 5 (1858–1865), Rome, 1965
  Lettres Circulaires de notre Bienheureuse Mère
  vol. 1, pour Toutes les Religieuses. Roehampton, 1904.
  vol. 2, pour les Seules Supérieures. Roehampton, 1917.
  Recueil de Pensées et de Maximes de la Vénérable Mère Madeleine Sophie Barat. Rome: Maison Mère, 5th edition, 1955.
  Thoughts and Sayings of Blessed Madeleine Sophie Barat. Roehampton, 1908.
[Barbaren, Marie, RSCJ] *Vie de la Révérende Mère Elizabeth Lamb*. Rome: Maison Mère, 1935.

Vie de la Révérende Mère Jeanne de Lavigerie. Rome: Maison Mère, 1935.

Vie de la Très Révérende Mère Marie de Loë. Rome: Maison Mère, 1932.

Vie de la Révérende Mère Catherine de Montalembert, Roehampton, 1930.

Vie de la Révérende Mère Marthe de Pichon, Roehampton, 1916.

Barham, Enid, RSCJ. *Some Chosen Sisters.* New York: Manhattanville College, 1947.

Barry, Agnes, RSCJ. *Saint Madeleine Sophie Barat.* New York: Manhattanville College, 1945.

Bascom, Marian, RSCJ. *Blessed Philippine Duchesne.* New York: Manhattanville College, 1946.

Baunard, Louis. *Histoire de Madame Barat, Fondatrice de la Société du Sacré Coeur,* 2 vols. Paris, Poussielgue, 1876. Centenary Edition, *Histoire de la Vénérable Mère Barat,* 1900. 7th ed. *Histoire de la Bienheureuse Mère Barat,* 1910. 8th ed. *Histoire de Sainte Madeleine Sophie Barat.* Gigord, 1925.

Histoire de Madame Duchesne. Paris: Poussielgue, 1873. 2nd ed. Gigord, 1926.

    Life of the Very Reverend Mother Madeleine Louise Sophie Barat, 2 vols. tr. Lady Georgiana Fullerton. Roehampton, 1876.

    Life of Mother Duchesne. tr. Lady Georgiana Fullerton, Roehampton, 1879.

Biolley, Odette, RSCJ. *Une Ame d'Elite, Mère Hélène de Burlet.* Bruges: Desclée de Brouwer, 1964.

Brou, Alexandre, S. J. *Travail et Prière: Sainte Madeleine Sophie Barat.* Paris: Beauchesne, 1926.

    Saint Madeleine Sophie, her Life of Prayer and her Teaching. tr. Jane Wynne Saul, RSCJ. New York: Desclée, 1963.

[Burlet, Hélène de, RSCJ.] *Lettres et Souvenirs de Mère Hélène de Burlet,* ed. Odette Biolley, RSCJ. Brussels: Casterman, 1951.

[Cahier, Adèle, RSCJ.] *Vie de la Vénérable Mère Barat.* 2 vols. Paris: De Soyes, 1884.

    L'Esprit et les Vertus de la Vénérable Madeleine Sophie Barat. No imprint. Reprint of chapters 54–62 of biography.

Callan, Louise, RSCJ. *Philippine Duchesne, Frontier Missionary of the Sacred Heart.* Westminster: Newman Press, 1957. Abridged edition 1965.

    The Society of the Sacred Heart in North America. New York: Longmans Green, 1937.

Caritas. "Dans le Sillage de Sainte Madeleine Sophie, Hier-Aujourd'hui 25 Mai, 1865–1965." Numéro Spécial, May 1965.

Cave, Angela. *Janet Stuart.* New York: Manhattanville College, 1946.

Charmot, François, S. J. *Les Constitutions de la Société du Sacré Coeur, Commentées.* Vatican City: Typis Polyglottis Vaticanis, 1954. Translated into English at the same date.

    La Société du Sacré Coeur de Jésus: Lyons: Lescuyer, 1953. Translations into English, Spanish and Portuguese.

de Charry, Jeanne, RSCJ. *Histoire des Constitutions de la Société du Sacré Coeur: La Formation de l'Institut,* vol. II, *Textes.* No imprint.

    Sainte Madeleine Sophie. Tournai: Casterman, 1965.

Circular Letters, Extracts. Brighton.

    vol. I. *Circular Letters of Saint Madeleine Sophie,* 1947

vol. II. *Circular Letters of Mothers Josephine Goetz, Adèle Lehon, Augusta de Sartorius*, 1947

vol. III. *Circular Letters of Mothers Mabel Digby and Janet Stuart*, 1948.

Constitutions et Règles de la Société du Sacré Coeur de Jésus. 3rd edition Lyons: Pelagaud, with the date 1852 retained from the 2nd edition but printed after 1922 in accordance with the new Code of Canon Law.

Constitutions and Rules of the Society of the Sacred Heart of Jesus, Roehampton, 1922.

Corcoran, Loretta, RSCJ. *God's Middlemen.* New York: Manhattanville College, 1948.

   Other Worlds. New York: Manhattanville College, 1951.

Décrets des Congrégations Générales de la Société du Sacré Coeur de Jesus, Parts I and II. Rome: Maison Mère, 1953.

[Demandolx, Marie, RSCJ.] *Vie de la Révérende Mère Maria Zaepffel.* Rome: Maison Mère, 1953.

Lettres Circulaires de notre Vénérée Mère Marie Joséphine Mabel Digby, Edition complète pour les seules supérieures. Roehampton, 1914. (in the same volume: *Lettres Circulaires de notre Vénérée Mère Janet Erskine Stuart.*) Edition pour toutes les religieuses: Rome: Maison Mère, 1960.

Directives de notre Très Révérende Mère, XXIV Congrégation Générale. Rome: Maison Mère, 1952.

Directives et Décisions de la XXV Congrégation Générale. Rome: Maison Mère, 1958.

Directives et Décisions du XXVI Chapitre Générale. Rome: Maison Mère, 1964.

[Dufour, Marie, RSCJ.] *Vie de la Mère Catherine de Charbonnel.* Paris, n. d.

   Vie de la Très Révérende Mère Marie-Joséphine Goetz. Roehampton, 1895.

   Vie de la Révérende Mère du Rousier. Mimeographed, n. d.

   Vie de la Très Révérende Mère Adèle Lehon. Roehampton, 1895.

   Vie de la Très Révérende Mère Marie-Augusta de Sartorius. No imprint.

[Duval, Marie-Thérèse, RSCJ.] *Histoire Abrégée de la Société du Sacré Coeur.* Rome: Maison Mère, 1926.

Enfants de Marie du Sacré Coeur, 2 vols. Paris: Gigord, 1932.

Ernemont, Madeleine d', RSCJ. *La Vie Voyageuse et Missionaire de la Révérende Mère Anna du Rousier.* Paris: Beauchesne, 1932.

Erskine, Marjorie, RSCJ. *Mother Philippine Duchesne.* New York, 1926.

Escartin, Maria Josefa, RSCJ. *El Misterio de Cristo en la Spiritualidad de Santa Magdalena Sofia Barat.* Rome: Regina Mundi, 1966.

Esprit et Plan d'Etudes de la Société du Sacré Coeur. Rome: typis Polyglottis Vaticanis, 1954.

Galindo, Maria Luisa, RSCJ. *La Bienventurada Filipina Duchesne.* Barcelona: Tipografia Catolica Casals, n. d.

   La Glorificadora del Sagrado Corazon de Jésus. Barcelona: Tipografia Catolica Casals, 1912. 1934.

Galitzin, Demetrius Augustin de. *Vie d'une Religieuse du Sacré Coeur, la Princesse Elizabeth Galitzin.* Paris: Techener, 1869.

Garvey, Mary, RSCJ. *Mary Aloysia Hardey.* New York: Longmans Green, 1925.

[Goetz, Josephine, RSCJ.] *Lettres Circulaires de la Très Révérende Mère Joséphine Goetz.* Paris, n. d.

Grandmaison, Geoffroy de. *La Bienheureuse Mère Barat.* Paris, 1909. Grant Sara RSCJ. *Life of Reverend Mother Catherine Andersson,* Bombay: St Paul's Publications, 1962.

Guidée, Achille, S. J. *Notices Historiques sur quelques Membres de la Société des Pères du Sacré Coeur,* 2 vols. Paris: Doumol, 1860.

   Vie du Père Joseph Varin. Paris: Poussielgue, 1854.

Jarmai, Edith, RSCJ. *Tuzben Izzo Elet.* Budapest: Varitas, 1944. German version: *Magdalena Sophia Barat.* Vienna: Herder, 1963.

Karam, Sharon, RSCJ. *Philippine Duchesne, RSCJ: FrontierMissionary. 1769–1852.* Sesquicentennial Booklet, 1818–1968. Saint Louis, 1968.

Kerr, Henrietta, RSCJ. *Notes of Retreat.* Roehampton, 1887.

[Landresse, Juliette, de, RSCJ.] *Vie de la Digne Mère Marie le Bail.* Roehampton, 1924.

   Vie de la Révérende Mère Juliette Désoudin. Roehampton, 1904.

   Vie de la Très Révérende Mère Josephine Mabel Digby. Aix-la-Chapelle, 1915.

   Vie de la Révérende Mère Janet Erskine Stuart. Roehampton, 1921.

Latgé, Maria Teresa. *Sob o Signo do Fogo.* Paulina, 1965.

[Lehon, Adele, RSCJ.] *Lettres Circulaires de notre Très Révérende Mère Adèle Aimée Thérèse Lehon.* Edition complète, et edition à l'usage de toutes les religieuses. Roehampton, 1914.

[Lescure, Marie-Thérèse de, RSCJ.] *Un Appel à l'Amour* Toulouse: Apostolat de la Prière, short edition 1938, complete edition 1944.

   Lettres Circulaires de la Très Révérende Mère Marie-Thérèse de l'Escure. Rome: Maison Mère, edition pour les seules supérieures, edition pour toutes les religieuses, 1958. English version, 1959.

   The Way of Divine Love. Westminster: Newman Press, 1949, 1955. translation of *Un Appel à l'Amour.*

Lettres Annuelles de la Société du Sacré Coeur. Maison Mère, 1805–1965.

Life of Mother Henrietta Kerr. Roehampton, 1886.

Life at the Sacred Heart (School Rule). White Plains: Sutherland, 1953.

[de Loë, Marie, RSCJ.] *Lettres Circulaires de notre Très Révérende Mère Marie de Loë,* pour toutes les religieuses. Roehampton, 1929. Supplement: Pour les Révérendes Mères Vicaires et Supérieures.

Maguire, Catherine, RSCJ. *Saint Madeleine Sophie Barat.* New York: Sheed and Ward, 1960.

Mère Elizabeth Zurstrassen, à travers sa Vie, à travers sa Correspondance. No imprint.

[Merle, Marguerite du, RSCJ.] *Vie de la Révérende Mère Marie-Thérèse de Lescure.* Rome: Maison Mère, 1961.

Mission and Justice. Rome: Maison Mère, 1973. Versions in French and Spanish.

Monahan, Maud, RSCJ. *Life and Letters of Janet Erskine Stuart.* New York: Longmans Green 1922.

   Life of Reverend Mother Rose Thunder. Roehampton, 1930. Version in French at the same date.

[Morineaux, Louise de, RSCJ.] *Vie de la Mère Henriette Montlivault.* Rome: Maison Mère, 1935.

   Vie de la Très Révérende Mère Manuela Vicente. Rome: Maison Mère, 1950.

Notice sur le Révérend Père Léonor de Tournély. Vienna, 1886.

O'Leary, Mary. *Education with a Tradition.* New York: Longmans Green, 1936.

[Passage, Antoinette du, RSCJ.] *Vie de la Révérende Mère Jeanne Dupont.* Rome: Maison Mère, 1940.

Percy-Dove, Clare, RSCJ. *Mother Mary Sheldon.* Brighton: Dolphin Press, n. d.

[Perdrau, Pauline, RSCJ.] *Les Loisirs de l'Abbaye.* Rome: Maison Mère, 1935.
   vol. I, Souvenirs de Notre Sainte Mère, vol. II, Souvenirs de notre Vénérée Mère Goetz.

Plan d'Etudes de la Société du Sacré Coeur. Roehampton, 1922.

Pollen, Ann, RSCJ. *Mother Mabel Digby.* New York: Longmans Green, 1914.

Poncelet, Genevieve, RSCJ. *Qui Est-Elle?* Rome: Apulia, 1965.

Réglement des Pensionnats et Plan d'Etudes de la Société du Sacré Coeur. Orleans: Alex Jacob, 1852.

Religieuses du Sacré Coeur. Paris: Gigord.
   vol. 1, Quelques Contemporaines de la Fondatrice, 1924.
   vol. II, Apostolat et Vie Cachée, 1927.
   vol. III, Dévoument Quotidien, 1931.

Richardson, M. K. RSCJ. *Heaven on Thursday.* London: Burns and Oates, 1948.
   Joseph Varin, Soldier. London: Burns and Oates, 1954.
   Life of our Venerated Mother Adèle Lehon. No imprint.
   Life of our Venerated Mother Augusta von Sartorius. No imprint.
   Life of our Venerated Mother Josephine Goetz. No imprint.
   Life of our Venerated Mother Marie de Loë. No imprint.
   Mabel Digby. New York: Longmans Green, 1957. Reprinted as Sudden Splendour. 1957.
   Redskin Trail. London: Burns and Oates, 1952.
   Tommasini. London: Sands, 1960.

[Sartorius, Augusta de.] *Lettres Circulaires de la Très Révérende Mère Marie-Augusta de Sartorius.* Roehampton, 1914.

Schaffgotch, Marie Anne de, RSCJ. *Die Heilige Magdalena Sophia Barat und ihre Stiftung.* Heiburg-Herder. 1925.

Souvenirs du Premier Noviciat de Poitiers. Roehampton, 1896.

Soeur Josefa Menendez à l'Ecole du Coeur de Jésus. Rome: Maison Mère, 1933.

Spirit and Plan of Studies in the Society of the Sacred Heart. England, 1958.

Spruit, Cornelius. *Etude sur les Provinces.* Rome: Maison Mère, 1970.
   La Société du Sacré Coeur: Questionnaire Résultats et Interpretation. Rome: Maison Mère, 1970.

Statistiques, 1965, Société du Sacré Coeur. Rome: Maison Mère, 1965.

Stuart, Janet Erskine, RSCJ. *Education of Catholic Girls.* London: Longmans Green, 1911. 6th impression, Newman Press, 1964. Translated into French, Dutch and Polish.
   Essays and Papers, 1880–1910. Roehampton, 1915.
   Highways and Byways in the Spiritual Life. London: Longmans, 1923.
   Lettres Circulaires de notre Vénérée Mère Janet Erskine Stuart. Rome: Maison Mère, 1963. Also in same volume as the Circular Letters of Mother Digby, for superiors only.
   Prayer in Faith. 2 vols. New York: Longmans Green, 1936.
   The Society of the Sacred Heart. Roehampton, 1914, reprinted 1927. Translated into Spanish and French.

Spiritual Instructions Based on the Rule, 2 vols. Hammersmith, 1938.

Symon, Marie, RSCJ. *La Vénérable Mère Philippine Duchesne*. Louvain, 1926.

[Thoreau, Gabrielle, RSCJ.] *Vie de la Très Révérende Mère Marie Symon*. Rome: Maison Mère, 1948.

Tommasini, Maria Stanislaus, RSCJ. *Mèmoires de la Mère Maria Stanislaus Tommasini*. Roehampton, 1918.

Two Manhattanville Nuns. Lives of Mothers Claude Stephens and Georgia Stevens, New York: Manhattanville College, 1947.

Valon, Sabine de. *Lettres Circulaires de la Très Révérende Mère Sabine de Valon*. Rome: Maison Mère, 1967.

Vermehren, Isa, RSCJ, and Smith, Eileen, RSCJ. *Mutter Barat*. Berlin: Morus Verlag, 1966.

[Vétillard, Louise, RSCJ.] *Vie de la Révérende Mère Giulia Datti*. Rome: Maison Mère, 1956.

Vie de la Révérende Mère Elena Yturralde. Rome: Maison Mère, 1962.

Vicente, Manuela, RSCJ. *Lettres Circulaires de notre Très Révérende Mère, Manuela Vicente*. Rome: Maison Mère, 1947.

Vie de la Digne Mère Marie le Bail. Roehampton, 1924.

Vie de la Révérende Mère Césarine Borget. Rome: Maison Mère, 1927.

Vie de la Réveende Mère Adèle Cahier. Paris, n. d.

Vie de la Révérende Mère Félicité Desmarquest. Paris, n. d.

Vie de la Révérende Mère Clémence Fornier de Mairard. Roehampton, 1896.

Vie de Madame Suzanne Geoffroy. Poitiers: Oudin, 1854.

Vie de la Mère la Comtesse de Gramont. Paris: 1836.

Vie de la Révérende Mère Aloysia Hardey. Paris, n. d.

Vie de la Révérende Mère Pauline de Limminghe. Paris, n. d.

Vie de la Digne Mère Henriette de Montlivault. Rome: Maison Mère, 1953.

Vie de la Révérende Mère Mathilde Nérincx. Roehampton, 1924.

Vie de la Mère Pauline Perdrau. No imprint.

Vie de la Révérende Mère Constance Perry. Rome: Maison Mère, 1954.

Vie de la Révérende Mère Helen Rumbold. Roehampton, 1925.

Vie de la Révérende Mère Anna Josephine Shannon. Roehampton, 1929.

Vita della Santa Maddelena Sofia Barat. Florence, 1925.

Virnot, Marie Thérèse, RSCJ. *Le Charisme de Sainte Madeleine Sophie*, with *Documents Annexes*. No imprint.

Ward, Margaret, RSCJ. *Life of Blessed Madeleine Sophie Barat*. Roehampton, 1925.

Williams, Margaret, RSCJ. *Life of Mother Gertrude Bodkin*. No imprint.

Mother Aloysia Hardey. New York: Manhattanville College, 1945.

Mother Anna du Rousier. New York: Manhattanville College, 1946.

Saint Madeleine Sophie: her Life and Letters. New York: Herder and Herder, 1965.

Second Sowing: the Life of Mary Aloysia Hardey. New York: Sheed and Ward, 1942.

Wolff-Salin, Mary, RSCJ. *Prayer according to Saint Madeleine Sophie Barat*, an analytical and structural study of her conferences. University of Louvain, 1971.

A Question in the Theology of Religious Life. University of Louvain, 1975.

Index